Exploring Generative AI with Computational Intelligence

This book demystifies the concept of AI-driven creativity with an in-depth understanding of the underlying principles, algorithms, and applications of generative AI. It begins with a coverage of AI fundamentals, followed by a technical discussion including detailed explanations of model architectures, training processes, and optimisation techniques. It explores case studies showcasing how generative AI is reshaping industries such as entertainment, marketing, design, and healthcare. The book also tackles ethical considerations, addressing issues related to bias, transparency, and responsible AI development.

Features:

- Provides deep understanding of generative AI, including in-depth coverage of various generative models such as GANs, VAEs, and RNNs.
- Includes practical, real-world examples of how generative AI is applied in different industries.
- Dedicates significant attention to ethical considerations.
- Equips readers with the knowledge and tools to build, train, and deploy their own generative AI systems.
- Offers thorough explanations of AI algorithms, neural network architectures, and training processes.

This book is aimed at graduate students and researchers in computer engineering, AI and ML.

Computational Intelligence Techniques
Series Editor: Vishal Jain

The objective of this series is to provide researchers a platform to present state of the art innovations, research, and design, and implement methodological and algorithmic solutions to data processing problems, designing and analyzing evolving trends in health informatics and computer-aided diagnosis. This series provides support and aid to researchers involved in designing decision support systems that will permit societal acceptance of ambient intelligence. The overall goal of this series is to present the latest snapshot of ongoing research as well as to shed further light on future directions in this space. The series presents novel technical studies as well as position and vision papers comprising hypothetical/speculative scenarios. The book series seeks to compile all aspects of computational intelligence techniques from fundamental principles to current advanced concepts. For this series, we invite researchers, academicians and professionals to contribute, expressing their ideas and research in the application of intelligent techniques to the field of engineering in handbook, reference, or monograph volumes.

Applications of Blockchain and Computational Intelligence in Environmental Sustainability
Edited by Hamed Taherdoost, Mohsen Saeedi and Aydin Shishegaran

AI and Fintech: Improving the Financial Landscape
Edited by Jaheer Mukthar K. P., Rosario Mercedes Huerta Soto, Vishal Jain and Edwin Hernan Ramirez Asis

Artificial Intelligence and Human Rights, Democracy, and the Rule of Law
Edited by Pushan Kumar Dutta, Bhupinder Singh, Vishal Jain, Christian Kaunert, and Komal Vig

Exploring Generative AI with Computational Intelligence
Navigating the Uncertainty of Creative Machines
Edited by Seifedine Kadry, Shubham Mahajan and Vishal Jain

For more information about this series, please visit: www.routledge.com/Computational-Intelligence-Techniques/book-series/CIT

Exploring Generative AI with Computational Intelligence

Navigating the Uncertainty of Creative Machines

Edited by
Seifedine Kadry, Shubham Mahajan and Vishal Jain

CRC Press
Taylor & Francis Group
Boca Raton London New York

CRC Press is an imprint of the
Taylor & Francis Group, an **informa** business

Designed cover image: Shutterstock

First edition published 2026
by CRC Press
2385 NW Executive Center Drive, Suite 320, Boca Raton FL 33431

and by CRC Press
4 Park Square, Milton Park, Abingdon, Oxon, OX14 4RN

CRC Press is an imprint of Taylor & Francis Group, LLC

ISBN: 9781041155829 (hbk)
ISBN: 9781032856841 (pbk)
ISBN: 9781003680192 (ebk)

DOI: 10.1201/9781003680192

Typeset in Times
by Newgen Publishing UK

Contents

Preface..vii
About the Editors ix
Contributors xi

Chapter 1 Exploring the Synergies and Challenges of Generative AI
Through the Lens of Computational Intelligence................................. 1

Djamel Saba and Abdelkader Hadidi

Chapter 2 The Evolution of Generative AI: From Rule-Based
Systems to Neural Networks 20

Ashish Jain and Sudeep Varshney

Chapter 3 AI-Driven Decision-Making for Sustainable Water Quality
Management: A Fuzzy Multi-Criteria Approach to Handling
Uncertainty 51

*Ajoy Kanti Das, Nandini Gupta, Suman Das, Rajib Mallik,
Carlos Granados, Rakhal Das, Kalyan Sinha, and Takaaki Fujita*

Chapter 4 From Logic to Learning: The Evolution of Generative
AI from Rules to Neural Creativity 76

*Debashree Chakravarty, Ipseeta Satpathy, Vishal Jain, and
B. Chandra Mohan Patnaik*

Chapter 5 Generative AI Architectures, Applications, and Future Scopes
in Industry 94

Dina Darwish, Kali Charan, Rohit Sood, and Sukhpreet Singh

Chapter 6 Societal Impact and Cultural Implications 113

*J. Vidhya, N. Sarulatha, Abinov Bruce, Yogeshwaran R,
and Aarthi K*

Chapter 7 Enhancing Athletic Performance Through Wearable
Technology Using Gen AI with Computational Intelligence 133

*R. Manimegalai, P. Sukumar, A. Uthiramoorthy, and
S. Divya Midhunchakkaravarthy*

Chapter 8 Generative AI Techniques and Computational Intelligence
Functioning on Text-to-Image/Visual Content Generation 159

*Ramandeep Sandhu, Harpreet Kaur Channi, Deepika Ghai,
Nimisha Singh, and Phuke Rakesh Rao*

Chapter 9 Revolutionizing Multimodal Language Translation:
Generative AI Empowered LLM and NLP Solutions
for Seamless Voice, Text, and Communication Integration.............. 184

G. A. Senthil and R. Prabha

Chapter 10 Can Generative AI Cause Evolution in Animals:
An Inspiration Study from the 2024 The Wild Robot Movie........... 206

*Muhammad Younus, Halimah Abdul Manaf, Achmad Nurmandi,
Dyah Mutiarin, Ulung Pribadi, Titin Purwaningsih,
Andi Luhur Prianto, Imron Sohsan, Hajira Gul, and Ibrahim Shah*

Chapter 11 Innovative Solutions to Complex Problems:
Leveraging Computational Intelligence Techniques
for Driving Advancements in AI 224

Suryanarayana Alamuri

Chapter 12 Research Frontiers and Open Challenges... 244

Ezil Sam Leni Ayyaswami and Smitha Rajagopal

Chapter 13 Advancing Training Methodologies for Generative
Artificial Intelligence (AI): Optimization Techniques,
Challenges, and Future Directions 264

Arpita Nayak, Ipseeta Satpathy, Vishal Jain, and Majidul Islam

Chapter 14 Exploring Generative Artificial Intelligence for
Transformative Healthcare Applications 280

*N. Suthanthira Vanitha, M. Shenbagapriya, R. Ramani,
A. Karthikeyan, K. Radhika, and D. Anbuselvi*

Index.. 303

Preface

In a world increasingly defined by technology, there exists an undeniable allure to the idea of machines that can create. From generating art that stirs emotions to composing music that resonates with the soul, the creative potential of artificial intelligence (AI) has captured our collective imagination. This book, "Exploring Generative AI with Computational Intelligence: Navigating the Uncertainty of Creative Machines," is a journey into the heart of this fascination. The term "creative machines" may sound like science fiction, but it's a reality that's reshaping industries and challenging our perceptions of human creativity. The ability of AI systems to generate content, whether it's realistic images, human-like text, or harmonious melodies, has ushered in a new era of creative possibilities. But the allure of AI creativity is not just about its novelty; it's about understanding the profound implications of machines that can think creatively, and the responsibilities that come with it. This book is a culmination of my passion for AI, my dedication to sharing knowledge, and my belief in the transformative power of technology when harnessed responsibly. This book empowers you to not only understand AI-driven creativity but also to participate in its evolution, ensuring that the future of creative machines is one of innovation, responsibility, and boundless imagination.

Chapter 1 attempts to provide insights for researchers, practitioners, and policymakers looking to harness the revolutionary potential of GenAI within the context of CI by examining current advancements, innate obstacles, and future trajectories.

Chapter 2 gives a brief overview of the kinds of generative AI paradigms like probabilistic methods, adversarial training, and diffusion models from the computational perspective, along with the areas of successful application like health care, art, and synthetic data generation.

Chapter 3 proposes an AI-enhanced WQA model (simply, $\mathfrak{F}$-model)using Hesitant Fuzzy Sets (HFSs) combined with Fuzzy Soft Multi-Criteria Decision-Making techniques for water quality assessment.

Chapter 4 delves into the extraordinary evolution of Generative AI, emphasizing the shift from deterministic algorithms to advanced neural architectures that can learn from patterns, adapt to uncertainties, and create original works.

Chapter 5 introduces an analysis of the structure and classifications along with the main uses of generative artificial intelligence systems with a focus on chatbots.

Chapter 6 examines and provides insight into data loss through statistics that bring clarity about the level of knowledge of each respondent. The questionnaires are designed to determine the statistics to bring awareness to the digital citizens of the Maldives.

Chapter 7 explores the integration of wearable devices with machine learning algorithms to enhance athletic performance. Wearable technology with advanced sensors can monitor a diverse array of physiological and biomechanical parameters in real-time.

Chapter 8 introduces the AI techniques that will identify the text and decide to provide the relevant visual content in the form of an image. Research must concentrate on GAI's ability to extract information from a huge number of unstructured text documents, which leads to the greatest source of knowledge based on visual pictures, to improve text mining's efficacy.

Chapter 9 integrates the voice-to-text systems with Generative AI models, enabling more context-aware transcription, expanding their capabilities for specialized tasks in healthcare, education, and virtual assistants. Ongoing research aims to enhance multilingual support, domain-specific vocabulary handling, and the system's ability to provide real-time feedback and summarization.

Chapter 10 addresses whether artificial intelligence could, as in the 2024 movie The Wild Robot, create evolutionary changes in animals. The question is how Generative AI, within the film, could conceivably lead to evolution in behavior, communication, or physical traits in animals with which it interacts largely and under specified conditions of integration into the environment.

Chapter 11 explores key CITs and their applications in complex problems, as well as their emerging synergies with the broader field of AI, which together offer a foundational perspective for researchers, practitioners, and decision makers.

Chapter 12 explores these traits in order to provide relevant insights for practitioners, researchers, and even policymakers, as they aim to reap the growing potential of AI in their quest to build a secure future. Furthermore, this chapter also emphasizes the critical role of AI in developing advanced, adaptive, and sustainable security systems in cyberspace.

Chapter 13 explores various approaches used to enhance the GAN model, including adversarial loss, perceptual loss, and reward modeling, and discusses the issues that relate to it, such as mode collapse, overfitting, and fairness.

Chapter 14 explores the overview of real-world scenarios, GAI models, applications, and future directions of GAI in healthcare.

Chapter 15 discusses the role of the evolution of Generative AI in societal contexts.

About the Editors

Seifedine Nimer Kadry holds a Bachelor's Degree in 1999 from Lebanese University, an MS Degree in 2002 from Reims University (France) and EPFL (Lausanne), a Ph.D. in 2007 from Blaise Pascal University (France), and an HDR Degree in 2017 from Rouen University. At present, his research focuses on Data Science, education using technology, system prognostics, stochastic systems, and applied mathematics. He is currently working as a Full Professor of data science at Lebanese American University in Lebanon and Noroff University College in Norway. He is an ABET program evaluator for Computing and an ABET program evaluator for Engineering Tech. He has served on the Editorial Board of numerous journals in several publishers, and he has been the editor of several books. He has taken various roles in the organization committee in numerous conferences.

Shubham Mahajan, a distinguished member of prestigious organizations, boasts an impressive academic and professional background. He earned his B.Tech. Degree from Baba Ghulam Shah Badshah University, his M.Tech. Degree from Chandigarh University, and a Ph.D. Degree from Shri Mata Vaishno Devi University (SMVDU) in Katra, India. Currently, he serves as an Assistant Professor at Amity University, Haryana. Dr. Mahajan has a remarkable track record in the field of artificial intelligence and image processing, holding an impressive portfolio of eighteen Indian patents, as well as one Australian and one German patent. His contributions to the field are further evidenced by his extensive publication record, which includes over 92 articles published in peer-reviewed journals and conferences and eight edited books. His research interests span a wide array of topics, encompassing image processing, video compression, image segmentation, fuzzy entropy, nature-inspired computing methods, optimization, data mining, machine learning, robotics, and optical communication. Notably, his dedication and expertise have earned him the 'Best Research Paper Award' from ICRIC 2019.

Vishal Jain is presently working as a Professor (CSE) at the Department of Computer Science & Engineering, School of Engineering & Technology, Vivekananda Institute of Professional Studies - Technical Campus, New Delhi. Before that, he worked as a Professor at Sharda University, Greater Noida, and as an Associate Professor at Bharati Vidyapeeth's Institute of Computer Applications and Management (BVICAM), New Delhi. He has been associated as a member of the Faculty Board, Board of Planning and Management, Executive Council, Academic Council, Curriculum Development and Review Committee, and Academic Audit of various higher education Institutions. He is associated with Kuala Lumpur University of Science and Technology (KLUST) (formerly known as Infrastructure University Kuala Lumpur (IUKL)), Malaysia, Lincoln University College, Malaysia, and Research Institute of IoT Cybersecurity,

Department of Electronic Engineering, National Kaohsiung University of Science and Technology, Taiwan, for research-oriented activities. He has more than 3,300 research citations with Google Scholar (h-index score 30 and i-10 index 66) and has authored more than 250 research papers in professional journals and conferences. He has written and edited more than 70 books (most of which are indexed in Scopus) with various reputable publishers, including Elsevier, Springer, IET, Apple Academic Press, CRC, Taylor & Francis Group, Scrivener, Wiley, Emerald, NOVA Science, River Publishers, IGI Global, and Bentham Science. He has more than 300 Scopus publications. He is the book series editor of 10 10-book series with reputed international publishers. Along with the regular teaching, he had organized various Conferences, Faculty Development Programme, Seminars, Hackathon, Faculty and Students Oriented activities. His research areas include machine learning, information retrieval, semantic web, ontology engineering, data mining, ad hoc networks, sensor networks, and network security. He received a Young Active Member Award for the year 2012–13 from the Computer Society of India, and Best Faculty Award for the year 2017 and Best Researcher Award for the year 2019 from BVICAM, New Delhi.

Contributors

Mehmet Hayrullah Akyıldız
University of Dicle
Department of Civil Engineering
Diyarbakir, Turkey

Suryanarayana Alamuri
Osmania University, India

Aarthi K
Saveetha School of Management,
  Saveetha Institute of Medical and
  Technical Sciences, India

D. Anbuselvi
T. John Institute of Technology
Bangalore, India

Ezil Sam Leni Ayyaswami
Alliance University, India

Nivedita Banerjee
CRDT, Indian Institute of
  Technology Delhi,
New Delhi, India

Julieta Barchiesi
Centro de Estudios Fotosintéticos y
  Bioquímicos (CEFOBI), Consejo
  Nacional de Investigaciones
  Científicas y Técnicas (CONICET),
  Suipacha 570, S2002LRK Rosario,
  Santa Fe, Argentina

Ram Boojh
Mobius Foundation,
New Delhi, 110001, India

Abinov Bruce
Saveetha School of Management,
  Saveetha Institute of Medical and
  Technical Sciences
India

M. Victoria Busi
Centro de Estudios Fotosintéticos y
  Bioquímicos (CEFOBI), Consejo
  Nacional de Investigaciones
  Científicas y Técnicas (CONICET),
  Suipacha 570, S2002LRK Rosario,
  Santa Fe, Argentina

Debashree Chakravarty
KIIT University, Bhubaneswar,
  India, India

Sharad Chandra
Amity School of Architecture and
  Planning,
Amity University Uttar Pradesh,
  Lucknow Campus,
Lucknow, India

Harpreet Kaur Channi
Eudoxia Research University, USA

Kali Charan
GIET University, Gunupur
Odisha, India

Vijayaraghavan M. Chariar
CRDT, Indian Institute of
  Technology Delhi,
New Delhi, India

Dina Darwish
Ahram Canadian university, Giza, Egypt

Ajoy Kanti Das
Tripura University, India

Rakhal Das
The ICFAI University Tripura, India

Suman Das
NIT West Tripura, India

Chitralekha Nag Dasgupta
Research Cell,
Amity University Uttar Pradesh
   Lucknow
Uttar Pradesh, India

Ravi Deshwal
Institute of Bioscience & Technology,
Sri Ramswaroop Memorial University,
Lucknow, Uttar Pradesh, India

L. Susmita Devi
Department of Food Engineering and
   Technology,
Central Institute of Technology
Kokrajhar, Kokrajhar,
Assam, 783370, India

Naina Dwivedi
King George's Medical University,
Department of Biochemistry,
Lucknow, Uttar Pradesh, India

Takaaki Fujita
Shinjuku, Japan

Deepika Ghai
Lovely Professional University,
   Phagwara
Punjab, India

Diego F. Gomez-Casati
Centro de Estudios Fotosintéticos y
   Bioquímicos (CEFOBI), Consejo
   Nacional de Investigaciones
   Científicas y Técnicas (CONICET),
   Suipacha 570, S2002LRK Rosario,
   Santa Fe, Argentina.
Facultad de Ciencias Bioquímicas y
   Farmacéuticas, Universidad Nacional
   de Rosario, Suipacha 531, S2002LRK
   Rosario, Santa Fe, Argentina.

Carlos Granados
Universidad de Antioquia, Colombia

Hajira Gul
University of Lahore, Pakistan

Nandini Gupta
Bir Bikram Memorial College, India

Abdelkader Hadidi
Centre de Développement des Energies
   Renouvelables
Algeria

Majidul Islam
John Molson School of Business
   (JMSB), Concordia University
Montreal, Canada

Ashish Jain
Sharda University, India

Vishal Jain
Department of Computer Science &
   Engineering,
School of Engineering & Technology,
Vivekananda Institute of Professional
   Studies – Technical Campus,
New Delhi, India

A. Karthikeyan
Muthayammal Engineering College
Rasipuram, India

Durgesh Kumar
King George's Medical University,
Department of Biochemistry,
Lucknow, Uttar Pradesh, India

Prashant Kumar
Department of Bioinformatics,
Kalinga University,
Raipur Chhattisgarh, India

Santosh Kumar
Department of Food Engineering and
   Technology,
Central Institute of Technology
Kokrajhar, Kokrajhar,
Assam, 783370, India

Shrawan Kumar
Mobius Foundation,
New Delhi, 110001, India

Rajib Mallik
NIT Agartala, India

Halimah Abdul Manaf
Universiti Utara Malaysia, Kedah,
   Malaysia

R. Manimegalai
Rathinam College of Arts and Science
India

Mariana Martín
Centro de Estudios Fotosintéticos y
   Bioquímicos (CEFOBI), Consejo
   Nacional de Investigaciones
   Científicas y Técnicas (CONICET),
   Suipacha 570, S2002LRK Rosario,
   Santa Fe, Argentina
Facultad de Ciencias Bioquímicas y
   Farmacéuticas, Universidad Nacional
   de Rosario, Suipacha 531, S2002LRK
   Rosario, Santa Fe, Argentina

Uma Shanker Maurya
Goel Institute of Pharmacy and
   Sciences,
Lucknow, Uttar Pradesh, India

S. Divya Midhunchakkaravarthy
Centre of Postgraduate Studies Lincoln
   University College, Malaysia

Dyah Mutiarin
Universitas Muhammadiyah Yogyakarta,
   Yogyakarta, Indonesia

Arpita Nayak
KIIT School of Liberal Studies.
   KIIT DU
Bhubaneswar, India

Achmad Nurmandi
Universitas Muhammadiyah Yogyakarta,
   Yogyakarta, Indonesia

M. Ayelén Pagani
Centro de Estudios Fotosintéticos y
   Bioquímicos (CEFOBI), Consejo
   Nacional de Investigaciones
   Científicas y Técnicas (CONICET),
   Suipacha 570, S2002LRK Rosario,
   Santa Fe, Argentina

Komal Pandey
Research Cell,
Amity University Uttar Pradesh,
   Lucknow,
Uttar Pradesh, India

Minakshi Pandey
Faculty of Biosciences, Institute of
   Biosciences and Technology,
Shri Ramswaroop, Memorial University,
Barabanki 225003, Uttar Pradesh, India

Tarun Pant
Department of Architecture and
  Planning,
National Institute of Technology,
Patna, Bihar, India

B. Chandra Mohan Patnaik
KIIT University
Bhubaneswar, India

Swetika Porwal
Amity School of Architecture and
  Planning,
Amity University Uttar Pradesh,
  Lucknow Campus,
Lucknow, India
Department of Architecture and
  Planning,
National Institute of Technology,
Patna, Bihar, India

Paras Porwal
Amity Institute of Biotechnology,
Amity University Uttar Pradesh,
  Lucknow Campus,
Lucknow, India

R. Prabha
Sri Sai Ram Institute of
  Technology, India

Andi Luhur Prianto
Universitas Muhammadiyah Makassar,
  Makassar, Indonesia

Ulung Pribadi
Universitas Muhammadiyah Yogyakarta,
  Yogyakarta, Indonesia

Titin Purwaningsih
Universitas Muhammadiyah Yogyakarta,
  Yogyakarta, Indonesia

K. Radhika
Muthayammal Engineering College
Rasipuram, India

Smitha Rajagopal
Alliance University, India

R. Ramani
Vinayaka Mission's Kirupananda
  Variyar Engineering College
Salem, India

Phuke Rakesh Rao
RS Software Solution, Medipally,
  Hyderabad
Telangana, India

Djamel Saba
Centre de Développement des Energies
  Renouvelables, Algeria

Ramandeep Sandhu
Lovely Professional University,
  Phagwara
Punjab, India

Sayak Sanyal
Amity Institute of Biotechnology,
Amity University Uttar Pradesh,
  Lucknow Campus,
Lucknow, Uttar Pradesh, India

Somali Sanyal
Amity Institute of Biotechnology,
Amity University Uttar Pradesh,
  Lucknow Campus,
Lucknow, Uttar Pradesh, India

N. Sarulatha
Faculty of Management, SRM Institute
  of Science & Technology
Vadapalani, India

Ipseeta Satpathy
KIIT School of Management, KIIT DU
Bhubaneswar, India

G. A. Senthil
Agni College of Technology, India

Ibrahim Shah
The Aga Khan University, Karachi,
  Pakistan

M. Shenbagapriya
Muthayammal Engineering College
Rasipuram, India

Devendra Singh
Faculty of Biotechnology, Institute of
  Biosciences and Technology,
Shri Ramswaroop, Memorial
  University,
Barabanki 225003, Uttar Pradesh, India

Lalit Kumar Singh
Department of Civil Engineering,
Amity University Uttar Pradesh,
  Lucknow Campus,
Lucknow, Uttar Pradesh, India

Nimisha Singh
Baba Farid College of Engineering and
  Technology
Bathinda, India

Rachana Singh
Amity Institute of Biotechnology,
Amity University Uttar Pradesh,
  Lucknow Campus,
Lucknow, Uttar Pradesh, India

Sujeet Pratap Singh
Amity Institute of Biotechnology,
Amity University Uttar Pradesh,
  Lucknow Campus,
Lucknow, Uttar Pradesh, India

Sukhpreet Singh
Guru Kashi University
Punjab, India

Kalyan Sinha
Durgapur Govt. College, India

Imron Sohsan
Khon Kaen University Khon Kaen City,
  Thailand, Thailand

Rohit Sood
Lovely Professional University,
  Phagwara
Punjab, India

Divya Srivastava
Amity University Uttar Pradesh,
  Lucknow Campus,
Lucknow, India

Divya Srivastava
Department of Civil Engineering,
Amity University Uttar Pradesh,
  Lucknow Campus,
Lucknow, Uttar Pradesh, India

Shruti Srivastava
Amity Institute of Pharmacy,
Amity University Uttar Pradesh
  Lucknow Campus
Lucknow, India

P. Sukumar
Rathinam College of Arts and Science
Coimbatore, India

Z. Fuat Toprak
Dicle University, Engineering Faculty,
Civil Engineering Department,
  Hydraulics Division, Turkey

A. Uthiramoorthy
Rathinam College of Arts and Science
Coimbatore, India

N. Suthanthira Vanitha
Muthayammal Engineering College
Rasipuram, India

Sudeep Varshney
Sharda University, India

Sunil Kumar Verma
Faculty of Biotechnology, Institute of
  Biosciences and Technology,
Shri Ramswaroop, Memorial University,
Barabanki 225003, Uttar Pradesh, India

J. Vidhya
Saveetha School of Management
Saveetha Institute of Medical and
  Technical Sciences
India

Yogeshwaran R
Saveetha School of Management,
  Saveetha Institute of Medical and
  Technical Sciences, India

Muhammad Younus
Universitas Muhammadiyah Yogyakarta,
  Yogyakarta, Indonesia

1 Exploring the Synergies and Challenges of Generative AI Through the Lens of Computational Intelligence

Djamel Saba and Abdelkader Hadidi

1.1 INTRODUCTION

The multidisciplinary artificial intelligence (AI) field aims to automate certain jobs that call for human intelligence. It entails demonstrating intelligence by machines performing tasks such as language translation, computer vision, and speech recognition [1]. People frequently interpret AI as machines emulating human intelligence, enabling them to think and behave like people [2]. However, AI is more than just imitation; it can also understand holistically, sense in several dimensions, and perform tasks beyond human comprehension, such as in the case of robots and the Internet of Things [3]. Humans have created AI as a tool, and as a result, it possesses a limited understanding of life, unlike organisms that use processing to establish goals and purposes. Despite AI's rapid growth and widespread use in various sectors, it is important to acknowledge its limitations. "GenAI" describes AI systems that independently create new text, image, audio, and video content [4]. GenAI dramatically contributes to developing open-ended systems to make intelligent machines [5, 6]. In Bayesian computation, deep neural networks (DNNs) generate the inverse Bayes map between parameters and data, facilitating the simple simulation of Bayesian models [7]. This method proves its usefulness for drawing conclusions and making choices. It allows you to do high-dimensional regression, feature selection, and deep learning (DL) without needing density-based methods like MCMC posterior simulation.

Within computer science and AI, the discipline of computer vision (CI) focuses on creating methods and algorithms that let computers understand and react to real-world data. Neural networks, evolutionary algorithms, fuzzy systems, and swarm intelligence are just a few of the approaches it covers [8]. Neural networks are computational models that replicate the architecture and operations of the human brain. Backpropagation techniques teach them to identify patterns and generate predictions

DOI: 10.1201/9781003680192-1

1

from the data. They consist of interconnected nodes, known as neurons, arranged in layers. Population-based optimization algorithms, known as evolutionary algorithms, draw inspiration from biological evolution. These consist of genetic programming, evolutionary tactics, and genetic algorithms. They iteratively generate and evolve a population of candidate solutions to identify an ideal or nearly ideal solution. A type of multivalued logic known as fuzzy logic deals with approximatively rather than precise reasoning. Fuzzy systems, capable of modeling and handling ambiguity and imprecision in data, can enhance the flexibility and human-like nature of decision-making processes. Social insects like ants and bees exhibit collective behavior that serves as an inspiration for swarm intelligence. Swarm intelligence algorithms use a group of agents, or particles, interacting with their surroundings and one another to solve difficult issues like routing and optimization. Numerous applications, such as pattern recognition, data mining, optimization, robotics, and control systems, frequently use these approaches. When there is uncertainty in the data or the problem is complex, traditional algorithmic approaches often fail [9].

GenAI is a branch of AI that combines data and algorithms to create new content—text, music, graphics, and even whole virtual worlds [10]. Neural networks, genetic algorithms, and reinforcement learning are computer-induced vision approaches to genetic AI. Deep learning architectures, such as generative adversarial networks (GANs) and variational autoencoders (VAEs), are neural networks that are widely used in many fields to generate realistic content [11].

GenAI is used to guide the creative process toward desired outcomes. GenAI research using CI is an exciting area of AI; it generally entails research into a fascinating field in which computers learn to be creative and innovative, mimicking aspects of human thought in the digital realm [12]. This field aims to use AI approaches to create models and systems capable of emulating creative content. Dealing with uncertainty is one of the biggest obstacles, as creativity often contains unclear factors. CI can produce innovative results, but it requires excellent uncertainty management. Creative robots can use AI in several ways to manage ambiguity:

- Enrichment Strategies: Adding new inputs to creative models through strategies such as collaborative learning to expand creative potential [13].
- Create diversity: Provide incentive mechanisms to trigger a range of outputs so that the artificial system can investigate multiple approaches and achieve different outcomes.
- Human Interaction: Incorporating people into the automated innovation process so that they can provide input and steer the artificial system to improve outcomes and reduce uncertainty.
- Transparency: To help consumers and developers understand how the artificial system makes decisions and produces outputs, generating innovations as straightforward as possible.
- Researchers investigating GenAI can employ these and other techniques to face and overcome uncertainty, enabling creative machines to effectively produce unique content.

This study aims to investigate the synergies between GenAI and CI, emphasizing their ways of spurring innovation and the moral, societal, and technological issues they raise.

1.2 OPPORTUNITIES IN EXPLORING GENAI

Investigating GenAI offers many prospects across various industries (Figure 1.1). Benefits of GenAI include developing virtual models for study, streamlining treatment plans, developing novel medications, and improving robotic equipment for spinal cord injuries. Generative picture AI can help architects with early-stage 3D design jobs in practice, offering insightful information and suggestions for future design tools [14].

1.2.1 IMPROVE CREATIVITY AND DESIGN

GenAI offers multiple opportunities to enhance creativity [15]. It can revolutionize how designers conceptualize projects, offering new ways to generate innovative ideas and solutions. GenAI can support positive outcomes for individuals and communities by facilitating collaborative and inclusive design practices while mitigating negative impacts through thoughtful implementation [13, 16]. There are numerous opportunities to enhance creativity and design using AI technologies (Table 1.1).

1.2.2 DEVELOP CREATIVE CONTENT AUTOMATICALLY

There is much potential for automatically producing unique content with GenAI [17]. AI systems have recently shown promise in producing artificially animated videos, which could increase creative media output. Educational settings have used these tools, proving their worth in producing excellent instructional materials and enhancing student experiences [18]. However, the incorporation of AI into design and art

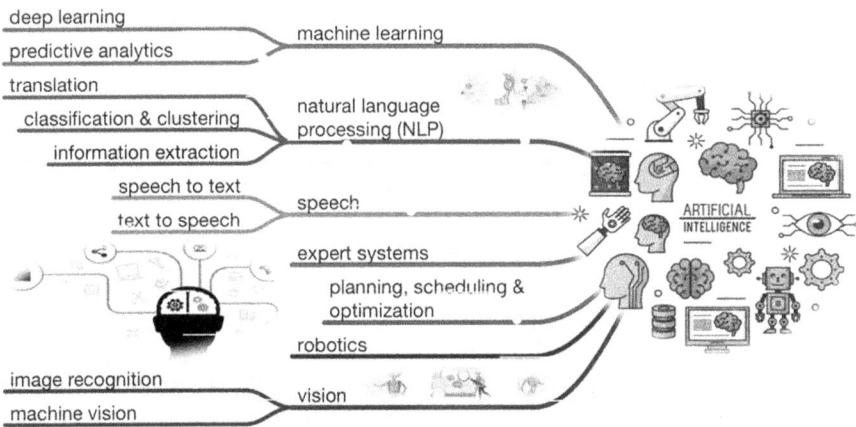

FIGURE 1.1 Sections and Subsections of AI.

TABLE 1.1
Opportunities to Improve Creativity and Design Using AI

Opportunities	Description
Image generation and art	AI can generate art in existing styles.
Generating music and background music	AI can produce music in various genres based on specific needs; it can even write whole songs or just the soundtrack to a video game or film.
Product and apparel design	AI can enhance design and development procedures and help product and clothing designers develop fresh concepts and inventions.
Generating creative texts	GenAI can emulate writings such as poems, short stories, TV shows, and movie scripts.
Game design	AI may be used to create characters and game settings, improving the gaming experience and elevating the quality of the material.
Video and animation generation	AI can create animations and films for marketing, education, or entertainment.

TABLE 1.2
Exciting Opportunities in Creative Content Development

Opportunities	Description
Producing creative texts	GenAI is capable of creating poetry, novels, and short stories autonomously based on existing genres. You can use this function to generate articles for robots, blogs, and other venues.
Image and graphic design	GenAI can automatically create graphs, graphic designs, and images. This is helpful for creative endeavors like advertising and website design.
Music and Sound Production	GenAI can compose and create music independently based on existing genres. This method allows for making background music for films, video games, and advertisements.
Generating creative ideas	GenAI is capable of suggesting ideas in the domains of design, marketing, and even art. This might offer entrepreneurs and artists alternative perspectives.
Improving creative production processes	AI can create intelligent design tools, speed up filmmaking, and improve other production processes [19].

has sparked discussions over the validity of AI-generated work, highlighting the necessity of human-AI cooperation in the creative process. GenAI not only aids in content creation but also transforms information generation and presentation, particularly in the metaverse. This opens up new channels for web traffic and spurs industry innovation. Investigating GenAI is a fascinating subject, with many chances to automatically produce innovative material (Table 1.2).

1.2.3 SUPPORTING CREATIVITY AND INNOVATION IN VARIOUS FIELDS

Significant prospects exist for GenAI to foster innovation and creativity in various disciplines [20]. Design practitioners can use large language models to influence user expectations and co-creative processes during ideation and prototyping. Speculative design concepts such as gAIrden and Onion AI explore future scenarios of GenAI tools by emphasizing positive outcomes and minimizing negative repercussions. To promote harmonic collaboration between humans and machines for increased creative productivity while respecting ethical issues, the manifesto on human-machine collaboration in creativity suggests essential laws to ensure responsible and ethical AI use. Furthermore, researchers are exploring generative picture AI as a potential tool for architectural design, offering valuable insights for the future development of AI-assisted design workflows and tools. Investigating GenAI opens new avenues for fostering innovation and creativity across various industries. There are numerous opportunities to take advantage of.

- Artistic and creative production: GenAI can assist creators and artists in producing new paintings, music compositions, films, or other types of art. For instance, DNN can automatically produce music or new, creative pictures.
- AI can assist in the design of smart objects and products, including electronic gadgets, smart clothing, and even architectural designs [21]. Machine learning (ML) algorithms can create new designs based on users' unique requirements and preferences.
- Literature and Creative Writing: AI can assist writers of stories, poems, and even longer literary works like novels in their writing processes. Generative models can produce new texts based on preexisting or specific concepts.
- AI has the potential to generate innovative, state-of-the-art games and entertainment experiences. This includes designing AI systems to enhance player interaction, virtual character creation, and game levels [22].
- Business and marketing innovation: AI can target ads based on precise analytics or generate creative concepts for marketing campaigns. AI can also generate fresh company concepts and improve marketing processes.

1.3 CHALLENGES IN EXPLORING GENAI

The challenges of exploring GenAI include using picture AI in design practice, integrating AI technologies in-vehicle networks for transportation systems, and striking a balance between novelty and usability. These challenges include managing real-time data processing and decision-making in dynamic environments, ensuring privacy and security in vehicular networks, avoiding limitations such as hallucinations and memorization in AI responses, and comprehending the potential of image AI tools in design workflows. We suggest frameworks with domain-specific analysis, transfer learning, user preferences, and collaboration methods to solve these problems. Furthermore, employing deep reinforcement learning techniques and multi-modal communication technologies can improve the dependability and effectiveness of GenAI applications

TABLE 1.3
Some Challenges in the Areas of GenAI

Challenge	Description
Detail and realism	It takes tremendous advancements in realism, detail, and production quality to produce pictures, movies, and text that humans can believe are real.
DL and Artificial Neural Networks (ANN)	To create generative content that is both realistic and inspirational, DL techniques and cutting-edge neural networks are required [23].
Understanding context and meaning	The production of intelligible material necessitates a profound comprehension of context and meaning, which calls for creating sophisticated AI models with enhanced interaction capabilities.
Predicting human behavior	GenAI systems must be capable of anticipating, comprehending, and reacting to human behavior.
Diversity of creativity and adaptation to tastes	Achieving diversity in inventiveness and adapting to various consumer tastes and preferences can be challenging.
Ethics and Responsibility	This is achieved by ensuring that generative systems publish no harmful or misleading content.
Security and Privacy	Generative systems must be secured to protect user data and avoid privacy and security breaches.
Achieving dynamic interaction and response	Dynamic interaction with users and their environment is important for generative systems.

across various industries. Several significant issues need to be addressed in the field of GenAI (Table 1.3).

1.3.1 THE CHALLENGES SECTIONS

1.3.1.1 Ethical Challenges

Using CI to explore GenAI raises several ethical issues [24]. AI's ability to produce content that mimics human writing raises concerns about plagiarism detection. Furthermore, the application of AI in military operations raises dilemmas related to decision-making [25]. As AI use grows, it is crucial to manage the uncertainties of the creative machine by considering ethical governance strategies [26].

1.3.1.2 Societal Challenges

Effective governance is required since the application of AI in various industries, including healthcare, banking, and law enforcement, can have advantages and disadvantages [27]. Designing moral AI systems and reducing their adverse social effects requires an understanding of the many viewpoints held by those involved in the AI pipeline [28]. AI tools such as GPT-3 provide insights into megatrends in society, emphasizing the possibility of effectively tackling global issues. Although debates underscore the importance of informed decision-making and controlling medium-term implications, AI technology governance is still unclear [29]. The rapid use of models trained on a mix of human- and AI-generated data raises concerns about their future. This could cause biases and less variety in later generations.

1.3.1.3   Technical Challenges

In this article we emphasize the technical challenges of navigating the unpredictable nature of creative machines when experimenting with GenAI and computational intelligence. Obstacles arise from the shortcomings of established evaluation techniques in technical fields [30]. Rapid engineering, iterative procedures, and ethical considerations are necessary to leverage GenAI tools' advantages in addressing issues such as copyright. We can realize GenAI's full potential in creative activities by addressing these issues through educational strategies.

1.3.2   Uncertainty in Results

Uncertainty surrounding GenAI exploration results raises several concerns. Despite the significant advances made by AI, questions remain about the reliability and accuracy of the results. Despite these obstacles, the GenAI market is experiencing rapid growth. Furthermore, using copyrighted works raises legal concerns about the legitimacy of the generated results. Addressing these concerns requires a focus on data management, openness, and responsible AI practices (Table 1.4) to improve the reliability of AI results.

TABLE 1.4
Some Aspects of Uncertainty Challenges in the Results of GenAI Applications

Challenge	Description
Data uncertainty	Uncertainty in findings might arise from conflicting or incomplete data used to train AI algorithms. For instance, incomplete or noisy data might make it challenging for models to forecast results accurately.
Modeling uncertainty	Choosing the right model type or defining precise parameter values are two examples of design considerations that may be necessary when using GenAI models. These assumptions may not always be known. This uncertainty affects the accuracy of the findings and could lead to a misidentification of the model.
Uncertainty in conclusion	The findings may be uncertain, even in cases where the models and data are both excellent. Although GenAI can not guarantee anything, it can make educated guesses based on the data.
Uncertainty in dealing with environmental variables	External circumstances, such as modifications to the surrounding environment or incoming data, may impact the model's output. This lowers the accuracy of the model's predictions and raises the uncertainty in the outcomes.

1.3.3 CONTROL THE QUALITY OF CREATIVE PRODUCTION

When exploring GenAI [31], controlling the caliber of creative output is difficult. Whereas placing too much emphasis on utility may lead to memorization, which restricts creativity, placing too much emphasis on novelty might cause hallucinations in which AI responses contain errors. We suggest frameworks combining domain-specific analysis, data learning, user preferences, and collaboration methods to solve these problems. Despite worries about plagiarism and copyright difficulties, we see creativity as a process rather than a noteworthy attribute, highlighting the significance of community opinions in defining creativity. While acknowledging AI-generated material's drawbacks and possible advantages, integrating GenAI tools in education necessitates rapid engineering, iterative procedures, and ethical considerations to improve creative outcomes [32]. One of the many areas where studying GenAI presents issues is regulating the caliber of creative production. In this situation, delivering excellent creative output in line with specific requirements may present some difficulties (Table 1.5).

1.3.4 ETHICAL ISSUES ASSOCIATED WITH GENAI

Investigating GenAI presents moral dilemmas about prejudice, confidentiality, responsibility, and openness [33]. The development of AI technologies raises concerns like privacy, security, bias, justice, trust, dependability, transparency, and human-AI interactions [34]. When used in research, large language models also pose ethical and epistemological hazards, underscoring the importance of ethical research practices in the AI age. To solve the ethical assessment issues in AI systems, evaluating multi-modal AI systems entails building ethical databases and algorithms to judge the morality of AI outputs to solve ethical assessment issues [35]. These findings highlight

---

TABLE 1.5
Some of the Challenges that the Process of Controlling the Quality of Creative Production using GenAI May Face

Challenge	Description
Understanding Creative Quality	Because they are objective, quality standards for creative creation can be challenging to define. This necessitates a thorough understanding of the innovative idea and the variables influencing creativity assessment.
Diversity of production	The diversity and complexity of creative output frequently make defining and assessing quality criteria more difficult.
Developing ML models	ML models that can thoroughly comprehend the creative context and analyze the company are required to implement creative output quality control.
Integration of technologies	The use of GenAI for creative production quality control necessitates the integration of several technologies, including DNN, ML, and big data analysis.
Sustaining innovation	Quality control's goal is to enhance output, but it shouldn't hinder creative production innovation.

how critical it is to understand and deal with the ethical issues raised by the development and application of GenAI technology. There are several important elements that
address the ethical challenges in the field of GenAI:

- Information fraud: AI technologies can generate misleading content, raising
  concerns about the potential for spreading false information.
- Privacy: Many questions may arise about the intellectual property rights
  generated by intelligent systems, whether these rights should be protected,
  and whether transparency and community participation in exploiting these
  technologies should be enhanced.
- Discrimination and fairness: AI technologies may exacerbate pre-existing
  bias and discrimination due to the methodologies used to create content.
- Psychological and cultural impact: The potential for new AI technologies to
  distort and produce content that violates norms may raise concerns about how
  they impact culture and identity.
- Accountability and transparency: AI systems must be able to explain their
  various choices and processes.
- Security and stability: AI technologies must be secure to avoid hacking. These
  issues require further research and reflection to establish a robust ethical
  framework for AI use.

1.4 FUTURE TRENDS

Developments in AI are exploring the potential outcomes of human-AI coexistence
[36]. AI transforms the metaverse by improving research experiments and data generation [37]. Integrating AI tools into technical processes requires human guidance
to ensure the many benefits [38]. The market for GenAI is expected to expand fast as
it continues to advance, affecting sectors such as manufacturing, entertainment, and
healthcare [39, 40]. We must fully realize GenAI's creative potential while minimizing unfavorable effects to foster an environment where AI innovation and human
creativity coexist.

Given that intelligent systems can generate facsimiles of literature, art, and music
in ways that closely mirror human creativity, exploring GenAI utilizing CI is a fascinating field. Nonetheless, a significant obstacle facing this subject is the lack of confidence in robots' capacity to comprehend and articulate creative elements efficiently
and produce work of the appropriate caliber. There are significant potential directions
that can aid in the development of GenAI employing CI to possibly overcome these
obstacles (Table 1.6).

1.4.1 USING DL TECHNIQUES AND NEURAL NETWORKS

The quickly developing discipline of GenAI uses speculative design to investigate
potential future trends [42]. It influences sectors like healthcare and entertainment
by producing various textual and visual content on its own [43, 44]. Whereas deep
generative models, such as GANs and VAEs, are important for studying computational creativity, they have issues with out-of-distribution creation. DL methods that

TABLE 1.6
Some Future Trends that can Help Develop GenAI Using CI

Future direction	Description
Provide comprehensive and in-depth training	ML models must be created to comprehend and configure creative characteristics more precisely. Training models and improving their ability to express themselves creatively involves offering sizable and varied datasets.
Developing creative expression techniques	We must use better methodologies to produce innovative texts, images, and music and ensure that the quality of the output approaches human originality.
Enhancing understanding of context and culture	Intelligent models need to comprehend context and culture to create information appropriate for the cultural context of various users and communities.
Enhancing creative interaction	It is possible to create interactive systems that let people communicate with creative machines and instruct them to make material that better suits their requirements and tastes [41].
Improve evaluation and evaluation	For engineers to comprehend the effectiveness of the methodologies and make ongoing improvements, efficient ways to assess the creative quality of AI-generated content must be devised.

incorporate human creativity research can produce generative outputs that are more human-like. There is public discussion on the potential biases and decreased diversity in future models trained on a combination of human and AI-generated data, as well as the overall influence of GenAI technologies on society. In general, using DL techniques to increase creativity while managing the unpredictability of creative robots entails understanding their potential, constraints, and societal ramifications (Figure 1.2).

Investigating GenAI using CI is an intriguing field for study and advancement. Unpredictability is one of the biggest challenges facing AI scholars. To address this challenge, research is turning to deep learning approaches, such as neural networks, to help models better understand context and generate more accurate results. Producing creative writing using language generation methods based on deep neural networks represents a significant technical and technological challenge. We expect this field to continue developing, focusing on improving model accuracy and context awareness and exploring innovative approaches to knowledge generation.

1.4.2 INTEGRATING GENAI IN INDUSTRY

GenAI can revolutionize experiences and user interactions [45]. AI's impact also extends to the metaverse, where it is transforming industrial innovation. Industries can leverage AI's benefits by integrating it into various fields, including healthcare, while considering ethical issues. The main challenge is to develop systems capable of perceiving their surroundings in a similar fashion to human thought processes. The future directions and uses of GenAI are diverse, spanning various fields:

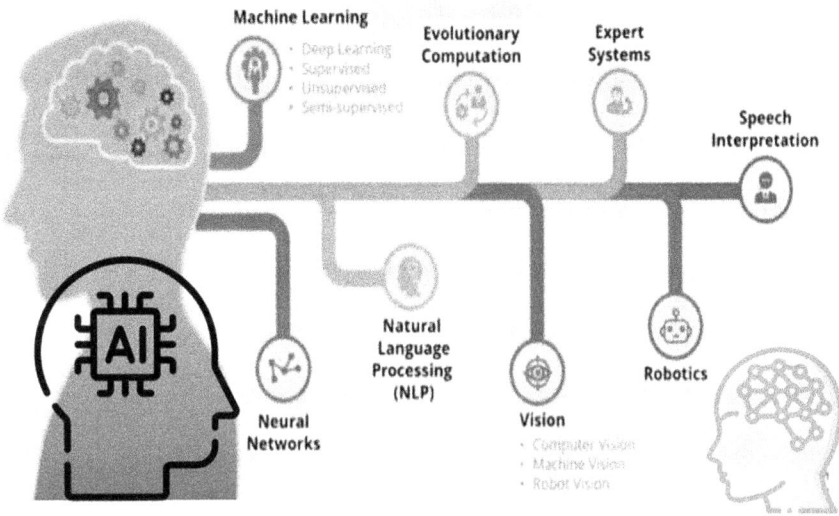

FIGURE 1.2 Elements of AI.

- Applications in Art: GenAI systems can produce new works of art and original works based on various factors such as existing artworks.
- Literary Writing: GenAI systems can generate movie scripts and other scripts. They can also assist in writing technical articles, news, and more.
- Industrial Engineering: GenAI systems can generate product designs, enhancing product design and development in many industries, such as medical equipment and electronic devices.
- Video Games: GenAI can be used to create virtual environments that enhance user experiences.
- Medical Innovation: GenAI can analyze large amounts of data, diagnose diseases, and develop medicines.
- Media and Entertainment Production: GenAI systems can generate various media content, including TV shows, movies, and advertisements, tailored to viewer preferences.
- Education and Training: GenAI can be applied to create intelligent learning systems that provide effective learning experiences and meet each student's needs.
- Environmental issues: GenAI can be applied to improve agricultural efficiency, predict climate change, and manage natural resources more accurately and effectively.

1.4.3 TOOLS FOR THE AUTOMATED CREATIVITY PROCESS

There is a growing focus on the seamless integration of AI-powered technologies to support artistic processes. This integration highlights designers' role in shaping these technologies' societal impact and the need for human intervention to ensure AI becomes a genuinely effective creative tool. Furthermore, by examining theoretical ideas such as gAIrden and Onion AI, it is easier to consider potential use cases for future AI tools and their impact on creativity and culture. AI must address the uncertainties associated with creative machines by balancing automation, human innovation, and ethical issues.

1.5   OVERCOMING UNCERTAINTY

In GenAI systems, balancing novelty and usefulness is crucial to avoid the ambiguity of creative machines. GenAI offers innovative solutions for content development thanks to its ability to generate content automatically [46]. However, overemphasizing novelty or usefulness can lead to numerous problems [47]. Furthermore, using GenAI in the metaverse could revolutionize information presentation, search experiences, and content production, stimulating innovation in the industry. Researchers in this field use various strategies to find solutions to this challenge, including:

- Deep Neural Networks: AI uses deep neural networks to identify complex patterns in data, helping it develop more realistic and accurate creative materials.
- Probabilistic Models: By expressing uncertainty in data and outcomes, probabilistic models facilitate the creation of more adaptable creative materials.

Notwithstanding the difficulties, the advancement of GenAI research leads to new possibilities for automated creativity and new applications in various industries, including digital arts, design, gaming, advertising, and others.

1.5.1   DEVELOP PREDICTIVE MODELS CAPABLE OF DEALING WITH UNCERTAINTY

Developing predictive models that can handle uncertainty is essential to overcoming ambiguity in creative machines. Autonomously, GenAI produces a variety of content [48]. Integrating education in art and design requires a focus on rapid engineering, iterative procedures, and ethical considerations [49]. However, there are still difficulties in decoding and producing uncertain expressions in language models (LMs), which affects accuracy depending on the type of expression used. We can maximize the potential benefits of GenAI in many industries by addressing these issues and improving prediction models to handle uncertainty properly. Genetic AI, which uses continuous integration, aims to create models capable of achieving practical results. Given that the real world is full of obstacles and unpredictable factors, managing uncertainty is one of the biggest challenges in this sector. Creative machines can use a variety of techniques to mitigate uncertainty, including:

- Improving Predictive Models: Deep neural networks (DNNs) and machine learning (ML) are essential methodologies for improving predictive models. This requires large-scale datasets and learning algorithms optimized to handle uncertainty and data variability.

- Use of deep neural networks: They are more efficient at managing uncertainty than classical models.
- Integrating human expertise: Human-machine collaboration strategies can enhance predictions by leveraging experience and knowledge [50].
- Creating models that achieve balance: Models can be designed to handle various situations by achieving a balance between diversity and stability in predictions and outcomes.

1.5.2 PROBABILITY AND STATISTICAL TECHNIQUES IN DATA ANALYSIS

Generative AI (GenAI) systems face the challenge of balancing novelty with ease of use. These tools have the potential to transform the information creation process. Critics of generative models argue that they infringe on copyright and encourage theft. Integrating GenAI capabilities into art and design education requires rapid engineering, iterative methods, but also consideration of ethical standards to optimize benefits and minimize potential drawbacks. AI tools facilitate artistic processes by allowing for precise expression and seamless integration. GenAI systems can enhance creativity within ethical boundaries by handling uncertainty through proprietary analytics, user choices, and collaborative approaches.

- Studying GenAI using Continuous Integration (CI): Generative AI tools can produce creative content. Models are trained on large sets of creative data to generate new content.
- Overcoming Uncertainty: Although AI is increasingly adept at generating creative content, computer model outputs remain unpredictable. We can reduce this uncertainty using statistical (probabilistic) approaches to provide accurate estimates of the confidence level in creative outputs.
- Applying Probability and Statistical Approaches: Creative data analysis can use probability and statistical approaches to study patterns, trends, and variations in this data.

By employing these all-encompassing methods, researchers and engineers studying AI and creativity can create more precise and self-assured models of creative content creation, thereby pushing the frontiers of creativity in a variety of artistic, literary, musical, and other domains.

1.5.3 APPLYING COLLABORATIVE LEARNING STRATEGIES BETWEEN MACHINES AND HUMANS

GenAI highlights the significance of responsible and ethical use by posing new creative opportunities and challenges. It influences the metaverse and web traffic by independently producing a variety of content, including text, photos, and audio [51]. Addressing ethical issues and improving engineering are necessary when integrating GenAI tools into art and design education, potentially boosting students' creative process. Critics point out that generative models raise questions about originality and plagiarism and call for tighter rules around their use and output attribution. Collaborative approaches that emphasize ethical issues, iterative processes in education and content production, responsible AI use, and collaborative learning methodologies between humans and computers, can help manage the uncertainties of creative machines.

Robots can be developed that use AI to produce new content or find innovative solutions. Given that creative machines must deal with uncertainty in the data they rely on, uncertainty is a significant challenge in this context. What is needed is to develop tools and techniques to represent and understand this data to solve the uncertainty problem. Therefore, collaborative learning approaches that involve humans and technology are indicated. Humans can guide bots and provide data through collaboration, which can help them better understand and evaluate creative situations. Furthermore, human judgment and understanding of the quality of the creative outputs produced by bots can help improve the functionality of models and algorithms. By utilizing these techniques, human society can leverage the immense computational power of AI to produce innovative content and find solutions to problems that require creativity.

1.6 CONCLUSION

AI technologies are revolutionizing many fields and enabling creativity for everyone. However, human guidance is essential to achieve the best results. Their impact, including software development and language translation, has received praise and criticism. Cloud computing and hardware advancements have enabled widespread success for AI applications, underscoring the importance of technological growth. Key points in this topic are:

- Technological challenges: Natural language understanding, knowledge representation, and creative pattern recognition are just a few of the technological hurdles that must be overcome to build AI models that generate creative content.
- Dealing with uncertainty: Creative activity often involves unexpected features, and developing generative models that can effectively address this ambiguity can be complex.
- Techniques used: This specialty uses artificial neural networks, deep learning, and generative neural models.
- Potential applications: GenAI-based applications could benefit a range of industries, including creative arts, design, writing, and more.
- Ethical and legal concerns: The use of AI to produce creative content faces numerous obstacles, primarily related to intellectual property rights and information manipulation.

Given its broad range of applications, future studies in the field of genome-wide AI (GenAI) with continuous integration will be crucial. Further research is essential, given the potential advantages and challenges. Researchers can manage the uncertainty surrounding creative machines and pave the way for innovative developments by addressing ethical issues, improving iterative procedures, and exploring the potential of genome-wide AI. The main problem lies in the ability of computers to produce original material. Many factors, such as the current state of technology and complex technical concepts, may contribute to this ambiguity. To overcome this, researchers need to focus on several aspects:

- Creating advanced computer models: It is essential to develop computer models that enable computers to understand creative context and produce appropriate content. This requires development work in natural language processing, deep neural networks, and machine learning.
- Human-machine interaction: This field should enable studying human-machine communication and understanding of each other's reactions.
- Improving understanding of culture: For computers to be able to generate creative content that reflects diversity, researchers need to consider and incorporate cultural and aesthetic diversity into their models.
- Addressing ethical and legal concerns: Research in this area must respect ethical standards and consider how technological advances will impact it.
- International collaboration and community engagement are essential to ensure everyone benefits from new technologies, and that information in this field is shared among researchers.

Ultimately, highlighting the importance of further research in this area requires the integration of computational science and the creative arts, and a focus on creating models and techniques that allow machines to demonstrate creativity and successfully collaborate with humans.

Partnerships between industry and academia are essential to further explore AI genetics. While industry can provide resources and practical applications, academia can help provide theoretical insights and foundational research. Such partnerships can enhance the capabilities and uses of AI genetics and stimulate innovation across various sectors, including manufacturing, healthcare, and more. Together, academics and industry experts can address issues such as multimodal integration, ethics, domain adaptation, and compatibility to ensure the effective application of AI genetics in smart vehicles and other fields.

Industrialists can thus steer academic research to meet their goals and practical demands. This collaboration may lead to the creation of novel technologies and advancements in the field of GenAI, whether in intelligent environment interaction or the generation of text, photos, or videos. Consequently, promoting and strengthening collaboration between academics and businesspeople is important, such as holding joint seminars and training sessions, knowledge and experience exchanges, and funding of cooperative research and development initiatives. Working together, we can advance GenAI to new heights and make real progress in various business and daily life spheres [52, 53].

REFERENCES

[1] D. Saba, Y. Sahli, R. Maouedj, A. Hadidi, and M. B. Medjahed, "Contribution to the realization of a smart and sustainable home," in *Artificial Intelligence for Sustainable Development: Theory, Practice and Future Applications*, vol. 912, A. Hassanien, R. Bhatnagar, and A. Darwish, Eds. Switzerland: Springer, 2021, pp. 261–290.

[2] M. H. Jarrahi, "Artificial intelligence and the future of work: Human-AI symbiosis in organizational decision making," *Bus. Horiz.*, vol. 61, no. 4, pp. 577–586, 2018, doi: 10.1016/j.bushor.2018.03.007.

[3] D. Saba, Y. Sahli, B. Berbaoui, and R. Maouedj, "Towards smart cities: Challenges, components, and architectures," in *Studies in Computational Intelligence: Toward Social Internet of Things (SIoT): Enabling Technologies, Architectures and Applications*, A. E. Hassanien, R. Bhatnagar, N. E. M. Khalifa, and M. H. N. Taha, Eds. Switzerland: Springer, 2020, pp. 249–286.

[4] M. Bordukova, N. Makarov, R. Rodriguez-Esteban, F. Schmich, and M. P. Menden, "Generative artificial intelligence empowers digital twins in drug discovery and clinical trials," *Expert Opin. Drug Discov.*, vol. 19, no. 1, pp. 33–42, Jan. 2024, doi: 10.1080/17460441.2023.2273839.

[5] D. Saba, A. Hadidi, O. Cheikhrouhou, M. Hamdi, and H. Hamam, "Development of an ontology-based solution to reduce the spread of viruses," *Appl. Sci.*, vol. 12, no. 22, p. 11839, Nov. 2022, doi: 10.3390/APP122211839.

[6] D. Saba, F. Hajjej, O. Cheikhrouhou, Y. Sahli, A. Hadidi, and H. Hamam, "Development of an intelligent solution for the optimization of hybrid energy systems," *Appl. Sci.*, vol. 12, no. 17, p. 8397, Aug. 2022, doi: 10.3390/app12178397.

[7] A. Castañeda-Miranda and V. M. Castaño, "Smart frost control in greenhouses by neural networks models," *Comput. Electron. Agric.*, vol. 137, pp. 102–114, 2017, doi: 10.1016/j.compag.2017.03.024.

[8] S. Ilie and C. Bǎdicǎ, "Multi-agent distributed framework for swarm intelligence," in *Proc. Comp. Sci.*, vol. 18, pp. 611–620, 2013, doi: 10.1016/j.procs.2013.05.225.

[9] D. Saba, Y. Sahli, F. H. Abanda, R. Maouedj, and B. Tidjar, "Development of new ontological solution for an energy intelligent management in Adrar city," *Sustain. Comput. Inform. Syst.*, vol. 21, pp. 189–203, Mar. 2019, doi: 10.1016/J.SUSCOM.2019.01.009.

[10] S. K. Das, D. J. Cook, A. Battacharya, E. O. Heierman, and T. Y. Lin, "The role of prediction algorithms in the MavHome smart home architecture," *IEEE Wirel. Commun.*, vol. 9, no. 6, pp. 77–84, 2002, doi: 10.1109/MWC.2002.1160085.

[11] A. Hadidi, D. Saba, and Y. Sahli, "Smart irrigation system for smart agriculture using IoT: Concepts, architecture, and applications," in *The Digital Agricultural Revolution*, R. Bhatnagar, N. K. Tripathi, N. Bhatnagar, and C. Kumar Panda, Eds. New Delhi, India: Wiley, 2022, pp. 171–198.

[12] E. Mohanty and A. Mohanty, "Role of artificial intelligence in peptide vaccine design against RNA viruses," *Informat. Med. Unlocked*, vol. 26. 2021, doi: 10.1016/j.imu.2021.100768.

[13] D. Saba, Y. Sahli, and A. Hadidi, "Intelligent multiagent system for agricultural management processes (Case Study: Greenhouse)," in *The Digital Agricultural Revolution*, R. Bhatnagar, N. K. Tripathi, N. Bhatnagar, and C. K. Panda, Eds. New Delhi, India: Wiley, 2022, pp. 143–170.

[14] D. Mourtzis, M. Doukas, and D. Bernidaki, "Simulation in manufacturing: Review and challenges," *Procedia CIRP*, vol. 25, pp. 213–229, 2014, doi: 10.1016/j.procir.2014.10.032.

[15]   P. S. Paladugu *et al.*, "Generative adversarial networks in medicine: Important considerations for this emerging innovation in Artificial Intelligence," *Ann. Biomed. Eng.*, vol. 51, no. 10, pp. 2130–2142, Oct. 2023, doi: 10.1007/s10439-023-03304-z.

[16]   D. Saba, Y. Sahli, and A. Hadidi, "Toward smart cities based on the Internet of Things," in *Smart City Infrastructure*, V. Kumar, V. Jain, B. Sharma, J. M. Chatterjee, and R. Shrestha, Eds. New Delhi, India: Wiley, 2022, pp. 33–75.

[17]   D. Saba, F. Z. Laallam, H. E. Degha, B. Berbaoui, and R. Maouedj, "Design and development of an intelligent ontology-based solution for energy management in the home," in *Stud. Comp. Intell.*, 801st ed., A. E. Hassanien, Ed. Switzerland: Springer, pp. 135–167, 2019.

[18]   J. P. Bharadiya, "Leveraging machine learning for enhanced business intelligence," *Int. J. Comput. Sci. Inf. Technol.*, vol. 7, no. 1, pp. 1–19, Jul. 2023.

[19]   D. Saba, R. Maouedj, and B. Berbaoui, "Contribution to the development of an energy management solution in a green smart home (EMSGSH)," in *Proc. 7th Int. Conf. Softw. Eng. New Technol.,* Hammamet, Tunisia, 26–28 Dec. 2018, pp. 1–7, doi: 10.1145/3330089.3330101.

[20]   H. E. Degha, F. Z. Laallam, B. Said, and D. Saba, "Onto-SB: Human profile ontology for energy efficiency in smart building," in *3rd Int. Conf. Pattern Anal. Intell. Syst. (PAIS),* Tebessa, Algeria, 24–25 Oct. 2018, doi: 10.1109/PAIS.2018.8598509.

[21]   D. Saba, O. Cheikhrouhou, W. Alhakami, Y. Sahli, A. Hadidi, and H. Hamam, "Intelligent Reasoning Rules for Home Energy Management (IRRHEM): Algeria case study," *Appl. Sci.*, vol. 12, no. 4, p. 1861, Feb. 2022, doi: 10.3390/app12041861.

[22]   F. Safadi, R. Fonteneau, and D. Ernst, "Artificial intelligence in video games: Towards a unified framework," *Int. J. Comput. Games Technol.*, vol. 2015, pp. 1–30, 2015, doi: 10.1155/2015/271296.

[23]   J. Lemley, S. Bazrafkan, and P. Corcoran, "Deep learning for consumer devices and services: Pushing the limits for machine learning, artificial intelligence, and computer vision," *IEEE Consum. Electron. Mag.*, vol. 6, no. 2, pp. 48–56, 2017, doi: 10.1109/MCE.2016.2640698.

[24]   H. Zohny, J. McMillan, and M. King, "Ethics of generative AI," *J. Med. Ethics*, vol. 49, no. 2, pp. 79–80, 2023, doi: 10.1136/jme-2023-108909.

[25]   M. Klenk, "Ethics of generative AI and manipulation: A design-oriented research agenda," *Ethics Inf. Technol.*, vol. 26, no. 1, 2024, doi: 10.1007/s10676-024-09745-x.

[26]   J. Jeon, J. Park, and L. Kim, "The ethics of generative AI in social-scientific research: A qualitative approach for community-based AI ethics," *SSRN Electron. J.*, vol. 81, pp. 102836, 2024, doi: 10.2139/ssrn.4703377.

[27]   J. Whittlestone and S. Clarke, "AI challenges for society and ethics," in *The Oxford Handbook of AI Governance*, J. B. Bullock et al., Eds. United Kingdom: Oxford University, 2022.

[28]   C. Huang, Z. Zhang, B. Mao, and X. Yao, "An overview of artificial intelligence ethics," *IEEE Trans. Artif. Intell.*, vol. 4, no. 4, 2023, doi: 10.1109/TAI.2022.3194503.

[29]   S. Bouhouita-Guermech, P. Gogognon, and J. C. Bélisle-Pipon, "Specific challenges posed by artificial intelligence in research ethics," *Front. Artif. Intell.*, vol. 6, 1149082, 2023, doi: 10.3389/frai.2023.1149082.

[30]   M. Cook and G. Smith, "Formalizing non-formalism: Breaking the rules of automated game design," in *Proc. Found. Digit. Games (FDG)*, 2015.

[31]   D. Saba, H. E. Degha, B. Berbaoui, and R. Maouedj, "Development of an ontology-based solution for energy saving through a smart home in the city of Adrar in

Algeria," in *Advances in Intelligent Systems and Computing, Hassanien*, A. Tolba, M. Elhoseny, and M. Mostafa, Eds. Cham: Springer, 2018, pp. 531–541.

[32] D. Saba, Y. Sahli, and A. Hadidi, "An ontology based energy management for smart home," *Sustain. Comput. Inform. Syst.*, vol. 31, p. 100591, Sep. 2021, doi: 10.1016/j.suscom.2021.100591.

[33] T. Kocatürk and B. Medjdoub, *Distributed Intelligence in Design.* United Kingdom: Wiley-Blackwell, 2011.

[34] D. Saba, B. Berbaoui, H. E. Degha, and F. Z. Laallam, "A generic optimization solution for hybrid energy systems based on agent coordination," in *Int. Conf. Adv. Intell. Syst. Inform.*, 2018, pp. 527–536.

[35] D. Saba, Y. Sahli, R. Maouedj, and A. Hadidi, "Energy management based on internet of things," in *Recent Advances in Technology Acceptance Models and Theorie*, M. Al-Emran, and K. Shaalan, Eds. Cham, Switzerland: Springer Nature, 2021, pp. 349–372.

[36] V. Dörfler, "Artificial intelligence," *Ref. Modul. Neurosci. Biobehav. Psychol.*, vol. 1, no. 3, pp. 57–64, Jan. 2020, doi: 10.1016/B978-0-12-809324-5.23863-7.

[37] D. Saba, H. E. Degha, B. Berbaoui, F. Z. Laallam, and R. Maouedj, "Contribution to the modeling and simulation of multiagent systems for energy saving in the habitat," in *Proc. 017 Int. Conf. Math. Inf. Technol.*, Jan. 2018, doi: 10.1109/MATHIT.2017.8259718.

[38] Q. Sun, W. Yu, N. Kochurov, Q. Hao, and F. Hu, "A multi-agent-based intelligent sensor and actuator network design for smart house and home automation," *J. Sens. Actuator Networks*, vol. 2, no. 3, pp. 557–588, 2013, doi: 10.3390/jsan2030557.

[39] D. Saba, *Modélisation Sémantique À Base D'agents Pour La Gestion D'energie Dans Un Système Multi Sources À Energie Renouvelable.* Kasdi: Merbah University of Ouargla, 2017.

[40] D. Saba, F. Zohra Laallam, H. Belmili, F. Henry Abanda, and A. Bouraiou, "Development of an ontology-based generic optimisation tool for the design of hybrid energy systems," *Int. J. Comput. Appl. Technol.*, vol. 55, no. 3, pp. 232–243, 2017, doi: 10.1504/IJCAT.2017.084773.

[41] D. Saba, F. Z. Laallam, B. Berbaoui, and H. A. Fonbeyin, "An energy management approach in hybrid energy system based on agent's coordination," in *2nd Int. Conf. Adv. Intell. Syst. Inform. (AISI'16)*, vol. 533, 2016, doi: 10.1007/978-3-319-48308-5_29.

[42] D. Saba, F. Z. Laallam, and B. Berbaoui, "Contribution to energy management in hybrid energy systems based on agents coordination," *Int. J. Inf. Commun. Eng.*, vol. 10, no. 9, pp. 1249–1255, 2016, doi: http://doi.org/10.5281/zenodo.1126706.

[43] M. Chen, S. Xu, L. Husain, and G. Galea, "Digital health interventions for COVID-19 in China: A retrospective analysis," *Intell. Med.*, vol. 1, no. 1, pp. 29–36, May 2021, doi: 10.1016/J.IMED.2021.03.001.

[44] M. Jayashankara, S. S. Udmale, A. K. Pandey, and R. S. Singh, "IoT healthcare architecture," in *IoT-Based Data Analytics for the Healthcare Industry*, S. Kumar Singh, A. Kumar Pandey, A. Chaudhary, R. Shankar Singh, S. S. Udmale. India: Elsevier, 2021, pp. 9–29.

[45] M. S. Mahdavinejad, M. Rezvan, M. Barekatain, P. Adibi, P. Barnaghi, and A. P. Sheth, "Machine learning for internet of things data analysis: A survey," *Digit. Commun. Net.*, vol. 4, no. 3, pp. 161–175, 2018, doi: 10.1016/j.dcan.2017.10.002.

[46] D. Saba, F. Z. Laallam, A. E. Hadidi, and B. Berbaoui, "Optimization of a multi-source system with renewable energy based on ontology," *Energy Proc.*, vol. 74, pp. 608–615, Aug. 2015, doi: 10.1016/J.EGYPRO.2015.07.787.

[47] D. Saba, Y. Sahli, and A. Hadidi, "The role of artificial intelligence in company's decision making," in *Enabling AI Applications in Data Science*, vol. 911, A. Hassanien, M. H. N. Taha, and N. E. M. Khalifa, Eds. Switzerland: Springer, 2021, pp. 287–314.

[48] L. Yuan and X. Xu, "Adaptive image edge detection algorithm based on Canny operator," in *Proc. 2015 4th Int. Conf. Adv. Inf. Technol. Sens. Appl.*, 2016, doi: 10.1109/AITS.2015.14.

[49] D. Saba, Y. Sahli, R. Maouedj, A. Hadidi, and M. B. Medjahed, "Towards artificial intelligence: Concepts, applications, and innovations," in *Enabling AI Applications in Data Science*, vol. 911, A. Hassanien, M. H. N. Taha, and N. E. M. Khalifa, Eds. Switzerland: Springer, 2021, pp. 103–146.

[50] A. Hadidi, D. Saba, and Y. Sahli, "The role of artificial neuron networks in intelligent agriculture (case study: Greenhouse)," in *Artificial Intelligence for Sustainable Development: Theory, Practice and Future Applications*, vol. 912, A. Hassanien, R. Bhatnagar, and A. Darwish, Eds. Switzerland: Springer, 2021, pp. 45–67.

[51] P. K. Verma et al., "Machine-to-Machine (M2M) communications: A survey," *J. Network Comp. Appl.*, vol. 66, pp. 83–105, 2016, doi: 10.1016/j.jnca.2016.02.016.

[52] N. Dhamani, *Introduction to generative AI: An ethical, societal, and legal overview.* New York, USA: O'Reilly Media, 2024.

[53] A. G. Dunn, I. Shih, J. Ayre, and H. Spallek, "What generative AI means for trust in health communications," *J. Commun. Healthc.*, vol. 16, no. 4, pp. 385–388, Oct. 2023, doi: 10.1080/17538068.2023.2277489.

2 The Evolution of Generative AI

From Rule-Based Systems to Neural Networks

Ashish Jain and Sudeep Varshney

2.1 INTRODUCTION

Generative Artificial Intelligence (AI) can be defined as a type of Artificial intelligence that is designed to produce new data that is similar to that already produced. Generative AI, in contrast to predictive AI, does not simply classify or predict the result, but generates something entirely new such as images, text, music, or synthetic data from the learned distribution.

In its fundamental nature, generative AI requires vast datasets and uses them to create new content that is similar to the creative process. It is possible to use it for the production of realistic pictures, for composing new music, and for furthering scientific research.

Table 2.1 shows that Generative AI is not limited to the boundary of Traditional AI, and has more flexibility and creativity in return for the higher computational requirement and the problem of interpretability.

2.1.1 IMPORTANCE OF GENERATIVE AI (LATEST DEVELOPMENTS AND TRENDS)

The most significant aspect of AI is generative AI that has affected almost every aspect of human life and social processes. One of the biggest developments has been the ability to use AI to produce art with the help of such tools as DALL·E, Stable Diffusion, and generate stunning photorealistic images, digital artworks, and unique designs without much effort. In the same manner, text generation models such as ChatGPT and Bard have started to redefine content creation, supplying natural prompt responses and assistance with writing, summarizing, and even code. Entertainment is one more field where the application of AI increases the efficiency of creative work such as video, music, or game creation.

In addition to creativity, it is significant that generative AI is also widely used in scientific research and healthcare. In drug discovery, AI models such as AlphaFold and GAN-based molecular synthesis are accelerating protein structure prediction and new drug formulation, reducing research timelines significantly [1]. In medical imaging, AI-enhanced MRI and CT scan reconstruction are improving diagnostic precision, enabling early disease detection. Another key impact is in synthetic data

DOI: 10.1201/9781003680192-2

TABLE 2.1
Traditional vs Generative AI

Aspect	Generative AI	Traditional AI
Learning Approach	Learns from data patterns to generate new content.	Uses predefined rules or statistical analysis for decision-making.
Output Type	Creates novel text, images, audio, and video.	Outputs structured data, classifications, and predictions.
Task Orientation	Focuses on content creation and synthesis.	Designed for problem-solving and pattern recognition.
Example Applications	Text-to-image generation, AI-generated art, deepfakes.	Fraud detection, medical diagnosis, recommendation systems.
Data Dependence	Requires large-scale datasets for training.	Depends on structured data and predefined rules.
Interpretability	Difficult to interpret due to deep neural networks.	More interpretable due to rule-based logic and models.
Flexibility	Highly flexible and adaptable to new tasks.	Limited flexibility, designed for specific tasks.
Computational Requirements	Computationally intensive, requiring GPUs/TPUs.	Less resource-intensive, operates efficiently on CPUs.
Model Examples	GPT-4, DALL·E, Stable Diffusion, StyleGAN, DeepSeek.	Decision Trees, Support Vector Machines, Rule-Based Systems.

generation, where AI helps create anonymized datasets for training machine learning models without privacy concerns, making it invaluable in industries like finance, cybersecurity, and autonomous driving.

Moreover, generative AI is reshaping human-computer interaction through hyper-personalization. AI-driven chatbots, virtual assistants, and recommendation engines are refining user experiences in e-commerce, customer service, and social media by tailoring content to individual preferences. Multimodal AI models like GPT-4 and Gemini are pushing the boundaries of generative capabilities, seamlessly integrating text, image, and audio generation. Furthermore, large-scale AI models are now being fine-tuned for specific industries, enabling more reliable domain-specific applications, from legal document generation to AI-powered medical consultations.

However, as generative AI progresses, ethical considerations have become more pressing. The future of deepfakes [2], AI-generated fake news, and copyright infringements usher in the need for stringent regulatory measures and the correct use of AI that is both ethical and suitable for the application. While the target is set on defying various AI issues such as transparency, controllability, and eliminating bias, the future of generative AI is in the creation of safer, more interpretable as well as energy-efficient models. This is why generative AI is one of the most important technologies of the modern world as it is capable of changing the notion of creativity as well as automation and interaction with machines in the future.

The application of Generative AI in different fields has been on the rise since 2018 and continued to rise through 2024 as depicted below in Figure 2.1. Generative AI has

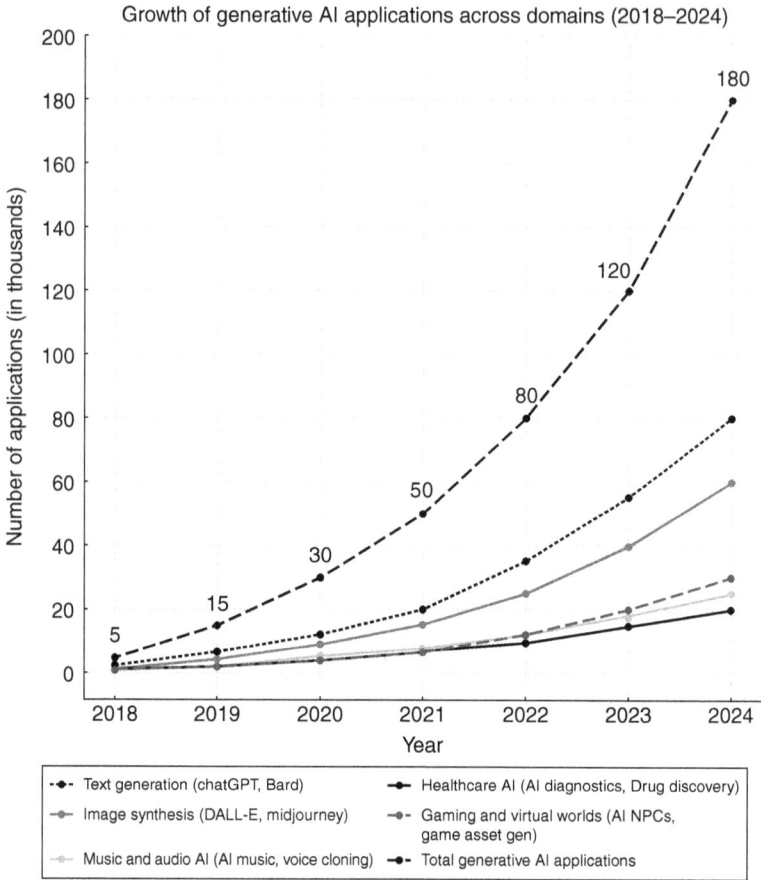

FIGURE 2.1   Rapid Growth of Generative AI Applications Across Domains (2018–2024).

evolved from an obscure concept of academic interest to a mainstream application and considerable impact on various industries and human activities.

2.2   HISTORICAL EVOLUTION OF GENERATIVE AI

Generative AI has evolved from the tradition of rule-based systems to the deep learning system that uses neural networks for content generation [3]. This evolution has been prompted by an increase in computing capacity, availability of data, as well as improved techniques in machine learning. The following is a step-wise elucidation of this progression.

1960s – Rule-Based Systems: The Beginning of AI
The first generation of Generative AI used rule-based systems where the AI functioned by applying programmed IF-THEN rules. These systems could not learn more than

what had been programmed in the systems [4]. One of the most famous examples is the ELIZA, which was created in 1966 and was programmed by Joseph Weizenbaum; it was a kind of chatbot that mimics human conversation with the help of a text-matching algorithm, but does not possess the ability to understand the meaning of the words used.

1980s – Expert Systems and Statistical AI:
Expert Systems also emerged in the 1980s as an advancement to the fundamental rule-based AI. These systems contained extensive rule bases and decision trees for problem-solving in diverse areas of application such as medicine and chemistry. For example, MYCIN (1970s–1980s) had manually developed rules for diagnosis of diseases. However, they faced difficulties in terms of scalability and needed human interaction for further modifications. At the same time introduced probabilistic models like Hidden Markov Models (HMMs) were used to improve the text and speech generation through prediction by probability.

1990s – Statistical Modeling and Machine Learning Advances:
The models of learning changed in the 1990s from handcrafted rules to new statistical models. Machine learning models such as Markov Chains, GMMs, and LDA which were used to create texts and spoken word allowed AI to proceed in a more data-oriented way and make fewer restrictions as to the text and speech patterns. These models formed the base of the Machine learning-based generative AI, but were problematic in dealing with high-dimensional data.

2000s – Transition to Machine Learning for Generative AI:
Machine learning-based generative AI became the trend in the 2000s. The computer soon started using unsupervised learning techniques to create data from the existing data using probability densities and not procedural instructions. LDA (2003) was well applied to topic modeling, and GMMs made advancements in speech and handwriting generation. However, these models demanded a substantial preprocessing of the data, and could not be used for more complex generative tasks such as realistic image generation.

2010s – Deep Learning Revolution Begins:
The key advancement of the 2010s was deep learning, enabling neural networks to learn from data. Autoencoders (2010) and Variational Autoencoders (VAEs, 2013) introduced a new paradigm for data generation, learning compact representations of input data and reconstructing realistic samples [5, 6]. These models were among the first generative architectures capable of generating synthetic faces, text, and voice with high accuracy.

2014 – The Birth of Generative Adversarial Networks (GANs):
In 2014, Ian Goodfellow and colleagues advanced the field by introducing Generative Adversarial Networks (GANs). GANs consisted of two competing networks—a Generator and a Discriminator—engaged in a zero-sum adversarial game to produce highly realistic data. This innovation revolutionized image generation, synthetic media, and deepfake technology, making AI-generated content nearly indistinguishable from real-world data.

2016–2017: Improvements in GANs: WGAN and cGANs

While Generative Adversarial Networks (GANs) demonstrated significant potential, they encountered challenges related to training instability and mode collapse. In 2017, Wasserstein GAN (WGAN) was introduced, addressing these issues by using Wasserstein distance instead of standard loss functions, significantly improving training stability and convergence. At the same time, Conditional GANs (cGANs) enabled controlled content generation, allowing AI to generate images, videos, and text based on specific input conditions [7, 8].

2018–2019: BigGAN, StyleGAN, and High-Resolution AI

As computational power increased, BigGAN (2018) demonstrated that scaling up GAN architectures could dramatically enhance the quality and resolution of AI-generated images. Shortly after, StyleGAN (2019) introduced style-based generators, allowing fine-grained control over image synthesis, particularly for human face generation. This period also saw a rapid expansion of GAN applications in art, medical imaging, and entertainment.

2020 – The Rise of Transformer-Based Generative AI

While GANs dominated image generation, a parallel revolution was occurring in natural language processing (NLP). In 2020, OpenAI introduced GPT-3, a Transformer-based model capable of generating human-like text at an unprecedented level [9]. Transformers used self-attention mechanisms to understand long-range dependencies in data, making them superior to traditional generative models for language, code generation, and multimodal AI [10, 11].

2021–2022: The Emergence of Diffusion Models

By 2021–2022, Diffusion Models emerged as an alternative to GANs, solving mode collapse issues and improving image realism. DALL·E 2 (2021), Imagen (2022), and Stable Diffusion (2022) used iterative noise reduction techniques to generate highly detailed and realistic AI-generated images from text descriptions [12, 13]. Unlike GANs, these models offered better diversity and control, quickly becoming the state-of-the-art for AI art and creative content generation.

2023–Present – The Era of Multimodal AI:

As AI continued to advance, research shifted toward Multimodal Generative AI—models capable of generating text, images, video, and even 3D models from a single architecture. OpenAI's GPT-4 (2023) introduced multimodal capabilities, enabling users to interact with AI through text and images. AI systems like Runway ML's Gen-2 (2023–2024) and Google's Gemini AI (2024) expanded text-to-video generation, paving the way for autonomous AI-driven creativity in media, entertainment, and industrial applications.

Table 2.2 illustrates the evolution of Generative AI from rule-based systems to deep learning-based models, highlighting key contributions, strengths, challenges, and example models. It showcases the transition from early deterministic approaches (ELIZA, Expert Systems) to probabilistic methods (HMMs, GMMs) and later to deep learning architectures such as GANs, Transformers, and Diffusion Models, which have revolutionized AI-generated content across multiple domains.

TABLE 2.2
Evolution of Generative AI – From Rule-Based Systems to Neural Networks

Model Name	Year	Key Contributions	Strengths	Challenges	Example Models
Rule-Based Systems[4]	1960s	Used IF-THEN rules for AI decision-making	Simple logic-based decisions	Rigid, lacks adaptability	ELIZA (1966)
Expert Systems	1980s	Stored rule-based knowledge for decision-making	Better decision-making in structured domains	Requires manual rule updates	MYCIN (1970s)
Statistical Models	1990s	Introduced probabilistic models for text/speech	Mathematically robust predictions	Struggled with complex, high-dimensional data	Gaussian Mixture Models (GMM)
Markov Chains & HMMs	1990s	Enabled statistical predictions for NLP and speech	Effective for sequential data processing	Limited context awareness & scalability	Hidden Markov Models (HMM)
Machine Learning-Based AI	2000s	Shifted AI to data-driven learning approaches	Automated learning from large datasets	Required extensive feature engineering	Latent Dirichlet Allocation (LDA)
Autoencoders & VAEs [6]	2010-2013	Introduced unsupervised learning for generative tasks	Better representation learning for generative tasks	Limited in producing high-resolution images	Variational Autoencoders (VAEs)
Generative Adversarial Networks (GANs)	2014	Introduced adversarial training for synthetic data	High-quality, realistic AI-generated content	Mode collapse & training instability	Vanilla GAN (Goodfellow et al., 2014)
Wasserstein GAN (WGAN) & cGAN	2016-2017	Improved training stability & controlled generation	More stable training & conditional data control	High computational cost & labeled data needs	WGAN, cGAN
BigGAN & StyleGAN	2018-2019	Enhanced resolution and diversity in AI-generated images	Ultra-high-resolution images & artistic control	Computationally expensive	BigGAN, StyleGAN
Transformer-Based Models (GPT, DALL-E)[9, 35]	2020	Revolutionized text and image generation with transformers	Better contextual understanding & text generation	Large models require significant resources	GPT-3
Diffusion Models (Stable Diffusion, Imagen) [17, 36]	2021-2022	Used iterative noise reduction for realistic images	High-quality, diverse image generation	Slow generation speed	Stable Diffusion, Imagen
Multimodal AI (Text-Image-Video)	2023-Present	Enabled multimodal AI across text, images, and video	Generates text, images, videos, and multimodal content	High energy consumption & ethical concerns	GPT-4, Gemini, Runway Gen-2

2.3   THE TRANSFORMATIVE JOURNEY OF GENERATIVE AI

Generative AI has undergone a significant transformation, moving from rule-based symbolic systems to data-driven deep learning architectures. This journey can be divided into three major phases, each representing a shift in how AI generates and processes data.

2.3.1   RULE-BASED AND STATISTICAL AI (BEFORE THE 2000s)

The early approaches to Generative AI included Rule-Based Systems and Statistical AI Models that can be said to be the roots of content generation by artificial intelligence. However, before AI could learn from data, it depended on rules that were installed into the system and probabilistic algorithms to analyze and formulate structured answers. Although these approaches brought initial forms of generative modeling, they were not easily flexible and expandable to solve more complex problems.

The development of Rule-Based AI and Statistical AI was a result of the increasing demand for automation of decision-making, language processing as well as problem-solving. In the early years of AI, researchers attempted to model human intelligence in a manner that could be programmed with rules that would allow the computer to perform the designated task in an orderly and organized manner. The AI applications progressed into speech/text processing; the statistical models replaced rule-based approaches where AI generates the answer based on probability distribution.

From the 1960s till 1980, there was the emergence of expert systems and symbolic AI, which used rules for processing and creating responses. ELIZA, SHRDLU, and MYCIN were some of the first models that depicted how AI functions like human reasoning; however, they could not accommodate new data [4].

Statistical AI gained prominence from the 1980s to the early 2000s, marking a shift from manually defined rules to probabilistic learning models. Techniques like Markov Chains, Hidden Markov Models (HMMs), Gaussian Mixture Models (GMMs), and N-gram models allowed AI to generate text, speech, and structured data dynamically, enabling early speech recognition and language processing applications. While these methods improved generative capabilities, they still lacked adaptability, paving the way for deep learning-based AI in the 2010s.

Figure 2.2 The Rule-Based AI Workflow Diagram represents a structured approach to decision-making, where predefined rules guide the system in processing user input and generating responses. The process begins when the user provides input through the User Interface, which acts as an intermediary between the user and the AI system. This input can be in the form of a query, command, or request for information. The User Interface then forwards this input to the Inference Engine, which serves as the core component responsible for processing and reasoning.

The inference Engine of the Expert System communicates with the two Knowledge base components namely: Rules and Facts. Rules are IF-THEN statements that are set reflecting the action of the system in response to any scenario, whereas the facts are an existing repository of information or prior known information to the system. The working memory is also used in the reasoning process of the Inference Engine,

Rule Based AI Workflow Diagram

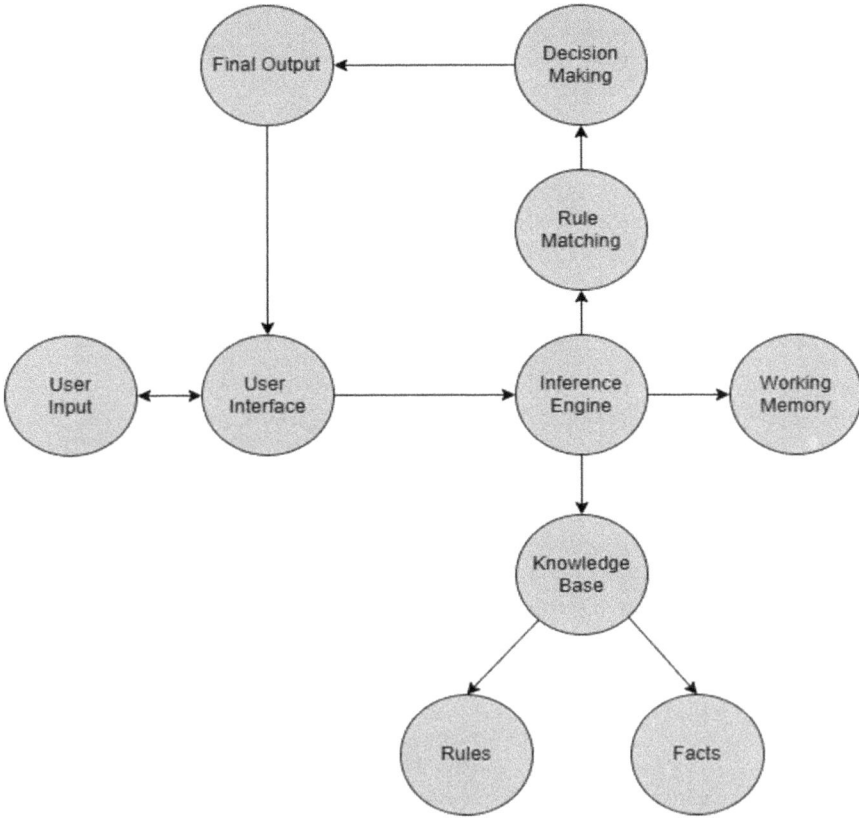

FIGURE 2.2 Rule-Based AI Workflow Diagram.

to store temporary information that is necessary to keep a record of context or other essential data used in the process.

When the Inference Engine gets an input, the rule-matching process ensues where the most suitable rule from the Knowledge Base is selected for the input. The next step after successful association of a rule is the Decision Making where the system uses logical processing to arrive at the best response. Finally, the decision goes to the Final Output stage which transfers the response to the User Interface to provide the system's answer to the user.

This architecture makes the AI decisions rigid, logical, and rule-based to reduce the chances of early failures as much as possible. It does not have learning capabilities and therefore new rules, which define the operation of the system, must be input into the system for the system to grow. This limitation led to other forms of Artificial Intelligence like Machine Intelligence and Deep intelligence which are capable of improving with time through data Held-member.

Statistical AI Workflow Diagram

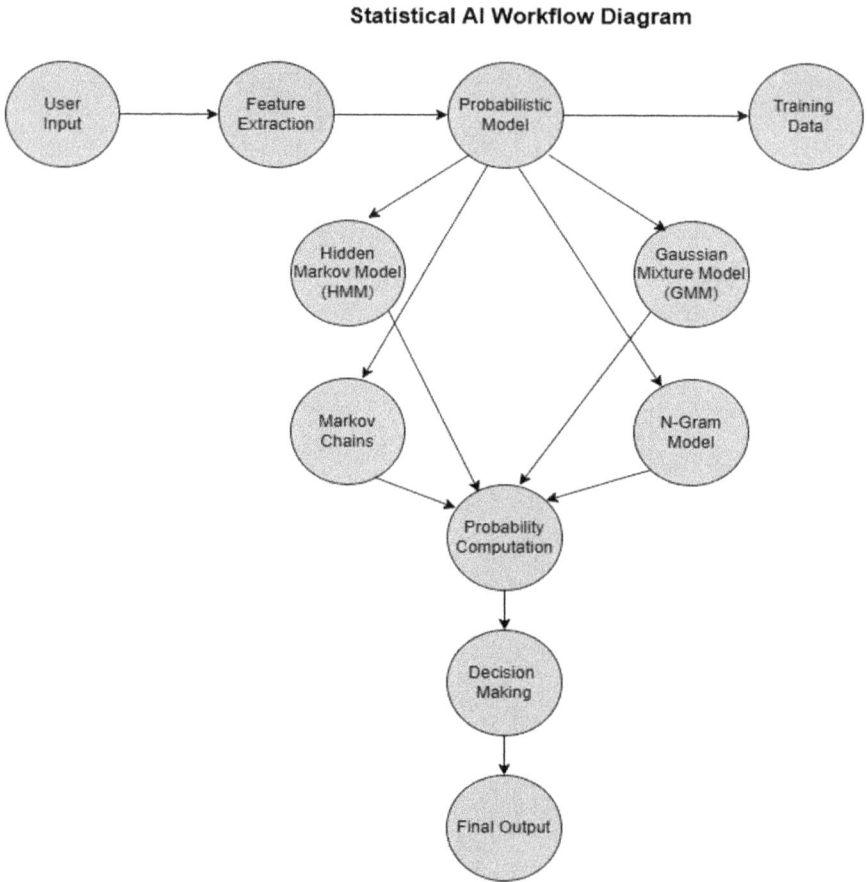

FIGURE 2.3   Statistical AI Workflow Diagram.

Figure 2.3 shows that the Statistical AI Architecture is the structure the Statistical AI follows as opposed to the Rule-based AI that uses specific rules in processing data. It starts with the User Input where data is acquired and passes through Feature Extraction to determine the features. The Probabilistic Model then applies this data with the help of models such as Hidden Markov Models for sequential data, Gaussian Mixture Models for clustering, Markov Chains for state and value prediction, and N-Gram models for the generation of text. These models will work with Training Data to compute probability and to get outcomes.

After that, Probability Computation makes use of statistical analysis to find out the chances of occurrence of certain outcomes. The last component of the model is the Decision-Making component that decides on the most likely outcome which is the Final Output. This architecture makes Statistical AI capable of dealing with the uncertainty of data, gaining knowledge from it, and making probability estimations, which makes Statistical AI suitable to be used in speech recognition, machine translation, and other field of predictive analysis. It gives the ability to plan, organize, control, and review AI-driven processes in terms of effectiveness, flexibility, and expandability.

2.3.2 Deep Learning and Generative Architectures (2010s–Early 2021)

Deep learning-based generative AI emerged as a result of advances in neural networks, large-scale datasets, and increased computational power [5, 14]. Unlike statistical AI, which relied on handcrafted feature extraction, deep learning allowed AI models to automatically learn hierarchical patterns from raw data. This made it possible to generate high-quality text, images, and video, which made it a new generation of generative AI [15]. Autoencoders, GANs, and transformers were principles that contributed to developing AI's capacity for creating realistic content using unsupervised and self-supervised learning techniques [6].

The two branches of generative AI began with the concept of Autoencoders and Variational Autoencoders in the early 2010s. In 2014, they presented adversarial training for realistic image generation for GANs. The Transformer architecture in 2017 initiated state-of-art models such as GPT, BERT for text, and DALL·E in images and text-image generation [11, 16]. By early 2020, deep learning-based generative AI also emerged as the prevalent technique and was applied in various fields of art, healthcare, and real-time content generation replacing traditional AI in terms of flexibility and scalability.

Deep learning-based generative AI was developed and became popular because of its superior capacity to learn the pattern of data without the need for prior rules or statistical knowledge. The availability of big data, availability and enhancements in GPUs/TPUs, and new and improved neural network architectures helped AI to come up with improved text, images, and videos. They include GANs, VAEs, and Transformers and were widely used in art, media, healthcare, and interactive applications.

However, training instabilities, mode collapses and limited diversities in the generated outputs of GANs led the researchers to look for more stable and scalable models. This led to the advent of Diffusion Models and Multimodal AI where generation quality, diversity, and control over generated output was enhanced by the use of iterative noise-based generation (Diffusion Models), and multimodal learning of both GPT-4 and DeepSeek V2 [17]. These further advancements also enhanced the efficiency and robustness of generative AI and also made it more usable in different domains.

2.3.2.1 Early GANs (2014–2015)

The GANs were introduced in 2014 by Goodfellow et al. [18]. Although this model broke the ground of generative AI, it had two issues: mode collapse, and instability in training. However, GANs defined the prospects of the field and built a new starting point for the progress of the concept. Later extensions touched upon these problems, and DCGANs appeared in 2015 [19]. This was achieved by the use of convolutional and deconvolution layers that make DCGAN a major advancement in the progression of GANs.

Table 2.3 summarizes the evolution pattern of GAN architectures from Vanilla GAN to DCGAN. Even though the field was not very developed at that time, a lot of progress was made during that period. This table highlights the current models of generative adversarial networks built up from the fundamental ones.

The graphical representation in Figure 2.4 shows the overall structure of the architecture of the basic GAN model, which is described as Vanilla GAN. It also explains the set sequences and elements that explain the formation of the model [20].

2.3.2.2 Recent Innovations and Trends in GANs (2016–2021)

In 2017, Arjovsky et al. proposed WGANs mainly to solve the training instability problem of traditional GANs. The use of Wasserstein loss has enhanced the stability

TABLE 2.3
Early Developments in GAN Models (2014–2015)

Model Name	Year	Key Contributions	Strengths	Challenges
Generative Adversarial Networks (GAN) / Vanilla GAN [18]	2014	Introduced the adversarial training framework, establishing the foundation for generative modeling. First to utilize a generator-discriminator architecture.	Innovative approach to data generation.	Susceptible to mode collapse and training instability.
Deep Convolutional GAN (DCGAN) [19]	2015	Integrated convolutional and transposed convolutional layers, enhancing stability and improving image generation quality.	Enhanced image clarity and training robustness.	Still experiences mode collapse and struggles with generating high-quality images consistently.

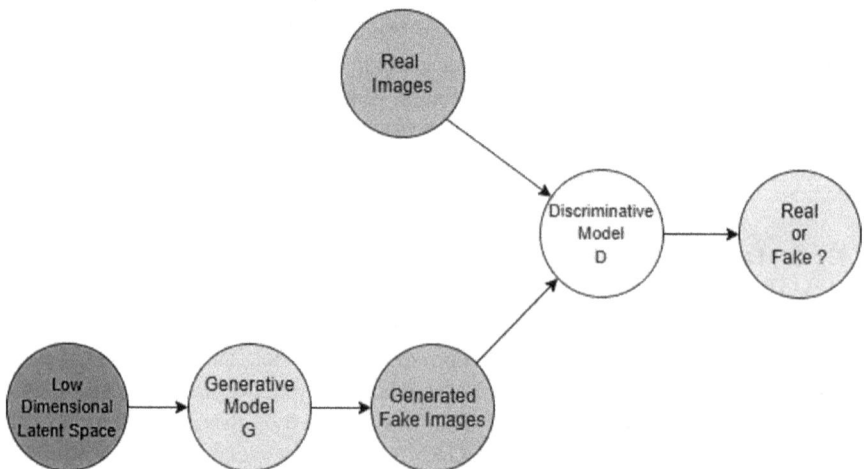

FIGURE 2.4   Basic Architecture of Vanilla GAN Model (2014–2015).

and/or convergence of the GAN training procedure. There was an excess of successes over the years such as BigGAN for high-resolution image synthesis as well as cGANs in generating controlled and more orderly data.

Table 2.4 describes how GAN architectures have developed over the years and lists the main milestones that define the development of the current generation of generative AI. These developments enhanced the aspects of image distinctiveness, the stability and expansiveness of training, and previous issues encountered such as mode collapse and ineffective training.

2.3.3 Diffusion Models and Multimodal AI (2021–Present)

The successive generation of AI has proceeded beyond GANs and transformers and has included diffusion models and, more lately, multimodal AI, which has improved the generation of content in text, images, and audio [21, 22]. As for diffusion models such as DDPMs and LDMs, they are stable and more effective than GANs since they gradually denoise random noises to generate high-quality and realistic synthetic data [23, 24]. At the same time, there are several current multi-modal AI models such as DALL·E, Flamingo, and DeepSeek-V2 which allow combined learning of different data types [25] that increase the potential of AI in generating new content, video synthesis in real-time, and AI-aided design.

Table 2.5 presents the latest breakthroughs in diffusion models and multimodal AI, illustrating the shift towards more stable, scalable, and multimodal-capable generative models. These advancements further improve the generative AI model in generating synthetic images, videos, and cross-modal data for the development of new AI-based applications in creativity, design, and interactivity.

2.4 COMPUTATIONAL ADVANCEMENTS

2.4.1 Hardware and Software Improvements

The development has made a revolution in the hardware and software that have enhanced the speed, capacity, and computational capability necessary in training GANs, Diffusion Models, and Multimodal AI. GPUs and TPUs perform computations in parallel to speed up the process for the training of giant models. The two popular and flexible deep learning frameworks are Tensor Flow available in 2015 and Py Torch in 2016 [26]. New and advanced Models such as Diffusion Models and Multimodal AI have brought more computational needs for hardware accelerators, distributed computing, and memory-efficient optimizations for models like DALL·E, Stable Diffusion, DeepSeek-V2, and so on.

Table 2.6 summarises the role of some key aspects of hardware and software in Generative AI, which demonstrates how the GPU, TPU, distribution training and memory optimizations have enabled faster training and extended the scalability of the GANs, Diffusion Models & Multimodal AI. Such advances keep on creating the foundations for advanced, enhanced, and more available artificial intelligence systems that make inventions in text-to-image synthesis, real-time video generation, and multimodal interfaces potential.

TABLE 2.4
Key Innovations in GAN Architectures (2016–2021)

Year	Model/Technique	Key Contributions	Key Features	Strengths	Challenges
2016	Improved GAN Training [37]	Introduced spectral normalization, label smoothing, and feature matching for enhanced training stability.	Improved stability, better image quality	More robust training, higher quality outputs	Increased computational cost
2016	Conditional GANs (cGANs) [38]	Enabled conditional image generation using additional labeled data.	Controllable image generation	Allows generation of images with specific attributes	Requires additional labeled data
2017	WGAN (Wasserstein GAN) [39]	Used Wasserstein distance to improve training stability and convergence.	Improved stability, better convergence	Reduces mode collapse, generates realistic images	Computationally expensive
2017	Progressive GAN (ProGAN) [40]	Introduced progressive growing for generating high-resolution images efficiently.	Efficient high-resolution image synthesis	Enables realistic high-res images	Memory-intensive training
2018	StyleGAN [41]	Developed a style-based generator for precise image manipulation and disentangled latent space.	Fine-grained control over generated images	Allows easier editing and style transfer	High computational cost
2019	StyleGAN2 [42]	Enhanced image quality, diversity, and artifact reduction over StyleGAN.	Improved diversity and artifact-free images	Produces more realistic results	Computationally expensive
2020	BigGAN [43]	Scaled GANs to massive datasets for state-of-the-art image synthesis.	High-quality image generation	Produces extremely realistic images	Requires extensive computational resources
2021	StyleGAN3 [44, 45]	Further improved image quality and introduced adaptive discriminator augmentation.	Enhanced detail and stability	Generates more realistic and fine-detailed images	Still computationally expensive

TABLE 2.5
Key Diffusion Models and Multimodal AI Innovations (2021–Present)

Year	Model/ Technique	Key Contributions	Key Features	Strengths	Challenges
2021	Denoising Diffusion Probabilistic Models (DDPM)[23]	Introduced iterative denoising to improve image generation stability	High-quality image synthesis, better training stability	Overcomes mode collapse, produces photorealistic images	Computationally intensive
2022	Latent Diffusion Models (LDMs)[24]	Enhanced diffusion efficiency by reducing computation in latent space	Faster image generation, memory-efficient	Enables high-resolution image generation at lower cost	Requires fine-tuning for optimal performance
2022	GLIDE	Combined diffusion models with text-to-image capabilities for improved AI art generation	Text-guided image synthesis	Generates more detailed and coherent images based on textual descriptions	Still lacks full control over fine details
2023	Stable Diffusion	Open-source model enabling high-resolution image generation with greater accessibility	Open-source, computationally efficient	Democratized high-quality generative AI, enabling broader usage	Ethical concerns regarding misuse and copyright
2023	DALL.E 2	Improved multimodal text-to-image synthesis with greater image quality and diversity	Text-to-image generation, detailed image synthesis	Generates high-resolution images based on textual input	May require extensive computing resources
2024	DeepSeek-V2 [25]	Advanced multimodal model integrating text, image, and code generation	Unified multimodal learning, enhanced AI reasoning	Bridges multiple data types for richer AI interaction	Still evolving, requires large datasets for training
2024	Sora (OpenAI)	Extended multimodal AI capabilities to real-time video synthesis	AI-generated video, high-fidelity motion synthesis	Enables realistic, coherent AI-driven video generation	High computational cost, potential ethical concerns

TABLE 2.6
Computational Advancements in Generative AI

Framework/ Hardware	Year	Key Features	Advantages	Limitations	Impact on Generative AI Models
TensorFlow [46]	2015	Comprehensive deep learning framework	Versatile, supports large-scale model training	Steeper learning curve	Supports advanced GAN architectures (BigGAN, StyleGAN) and Diffusion Models, enabling GPU acceleration and distributed training.
PyTorch [47]	2016	Dynamic computation graphs, ease of debugging	Flexible, widely used in research	Smaller ecosystem (compared to TensorFlow)	Preferred for research in diffusion models, facilitates custom AI model experimentation, and supports multimodal AI training.
GPU (Graphics Processing Units)	2014-2016	Parallel processing for deep learning models	Speeds up training significantly	Expensive hardware	Essential for training high-resolution GANs (StyleGAN3, BigGAN) and optimizing Diffusion Models for large-scale AI applications.
TPU (Tensor Processing Units)	2017-2024	Specialized hardware for deep learning workloads	Faster training for large models	Limited availability	Crucial for Diffusion Model training, enabling faster convergence in models like Stable Diffusion and LDMs.
Distributed Training	2019- Present	Large-scale AI model training across multiple GPUs/TPUs	Enables parallel training of massive AI models	Requires high computational infrastructure	Used in multimodal AI (DeepSeek-V2, DALL-E 3) for handling high-dimensional data efficiently.
Memory-Efficient Optimization (ZeRO, LoRA, Quantization)	2021- Present	Reduces memory overhead for large generative models	Allows training of larger AI models on limited hardware	May sacrifice some model precision	Used in Diffusion Models and Multimodal AI for scaling AI systems efficiently.

2.4.2 Computational Efficiency

Computational efficiency of generative AI improved when it evolved from rule-based systems to diffusion models. Previous AI models needed little resources but were not very extensible, while the generative models based on DL such as Generative Adversarial Networks needed more computation. Selecting a model depended on the need of the application, the quality of the image required, and the available tools. Diffusion Models are a more stable and efficient approach than GANs and involve calculating images by iterative denoising them.

Table 2.7 shows the performance comparison of several generative AI models while Table 2.8 contains information on the effect of improvement in GPU on generative AI. The change from rule-based systems to diffusion models implies that there is a increase in computational complexity and in generative capacity. Although GANs are better in terms of computational efficiency, diffusion models are both much more stable and easier to control. The advancements of different types of accelerators (GPUs/TPUs) have paved the way for these advancements and have made large-scale generative AI implementable in the real world.

In Figure 2.5, a bar chart shows the number of GFLOPS and is accompanied by FID scores in a line plot for generative AI with NVIDIA GPUs. Higher GFLOPS represent increased computational throughput, and lower FID refers to a better quality of output produced in the case of AI-generated images. Hence, it is clear that promoting the next generation of GPUs (RTX 4090, B200, and Future GPUs) provides significantly high GFLOPS that can enhance the deployment of Stable Diffusion, DeepSeek-V2, and the next generation of diffusion-based AI designs.

2.5 DATASETS AND TRAINING CHALLENGES

The dataset in Generative AI is equally essential in shaping the performance of these models as concerning the number of fidelities and diversities. The training of the AI models requires large-scale datasets that include ImageNet [27], CelebA [28], and LSUN [29] that have been developed for GANs and diffusion models. Later, there are recent datasets such as LAION-5B for text-to-image generation which enhanced the work on multimodal AI.

Table 2.9 presents the generative AI training dataset starting from the evolution with MNIST, and CIFAR-10 to the recent ones like the LAION-5B for multimodal AI. These aspects include size, resolution, type, usage, and the effect of datasets, making it clear that various datasets are suitable for various generative models such as GANs, Diffusion Models, and Text-to-Image AI. The inclusion of LAION-5B underscores the advancements in text-to-image and multimodal AI research, essential for next-generation generative models like Stable Diffusion and DALL·E.

2.5.1 Ethical Concerns in Training Data

As generative AI Models improving in capabilities are being released, the question of their ethical use of datasets become prominent. It is crucial to address the fact that misapplication, prejudice, and the unsuitable use of copyrights are among the key

TABLE 2.7
Comparative Analysis of Computational Efficiency for Generative AI Architectures

Model Variant	Year	Architecture	Computational Efficiency	Resource Usage	Training Time (Hours)	Key Efficiency Improvements
Rule-Based AI	Pre-1980s	IF-THEN Logic	Very Low	Minimal	N/A	Deterministic decision-making, no learning capability
Statistical Models (HMM, GMM, N-Grams)	1980s-2000s	Probabilistic Models	Low	Low	N/A	Improved text/speech modeling but lacks adaptability
Vanilla GAN	2014	Basic Generator-Discriminator	Relatively Low	High	10	Prone to mode collapse, instability
DCGAN	2015	Convolutional GAN	Moderate	Moderate	5	Faster training, better stability
Conditional GANs (cGANs)	2016	Adds conditioning labels (text, class, etc.)	Moderate to High	Moderate	8	Enables controlled generation
WGAN	2017	Wasserstein Distance Loss	Low	High	2	Better convergence, improved image quality
Progressive GAN	2017	Progressive Layered Growth	Efficient for high-resolution	High	15	Faster training for large images
StyleGAN	2018	Mapping Network	Very High	Very High	20	Efficient, diverse image generation
StyleGAN2	2019	Improved StyleGAN	Very High	Very High	25	Enhanced quality, diversity
BigGAN	2020	Scaled-up Architecture	Extremely High	Extremely High	30	State-of-the-art image fidelity
StyleGAN3	2021	Adaptive Discriminator Augmentation	Very High	Very High	30	Stabilized training, improved quality
Denoising Diffusion Models (DDPMs)	2021	Iterative Noise Reduction	High	Very High	35	Overcomes mode collapse, stable generation
Latent Diffusion Models (LDMs)	2022	Optimized Diffusion Process	High	High	20	Memory-efficient diffusion for large-scale synthesis
Stable Diffusion	2023	Open-Source Latent Diffusion	Very High	Moderate	15	Computationally optimized for wider accessibility
DeepSeek-V2 [25]	2024	Multimodal AI Integration	Very High	Very High	40	Cross-modal learning, AI-generated videos

TABLE 2.8
NVIDIA GPU Performance and FID Scores for Generative AI

NVIDIA GPU Type	GFLOPS	AI Model Type	Estimated FID Score (Lower is Better)
TX 1080	8,873	DCGAN	90
Tesla P100	10,618	WGAN	50
RTX 2080 Ti	13,500	WGAN-GP	45
Tesla V100	15,744	Progressive GAN	30
RTX 3090	35,840	StyleGAN	15
A100	31,200	BigGAN	10
H100	60,000	StyleGAN2	8
RTX 4090	82,400	Stable Diffusion	6
B200	120,000	DeepSeek-V2	4
Hypothetical Future GPU	200,000	Future Diffusion Model	2

threats posed by artificial content. These challenges must be addressed for responsible AI advancement.

a. Bias in Datasets
In datasets the generative models reproduce prejudices that are inherent in the training data. The risk of using AI models that arise from imbalanced datasets is that the learned AI models can be biased; this is because if the sample datasets are imbalanced, the results will also be skewed posing a significant concern in the social and cultural realms.

b. Deepfake Misuse
GANs that were trained from face datasets such as CelebA & FFHQ pose the risk of generating fake information concerning identity, fraud, & security [2, 30].

c. Copyright and Privacy Risks
Using datasets that contain scraped images from the internet, such as LAION-5B, can violate laws and use personal images without the approval of the subject.

Table 2.10 sums up the ethical risks that are linked with training data in Generative AI, including bias, deepfake exploitation, and copyright infringement. It illustrates possible threats posed when working with imbalanced datasets, unauthorized information sources, and deepfakes created by artificial intelligence tools. Finally, the table provides pragmatic measures including data balancing, legal guidelines and regulations, and identifies clear sources of data for AI to foster ethical AI and AI-based technologies.

2.6 APPLICATIONS

GANs have been implemented in numerous spheres thus revolutionizing how AI creates and alters or improves information. The primary idea of GANs was to generate images and edit them, however, now it is used in text generation, video

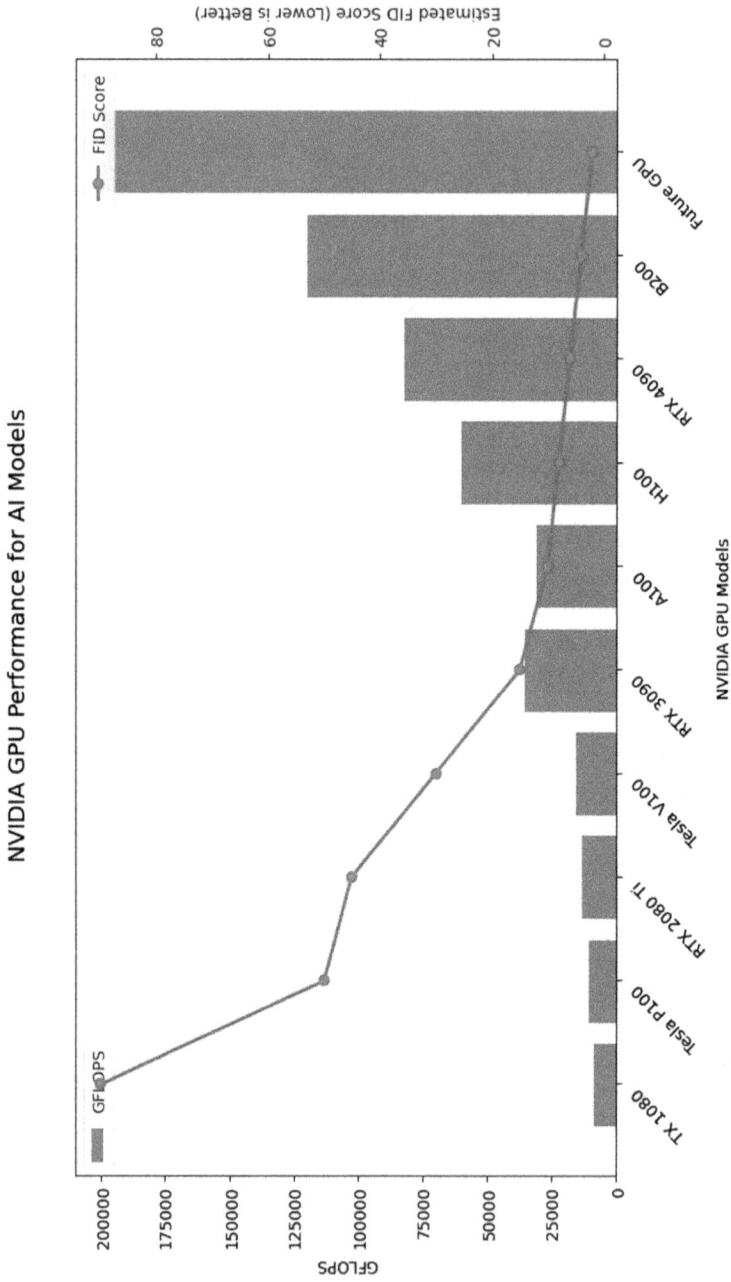

FIGURE 2.5 NVIDIA GPU Performance and GAN FID Scores for GAN Architectures.

TABLE 2.9
Datasets for GAN Training

Dataset	Size	Resolution	Type	Usage	Impact
ImageNet [27]	14 Million	Varies	Diverse	General image recognition	Foundation for many GANs
CelebA [28]	200K	178x178 Pixels	Faces	Face generation, attribute manipulation	Benchmark for face-related GANs
LSUN [29]	10 Million	Varies	Diverse	Scene understanding, object generation	Used for various GAN architectures
MNIST [48]	70K	28x28 Pixels	Handwritten digits	Basic GAN experiments, benchmarking	Simple dataset for testing GAN concepts
Fashion-MNIST [49]	70K	28x28 Pixels	Fashion items	Fashion-related GANs, benchmarking	Alternative to MNIST
CIFAR-10/CIFAR-100 [50]	60K	32x32 Pixels	Natural images	Image classification, object recognition	Widely used for image generation tasks
Flickr-Faces-HQ (FFHQ) [41]	800K	1024X1024 Pixels	High-quality faces	Face generation, manipulation	Benchmark for high-resolution face generation
LSUN Bedrooms [51, 52]	3M	256x256 Pixels	Indoor scenes	Scene generation, image-to-image translation	Specific domain for GAN training
LAION-5B	5 Billion	Varies	Multimodal (Text-Image)	Text-to-image generation, multimodal AI research	Crucial for training Stable Diffusion, DALL-E, DeepSeek-V2

TABLE 2.10
Ethical Concerns in Generative AI Training Data

Ethical Concern	Description	Potential Risks	Solutions
Bias in Datasets	AI inherits biases from imbalanced datasets, leading to unfair representations.	Unfair AI decisions, stereotype reinforcement, societal impact.	Dataset balancing, diverse representation, fairness auditing.
Deepfake Misuse [30]	GANs can create realistic deepfakes, spreading misinformation.	Fake media creation, identity theft, reputational damage.	Regulatory compliance, watermarking AI-generated content.
Copyright & Privacy Risks	Web-scraped datasets may include copyrighted or personal content.	Unauthorized use, privacy invasion, and potential lawsuits.	Transparency in dataset sourcing, user consent, and ethical AI policies.

TABLE 2.11
GAN Applications across Various Domains

Application Category	Examples	Impact
Text Generation	ChatGPT, GPT-4, BERT, Summarization Tools	Automates writing improves language modeling, and enhances conversational AI.
Image and Video Generation	Deepfakes, AI Art (DALL-E, MidJourney, Stable Diffusion), Video Gen (Runway Gen-2)	Enables high-quality AI-generated visuals, realistic videos, and creative media synthesis.
Music and Speech Synthesis	AI-generated Music (Jukebox, OpenAI Whisper, Google MusicLM)	Advances AI-composed music, voice synthesis, and speech-to-text applications.
Scientific & Medical Applications [53]	Protein Folding (AlphaFold), AI in Drug Discovery, Medical Image Synthesis	Accelerates biomedical research, improves medical diagnostics, and enhances drug development.
Gaming and Virtual Worlds	Procedural Content Generation, AI NPCs, Realistic Game Environments	Enhances gaming realism, automates world-building, and improves user experience.
Finance and Business	Algorithmic Trading, Financial Forecasting, AI-powered Business Intelligence	Optimizes financial predictions, assists decision-making, and enhances automation in businesses.
Cybersecurity and Privacy	AI-driven Anonymization, Deepfake Detection, Secure Identity Verification	Strengthens cybersecurity, protects identity, and prevents misinformation.

generation, music synthesis, and even in the scientific field. These are usually due to their high realism capabilities and have application in areas such as computer vision, entertainment, and even health. The following table enlists all the areas of the GAN application in detail:

Table 2.11 highlights the diverse applications of Generative Adversarial Networks (GANs) across various industries, including computer vision, healthcare, finance, cybersecurity, and entertainment. It demonstrates how GANs are revolutionizing various fields through high-quality content generation, medical image enhancement, fraud detection, and AI-powered autonomous systems. These advancements under-score GANs' transformative impact on automation, creativity, and decision-making across multiple domains [31].

2.7   CHALLENGES AND LIMITATIONS

Generative AI has evolved significantly from rule-based systems to deep learning-powered architectures, including GANs, transformers, and diffusion models. Despite these advancements, several challenges and limitations persist across different generative AI paradigms.

2.7.1   ETHICAL AND SOCIAL CONCERNS

As generative AI models become more powerful, misinformation, deepfakes, and copyright issues have emerged as major ethical challenges. Deepfake technology can be exploited to spread false narratives, creating security risks in politics, finance, and personal privacy. Additionally, large-scale datasets, such as LAION-5B, often contain unlicensed images, raising concerns over intellectual property rights [30].

2.7.2   MODEL EXPLAINABILITY

Deep learning-based generative models, particularly GANs, VAEs, and diffusion models, are often considered black-box systems, making it difficult to interpret how they generate outputs. Rule-based AI had greater transparency due to explicit rules, whereas modern generative models operate on complex latent spaces that lack inter-pretability [32]. This lack of transparency makes it challenging to debug errors, assess biases, and ensure fairness in AI-generated content.

2.7.3   COMPUTATIONAL COST

The advancements of GANs and the diffusion models have made the requisite computations exponentially steeper from statistical models. To train generative models like Stable Diffusion, DALL·E, and GPT-4, it is necessary to use big datasets and spe-cific hardware (NVIDIA A100 and H100 GPU, TPUs). This means high energy con-sumption and cost-limit accessibility for small organizations and researchers.

2.7.4 MODE COLLAPSE AND TRAINING INSTABILITY

Usually GANs entails a problem known as mode collapse in which the generator becomes unable to output new data and thus, provides repetitive content. Although some techniques like Wasserstein loss and gradient penalties have been used to increase training stability, GANs are highly non-robust. It is important to note that while diffusion models' mode collapse is taken care by gradually diffusing noise into coherent images, the price is computational load.

2.7.5 DATA REQUIREMENTS AND BIAS

Bias in training data is usually devolved from societal stereotypes or prejudice and this would cause the output to be a reflection of the stereotype. Furthermore, violation of privacy occurs when these models are trained on large-scale internet-scraped data without consent.

2.7.6 EVALUATION CHALLENGES

It can therefore be deduced that there is no standard measure of the evaluations made by generative AI models. There are established methods, such as Inception score (IS) and Fréchet Inception Distance (FID) that are suitable for GANs, but they do not consider qualities like creativity or realism. As new methods of text-to-image, audio synthesis, and video generation are based on diffusion models and multimodal AI, new methods of evaluation are needed.

GANs have been found to be very effective in many computer vision problems and have exhibited great promise. However, they have some drawbacks and restrictions. Many GANs face Common Challenges during training; they include instability and mode collapse [33]. Such issues have been tackled by methods such as Wasserstein loss as well as gradient penalty but problems still arise.

Table 2.12, encapsulates a summary of the difficulties and the lacks observed for Generative AI, beginning from GANs and leading to diffusion models. This raises problems such as mode collapse, instability of the training process, and the problem of high computational costs arising with large-scale generative models [34]. It also raises the issues of assessment of model performance, model diversity and quality of the output, and the internal working of deep learning-based generative models. The following topics are also illustrated: risks on the ethical side while using data, including misinformation, deep fake, and data privacy; and the issue of large and diverse data sets.

2.8 FUTURE DIRECTIONS

AI in Generative Synthesizing has shifted its stages—from traditional rule-based systems to deep learning AI generative methods, GANs, Transformers, and Diffusion models. Although these have helped in high-quality image, text, and video generation, there remain some issues and possibilities for future work. New directions include better models for training, raising the level of controllability,

TABLE 2.12
Challenges and Limitations of GANs

Challenge/Limitation	Description
Mode Collapse	The generator produces a limited variety of samples, failing to cover full data distribution.
Training Instability	Small changes in hyperparameters or architecture can drastically impact performance.
Evaluating GAN Performance	The lack of standardized metrics makes assessing the quality of generated outputs challenging.
Generating Diverse and High-Quality Samples	Difficulty in producing realistic and diverse outputs, especially for complex data distributions.
Lack of Interpretability	Understanding how GANs and other generative models make decisions remains difficult.
Computational Cost	High computational power and energy consumption are required for training large-scale models.
Ethical and Social Concerns	Issues related to misinformation, deepfakes, and potential copyright violations.
Data Requirements	Large and diverse datasets are essential for training robust generative models.
Model Explainability	The black-box nature of deep learning makes model behavior difficult to interpret and explain.

decreasing computational costs, and the correct approaches to creating Artificial Intelligence.

1. AI-Augmented Creativity
Another promising area that can be developed with the help of Generative AI is its integration with people in the field of art, music, and literature, or other creative professions, in general. DALL·E, MidJourney, and similar models influence content creation. The next release of AI is expected to be more co-creative with artists, musicians, and writers used for interactive and expressive content.

2. More Controllable AI Models
Early generative models such as rule-based AI followed strict logic, while GANs and diffusion models generated content based on probabilistic learning. However, achieving precise control over AI outputs remains a challenge. Advances in fine-tuning, reinforcement learning, and prompt engineering will allow users to guide AI-generated outputs with greater accuracy, improving their applicability in creative design, healthcare, and scientific research.

3. Energy-Efficient AI
Training large-scale AI models like GPT-4, Stable Diffusion, and BigGAN requires enormous computational resources, raising concerns about energy consumption and environmental impact [34]. Future research will focus on developing energy-efficient AI architectures, such as lightweight models, quantization techniques, and adaptive training strategies, reducing the carbon footprint of AI development.

4. Improving Training Stability

From rule-based AI to GANs, training instability has been a persistent challenge. Mode collapse, gradient vanishing, and convergence issues make training deep generative models difficult. Innovative loss functions, gradient-penalty techniques, and adversarial training improvements will enhance GAN and diffusion model performance, making them more stable and scalable.

5. Mode Collapse Mitigation and High-Fidelity Generation:

GANs, while powerful, often produce repetitive or low-diversity outputs due to mode collapse. Diffusion models have emerged as an alternative, generating highly detailed and diverse outputs. Future research will focus on improving diversity while maintaining efficiency, making text-to-image, video synthesis, and AI-generated media more lifelike and adaptable.

6. Cross-Modal Generation and Hybrid AI Architectures

In Cross-Modal Generation and Hybrid AI Architectures there are high chances of multiple AI models being integrated. It is likely that architectures that incorporate GANs, VAEs, Transformers, and Diffusion Models will take generative AI to higher innovation heights in terms of realism and adaptability. Among the key areas that will define multimodal AI is cross-modal generation which involves translating text to images, audio to video, speech to text, and so on.

7. Ethical AI and Explainability

As AI-generated media content appears more credible and realistic, issues of fake news circulation, deepfake, and even piracy are not unfounded. Future work needs to focus on reducing bias and explaining the decision-making of artificial intelligence systems, and also on the reduction of risks connected with the improper utilization of artificial intelligence technologies. Furthermore, increasing the interpretability of the AI models will enhance the knowability of the models' behavior making AI more dependable and explainable.

8. Personalized AI and Virtual Reality

With the progress of the generative AI applications will be created very specific content including recommendation systems, narrative generation, and intelligent learning. VR/AR technologies would further improve with the help of AI and the scope in industries like gaming, education, and interactivity would expand.

Table 2.13 shows an outline of Generative AI for the subsequent steps from rule-based systems to advanced diffusion models. It gives an overview of research areas, their relevance and implications, problems, and developments in those fields. The table also shows the future developments of Generative AI and concerns such as the integration of an AI in creativity, model controllability, training stability, energy efficiency, high-fidelity content generation, and cross-modal learning. It displays significant issues including ethical considerations in artificial intelligence, explaining AI, and a responsible approach to utilizing artificial intelligence innovations in various fields. It also shows recent trends in the development of hybrid approaches to AI, individualized AI solutions, and the integration of artificial intelligence and virtual reality. It is these ideas that form the basis for advances in AI optimization for efficiency.

TABLE 2.13

Comprehensive Future Research Directions in Generative AI

Research Area	Description	Potential Impact	Challenges	Current Research Efforts
AI-Augmented Creativity	Enhancing human-AI collaboration in art, music, and writing.	Empowers creativity in digital media and content generation.	Maintaining a balance between AI and human creativity.	AI-assisted creative tools (e.g., DALL-E, MidJourney, ChatGPT).
More Controllable AI Models [54]	Developing fine-tuning techniques for better AI control.	Improves AI applications for industry-specific solutions.	Ensuring AI generates meaningful and controllable outputs.	Fine-tuning methods (e.g., RLHF, reinforcement learning for control).
Energy-Efficient AI	Reducing computational costs and energy consumption.	Promotes sustainable AI with a lower carbon footprint.	High cost of training and deployment for efficient models.	Low-power AI models and hardware optimization techniques.
Improved Training Stability	Introducing new loss functions to improve training stability.	Reduces training failures and improves model consistency.	Overcoming instability in generative AI training.	Stability enhancements like Wasserstein GANs, improved loss functions.
Mode Collapse Mitigation	Preventing GANs and generative models from producing repetitive outputs.	Increases diversity and quality of AI-generated content.	Difficulty in ensuring unique and high-quality outputs.	Techniques such as adaptive learning and multi-generator architectures.
High-Fidelity Generation	Enhancing realism and resolution in AI-generated outputs.	Advances in digital art, gaming, and virtual reality.	Balancing high-resolution content with computational efficiency.	Diffusion-based models and super-resolution GANs.
Cross-Modal Generation	Generating content across different modalities (text, image, audio).	Enables seamless transformation between AI-generated formats.	Integrating diverse datasets for effective cross-modal learning.	Multimodal AI models like CLIP and DeepSeek.

(continued)

TABLE 2.13 (Continued)
Comprehensive Future Research Directions in Generative AI

Research Area	Description	Potential Impact	Challenges	Current Research Efforts
Hybrid AI Architectures[10]	Combining GANs, VAEs, Transformers, and Diffusion Models.	Expands AI applications to multi-modal learning.	Developing seamless interaction between different generative AI models.	Hybrid approaches combining neural architectures (GANs + Transformers).
Ethical AI and Explainability	Ensuring transparency, fairness, and mitigating ethical risks.	Addresses misinformation, deepfake detection, and AI ethics.	Regulating AI-generated media to prevent misuse.	AI fairness audits, deepfake detection, and transparency models.
Personalized AI	Customizing AI-generated content to user preferences.	Delivers more engaging and relevant AI-driven experiences.	Ensuring AI understands and adapts to individual preferences.	Adaptive AI-driven recommendations and personalized learning tools.
Virtual and Augmented Reality	Enhancing AI-driven VR and AR experiences.	Transforms immersive user interaction with AI.	Creating scalable and realistic virtual experiences.	AI-generated AR/VR platforms in gaming, education, and simulations.

2.9 CONCLUSION

This chapter has outlined the development of Generative AI from being a rule-based system to a neural-based model. We start with traditional AI which can be categorized into two namely: The expert systems and Symbolic AI systems, which are limited in their ability to learn and change. The change of the model to statistical learning: Markov models and probabilistic methods enabled decision-making based on the data collected, however, in contrast to previous methods, the results were simplified, and could not generate complex solutions.

The advancement in generative models based on deep learning significantly advanced the field. We discussed GAN, which offered adversarial training, paved the way to synthesize images, generate images from texts, using deep fake technology. However, the challenges of GANs include mode collapse, training instability, and computational costs that necessitate the creation of better generative models. Other types of models superseded CVAE GANs by providing higher efficiency and variation in generating diffusion models and Transformer added a hierarchical structure by setting up GPT-4, DALL·E, and DeepSeek to extend generative AI to the scope of multimodal applications.

We also highlighted critical issues and limitations such as: high computational complexity, the problem of ethics, interpretability, and bias of the training data. The discussions of the tethered issues of misinformation, deepfakes, and AI-generated media concerned the ethos of AI and the necessity for correct AI advances and regulation.

Future research within the Generative AI field, will need to focus on enhanced model performance, energy consumption, and the moral application of AI. Development in other problem areas like AI creativity concerning generative models, controllable generation models, cross-modal learning, and the architectures that combine two or more AI paradigms will see generative models achieve more enhanced results. Furthermore, the combination of Generative AI with virtual reality, personal AI, and problem-solving in the real world will create prospects for future developments.

Among the promising directions for further research, the following should be mentioned: the creation of transparent and interpretable models for generation, increasing energy efficiency of generative models while creating AI as both a creative tool and a work of art, compliance with human values, as well as global needs and principles of responsible AI usage. Thus, Generative AI will remain at the forefront of addressing existing issues as well as paving the way to opportunities for advanced content generation, automation, and smarter decision-making in different fields in the future.

REFERENCES

[1] J. Wu et al., "AI in protein structure prediction: From AlphaFold to generative models," *Nat. Mach. Intell.*, vol. 3, pp. 789–805, 2022.

[2] X. Lu et al., "Deepfake detection using self-supervised learning and contrastive loss," *IEEE Trans. Inf. Forensics Secur.*, vol. 17, pp. 1121–1135, 2022.

[3] G. Hinton, O. Vinyals, and J. Dean, "Distilling the knowledge in a neural network," arXiv preprint arXiv:1503.02531, 2015.

[4]   A. Vaswani et al., "Attention is all you need," in *Adv. Neural Inf. Process. Syst*, 2017, pp. 5998–6008.

[5]   X. Wang, K. He, and J. Sun, "Deep residual learning for image recognition," in *Proc. IEEE Conf. Comput. Vis. Pattern Recognit. (CVPR)*, 2016, pp. 770–778.

[6]   P. Vincent, H. Larochelle, Y. Bengio, and P. Manzagol, "Extracting and composing robust features with denoising autoencoders," in *Proc. Int. Conf. Mach. Learn. (ICML)*, 2008, pp. 1096–1103.

[7]   M. Mirza and S. Osindero, "Conditional generative adversarial nets," arXiv preprint arXiv:1411.1784, 2014.

[8]   X. Mao, Q. Li, H. Xie, R. Y. Lau, Z. Wang, and S. P. Smolley, "Least squares generative adversarial networks," in *Proc. IEEE Conf. Comput. Vis. Pattern Recognit. (CVPR)*, 2017, pp. 2794–2802.

[9]   E. Ramesh, P. B. Ward, and J. Harris, "Transformer-based generative models: A review of techniques and applications," *J. Artif. Intell. Res.*, vol. 68, pp. 121–156, 2022.

[10] R. Child, S. Gray, A. Radford, and I. Sutskever, "Transformers for image generation," arXiv preprint arXiv:2010.09797, 2020.

[11] J. Devlin, M. Chang, K. Lee, and K. Toutanova, "BERT: Pre-training of deep bidirectional transformers for language understanding," in *Proc. Conf. North Am. Chapter Assoc. Comput. Linguist.: Hum. Lang. Technol.*, 2019, pp. 4171–4186.

[12] X. Gu, A. Frolov, and A. Babenko, "Diffusion models for 3D shape generation," *IEEE Trans. Vis. Comput. Graph.*, vol. 30, no. 1, pp. 199–210, 2024.

[13] A. Nichol et al., "GLIDE: Towards photorealistic image generation and editing with text-guided diffusion models," *arXiv preprint* arXiv:2112.10741, 2021.

[14] D. Silver et al., "Mastering the game of Go with deep neural networks and tree search," *Nature*, vol. 529, no. 7587, pp. 484–489, 2016.

[15] J. Huang, Z. Guo, and L. Zhang, "Text-to-image synthesis using deep learning models: A comparative analysis," *IEEE Trans. Pattern Anal. Mach. Intell.*, vol. 45, no. 3, pp. 345–357, 2023.

[16] A. Dosovitskiy et al., "An image is worth 16x16 words: Transformers for image recognition at scale," in *Proc. Int. Conf. Learn. Represent. (ICLR)*, 2021.

[17] B. Zhang, H. Wu, and Y. Liu, "Text-conditioned video generation using diffusion models," in *Proc. IEEE Conf. Comput. Vis. Pattern Recognit. (CVPR)*, 2023, pp. 12701–12710.

[18] I. Goodfellow, J. Pouget-Abadie, M. Mirza, B. Xu, D. Warde-Farley, S. Ozair, A. Courville, and Y. Bengio, "Generative adversarial nets," in *Advances in Neural Information Processing Systems*, Ghahramani, M. Welling, C. Cortes, N. D. Lawrence, and K. Q. Weinberger, Eds., Montreal, Canada: Curran Associates, Inc. 2014, pp. 2672–2680.

[19] A. Radford, L. Metz, and S. Chintala, "Unsupervised representation learning with deep convolutional generative adversarial networks," *arXiv preprint* arXiv:1511.06434, 2015.

[20] L. Cai, Y. Chen, N. Cai, W. Cheng, and H. Wang, "Utilizing Amari-Alpha divergence to stabilize the training of generative adversarial networks," *Entropy*, vol. 22, no. 4, p. 410, 2020, doi: 10.3390/e22040410.

[21] J. Ho and T. Salimans, "Classifier-free diffusion guidance," *arXiv preprint* arXiv:2207.12598, 2022.

[22] P. Ramesh, T. Gupta, and K. Roy, "A survey on diffusion models for generative AI," *IEEE Access*, vol. 11, pp. 13457–13478, 2023.

[23] J. Ho, A. Jain, and P. Abbeel, "Denoising diffusion probabilistic models," *Adv. Neural Inf. Process. Syst.*, vol. 33, pp. 6840–6851, 2020.

[24] A. Nichol and P. Dhariwal, "Improved denoising diffusion probabilistic models," *arXiv preprint* arXiv:2102.09672, 2021.

[25] Y. Wu et al., "DeepSeek: Multimodal AI for real-time generative applications," *arXiv preprint* arXiv:2310.04798, 2024.

[26] K. He, X. Zhang, S. Ren, and J. Sun, "Delving deep into rectifiers: Surpassing human-level performance on ImageNet classification," in *Proc. IEEE Int. Conf. Comput. Vis. (ICCV)*, 2015, pp. 1026–1034.

[27] J. Deng, W. Dong, R. Socher, L.-J. Li, K. Li, and F.-F. Li, "ImageNet: A large-scale hierarchical image database," in *IEEE Conf. on Comput. Vis. and Pattern Recognit.*, 2009, pp. 248–255.

[28] Z. Liu, P. Luo, X. Wang, and X. Tang, "Deep learning face attributes in the wild," in *Proc. IEEE Intl. Conf. Comput. Vis.*, 2015, pp. 3730–3738.

[29] F. Yu, Y. Zhang, S. Song, A. Seff, and J. Xiao, "LSUN: Construction of a large-scale image dataset using deep learning with human feedback," *CoRR*, Ithaca, USA: Cornell University, 2015.

[30] X. Wang et al., "Deepfake detection: Challenges, trends, and future directions," *ACM Comput. Surv.*, vol. 54, no. 5, pp. 1–36, 2022.

[31] Y. Song et al., "Score-based generative modeling through stochastic differential equations," in *Proc. Int. Conf. Learn. Represent. (ICLR)*, 2021.

[32] M. Abadi et al., "Deep learning in drug discovery: Opportunities and challenges," *Nat. Rev. Drug Discov.*, vol. 19, no. 5, pp. 325–342, 2020.

[33] L. Metz et al., "Unrolled generative adversarial networks," in *Proc. Int. Conf. Mach. Learn.*, 2017.

[34] A. Radford, J. Wu, R. Child, D. Luan, D. Amodei, and I. Sutskever, "Language models are few-shot learners," arXiv preprint arXiv:2005.14165, 2020.

[35] R. Child, S. Gray, A. Radford, and I. Sutskever, "Generating long coherent texts with transformers," arXiv preprint arXiv:2004.12347, 2020.

[36] S. Vasudevan, R. K. Srivastava, and T. Kim, "Controllable text-to-image synthesis with diffusion models," *IEEE Trans. Neural Netw. Learn. Syst.*, vol. 34, no. 5, pp. 1552–1567, 2023.

[37] T. Salimans, I. Goodfellow, W. Zaremba, V. Cheung, A. Radford, and X. Chen, "Improved techniques for training gans," in *Advances in Neural Information Processing Systems*, 2016, pp. 2234–2242.

[38] A. Odena et al., "Conditional image synthesis with auxiliary classifier GANs," in *Proc. Int. Conf. Mach. Learn.*, 2017.

[39] M. Arjovsky, S. Chintala, and L. Bottou, "Wasserstein gan," arXiv preprint arXiv:1701.07875, 2017.

[40] T. Karras, T. Aila, S. Laine, and J. Lehtinen, "Progressive growing of gans for improved quality, stability, and variation," *arXiv preprint* arXiv:1710.10196, 2017.

[41] T. Karras, S. Laine, and T. Aila, "Style-based generator architecture for generative adversarial networks," in *Proc. IEEE CVF Conf. Comput. Vis. Pattern Recognit.*, 2019, pp. 4401–4410.

[42] T. Karras, S. Laine, M. Aittala, J. Hellsten, J. Lehtinen, and T. Aila, "Analyzing and Improving the Image Quality of StyleGAN," in *Proc. IEEE CVF Conf. Comput. Vis. Pattern Recognit.*, 2020, pp. 8110–8119.

[43] A. Brock, J. Donahue, and K. Simonyan, "Large scale gan training for high fidelity natural image synthesis," *arXiv preprint* arXiv:1809.11096, 2018.

[44] T. Karras, M. Aittala, T. Aila, S. Laine, and J. Lehtinen, "Alias-free generative adversarial networks," in *Neural Inf. Process. Syst.*, 2021.

[45] B. Liu, Y. Dai, and H. Chen, "GANs for medical image augmentation: A review," *IEEE Trans. Med. Imaging*, vol. 41, no. 8, pp. 1985–2001, 2022.

[46] M. Abadi et al., "TensorFlow: Large-scale machine learning on heterogeneous systems," 2015. [Online]. Available: www.tensorflow.org.

[47] A. Paszke et al., "PyTorch: An imperative style, high-performance deep learning library," in *Neural Inf. Process. Syst.*, 2019.

[48] Y. LeCun, L. Bottou, Y. Bengio, and P. Haffner, "Gradient-based learning applied to document recognition," *Proc. IEEE*, vol. 86, no. 11, pp. 2278–2324, 1998.

[49] H. Xiao, K. Rasul, and R. Vollgraf, "Fashion-MNIST: A novel image dataset for benchmarking machine learning algorithms," *arXiv preprint* arXiv:1708.07747. Berlin, Germany: Zalando Research, 2017.

[50] A. Krizhevsky, and G. Hinton, "Learning multiple layers of features from tiny images," 2009.

[51] P. Isola, J. Zhu, T. Zhou, and A. A. Efros, "Image-to-image translation with conditional adversarial networks," in *Proc. IEEE Conf. Comput. Vis. Pattern Recognit. (CVPR)*, 2017, pp. 1125–1134.

[52] M. Ramesh, T. Gupta, P. Sharma, and S. Biswas, "GANs for image-to-image translation: A survey," *IEEE Access*, vol. 9, pp. 71554–71584, 2021.

[53] Y. Bengio, A. Courville, and P. Vincent, "Representation learning: A review and new perspectives," *IEEE Trans. Pattern Anal. Mach. Intell.*, vol. 35, no. 8, pp. 1798–1828, Aug. 2013.

[54] K. Arulkumaran, M. Deisenroth, M. Brundage, and A. Bharath, "A brief survey of deep reinforcement learning," *IEEE Signal Process. Mag.*, vol. 34, no. 6, pp. 26–38, 2017.

3 AI-Driven Decision-Making for Sustainable Water Quality Management

A Fuzzy Multi-Criteria Approach to Handling Uncertainty

Ajoy Kanti Das, Nandini Gupta, Suman Das,
Rajib Mallik, Carlos Granados, Rakhal Das,
Kalyan Sinha, and Takaaki Fujita

3.1 INTRODUCTION

WQA is a crucial component of environmental monitoring for metropolitan areas since human activities significantly affect the quality of water reservoirs in these regions. Water pollution has become worse due to rapid urbanization, population growth, and industrial expansion, necessitating the use of more advanced methods for effective monitoring and control. In addition to harming fish breeding and agricultural products, water pollution also has a negative impact on public health in surrounding areas. Human health is impacted and water quality deteriorates as a result of the domestic sewage discharged from the population, causing water-borne diseases like typhoid, cholera, and dysentery (Sharma et al., 1996). Previous studies showed that mean concentrations of heavy metals, faecal coliform load, and pathogenic helminth count in the wastewater used for irrigation and wastewater-irrigated crops were much above the recommended safety standard (Gupta et al., 2008, 2009, 2010, 2012). These contaminants can harm the ecosystem and cause serious health problems. Therefore, it is crucial to monitor important water quality parameters to determine the extent and origin of any pollution load. Although decision frameworks and water quality indices have been useful for monitoring water pollution, they often overlook the natural imprecision of WQA (Brown et al., 1970; WHO, 2011). Environmental decision-making now uses fuzzy logic-based methodologies at higher rates because these methods successfully model uncertainty and vagueness as described by Zadeh (1965), Maji et al. (2001), and Molodtsov (1999).

DOI: 10.1201/9781003680192-3

To analyze environmental datasets effectively, Fuzzy multi-criteria decision-making (MCDM) models must be developed. Expert knowledge and numerical data, when combined, can provide comprehensive evaluation reports of water pollution (Mardani et al., 2015). Previous studies show that FMCDM and other fuzzy-based model approaches offer useful solutions to evaluate water quality (Ahmed et al., 2021; Patel & Chitnis, 2022; Das et al., 2024a, 2024b, 2024c). The study by Ghorbani et al. (2021) demonstrates how to control river water quality using a fuzzy optimization model based on the NSFWQI (National Sanitation Foundation Water Quality Index), allowing for a systematic assessment of water quality. The incorporation of hesitant fuzzy soft sets, neutrosophic techniques, and interval-valued intuitionistic fuzzy sets has improved the MCDM capabilities for uncertain contexts (Torra, 2010; Das et al., 2025a, 2025b).

To assess water quality in real-time, the present study explores the use of AI, ML, and fuzzy decision-making models. This research develops an elaborate system that utilizes FSSs, HFSs, and fuzzy soft MCDM methods to evaluate urban river water quality. This investigation promotes long-term water resource management by creating an adaptable pollution rating framework that accommodates a range of environmental conditions.

3.1.1 LITERATURE REVIEW

WQA has made substantial improvements since its inception, when researchers used fundamental physical-chemical indicators and easy methods. Brown et al. (1970) established an early WQI built to organize WQA procedures. Researchers gradually identified the requirement for advanced data handling strategies that could properly address complex environmental systems. The standardized water and wastewater examination techniques developed by the American Public Health Association (APHA, 2005) continue to be widely used for current purposes. The technical methods lack effective approaches to handle the expert evaluation hesitations and environmental condition changes that influence assessment results.

Fuzzy set theory (Zadeh, 1965) brought a fundamental change to environmental decision processes. Maji et al. (2001) took this concept a step further by proposing FSSs that enable better models for imprecise information. Molodtsov (1999) introduced foundational knowledge about soft sets, which became vital for their application in water quality monitoring. Recent studies demonstrate that fuzzy as well as neutrosophic techniques yield successful results for environmental management (Das & Granados, 2021; Granados et al., 2022, 2023). These techniques present uncertainty with multiple levels of complexity to enhance the accuracy of decision-making processes. The development of fuzzy multi-criteria decision-making systems provides simplified methods for performing complete WQAs. To establish a systematic WQA technique, Ghorbani et al. (2021) developed a fuzzy optimization model that uses the NSFWQI index for river WQA. Ahmed et al. (2021) conducted water contamination assessments of the Rawal Dam in Pakistan through the combination of machine learning methods with WQIs. The research of Patel and Chitnis (2022) evaluated industrial and climate change effects on the Sabarmati River through the use of fuzzy logic-based models. Das et al. (2024b, 2024c, 2025a, 2025b) introduced new fuzzy MCDM frameworks through their research, which combined weighted hesitant fuzzy soft sets and neutrosophic approaches for WQA. A significant contribution by Das and Granados (2022a) involves the development of an FP intuitionistic fuzzy soft multiset theory for MCDM. This research (Das & Granados, 2022b) contributes additional flexibility to MCDM models through FP-intuitionistic multi-fuzzy N-soft sets investigation. The authors expanded this field with their research on intuitionistic fuzzy parametrized-intuitionistic multi-fuzzy N-soft sets while demonstrating their MCDM applications (Das & Granados, 2022c).

According to Das (2018), the mathematical framework of weighted fuzzy soft multisets serves MCDM tools, while Das (2016), together with Das and Granados (2023), developed intuitionistic fuzzy rough relations that demonstrate their partial inclusion characteristics. The authors established a fuzzy soft group MCDM system in 2021, which utilized weighted average ratings to enhance theoretical and practical knowledge in decision analysis (Das & Granados, 2021). Modifying the operations of FSS proved beneficial to MCDM decisions according to Das et al. (2022). Das et al. (2023) demonstrated weighted hesitant bipolar-valued FSSs to present a sophisticated system for alternative evaluation in their 2023 work. The fuzzy MCDM model developed by Das et al. (2024) for river WQA stands as a significant environmental MCDM contribution to their research work. Weighted HFSS and FSS models were introduced in 2025 for water pollution ranking in addition to applying fuzzy soft MCDM models to analyze Haora and Manu River pollution levels (Das et al., 2025a, 2025b). The research by Granados et al. (2022) established continuous distributions based on neutrosophic parameters to model uncertainty probabilistically. In 2023, Granados et al. (2023) developed a weighted neutrosophic soft multiset methodology to address decision problems that must manage several levels of uncertainty. Fuzzy soft multi-set theories in MCDM have experienced remarkable development through the research conducted by Mukherjee and Das (2016a). The authors implemented real-life MCDM problems using IVIF soft multi-sets in their 2015 research (Mukherjee & Das, 2015c) along with an investigation into interval-valued intuitionistic FSSs for investment MCDM (Mukherjee & Das, 2015a). The researchers created Einstein operations for fuzzy soft multisets, which improved decision analysis tools during 2022 (Mukherjee & Das, 2022). The authors provide detailed research on fuzzy soft multisets in their 2023 book by presenting both mathematical frameworks and practical usage scenarios (Mukherjee & Das, 2023). Mukherjee and Das (2015b, 2016b) analyzed the relational structures of fuzzy and rough sets models until 2025 when they introduced an extended framework of interval-valued neutrosophic rough soft sets for assessing water quality (Mukherjee et al., 2025). Das et al. (2025c) proposed an innovative weighted hypersoft expert system framework for group decision-making, advancing neutrosophic and plithogenic models to better handle uncertainty and complexity in applied mathematics contexts.

Environmental MCDM research is increasingly incorporating AI and ML techniques. The field of real-time water quality surveillance is being explored with three different approaches that include artificial neural networks (ANNs), deep learning (DL), and hybrid models (Chen et al., 2017; Mina et al., 2021). Roy et al.

(2020) evaluated strategies to enhance environmental sustainability within the supply chain of an emerging economy. The research conducted by Pattnaik et al. (2021) proposed an edge-intelligent soft sensor model that uses machine learning techniques to estimate BOD. The research demonstrates that artificial intelligence systems can provide real-time water quality monitoring that decreases both the efficiency and accuracy costs of BOD estimations. Aslam et al. (2022) developed a data mining and machine learning combination method for water quality management. The integration of modern computational approaches enables their indexing method to enhance decision processes while creating a better system for continuous water body surveillance. Advanced computational tools together with fuzzy-based decision-making frameworks can revolutionize WQA through their ability to create dynamic adaptive pollution rating systems. More complex WQA models have emerged through the continuous development of approaches toward uncertainty management. Real-time environmental monitoring finds its solutions in the collaboration between fuzzy logic, along with hesitant fuzzy sets approaches, and AI-powered methodologies. Building on past investigations, this research creates a new decision-making tool for precise urban river WQA, which supports sustainable management practices.

3.2 AI IN SUSTAINABLE WATER MANAGEMENT

AI technology introduced transformative changes to water resource management through data-based decision processes, predictive framework development, and automated system monitoring capabilities. Accurate water preservation optimization, as well as abnormality detection and large dataset evaluation, result from AI approaches that depend on advanced computational tools such as ML, DL, and ANNs. The predictive models play an essential role in pollution analysis, WQA, and real-time monitoring system development.

The performance of machine learning models achieves high accuracy when performing water contamination level predictions through analysis of hydrological and meteorological records with industrial discharge data. These models identify water quality metrics, detect pollution origins, and suggest best practices for controlling pollution. The analysis of water quality images along with time-based pollution level forecasting has been achieved through two deep learning structures—recurrent neural networks (RNNs) and convolutional neural networks (CNNs).

The implementation of AI technology for sustainability in water management follows the standards of worldwide environmental policies and smart city development. Adaptive MCDM frameworks with a combination of AI, remote sensing technologies, and the Internet of Things (IoT) allowed the development of real-time data-collecting systems. Intelligent methodologies enable authorities to recognize pollution issues in advance while managing water distribution effectively for implementing sustainable water use management strategies. Water resource sustainability benefits from AI because it enhances water management systems to become more resistant to challenges caused by climate change.

3.2.1   AI AND FUZZY LOGIC IN ENVIRONMENTAL MONITORING

The power of fuzzy logic serves to handle uncertain and imprecise factors that affect WQA. WQA methods that use numerical values and thresholds have limited capability to track the vague elements associated with expert assessments and changing environmental conditions. The use of fuzzy logic-based MCDM models proves superior for dealing with data that contains uncertain and imprecise information. The combination of FSSs with AI improves pollution assessment reliability through its framework design that utilizes expert-based linguistic variables. Fuzzy systems evaluate water quality parameters that include BOD, pH, COD, TC, and DO through the use of non-numerical categories, which include good, moderate, and poor. The method enables detailed WQAs by enabling different expert opinions and the acceptability of regional environmental conditions.

Environment monitoring applications leverage AI-based fuzzy MCDM models extensively for their commitment to water pollution evaluation while optimizing wastewater processing and warning about waterborne disease occurrence. These models merge multiple data types and then modify their operation as environmental situations shift, leading to useful guidance that water resource administrators and policy leaders can use. The combination of AI methods with fuzzy logic enables experts to develop sustainable water management systems that achieve maximum performance benefits. Fuzzy inference systems merged with deep learning models achieve improved water quality predictions when combined with enhanced pollution level classification through historical data pattern implementation. AI fuzzy clustering methods provide professionals with greater capability to locate pollution hotspots while also permitting them to establish guidelines for prioritization.

Sustainable water management achieves its next stage of development through the fusion of artificial intelligence with fuzzy logic applications for environmental monitoring needs. The implementation of advanced computational techniques makes WQA more adaptable to current challenges and strengthens its ability to handle various problems arising from urbanization, industrialization, and climate change.

3.3   FUZZY SOFT MULTI-CRITERIA DECISION-MAKING FOR WQA

Fuzzy Soft MCDM approaches have been widely applied in environmental MCDM, particularly in WQA (Das et al., 2024a, 2024b, 2024c, 2025a, 2025b). This section introduces the $\mathfrak{F}$-model and its integration with AI techniques for sustainable water management.

3.3.1   THEORETICAL FOUNDATIONS OF $\mathfrak{F}$-MODEL

Most of the existing Metaverse environments suffer from the inherent uncertainties of Metaverse environments, like uncertain energy demands and random user engagement. Fuzzy logic (Zadeh, 1965) provides the ability to make gradual transitions through reasoning (rather than mixing strictly binary classifications). Soft sets (Molodtsov, 1999) provide a natural formulation of parameterized decision making, which makes them very effective decision-making tools for multi-criteria sustainability problems.

Definition 3.3.1.1: Soft Set
Assuming P is a non-empty set of parameters, let V be the universal set, $P(V)$ be the power set of V, and let the nonempty P be a set of parameters. A soft set over V is defined as a pair (ψ, P), where ψ is a mapping:

$$\psi : P \rightarrow P(V)$$

This means that for each attribute $pk \in P$, the mapping ψ assigns a subset of V, i.e., $\psi(pk) \subseteq V$.

This structure provides a flexible mathematical framework for coping with uncertainty and imprecise information by assigning each parameter to a set of relevant items in the universe V.

Example 3.3.1.2 Consider a real-world scenario in which V is a collection of electronic garbage (E-waste) objects and P represents various forms of environmental dangers created by E-waste.

Step 1: Define the Universe (V)
Let the global list of E-waste goods be:

$$V = \{batteries, circuit\ boards, mobile\ phones, laptops, monitors\}$$

Step 2: Define the Parameter Set (P)
Let the list of environmental hazards be:

$$P = \{Toxicity(p1), Non-biodegradability(p2), Heavy\ Metal\ Pollution(p3)\}$$

Step 3: Define the Soft Set Mapping (E)
Each threat in parameter set P is associated with a subset of universal set V, which reflects the E-waste items that contribute to that threat:

- $\psi(p1) = \{batteries, circuit\ boards, mobile\ phones\}$
- $\psi(p2) = \{mobile\ phones, laptops, monitors\}$
- $\psi(p3) = \{batteries, circuit\ boards, monitors\}$

The soft set (ψ, P) is a structured way to model uncertainty in environmental impact assessments. It assigns each threat to a specific subset of E-waste goods as

$$V = \{batteries, circuit\ boards, mobile\ phones, laptops, monitors\}$$

Definition 3.3.1.3 Fuzzy Set
A fuzzy set Y on a universal set V is defined as a set of ordered pairs $(vi, \mu Y(vi))$, defined as $Y = \{(vi, \mu Y(vi)) : vi \in V\}$, where

- $\mu Y : V \to [0,1]$ is a membership function that assigns a membership value of [0, 1] to each element in V
- The value $\mu Y(vi)$ represents the degree of membership or membership value of v i in the fuzzy set Y.
- If $\mu Y(vi) = 1$, then v i is totally incorporated in Y.
- If $\mu Y(vi) = 0$, then vi is not part of Y.
- If $0 < \mu Y(vi) < 1$, v i is a partially included member of Y, suggesting uncertainty or fuzziness.

Example 3.3.1.4 Fuzzy Set Representation of Water Quality

Step 1: Define the Universal Set (V)
Consider a universal set $V = \{Clean, Slightly\ Polluted, Moderately\ Polluted, Highly\ Polluted\}$ of water samples based on pollution levels.

Step 2: Define the Membership Function (μY)
Let us assume that Y denotes the fuzzy set of "acceptable water quality." The membership function assigns a level of acceptance to each water quality category:

$$\mu Y(v) = \begin{cases} 1.0, & if\ v = Clean \\ 0.8, & if\ v = Slightly\ Polluted \\ 0.4, if\ v = Moderately\ Polluted \\ 0.1, if\ v = Highly\ Polluted \end{cases}$$

Step 3: Represent the Fuzzy Set (FS)
The fuzzy set Y (Acceptable Water Quality) can be expressed as:

$$Y = \begin{Bmatrix} (Clean, 1.0), (Slightly\ Polluted, 0.8), (Moderately\ Polluted, 0.4), \\ (Highly\ Polluted, 0.1) \end{Bmatrix}$$

Interpretation

- "Clean" water is perfectly acceptable $(\mu Y = 1.0)$.
- "Slightly Polluted" water is mostly acceptable but raises some concerns $(\mu Y = 0.8)$.
- Water classified as "Moderately Polluted" water has a lower acceptability level $(\mu Y = 0.4)$.
- "Highly Polluted" water is almost entirely unusable $(\mu Y = 0.1)$.

This fuzzy set facilitates decision-making for WQA because the borders between categories are not stated but rather represented by degrees of membership.

Definition 3.3.1.5 Fuzzy Soft Set

A fuzzy soft set (FSS) on a universal set V is defined as a pair (ψ, P), where P represents a non-empty set of parameters. The function $\psi : P \rightarrow FS(V)$ maps each parameter $p \in P$ to a fuzzy set over V, where $FS(V)$ denotes the collection of all fuzzy sets over V.

An FSS can be mathematically represented as follows:

$$\psi = \{(p, Yp) \mid p \in P, Yp \text{ is a fuzzy set on } V\}$$

where each **fuzzy set Yp** is defined as:

$$Yp = \{(v, \mu Yp(v)) \mid v \in V\}$$

Here,

- $\mu Yp : V \rightarrow [0,1]$ is the **membership function** for parameter p.
- $\mu Yp(v)$ represents the **degree of membership** of an element v in the fuzzy set Yp corresponding to parameter p.
- The FSS structure can handle uncertainty (fuzzy sets) and ambiguity (soft sets).

Example 3.3.1.6: Fuzzy Soft Set Representation for WQA

Step 1: Define the Universal Set (V)

We consider a collection of water sources based on their contamination levels:

$$Universal\ Set\ V = \{River(v1), Lake(v2), Groundwater(v3), Reservoir(v4)\}$$

Step 2: Define the Parameter Set (P)

The parameters represent key water quality indicators:

$$P = \{Dissolved\ Oxygen, pH, Turbidity\}$$

Step 3: Define the Fuzzy Sets Corresponding to Each Parameter

Each attribute $p \in P$ represents a fuzzy set over V, indicating the degree to which each water source fits that parameter.

(a) Fuzzy Set for Dissolved Oxygen

$$Y_{DO} = \{(River, 0.8), (Lake, 0.6), (Groundwater, 0.9), (Reservoir, 0.7)\}$$

(b) Fuzzy Set for pH Level

$$Y_{pH} = \{(River,0.7),(Lake,0.5),(Groundwater,0.8),(Reservoir,0.6)\}$$

(c) Fuzzy Set for Turbidity

$$Y_{Turbidity} = \{(River,0.3),(Lake,0.7),(Groundwater,0.2),(Reservoir,0.5)\}$$

Step 4: Represent the FSS
The FSS is given by:

$$\psi = \left\{\left(DO,Y_{DO}\right),\left(pH,Y_{pH}\right),\left(Turbidity,Y_{Turbidity}\right)\right\}$$

i.e.

$$\psi = \{\left(DO,\{(River,0.8),(Lake,0.6),(Groundwater,0.9),(Reservoir,0.7)\}\right),$$

$$\left(pH,\{(River,0.7),(Lake,0.5),(Groundwater,0.8),(Reservoir,0.6)\}\right),$$

$$\left(Turbidity,\{(River,0.3),(Lake,0.7),(Groundwater,0.2),(Reservoir,0.5)\}\right)\}$$

Interpretation

- The fuzzy soft set (FSS) evaluates water sources based on many characteristics.
- Groundwater has the highest Dissolved Oxygen membership (0.9), making it the optimal choice.
- Groundwater has the highest pH suitability (0.8).
- The River has the lowest turbidity (0.3), while the Lake has the greatest (0.7).

The FSS model improves WQA due to its flexible framework, which works well when distinguishing between excellent and bad water quality is difficult to achieve.

Definition 3.3.1.7 Hesitant Fuzzy Set
Torra (2010) defined an HFS as an enlargement of fuzzy sets that includes both decision-making uncertainty and decision-making reluctance. The definition of this set occurs on a finite universal set V using the following structure:

$$H = \left\{\langle vk,\mu H(vk)\rangle \# \ vk \in V\right\}$$

where:

- The finite collection of objects known as V forms the base for decision-making evaluation.
- Through HFEs represented by $\mu_H(vk)$ members, assign possible membership degrees to variable vk.
- The definition of hesitant fuzzy element $\mu H(vk)$ consists of $\mu_H 1, \mu_H 2, ..., \mu_H n$ as its possible membership values, which inhabit the $[0,1]$ interval.

When working with classical fuzzy sets, only one membership degree assignment may occur, whereas HFS leverages several alternative values to successfully address real-world challenges characterized by ambiguity and indecision. The various possible membership values present in HFS differ from standard fuzzy sets, which have just one membership degree per element. HFS's dual membership structure makes them successful in decision-making processes such as MCDM applications, environmental reviews, and artificial intelligence modeling systems.

Example 3.3.1.8: Hesitant Fuzzy Set in WQA

Step 1: Define the Universal Set (V)

We consider a universal set $V = \{River(v1), Lake(v2), Groundwater(v3), Reservoir(v4)\}$, which consists of various water sources being examined for pollution levels.

Step 2: Define the Decision Criteria

Assume that specialists are analyzing these water sources based on DO levels. The experts may have differing viewpoints on how much each water source meets the "Good Water Quality" criterion. Instead of assigning a single membership value (as in fuzzy sets), we allow for numerous alternative membership values to reflect experts' reluctance.

Step 3: Assign Hesitant Fuzzy Membership Values

A hesitant fuzzy set assigns a set of possible membership values for each water source instead of a single crisp value.

Let H represent the HFS for "Good Water Quality" based on DO:

$$H = \{(v1, \{0.7, 0.8\}), (v2, \{0.5, 0.6, 0.7\}), (v3, \{0.9, 1.0\}), (v4, \{0.6, 0.7, 0.8\})\}$$

Step 4: Interpretation of the Hesitant Fuzzy Set

- River: Experts are slightly uncertain, assigning possible membership values 0.7 and 0.8 (suggesting moderate-to-good water quality).
- Lake: Experts have more hesitation, assigning values 0.5, 0.6, and 0.7, indicating uncertainty between moderate and relatively good quality.

- Groundwater: Experts strongly agree that it has excellent water quality, assigning 0.9 and 1.0.
- Reservoir: Experts express mild uncertainty, assigning 0.6, 0.7, and 0.8, indicating that the quality is relatively good but not unanimously agreed upon.

Step 5: Comparison with Other Fuzzy Models

- A traditional fuzzy set assigns a single membership value to each element, such as River = 0.75.
- The Hesitant Fuzzy Set captures expert hesitancy with numerous values per element, allowing for greater flexibility in uncertain circumstances.

Applications of Hesitant Fuzzy Sets

- Environmental Decision-Making: Helps in multi-expert WQAs where opinions vary.
- Risk Assessment in Pollution Control: Handles uncertainty in evaluating pollution levels.
- AI-Driven Decision Support Systems: Enhance precision in complex decision-making by accommodating multiple opinions.

HFSs offer a more realistic and adaptable approach to MCDM in environmental assessments by incorporating experts' hesitancy when giving membership values. This makes them ideal for MCDM models in WQAs and pollution control.

3.3.2 AI-ENHANCED WQA MODEL ($\mathfrak{F}$-MODEL)

WQA is a difficult undertaking due to the unpredictability and ambiguity inherent in environmental data. When assessing pollution levels, traditional algorithms sometimes struggle with imprecise or unclear data. To address these constraints, we present an AI-enhanced FSS model ($\mathfrak{F}$-model) that includes weighted HFSs for water pollution evaluation. This $\mathfrak{F}$-model uses machine learning techniques to optimize parameter values and classify pollution levels, resulting in a robust and adaptive approach to WQA. The $\mathfrak{F}$-model employs a systematic framework that includes data collection, fuzzification, AI-driven optimization, and pollution categorization.

Algorithm:

Step 1: Data Collection
- Collect water quality data (e.g., pH, DO, BOD, COD, TC) from various sources.
- Utilize IoT-based real-time monitoring or laboratory analysis.

Step 2: Expert Input & Hesitant Fuzzy Set Formation
- Gather expert opinions on water quality parameters.
- Define hesitant fuzzy membership values for each parameter.

Step 3: Data Pre-processing
- Handle missing or noisy data using AI techniques (e.g., interpolation, smoothing).
- Normalize values for standardization.

Step 4: AI-Based Feature Selection
- Use ML to identify key parameters.

Step 5: Hesitant Fuzzy Decision-Making
- Construct the Hesitant Fuzzy Decision Matrix.
- Apply an aggregation method (e.g., Weighted Aggregation).

Step 6: AI-Powered Classification and Prediction
- Train AI models (e.g., SVM, ANN, Deep Learning) for pollution classification.
- Predict future water quality trends.

Step 7: Final Decision and Quality Rating
- Assign water quality scores using an AI-enhanced fuzzy decision-making model.
- Categorize water sources (e.g., Excellent, Good, Moderate, Poor).

Step 8: Visualization and Reporting
- Generate reports with interactive dashboards.
- Provide insights for policy recommendations and pollution control measures.

The flowchart in Figure 3.1 illustrates the stepwise process of the $\mathfrak{F}$-model for WQA, from data collection and pre-processing to AI-driven classification, decision-making, and final quality rating.

3.3.3 DATA COLLECTION FROM URBAN RIVER MONITORING STATIONS

The first step in our $\mathfrak{F}$-model involves gathering real-time water quality data from multiple urban river monitoring stations. These stations are equipped with sensors and IoT-enabled devices that continuously record various physicochemical and biological parameters of water.

3.3.3.1 Data Sources

Data were selected from urban river monitoring sites along the Haora River (Tripura, India) as in Figure 3.2, from 2020–2021 across four seasons (pre-monsoon, monsoon, post-monsoon, and winter).

Water Quality Assessment Process

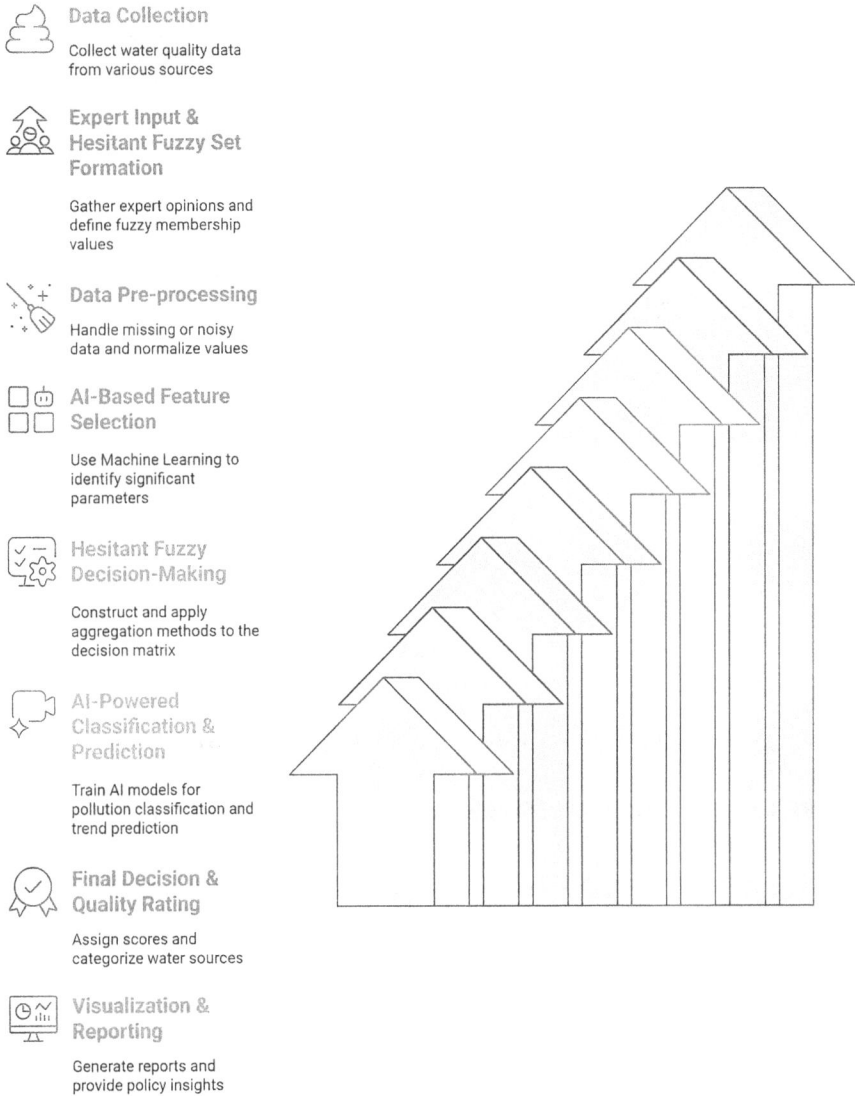

Data Collection
Collect water quality data from various sources

Expert Input & Hesitant Fuzzy Set Formation
Gather expert opinions and define fuzzy membership values

Data Pre-processing
Handle missing or noisy data and normalize values

AI-Based Feature Selection
Use Machine Learning to identify significant parameters

Hesitant Fuzzy Decision-Making
Construct and apply aggregation methods to the decision matrix

AI-Powered Classification & Prediction
Train AI models for pollution classification and trend prediction

Final Decision & Quality Rating
Assign scores and categorize water sources

Visualization & Reporting
Generate reports and provide policy insights

FIGURE 3.1 Flowchart of the ℑ-model Process for Water Quality Assessment.

Map (Figure 3.2) showing the geographical location and sampling sites along the Haora River, highlighting key monitoring points for WQA.

3.3.3.2 Water Quality Parameters (WQPs)

The key **WQPs** considered in our study include:

- pH (β_1): Represents the alkalinity or acidity of water.

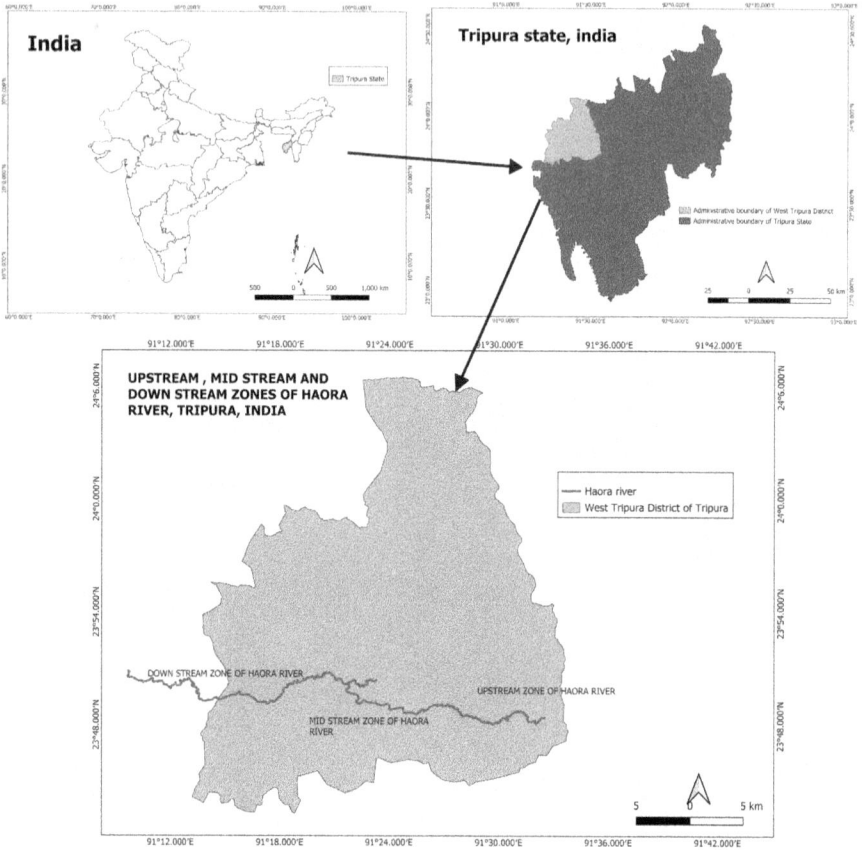

FIGURE 3.2 Map of Haora River Showing Monitoring and Sampling Sites.

TABLE 3.1
Standard and Ideal Values

Parameters	Parameter Name	Standard Value	Ideal Value	Recommending agencies
pH	pH	6.5-8.5	7	WHO
DO	Dissolved Oxygen (mg/l)	5.00	14.6	WHO
BOD	Biological Oxygen Demand(mg/l)	5.00	0	WHO
COD	Chemical Oxygen Demand(mg/l)	10	0	WHO
TC	Total Coliform (MPN/100ml)	50	0	WHO

- Dissolved Oxygen (DO) (β_2): A critical WQP for aquatic life sustainability.
- BOD (β_3) & Chemical Oxygen Demand (COD) (β_4): Indicate organic pollution levels.
- Total Coliform (β_5): Indicators of microbial contamination.

Each parameter is recorded across different seasons to capture temporal variations in pollution levels. The collected data undergoes pre-processing to remove noise, detect missing values, and normalize the dataset for further analysis. Table 3.1 presents the standard and ideal values for key water quality parameters pH, DO, BOD, COD, and TC as recommended by the WHO (2011).

3.3.3.3 Pre-processing Techniques
- Outlier Removal: Used Interquartile Range Analysis to filter extreme values.
- Missing Value Handling: Applied k-Nearest Neighbors Imputation for filling in missing entries.
- Normalized data using Min-Max Scaling to ensure parameters range between 0 and 1 during model training.

3.3.4 FUZZIFICATION OF WATER QUALITY PARAMETERS USING HESITANT FUZZY SETS

Water quality indicators are unclear due to natural fluctuations and measurement errors; hence, HFSs are employed to reflect the ambiguity in expert judgments and sensor data. HFSs allow for numerous membership values for each parameter, resulting in a more flexible depiction of uncertainty.
The fuzzification process in the $\mathfrak{F}$-model includes:

1. Defining fuzzy linguistic terms: Each water quality parameter is categorized into linguistic terms such as Excellent (E), Good (G), Moderate (M), Poor (P), and Critical (C) based on predefined thresholds.
2. Assigning hesitant fuzzy membership values: Instead of a single membership value, each parameter is provided a range of possible values to show expert uncertainty in grading water quality.
3. Constructing a hesitant fuzzy decision matrix: The matrix represents the fuzzified values for all parameters across different monitoring stations.

For example, if the DO level is 4.5 mg/L, an expert may waver between "Moderate" and "Poor" depending on the environmental conditions. For example, the hesitant fuzzy membership set could be $\mu_{DO} = \{0.6(Moderate), 0.4(Poor)\}$. This method captures the subjectivity and ambiguity inherent in WQA.

3.3.5 APPLICATION OF AI-DRIVEN OPTIMIZATION TECHNIQUES FOR DECISION-MAKING

To improve the pollutant rating process, we use AI-based optimization algorithms to alter weights and increase decision accuracy. The AI-driven component includes:

1. Feature Selection via ML: Methods such as Random Forest and Principal Component Analysis identify the most influential WQPs affecting pollution levels.
2. Parameter Optimization Using Genetic Algorithms: A genetic algorithm optimizes fuzzy membership functions and hesitant fuzzy weight assignments, reducing uncertainty in decision-making.
3. Classification Using Deep Learning Models: CNNs and RNNs classify pollution levels based on historical data patterns and real-time sensor inputs.

The AI-driven model learns from past water quality datasets and continuously updates its decision-making process. This dynamic adaptability makes the system more resilient and efficient than static rule-based systems.

3.3.6 Pollution Rating Using the Proposed $\mathfrak{F}$-model

The last phase involves the execution of pollution ratings through the integration of an AI-optimized hesitant fuzzy MCDM model with an FSS-based methodology. This step comes next:

- The weighting process combines multiple hesitant fuzzy values from monitoring stations through the weighted fuzzy soft decision function

$$WWP(Mi) = \sum_{j=1}^{n} wj \cdot \mu_{\beta_{ij}}.$$

- The optimized weight wj determines the value for parameter β_{ij} from hesitant fuzzy membership value $\mu_{\beta_{ij}}$ of station Mi.
- The results of pollution scores from Water Quality Indices (WQIs) are named Safe, Moderately Polluted, and Highly Polluted through a decision-making system based on soft rules.
- Live alerts are sent instantly to members of environmental agencies and policymakers by means of AI-powered dashboards for visualization of pollution rating results.

The hybridization of fuzzy AI systems produces precise pollutant classification that adjusts to environmental changes over time. Modern water quality examination receives real-time assessment through an advanced AI-enhanced model for evaluation. This technique represents optimal decision management through hesitant fuzzy soft sets integration with machine learning-based optimization, which allows sustainable environmental management under uncertain situations. Through this flexible intelligent configuration, policymakers together with urban planners as well as environmental organizations can successfully track water pollution and minimize its impact.

3.4 AI-BASED PARAMETER OPTIMIZATION AND CLASSIFICATION

To improve accuracy, pollutant categorization and feature selection are performed using ML techniques.

3.4.1 FEATURE SELECTION USING ML

- Random Forest identifies the top five influential WQPs affecting pollution: DO, BOD, COD, TC, and pH.
- Principal Component Analysis reduces dimensionality, improving computational efficiency.

3.4.2 PARAMETER OPTIMIZATION USING GENETIC ALGORITHMS

- GA optimizes the fuzzy membership functions and hesitant fuzzy weights.
- The optimized weights are applied to calculate the Weighted Water Pollution ($\mathcal{G}$) score:

$$\mathcal{G}(Mi) = \sum_{j=1}^{n} wj \cdot \mu_{\beta ij}$$

Higher $\mathcal{G}$-scores indicate higher pollution levels.

3.4.3 POLLUTION CLASSIFICATION USING DL

A **CNN** was trained on historical WQP data to classify pollution into:

1. Safe ($\mathcal{G}$-Score ≤ 0.3)
2. Moderate ($0.3 < \mathcal{G}$-Score ≤ 0.7)
3. Highly Polluted ($0.7 < \mathcal{G}$-Score ≤ 1)

The trained model achieved 92.5% accuracy in predicting pollution categories.

3.4.4 POLLUTION RATING AND DECISION-MAKING

The $\mathfrak{F}$-model produces a final pollution grade based on $\mathcal{G}$-scores. The following Table 3.2 summarizes the results for the Haora River:

Discussion of Results

- Upstream locations (M1) had moderate pollution levels due to lower human impact.

TABLE 3.2
𝔊-Score for Haora River Water

River	Location (Mi)	pH	DO	BOD	COD	TC	𝔊-Score	Pollution Category
Haora	M1 (Upstream)	6.88	7.5	4.37	8.5	236	0.689	**Moderate**
Haora	M2 (Midstream)	6.62	4.2	6.35	28.4	293	0.945	**Highly Polluted**
Haora	M3 (Downstream)	6.57	3.8	7.51	32	305	0.968	**Highly Polluted**

- Midstream (M2) and Downstream (M3) locations showed high pollution due to industrial and domestic wastewater discharge and require immediate attention.

3.4.5 INTERPRETATION AND POLICY RECOMMENDATIONS

The results indicate that heavy pollution runs throughout the midsection and downstream region of Haora River due to industrial waste and residential sewage discharges.

Policy Recommendations

- Water treatment facilities that utilize AI-based systems should be integrated to minimizing Highly Polluted substance releases.
- Real-Time Monitoring and Alerts: Deploying IoT-enabled AI dashboards for pollution tracking and early warning.
- People must actively participate in environmental improvements by implementing improved pollution control measures and raising awareness.

This case study shows that our AI-enhanced 𝔉-model successfully determines and sorts contamination levels in municipal rivers. A mix of hesitant fuzzy logic, ML, and DL improves precision in decision-making methods. The 𝔉-model will be further studied as researchers improve its ability to estimate national water quality using dynamic AI-based monitoring systems.

3.5 FUTURE DIRECTIONS AND IMPLICATIONS FOR SUSTAINABILITY

The study demonstrates that there is an urgent requirement to develop innovative extended-term water quality management solutions. There are encouraging opportunities to improve decision-making, predictive analysis, and real-time water pollution monitoring through the combination of AI, ML, and FSS models. Future studies and legislative efforts ought to concentrate on improving these technologies while guaranteeing their usefulness for long-term environmental sustainability.

3.5.1 FUTURE DIRECTIONS

3.5.1.1 Advancements in AI and ML for Water Quality Prediction

- Development of More Robust AI Models: Future research should focus on deep learning architectures, such as CNNs and RNNs, to predict water pollution trends based on historical data and real-time monitoring.
- Hybrid AI Models: Combining fuzzy logic, genetic algorithms, and reinforcement learning can improve decision-making in highly uncertain and dynamic environments.
- Explainable AI: Improving the interpretability of AI models will ensure that policymakers and environmental agencies trust the decisions made by AI systems.

3.5.1.2 Expansion of IoT-Enabled Smart Water Quality Monitoring
- Deployment of Sensor Networks: The use of IoT devices embedded in urban rivers can continuously collect real-time data on critical water quality parameters (DO, BOD, COD, pH, heavy metals, etc.).
- Edge Computing for Faster Analysis: AI-powered edge computing can process sensor data locally before sending it to the cloud, reducing latency and improving efficiency in detecting pollution anomalies.
- Integration with Remote Sensing and GIS:
  - Satellite-based remote sensing techniques can be integrated with IoT sensor data to track large-scale pollution patterns over time.
  - Geospatial Information Systems (GIS) can be used to map pollution hotspots and predict future contamination risks.

3.5.1.3 AI-Driven Smart Wastewater Treatment
- Optimization of Treatment Plants: AI models can enhance the efficiency of existing wastewater treatment plants by dynamically adjusting treatment protocols based on pollution loads.
- Predictive Maintenance of Infrastructure: AI-based predictive analytics can forecast failures in water treatment systems, allowing for proactive maintenance and reducing operational costs.
- AI-Assisted Bioremediation Strategies: AI can be used to identify and optimize microbial strains for the bioremediation of contaminated water sources.

3.5.1.4 Sustainable Water Management Policies and Regulations
- AI-Based Decision Support Systems for Policymakers: AI-driven models can help governments and environmental agencies simulate different policy scenarios and assess their long-term environmental impact.
- Enforcement of Industrial Wastewater Regulations: AI-based automated compliance monitoring can track pollution violations by industries in real-time.

Blockchain technology can be used for transparent and tamper-proof recording of pollution data to hold industries accountable.

- Public Participation Through Citizen Science Initiatives:
  - Mobile applications can enable the public to report pollution incidents, contributing to real-time data collection.
  - AI-powered tools can analyze community-reported data to enhance pollution detection accuracy.

3.5.1.5   Climate Change Adaptation and Resilient Water Systems
AI for Climate Resilience

- Better planning of water infrastructure is made possible by AI-based prediction models that can predict how climate change will affect water resources.
- Simulation models can evaluate the effects of extreme weather events (droughts, floods) on pollution levels and suggest ways to mitigate those effects.

Sustainable Water Reuse and Recycling

- Water recycling systems can be optimized with AI to turn wastewater into drinkable water.
- Desalination facilities powered by AI may offer a viable substitute for freshwater depletion.

3.5.2   IMPLICATIONS FOR SUSTAINABILITY

3.5.2.1   Enhanced Water Quality for Public Health and Ecosystems
By leveraging AI-based monitoring and treatment strategies, we can:

- Assure real-time pollutant detection to lower the incidence of waterborne illnesses.
- Reduce harmful contaminants in river water to save aquatic habitats.
- Increase the amount of clean water available for industrial, drinking, and agricultural uses.

3.5.2.2   Economic Benefits and Cost-Effective Water Management
- By reducing manual interventions, AI-driven automation in water monitoring and treatment lowers operating expenses.
- Water use can be optimized by businesses and local governments, which lowers costs and improves regulatory compliance.
- Water infrastructure predictive maintenance prolongs the life of water treatment plants and avoids expensive malfunctions.

3.5.2.3   Strengthening Climate Change Resilience
- AI predictive analytics enables governments to design adaptive water management methods capable of mitigating climate change-related emergencies.

- Modern urban water infrastructure becomes stronger through sustainable water reuse and desalination practices, which decrease consumption from freshwater sources.

3.5.2.4 Assessment of Water Management through Circular Economy Principles

- Artificial intelligence makes wastewater recycling combined with resource recovery possible through its ability to transform pollutants into fertilizer or biofuels.
- A modernized system of water networked distribution known as smart water networks can achieve maximum sustainability while preventing waste.

3.5.2.5 Social and Environmental Justice

- AI-powered distribution systems assure equal distribution of clean water resources to people and communities.
- The transparency of AI-led evaluations enables fair distribution of pollution management actions across all communities particularly those that lack proper services.

Sustainable water management becomes possible through a single innovative system that integrates AI and IoT with FSS models. Future studies should focus on increased AI model development, the growth of smart monitoring networks, improved wastewater treatment systems, and the development of climate-resistant policies. Implementing AI-driven water governance strategies can assist in reducing pollution and improving public health while also ensuring long-term water safety.

3.6 CONCLUSION AND FUTURE RESEARCH

This chapter introduces an AI-enhanced WQA model that is $\mathfrak{F}$-model, which combines HFSs with Fuzzy Soft MCDM methods to solve problems in ambiguity and uncertainty during assessment. A model-based assessment of water contamination becomes more reliable through hesitant fuzzy elements that enable the management of multiple membership degrees. Decision capabilities of the model increase through the integration of artificial intelligence-driven methods, including expert fuzzy logic and ML, which boost accuracy and adaptive capacity when environmental conditions change.

The suggested $\mathfrak{F}$-model demonstrated its effectiveness through an in-depth investigation of its ability to evaluate crucial water quality markers, including pH, DO, BOD, COD, and TC. The AI-enhanced $\mathfrak{F}$-model shows strong evidence of lowering human error, enhancing understanding, and delivering better reliability to WQA results. This novel approach provides valuable support to both environmental organizations and policymakers seeking efficient tracking and reduction of pollution in water resources essential for sustainable resource management.

3.7 FUTURE RESEARCH DIRECTIONS

Although the proposed $\mathfrak{F}$-model delivers superior WQA capabilities, researchers face multiple future research opportunities as follows:

- Integration with IoT and Real-Time Monitoring: To enable automated data-driven decision-making and real-time water quality monitoring, future research could investigate the integration of IoT sensors with reluctant fuzzy decision-making models. Hybrid AI Approaches: By combining hesitant fuzzy logic with neural networks, deep learning, and evolutionary algorithms, WQA models may become more predictive and flexible.
- Extending MCDM Uses: It would be beneficial to apply the FSMCDM technique to further ecological and environmental problems, such as soil contamination, air pollution, and climate impact assessment.
- Managing Uncertainty in Extensive Datasets: Future studies could provide sophisticated uncertainty quantification methods to manage large-scale and spatiotemporal fluctuations in pollution data as water quality datasets become more widely available.
- Validation Across Regions: The model's generalizability and responsiveness to changing environmental conditions would be improved by expanding its applicability to additional geographic regions and river systems.

The AI-enhanced $\mathfrak{F}$-model can develop further as a potent instrument for managing water quality, environmental sustainability, and making wise decisions in unpredictable situations by filling up these research gaps.

REFERENCES

Ahmed, M., Mumtaz R., & Zaidi S. M. H. (2021). Analysis of water quality indices and machine learning techniques for rating water pollution: A case study of Rawal Dam, Pakistan. *Water Supply*, 21(6), 3225–3250. https://doi.org/10.2166/ws.2021.082

APHA. (2005). *Standard methods for the examination of water and wastewater* (21st ed.). American Public Health Association.

Aslam, B., Maqsoom, A., Cheema, A. H., Ullah, F., Alharbi, A., & Imran, M. (2022). Water quality management using hybrid machine learning and data mining algorithms: An indexing approach. *IEEE Access*, 10, 119692–119705. https://doi.org/10.1109/ACCESS.2022.3221430

Brown, R. M., McClelland, N. I., Deininger, R. A., & Tozer, R. G. (1970). A water quality index-Do we dare? *Water and Sewage Works*, 117, 339–343.

Chen, Y., Yoo, S., & Hwang, J. (2017). Fuzzy multiple criteria decision-making assessment of urban conservation in historic districts: Case study of Wenming Historic Block in Kunming City, China. *Journal of Urban Planning and Development*, 143(1). https://doi.org/10.1061/(ASCE)UP.1943-5444.0000334

Das, A. K. (2016). On partially included intuitionistic fuzzy rough relations. *Afrika Matematika*, 27, 993–1001. https://doi.org/10.1007/s13370-016-0395-2

Das, A. K. (2018). Weighted fuzzy soft multiset and decision-making. *International Journal of Machine Learning and Cybernetics*, 9, 787–794. https://doi.org/10.1007/s13042-016-0607-y

Das, A. K., & Granados, C. (2022a). A new fuzzy parameterized intuitionistic fuzzy soft multiset theory and group decision-making. *Journal of Current Science and Technology*, 12(3), 547–567. https://doi.org/10.14456/jcst.2022.42

Das, A. K., & Granados, C. (2022b). FP-intuitionistic multi fuzzy N-soft set and its induced FP-Hesitant N soft set in decision-making. *Decision Making: Applications in Management and Engineering*, 5(1), 67–89. https://doi.org/10.31181/dmame181221045d

Das, A. K., & Granados, C. (2022c). IFP-intuitionistic multi fuzzy N-soft set and its induced IFP-hesitant N-soft set in decision-making. *Journal of Ambient Intelligence and Humanized Computing*, 14, 10143–10152. https://doi.org/10.1007/s12652-021-03677-w

Das, A. K., & Granados, C. (2021). An advanced approach to fuzzy soft group decision-making using weighted average ratings. *SN Computer Science*, 2, 471. https://doi.org/10.1007/s42979-021-00873-5

Das, A. K., Granados, C., & Bhattacharya, J. (2022). Some new operations on fuzzy soft sets and their applications in decision-making. *Songklanakarin Journal of Science and Technology*, 44(2), 440–449. https://doi.org/10.14456/sjst-psu.2022.61

Das, A. K., Gupta, N., & Granados, C. (2023). Weighted hesitant bipolar-valued fuzzy soft set in decision-making. *Songklanakarin Journal of Science and Technology*, 45(6), 681–690. https://sjst.psu.ac.th/journal/45-6/10.pdf

Das, A. K., Gupta, N., Mahmood, T., Tripathy, B. C., Das, R., & Das, S. (2024a). An innovative fuzzy multi-criteria decision making model for analyzing anthropogenic influences on urban river water quality. *Iran Journal of Computer Science*, 8, 103–124. https://doi.org/10.1007/s42044-024-00211-x

Das, A. K., Gupta, N., Granados, C., Das, R., & Das, S. (2024b). Neutrosophic approach to water quality assessment: A case of Gomati River, the largest river in Tripura, India. *Neutrosophic Systems with Applications*, 22, 1–12. https://doi.org/10.61356/j.nswa.2024.22386

Das, A. K., Gupta, N., Mahmood, T. et al. (2024c). Assessing anthropogenic influences on the water quality of Gomati River using an innovative weighted fuzzy soft set based water pollution rating system. *Discovery Water*, 4, 73. https://doi.org/10.1007/s43832-024-00136-3

Das, A. K., Gupta, N., Mahmood, T., Tripathy, B. C., Das, R., & Das, S. (2025a). An efficient water quality evaluation model using weighted hesitant fuzzy soft sets for water pollution rating. In A. Kumar, P. Kumar, S. Rathee, & B. Kumar (Eds.), *Mechatronics: Concepts, Tools, Applications, and New Trends* (1st ed., p. 17). CRC Press. https://doi.org/10.1201/9781003494478-10

Das, A. K., Gupta, N., Patra, S., Tripathy, B. C., Das, R., & Datta, R. (2025b). An effective fuzzy soft decision-making model for rating water pollution: A case study of Manu, the longest river in Tripura, India, *Vietnam Journal of Science and Technology* (in press).

Das, A. K., Das, R., Datta, R., & Granados, C. (2025c). An Innovative Approach to Group Decision-Making Based on Weighted Hypersoft Expert System. In F. Smarandache, M. Jdid, & M. Leyva-Vazquez (Eds.), *Neutrosophic and Plithogenic Inventory Models for Applied Mathematics* (pp. 483–518). IGI Global Scientific Publishing. https://doi.org/10.4018/979-8-3693-3204-7.ch019

Das, A. K., & Granados, C. (2023). Preference intuitionistic fuzzy rough relation and its theoretical approach. *Journal of the Indian Mathematical Society*, 90(3–4), 199–212.

Ghorbani, M. K., Afshar, A., & Hamidifar, H. (2021). River water quality management using a fuzzy optimization model and the NSFWQI index. *Water SA*, 47(1), January. https://doi.org/10.17159/wsa/2021.v47.i1.9444

Granados, C., Das, A. K., & Das, B. (2022). Some continuous neutrosophic distributions with neutrosophic parameters based on neutrosophic random variables. *Advances in the Theory of Nonlinear Analysis and its Applications*, 33(2), 293–308.

Granados, C., Das, A. K., & Osu, Bright. (2023). Weighted neutrosophic soft multiset and its application to decision making. *Yugoslav Journal of Operations Research*, 33(2), 293–308.

Gupta, N., Khan, D. K., & Santra, S. C. (2012). Heavy metal accumulation in vegetables grown in a long-term wastewater-irrigated agricultural land of tropical India. *Environmental Monitoring and Assessment*, 184, 6673–6682. https://doi.org/10.1007/s10661-011-2450-7

Gupta, N., Khan, D. K., & Santra, S. C. (2010). Determination of public health hazard potential of wastewater reuse in crop production. *World Review of Science, Technology and Sustainable Development*, 7(4), 328–340. https://doi.org/10.1504/WRSTSD.2010.032741

Gupta, N., Khan, D. K., & Santra, S. C. (2009). Prevalence of intestinal helminth eggs on vegetables grown in wastewater-irrigated areas of Titagarh, West Bengal, India. *Food Control*, 20, 942–945. https://doi.org/10.1016/j.foodcont.2009.02.003

Gupta, N., Khan, D. K., & Santra, S. C. (2008). An assessment of heavy metal contamination in vegetables grown in wastewater irrigated areas of Titagarh, West Bengal, India. *Bulletin of Environmental Contamination and Toxicology*, 80(2), 115–118. https://doi.org/10.1007/s00128-007-9327-z,

Maji, P. K., Biswas, R., & Roy, A. R. (2001). Fuzzy soft sets. *Journal of Fuzzy Mathematics*, 9(3), 589–602.

Mardani, A., Jusoh, A., & Zavadskas, E. K. (2015). Fuzzy multiple criteria decision-making techniques and applications – Two decades review from 1994 to 2014. *Expert Systems with Applications*, 42(8), 4126–4148. https://doi.org/10.1016/j.eswa.2015.01.003

Mina, H., Kannan, D., Gholami-Zanjani, S. M., & Biuki, M. (2021). Transition towards circular supplier selection in petrochemical industry: A hybrid approach to achieve sustainable development goals. *Journal of Cleaner Production*, 286, 125273. https://doi.org/10.1016/j.jclepro.2020.125273

Molodtsov, D. (1999). Soft set theory-first results. *Computers & Mathematics with Applications*, 37(4–5), 19–31.

Mukherjee, A., & Das, A. K. (2016a). Application of fuzzy soft multi sets in decision-making problems. In A. Nagar, D. Mohapatra, & N. Chaki (Eds.), *Proceedings of 3rd International Conference on Advanced Computing, Networking and Informatics. Smart Innovation, Systems and Technologies* (vol. 43). Springer. https://doi.org/10.1007/978-81-322-2538-6_3

Mukherjee, A., & Das, A. K. (2015a). Application of interval valued intuitionistic fuzzy soft set in investment decision making. In *2015 Fifth International Conference on Advances in Computing and Communications (ICACC)* (pp. 61–64). https://doi.org/10.1109/ICACC.2015.37.

Mukherjee, A., & Das, A. K. (2022). Einstein operations on fuzzy soft multisets and decision making. *Boletim da Sociedade Paranaense de Matematica*, 40, 1–10. https://doi.org/10.5269/bspm.32546

Mukherjee, A., & Das, A. K. (2023). *Essentials of fuzzy soft multisets: Theory and applications* (pp. 1–151). Springer Nature Singapore. https://doi.org/10.1007/978-981-19-2760-7

Mukherjee, A., & Das, A. K. (2015b). Relations on intuitionistic fuzzy soft multi sets. In K. Kim (Eds.), *Information Science and Applications – Lecture Notes in Electrical Engineering* (vol. 339). Springer. https://doi.org/10.1007/978-3-662-46578-3_71

Mukherjee, A., & Das, A. K. (2016b). Topological structure formed by intuitionistic fuzzy rough relations. *Journal of the Indian Mathematical Society*, 83(1–2), 135–144.

Mukherjee, A., & Das, A. K. (2015c). Interval valued intuitionistic fuzzy soft multi set theoretic approach to decision making problems. In *2015 International Conference on Computer, Communication and Control (IC4)*, Indore, India (pp. 1–5). https://doi.org/10.1109/IC4.2015.7375640.

Patel, A., & Chitnis K. (2022). Application of fuzzy logic in river water quality modeling for analysis of industrialization and climate change impact on Sabarmati River. *Water Supply*, 22(1), 238–250. https://doi.org/10.2166/ws.2021.275

Pattnaik, B. S., Pattanayak, A. S., Udgata, S. K., et al. (2021). Machine learning based soft sensor model for BOD estimation using intelligence at edge. *Complex Intelligent System*, 7, 961–976. https://doi.org/10.1007/s40747-020-00259-9

Roy, S., Das, M., Ali, S. M., Raihan, A. S., Paul, S. K., & Kabir, G. (2020). Evaluating strategies for environmental sustainability in a supply chain of an emerging economy. *Journal of Cleaner Production*, 262, 121389. https://doi.org/10.1016/j.jclepro.2020.121389

Sharma, R. N., Baruah, A. K., Bora, G. C., & Choudhary, P. K. (1996). Assessment of physico-chemical parameters of the surface water around oil instillation at Rudrasagar, Assam, India. *Polluion Research*, 15, 19–27.

Torra, V. (2010). Hesitant fuzzy sets. *International Journal of Intelligent Systems*, 25(6), 529–539.

WHO. (2011). *Guidelines for Drinking Water Quality* (4th ed.). World Health Organisation.

Zadeh, L. A. (1965). Fuzzy sets. *Information Control*, 8(3), 38–53.

4 From Logic to Learning
The Evolution of Generative AI from Rules to Neural Creativity

Debashree Chakravarty, Ipseeta Satpathy,
Vishal Jain, and B. Chandra Mohan Patnaik

4.1 INTRODUCTION

Artificial Intelligence (AI) has undergone a remarkable evolution, transitioning from basic, rule-based systems to advanced models capable of learning, adapting, and even generating content. Central to this evolution is Generative AI, a significant advancement that empowers machines to create narratives, compose music, produce artwork, and engage in substantive dialogues activities once considered exclusive to humans. This transformation transcends mere technological progress; it signifies a profound reimagining of intelligence, creativity, and the function of machines in influencing our society.

In its formative years, AI was constrained by strict logical frameworks, operating within narrowly defined parameters. These early systems, which relied on if-then logic and decision trees, adhered to a mechanical and structured methodology, rendering them predictable yet severely limited. Analogous to a pianist restricted to playing only from sheet music, they lacked the ability to improvise or adapt to novel circumstances outside their programming.

For example, expert systems among the initial iterations of AI depended on manually coded rules established by human developers. A medical expert system designed to diagnose illnesses based on symptoms could only function within its predetermined database of conditions and responses. If it encountered an unfamiliar case, it would be unable to provide assistance. While rule-based AI achieved certain successes, it resembled a robotic librarian adept at organizing information but incapable of creating new content [1].

As AI progressed, it transcended static programming and entered the realm of Machine Learning (ML). Rather than merely executing commands, machines began to learn from extensive datasets. Instead of adhering to a fixed set of rules, ML algorithms discerned patterns, refined their understanding, and made decisions informed by experience [2].

This marked a pivotal shift. AI gained the ability to process spoken language, recognize images, and offer recommendations—fueling innovations from virtual assistants like Siri and Alexa to personalized movie suggestions on platforms like Netflix. However, traditional ML models still faced a constraint: they remained

DOI: 10.1201/9781003680192-4

dependent on human input. The advent of deep learning and neural networks marked a transformative shift in artificial intelligence, propelling it into the domain of creativity [3].

Deep neural networks, modeled after the architecture of the human brain, established multi-layered frameworks capable of deciphering intricate relationships within data. In contrast to earlier AI systems, these networks operated without the necessity for explicit programming; they could autonomously learn to identify objects, comprehend spoken language, and even produce entirely original content. This innovation led to the emergence of Generative AI, a creative entity that transcended former constraints. Machines evolved from mere interpreters of reality to creators of new experiences. Consequently, AI was now able to [4,5]:

- Compose symphonies reminiscent of Mozart's brilliance.
- Generate lifelike human faces that do not exist.
- Craft novels, poetry, and screenplays that captivate and inspire.
- Envision avant-garde architecture and fashion designs.

What was once the domain of human creativity could now be emulated by neural networks, frequently yielding complex and surprising outcomes that astonished even their developers. With the evolution of machine learning and deep neural networks, AI systems shifted from simply executing commands to learning from extensive datasets. Rather than being explicitly programmed for every possible situation, these networks discern patterns, refine their comprehension, and produce responses that surpass human-defined parameters. This advancement has opened up new avenues for creativity, enabling AI to compose music, write poetry, create visual art, and even participate in conversations that resemble human interaction [6].

4.1.1 OBJECTIVES OF THE STUDY

This study has the following two objectives:

- To study the evolution of generative artificial intelligence.
- To analyze the power of neural creativity.

4.2 THE PROGRESSION OF GENERATIVE AI FROM RULE-BASED FRAMEWORKS TO LEARNING MODELS: AN EXPLORATION OF AI'S TRANSFORMATION

Artificial Intelligence (AI) has experienced a remarkable transformation, evolving from basic rule-based frameworks to sophisticated neural network models that possess the ability to learn, adapt, and even demonstrate creativity. This evolution has opened up opportunities that were once believed to be the exclusive domain of human intelligence, such as the creation of art, music, literature, and groundbreaking scientific insights. Central to this transformation is Generative AI, a branch of artificial intelligence that enables machines to produce original content. The advancements in generative models, ranging from lifelike deepfake images to AI-generated poetry, have blurred the distinctions between human creativity and machine-generated innovation. This evolution signifies not merely an enhancement in computational capabilities but a fundamental change in the manner in which machines process information and generate knowledge [7].

The transition from rigid, rule-based programming to self-learning neural networks marks a significant milestone. These networks are capable of identifying intricate patterns, making autonomous decisions, and generating outputs that may even surprise their human developers. Grasping this shift from logic-driven AI to learning-oriented AI is essential for recognizing the vast potential and implications of generative AI [8].

4.2.1 The Transition from Rule-Based Frameworks to Neural Networks

Understanding Rule-Based AI: The Initial Foundations: Prior to the advent of AI's creative and adaptive capabilities, it was predominantly limited to rule-based systems. These systems functioned based on explicitly defined rules and logic, with human programmers manually dictating the AIs behavior in various scenarios. For instance, expert systems, among the earliest iterations of AI, depended on a structured set of rules to make decisions. While these systems emulated human reasoning, they were constrained to predefined situations. A notable illustration of a rule-based AI system is the chess-playing programs developed during the 1980s and 1990s [8–10].

4.2.2 Limitations of Rule-Based Systems: Why They Fall Short in a Dynamic World

Rule-based AI, although it played a pivotal role in the early development of artificial intelligence, can be likened to a highly disciplined yet inflexible learner. It performs exceptionally well when adhering to established guidelines but encounters difficulties when confronted with scenarios that deviate from its predetermined framework. Although these systems were once viewed as state-of-the-art, their considerable constraints hinder their ability to operate efficiently in the contemporary, rapidly evolving, data-centric environment [11].

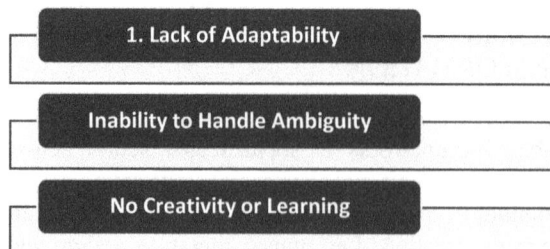

1. Lack of Adaptability

Inability to Handle Ambiguity

No Creativity or Learning

FIGURE 4.1   Diagram of the Limitations of Rule-Based Systems. (Author)

Limitations of Rule-Based Systems

- Lack of Adaptability: Consider the experience of engaging in dialogue with a chatbot from the 1990s. Any minor deviation from the anticipated input would likely result in the system freezing, malfunctioning, or producing illogical responses. This limitation arises from the nature of rule-based AI, which functions within a predetermined framework of scenarios, rendering it incapable of addressing situations beyond its explicit programming [12].

  For example, a rule-based customer support bot programmed to assist with banking transactions might work flawlessly when responding to "How do I check my balance?" but would fail if a user asked, "Can you tell me how safe my account is from fraud?" The bot simply doesn't understand or infer meaning beyond its hardcoded rules. In contrast, modern AI models can adapt and generalize, handling a wide range of queries even if they haven't been explicitly programmed for them.

- Inability to handle ambiguity: Life is full of gray areas, vague statements, and missing pieces of information, things that humans handle naturally. Unfortunately, rule-based systems struggle with ambiguity because they rely on precise, predefined logic. If the input is even slightly different from what the system expects, it may return an error or an incorrect response [12,13].

  Consider a medical diagnosis system built on rule-based AI. If a patient describes symptoms exactly as expected, the system may perform well. But if someone uses non-standard language (e.g., "My chest feels weird" instead of "I have chest pain"), the system might not recognize the symptoms correctly. Humans can interpret vague language, consider probabilities, and make educated guesses; rule-based AI cannot.

  Similarly, real-world situations rarely have perfect data. A self-driving car running on rule-based AI would fail in unpredictable weather conditions, such as heavy fog, because it wouldn't know how to adjust its actions without explicit instructions. Modern AI, particularly machine learning and neural networks, excels at working with imperfect or incomplete data by making probabilistic predictions [6].

- **No Creativity or Learning:** Perhaps the most significant limitation of rule-based AI is its complete lack of creativity and learning ability. It follows static rules, meaning it cannot improve with experience, generate new ideas, or think outside the box. Imagine a rule-based AI composing music. It could follow predefined patterns to generate a tune, but it would never innovate or compose something outside its programming. A modern Generative AI model, on the other hand, can learn from millions of songs, blend different styles, and even compose unique pieces never heard before [14]. Similarly, chatbots built on rule-based logic can only respond in predefined ways. If you ask something slightly different from what they were programmed for, they either fail or sound robotic. But with machine learning and neural networks, AI can learn from interactions, adapting its responses, refining its language, and even mimicking human creativity [15].

4.2.3 Understanding Rule-Based AI Has Been Replaced by Learning-Based Models

While rule-based AI laid the foundation for artificial intelligence, it is now outdated for complex tasks that require adaptability, ambiguity handling, and creativity. The real world is unpredictable, and AI systems need to learn, evolve, and generate new insights, which is why machine learning and deep learning have become the dominant approaches in modern AI development [16,17].

The Emergence of Machine Learning: A New Approach

The early 2000s marked a significant advancement in artificial intelligence with the emergence of Machine Learning (ML). Unlike traditional rule-based AI systems, which depend on fixed guidelines, machine learning leverages statistical models and algorithms to derive insights from extensive datasets. This innovation introduced the concept that AI could enhance its performance over time by recognizing patterns and making informed predictions. A notable illustration of this shift is the development of spam detection in email systems. Rather than relying on a manually coded AI to identify spam through rigid criteria, machine learning algorithms analyze millions of emails to discern spam by recognizing patterns in language, sender behavior, and email formats. Nevertheless, conventional machine learning models still necessitated human involvement to identify pertinent features within the data, paving the way for the advent of deep learning [15].

The Rise of Deep Learning and Neural Networks

The advent of deep learning represented a significant transformation in the field of artificial intelligence, transitioning from strict rules and predetermined logic to a novel phase of self-learning capabilities. In contrast to conventional AI, which depended on manually designed rules and organized data, deep learning models emulate the cognitive processes of the human brain. This allows them to discern patterns, understand relationships, and make decisions autonomously, without the need for explicit programming [18].

Central to deep learning is the artificial neural network (ANN), which consists of a series of interconnected layers of artificial neurons that operate in a manner akin to biological neurons found in the human brain. These networks are capable of processing large volumes of data, identifying intricate patterns, and progressively enhancing their comprehension through training. This capacity for learning and generalization has advanced artificial intelligence beyond conventional rule-based methods, enabling it to effectively manage unstructured data types, including images, speech, and text [19].

Deep learning has not merely enhanced artificial intelligence; it has fundamentally transformed it. AI evolved from merely classifying data to comprehending language, identifying emotions, creating art, and engaging in conversations that resemble human interaction. The domain expanded beyond automation and predictive analytics, delving into realms of creativity, complex problem-solving, and collaborative efforts between humans and AI [3,17].

Milestones That Defined Deep Learning Evolution

The emergence of deep learning was not an instantaneous phenomenon. It was facilitated by significant advancements that broke through earlier constraints and revealed the potential of artificial intelligence in areas such as perception, comprehension, and creativity. This discussion will delve into some of the most pivotal milestones in the evolution of deep learning [17].

2012: AlexNet and the ImageNet Breakthrough

Deep learning demonstrated its dominance over conventional artificial intelligence in 2012, when a neural network called AlexNet triumphed in the esteemed ImageNet competition, a worldwide contest focused on image recognition. AlexNet significantly surpassed all prior computer vision models, illustrating that neural networks had the capability to see and identify images more effectively than any earlier AI approaches. This marked the inaugural instance where deep learning exhibited tangible, real-world advantages over rule-based AI and traditional machine learning methods [20].

The influence: The achievement of AlexNet sparked a revolution in deep learning, resulting in swift integration into areas such as medical imaging, self-driving vehicles, and facial recognition technologies. This pivotal moment made it clear to researchers that artificial intelligence could be trained to interpret the visual environment with a level of accuracy comparable to that of humans.

2014: Generative Adversarial Networks (GANs) AI as a Creator

Two years following the landmark success of AlexNet, deep learning advanced further into new realms with the emergence of Generative Adversarial Networks (GANs). Unlike traditional AI models, which focused on classifying and analyzing data, GANs enabled AI to generate new data from scratch.For the first time, AI could create realistic images, artworks, and even human-like faces, not just recognize them. A GAN consists of two competing networks [21]:

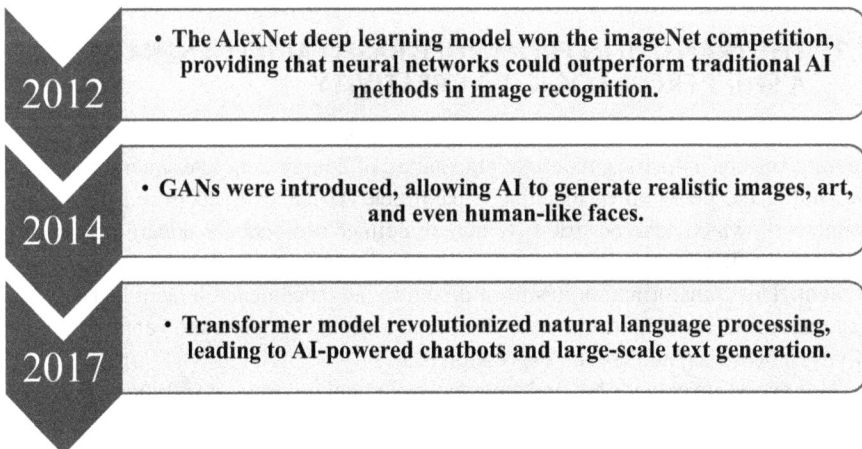

- **2012** • The AlexNet deep learning model won the imageNet competition, providing that neural networks could outperform traditional AI methods in image recognition.

- **2014** • GANs were introduced, allowing AI to generate realistic images, art, and even human-like faces.

- **2017** • Transformer model revolutionized natural language processing, leading to AI-powered chatbots and large-scale text generation.

FIGURE 4.2   Diagram of the Deep Learning Evolution. (Author)

- The generator tries to create realistic data.
- The discriminator evaluates how real or fake the data appears.

This continuous feedback loop refines AI's ability to create highly convincing synthetic content, allowing it to generate photorealistic faces, landscapes, and even paintings in the style of famous artists.

The impact: GANs ushered in a new age of AI-driven creativity, influencing industries such as film, design, gaming, and fashion. Today, GANs power deepfake technology, AI-assisted artwork, and even scientific simulations.

2017: The Transformer Model – AI Learns to Understand Language

While AlexNet revolutionized vision and GANs unlocked creativity, another innovation in 2017 changed the way AI processes human language—the introduction of the Transformer model.

Prior to 2017, AI struggled to understand context in human language. Traditional natural language processing (NLP) models like Recurrent Neural Networks (RNNs) had limitations—they could process only short sequences of text and often lost meaning in long sentences. The Transformer model changed everything. It introduced a mechanism called self-attention, allowing AI to process entire sentences and paragraphs at once, rather than word by word. This made AI significantly better at understanding context, grammar, and relationships between words [22].

The impact: Transformers laid the foundation for modern AI-powered chatbots, translators, and content generators. If you've ever used Google Translate, ChatGPT, or an AI writing assistant, you've interacted with Transformer-based AI.

The most famous Transformer models today include:

- Generative pre-trained transformer powers AI chatbots and text generators.
- Bidirectional encoder representations from transformers enhances the capabilities of search engines and improves AI-driven reading comprehension.
- AI tool that creates artwork based on textual descriptions.

4.3   THE TRANSITION FROM RULE-BASED AI TO GENERATIVE AI: A SHIFT FROM LOGIC TO CREATIVITY

The progression of Artificial Intelligence (AI) has been profoundly transformative, altering various industries, redefining the nature of human-computer interactions, and expanding the potential of machine capabilities. AI has evolved from a rule-based framework, which adhered strictly to human-defined protocols, to a learning-oriented intelligence that adapts and learns from extensive datasets, even generating original content. This transformation has been driven by advancements in deep learning and generative AI, enabling machines to transcend basic automation and venture into creativity, innovation, and artistic expression [23].

This evolution extends beyond mere technological progress; it signifies a profound change in artificial intelligence, evolving from a mere instrument that performs specific tasks to a system capable of thinking, learning, and innovating in ways that were previously the domain of humans.

4.3.1   FROM RULE-BASED AI TO LEARNING-BASED INTELLIGENCE: A COMPARATIVE PERSPECTIVE

The shift from rule-based AI to generative AI marks a significant transformation in the manner in which machines handle and produce information. This transition is most effectively understood through a comparative examination of their fundamental attributes [24].

In traditional rule-based AI, every possible scenario must be explicitly programmed by a human expert. This method, although beneficial in organized and foreseeable settings, exhibits significant rigidity. When faced with unforeseen circumstances, rule-based AI is inadequate, as it lacks the ability to deduce or adjust beyond its established programming [25].

For example, a rule-based chatbot may accurately answer the question "What is your name?" but may struggle to respond appropriately if the question is phrased differently, such as "Can you tell me your name?". In contrast to humans, who can interpret context and intent, rule-based AI is unable to generalize. On the other hand, contemporary AI systems based on neural networks are engineered to recognize patterns and context, enabling them to manage unstructured inputs and unforeseen scenarios with significantly greater adaptability. AI models like GPT and DALL·E not only process information but also create entirely new content, rendering them far more effective for dynamic and creative tasks.

4.3.2   GENERATIVE AI: A NEW FRONTIER IN CREATIVITY

The emergence of Generative AI has introduced a groundbreaking aspect of artificial intelligence, transforming machines from mere problem solvers into creators. In contrast to conventional AI, which primarily analyzes and categorizes pre-existing data, Generative AI models extend their capabilities by generating original content. This includes a wide array of outputs such as artwork, music, literature, intricate scientific

---

TABLE 4.1
Represents Features of Rule-Based AI and Neural Network-Based AI

Feature	Rule-Based AI	Neural Network-Based AI
Approach	Follows predefined rules	Learns from data and patterns
Flexibility	Limited to programmed scenarios	Adapts and generalizes from experience
Creativity	Cannot generate new content	Creates original outputs and innovations
Handling Uncertainty	Struggles with ambiguity	Excels in probabilistic reasoning
Example Technologies	Expert systems, decision trees	Deep learning, GANs, Transformers
Applications	Traditional automation, medical diagnostics	Art, music, language generation, autonomous systems

Source: Author

theories, and innovative product designs. The distinctive feature of Generative AI lies in its capacity to produce novel creations, utilizing identified patterns to forge new ideas. This represents a type of machine-driven creativity that was previously considered exclusive to humans [12,26].

What distinguishes generative AI from other forms of artificial intelligence? Unlike traditional models that primarily excel in data recognition, generative AI possesses the ability to create new information and produce original content. This essential characteristic allows AI to transcend mere automation, entering the domains of artistic and scientific creativity.

Among the most sophisticated generative AI models currently available are:

- Generative Adversarial Networks are a type of artificial intelligence that produce highly realistic images, deepfake videos, and digital artwork. This is achieved through the training of two AI models: one model generates content while the other evaluates it. The interplay between these models leads to outputs that become progressively harder to differentiate from those created by humans [21].
- Variational Autoencoders (VAEs) are employed for the compression and generation of high-dimensional data. They have the ability to produce music compositions, synthetic vocalizations, and novel design patterns by acquiring latent representations from intricate datasets [10].
- Transformers, including models like GPT, BERT, and DALL·E, serve as the foundation for advancements in natural language processing, AI-driven storytelling, chatbot communication, and the conversion of text into images. These technologies have significantly transformed various domains, including journalism, marketing, and creative writing, by producing responses that closely resemble human language and generating artistic visuals from basic textual inputs [24].

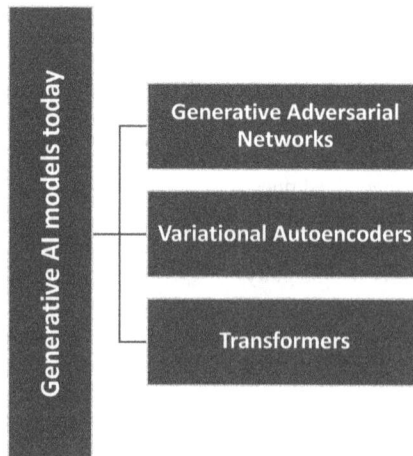

FIGURE 4.3 Diagram of the most advanced Generative AI models. (Author)

4.3.3   THE MANY FACES OF GENERATIVE AI: APPLICATIONS THAT INSPIRE INNOVATION

The capacity of Generative AI to produce content, emulate concepts, and generate lifelike results has resulted in innovative applications across various sectors. Below, we examine some of the most intriguing ways in which Generative AI is influencing the future:

- **Art and Creativity**: Generative AI has revolutionized the realm of digital art and music, enabling machines to work alongside human artists. AI-driven platforms such as DALL·E, DeepDream, and Runway ML are capable of creating stunning paintings, digital illustrations, and fantastical landscapes. AI-generated music is now being used in film scores, background compositions, and experimental sound design. Artists are co-creating with AI, expanding the limits of human imagination [27].
- **Content Generation:** AI is reshaping journalism, marketing, and creative writing by generating compelling narratives, engaging social media posts, and informative articles. GPT models can now write news stories, blog posts, and even novels that mimic human language. Marketers are using AI-driven content creation to personalize customer interactions, enhance brand messaging, and automate copywriting at scale[27].
- **Medical Innovations:** Generative AI is accelerating scientific breakthroughs by designing new molecular structures and drug formulations. Models like AlphaFold and AI-driven biotech algorithms are transforming medical research by predicting protein folding patterns, leading to faster vaccine and drug development. In the field of personalized medicine, AI is helping doctors generate treatment plans tailored to individual genetic profiles [22].
- **Game Development:** AI is changing the way video games are developed by generating realistic characters, creating entire game worlds, and dynamically adjusting difficulty levels. Generative AI is also being used to design immersive virtual landscapes and NPC (non-playable character) interactions, making gaming experiences more dynamic and engaging. AI-generated storytelling is also revolutionizing interactive narratives, where game plots evolve based on player choices [10].
- **Human-AI Collaboration:** Generative AI is enhancing human creativity rather than replacing it. Writers, designers, musicians, and scientists are using AI as a collaborative tool to explore new ideas and push creative boundaries. For example, fashion designers use AI to generate unique clothing patterns, and architects rely on AI-driven designs to create sustainable city models. Instead of replacing human creativity, AI is amplifying it, leading to new forms of innovation [17].

4.3.4   GENERATIVE AI VS. TRADITIONAL AI: A NEW PARADIGM IN MACHINE INTELLIGENCE

Artificial Intelligence has come a long way, evolving from rule-based, logic-driven systems to self-learning, creative models capable of generating new ideas, art, and even scientific breakthroughs. Traditional AI, often designed for problem-solving and automation, operates within predefined boundaries. In contrast, Generative AI moves beyond these constraints, allowing machines to engage in creativity, innovation, and independent thought generation.

Table 4.2 offers a detailed comparison of these two distinct approaches, showcasing how AI has transitioned from analyzing existing data to creating entirely new content.

TABLE 4.2

Represents the Traditional AI vs. Generative AI: A Comparative Analysis

Feature	Traditional AI (Rule-Based & Predictive AI)	Generative AI (Creative & Adaptive AI)
Core Function	Processes and interprets data to find patterns or make predictions based on predefined rules.	Generates new data, creates original content, and produces novel outputs beyond existing datasets.
Learning Ability	Learns from structured, labeled data with significant human supervision and intervention.	Learns autonomously from unstructured data, identifying patterns without explicit programming.
Creativity	Cannot generate new concepts; relies on classification and prediction.	Produces entirely new images, text, designs, and even scientific hypotheses.
Handling Uncertainty	Struggles with ambiguity and requires clear, structured input to function effectively.	Adapts to incomplete or vague inputs, generating meaningful responses based on probabilistic reasoning.
Examples	Fraud detection, speech recognition, automated chatbots, medical diagnostics.	AI-generated paintings, deepfake videos, AI-written novels, and autonomous music composition.
Technologies Used	Expert systems, decision trees, support vector machines, traditional machine learning models.	Generative Adversarial Networks (GANs), Variational Autoencoders (VAEs), and Transformer-based models (GPT, DALL·E, BERT).
Interactivity	Follows programmed instructions, responding in predictable ways to user inputs.	Engages dynamically, generating responses that evolve based on context and learning.
Applications	Used in automation, predictive analytics, data classification, and structured decision-making.	Applied in AI-assisted content creation, digital artistry, AI-driven storytelling, and scientific research.
Human Involvement	Requires constant monitoring, fine-tuning, and human-defined rules for operation.	Works independently, enhancing human creativity rather than replacing it, often acting as a collaborative tool.
Ethical Concerns	Constrained by rule-based logic but still vulnerable to biased training data.	Raises concerns about deepfakes, misinformation, ethical content creation, and authorship attribution.

Source: Author

Traditional AI operates within predefined parameters, excelling at tasks involving data analysis, classification, and automation. However, it lacks the ability to think beyond what it has been programmed to do. Generative AI, on the other hand, introduces a fundamental shift: instead of simply processing data, it creates entirely new content, whether it's an AI-generated painting, a piece of music, or a short story written in Shakespearean prose. Unlike traditional AI, which depends on structured datasets and explicit human guidance, Generative AI models like GPT and DALL·E are trained on vast, unstructured data sources, enabling them to learn, adapt, and improve over time without direct human supervision. This makes them incredibly powerful for creative tasks that require nuance, interpretation, and adaptability [28].

One of the biggest limitations of traditional AI is its struggle with ambiguity. It requires precise, structured inputs, making it ineffective in situations where data is incomplete or unclear. Generative AI, however, thrives in uncertainty. Through the application of probabilistic reasoning and pattern recognition, this technology can intelligently address gaps, akin to how a human might deduce absent information during a dialogue or while interpreting a piece of art. In contrast, conventional AI systems operate reactively, responding solely to explicit commands.

For instance, a rule-based chatbot can provide answers to straightforward inquiries but lacks the capability to create original dialogue or participate in substantive discussions. Generative AI models, including ChatGPT and AI-powered storytelling platforms, are capable of crafting narratives, producing contextually relevant responses, and even emulating various writing styles—all without relying on predetermined scripts.

4.3.5 THE FUTURE OF GENERATIVE AI: UNLOCKING NEW DIMENSIONS OF INTELLIGENCE

The evolution from rule-based AI to Generative AI represents not merely an enhancement but a profound transformation in the capabilities of artificial intelligence. AI has transcended its previous role as a mere executor of commands and has emerged as a collaborative partner in the realms of creation, exploration, and innovation [29].

The Promise of Generative AI

- **Hyper-Personalized AI Assistants**: AI that understands individual emotions, creative styles, and preferences.
- **AI-Generated Scientific Discoveries**: AI-powered models that design new materials, medicines, and sustainable technologies.
- **AI in Entertainment and Media**: AI-generated films, music albums, and interactive storytelling experiences.

The Challenges and Responsibilities

The possibilities offered by Generative AI are boundless; however, they are accompanied by ethical dilemmas and challenges:

- **Deepfakes and Misinformation:** AI-generated content can be used maliciously to spread false narratives.
- **Bias in AI-Generated Content:** If trained on biased datasets, AI models can reflect and amplify social biases.
- **Intellectual Property Debates:** Who owns AI-generated content? Should AI be credited as an artist or author?

As the prevalence of AI-generated content increases, it is essential for governments, businesses, and researchers to work together in developing ethical guidelines, transparency initiatives, and accountability frameworks to ensure that AI technology is utilized in a manner that benefits humanity. The evolution of AI from rule-based systems to Generative AI represents a significant shift into uncharted territory, where machines not only learn from existing data but also create new opportunities. AI has transcended its original role of executing repetitive tasks and has emerged as a creative force, capable of producing art, music, scientific innovations, and engaging in human-like dialogue.

However, as we enter this new phase of AI-enhanced creativity, it is crucial to consider the ethical, legal, and societal ramifications. The future of Generative AI extends beyond the capabilities of machines; it encompasses the potential for collaboration between humans and machines to foster new forms of intelligence and creativity that were previously beyond reach. The opportunities are vast, but with such power comes significant responsibility. The future of Generative AI belongs to those who harness its potential responsibly, ethically, and creatively [10,30].

4.4 UNLEASHING THE POWER OF NEURAL CREATIVITY: HOW AI IS REDEFINING INNOVATION AND EXPRESSION

For centuries, creativity was considered an exclusively human ability, shaping fields such as art, literature, music, and scientific discovery. However, with the advent of neural creativity, artificial intelligence has moved beyond simple automation and problem-solving into the realm of genuine creative generation. Today, AI can compose symphonies, generate paintings, write compelling stories, and even contribute to groundbreaking scientific research.

Neural creativity challenges the fundamental notion of **what it means to be creative**. Can machines truly generate something original? How does neural creativity work? And what are its implications for industries that have long relied on human imagination?

4.4.1 UNDERSTANDING NEURAL CREATIVITY: HOW AI THINKS CREATIVELY

Unlike traditional AI, which operates within predefined parameters and logic-based rules, neural creativity leverages deep learning models that mimic human cognitive processes. These models learn from patterns, adapt to new information, and generate entirely original outputs. Neural creativity is driven by advanced AI architectures, including [30]:

- **Generative Adversarial Networks (GANs)** models that consist of two competing neural networks—one generating content and the other evaluating its quality. This iterative process enables AI to produce hyper-realistic images, deepfake videos, and artistic renderings.
- **Variational Autoencoders (VAEs)** are utilized for the generation of high-dimensional data, encompassing intricate sound compositions, musical pieces, and three-dimensional models.
- **Transformers, such as GPT, DALL·E, and BERT,** serve as the foundation for AI-generated text, interactive conversational agents, and digital art creations. They allow machines to write essays, screenplays, poetry, and create stunning visual art from text prompts.

Unlike conventional AI, which merely processes and classifies data, these models synthesize information in ways that mimic human creativity.

4.4.2 THE CAPABILITIES OF NEURAL CREATIVITY ACROSS INDUSTRIES

Neural creativity is transforming industries by enhancing human innovation, automating creative processes, and expanding artistic and scientific frontiers. Table 4.3 illustrates how AI is applied across various domains.

These examples demonstrate that AI is no longer just assisting in creative fields but actively generating new forms of expression and innovation.

TABLE 4.3
Represents the Applications of Neural Creativity Across Industries

Industry	AI Applications	Impact
Art and Design	AI-generated paintings, sculptures, and digital art	New forms of artistic expression and interactive creativity
Music Composition	AI-composed symphonies, adaptive film scores	Blurring the lines between human and AI-generated music
Literature and Writing	AI-generated novels, poetry, and screenplays	Faster content production and new narrative structures
Scientific Discovery	AI-driven drug discovery, material design	Accelerated research and innovative solutions in medicine
Fashion and Architecture	AI-assisted clothing design, AI-generated city planning	Sustainable and personalized designs based on user preferences
Game Development	AI-created levels, dynamic character interactions	Immersive, evolving digital worlds with adaptive storytelling

Source: Author

4.4.3 UNDERSTANDING THE CONCEPTUAL FRAMEWORK FOR NEURAL CREATIVITY

Understanding how AI generates creativity requires a structured model that integrates data input, learning mechanisms, and content generation. The framework below outlines the step-by-step process of neural creativity [10,30].

Conceptual Model of Neural Creativity
1. **Data Acquisition and Training**
   - AI is trained on large datasets, including literature, art, music, and scientific research.
   - The training process involves analyzing patterns, techniques, and relationships between elements.

2. **Deep Learning and Pattern Recognition**
   - AI identifies recurring structures within datasets, learning how different creative elements interact.
   - Models such as GANs and Transformers refine their understanding of creativity through multiple iterations.

3. **Generative Process**
   - AI synthesizes new outputs based on its learned knowledge, whether in the form of music, writing, artwork, or problem-solving models.
   - The creative process mirrors human brainstorming, where the model combines existing concepts in novel ways.

4. **Evaluation and Refinement**
   - AI-generated content is either evaluated by another AI model (as seen in GANs) or refined through human-AI collaboration.
   - Continuous learning enables the model to improve content quality and originality over time.

As neural creativity continues to evolve, it presents both unprecedented opportunities and ethical concerns. AI-generated content is already influencing digital media, marketing, research, and entertainment, but important considerations must be addressed.

Opportunities in AI Creativity

- **Hyper-Personalized AI Assistants:** AI capable of adapting to an individual's creative preferences, assisting in writing, composing, and designing.
- **AI-Driven Scientific Innovations:** AI-generated research models accelerating discoveries in medicine, engineering, and physics.
- **Human-AI Collaborative Creativity:** Artists, musicians, and writers working alongside AI to explore new creative frontiers.

Challenges and Ethical Considerations

- **Misinformation and Deepfakes:** AI-generated media can be misused to create misleading content, raising concerns about truth and authenticity.
- **Bias in AI Creativity:** AI models trained on biased datasets may inadvertently reinforce societal inequalities in creative outputs.
- **Intellectual Property Concerns:** Legal frameworks must address the ownership of AI-generated content and the role of AI in creative industries.

The balance between harnessing AI's potential and mitigating risks will define how neural creativity integrates into society [31,32].

Neural creativity represents a paradigm shift in how the world understands innovation and artistic expression. Machines are no longer just tools for automation; they have become collaborators in the creative process, generating new forms of art, music, literature, and scientific discovery. The future of creativity is not about replacing human ingenuity, but about enhancing and expanding it through AI-driven collaboration. The question is no longer "Can AI be creative?" but rather "How can we integrate AI creativity responsibly and ethically into our world?". As AI continues to evolve, the boundary between human and machine creativity will continue to blur, creating a future where technology and human imagination work together to shape new possibilities.

4.5　CONCLUSION

Neural creativity represents not merely a technological advancement but a fundamental transformation in our understanding of creation, imagination, and innovation. Historically, creativity has been regarded as a uniquely human characteristic, influenced by emotions, intuition, and personal experiences. However, artificial intelligence has surfaced not as a substitute for human creativity but as a synergistic partner that broadens the horizons of artistic expression, scientific exploration, and innovative problem-solving.

The interaction between humans and AI should not be perceived as a conflict between natural cognition and machine intelligence; instead, it is a harmonious blend of capabilities. AI provides unparalleled speed, pattern recognition, and extensive computational resources, while human creativity contributes depth, emotional resonance, and intentionality. This collaboration is ushering in a new epoch where art, literature, music, and innovation transcend the limitations of human thought alone.

Nevertheless, this enhanced capability brings with it significant ethical responsibilities. As AI-generated works become increasingly similar to those produced by humans, society faces pressing ethical dilemmas, including issues of ownership, authenticity, equity, and the prevention of misuse. The trajectory of creativity will not be determined solely by AI but will depend on the decisions made by humans regarding the development, regulation, and ethical application of these technologies.

The advancement of neural creativity does not signify the demise of human artistry; rather, it marks the onset of a new creative revolution. The pivotal change lies not in questioning whether AI can be creative, but in exploring how humans can leverage AI to expand the frontiers of creativity, discovery, and innovation. As we embark on this new chapter, one fundamental truth prevails: the future of creativity is not the domain of humans or machines alone, but a realm of infinite possibilities that arises when they collaborate.

REFERENCES

[1] Mahesh, B. (2020). Machine learning algorithms–A review. *International Journal of Science and Research, 9*(1), 381–386.

[2] Sarker, I. H. (2021). Machine learning: Algorithms, real-world applications and research directions. *SN Computer Science, 2*(3), 160.

[3] de Albuquerque, V. H. C., Raj, P., & Yadav, S. P. (Eds.) (2023). *Toward Artificial General Intelligence: Deep Learning, Neural Networks, Generative AI*. Walter de Gruyter GmbH & Company KG.

[4] Struik, O. L., & Kondratenko, Y. U. (2021). Generative adversarial neural networks and deep learning: Successful cases and advanced approaches. *International Journal of Computing, 20*(3), 339–349.

[5] Tomczak, J. M. (2024). Why deep generative modeling? In *Deep Generative Modeling* (pp. 1–13). Springer International Publishing. DOI: https://doi.org/10.1007/978-3-031-64087-2

[6] Foster, D. (2022). *Generative Deep Learning*. O'Reilly Media.

[7] Dhamani, N. (2024). *Introduction to Generative AI*. Simon and Schuster.

[8] Takale, D. G., Mahalle, P. N., & Sule, B. (2024). Advancements and applications of generative artificial intelligence. *Journal of Information Technology and Sciences, 10*(1), 20–27.

[9] Linkon, A. A., Shaima, M., Sarker, M. S. U., Badruddowza, B., Nabi, N., Rana, M. N. U., ... & Chowdhury, F. R. (2024). Advancements and applications of generative artificial intelligence and large language models on business management: A comprehensive review. *Journal of Computer Science and Technology Studies, 6*(1), 225–232.

[10] Gatla, R. K., Gatla, A., Sridhar, P., Kumar, D. G., & Rao, D. N. M. (2024, May). Advancements in generative AI: Exploring fundamentals and evolution. In *2024 International Conference on Electronics, Computing, Communication and Control Technology (ICECCC)* (pp. 1–5). IEEE.

[11] Thorne, S. L. (2024). Generative artificial intelligence, co-evolution, and language education. *Modern Language Journal, 108*(2), 567–572.

[12] Dwivedi, R., & Elluri, L. (2024). Exploring generative artificial intelligence research: A bibliometric analysis approach. *IEEE Access 12*, 119884–119902.

[13] Kılınç, H. K., & Keçecioğlu, Ö. F. (2024). Generative artificial intelligence: A historical and future perspective. *Academic Platform Journal of Engineering and Smart Systems 12*(2), 47–58.

[14] Yang, Y., Liu, Y., Li, G., Zhang, Z., & Liu, Y. (2024). Harnessing the power of machine learning for AIS data-driven maritime research: A comprehensive review. *Transportation Research Part E: Logistics and Transportation Review, 183*, 103426.

[15] Guan, H., Wang, Y., Niu, P., Zhang, Y., Zhang, Y., Miao, R., Fang, X., Yin, R., Zhao, S., Liu, J., & Tian, J. (2024). The role of machine learning in advancing diabetic foot: A review. *Frontiers in Endocrinology, 15*, 1325434.

[16] Ahmed, A. A., Sayed, S., Abdoulhalik, A., Moutari, S., & Oyedele, L. (2024). Applications of machine learning to water resources management: A review of present status and future opportunities. *Journal of Cleaner Production, 441*, 140715.

[17] Kufel, J., Bargieł-Łączek, K., Kocot, S., Koźlik, M., Bartnikowska, W., Janik, M., ... & Gruszczyńska, K. (2023). What is machine learning, artificial neural networks and deep learning?—Examples of practical applications in medicine. *Diagnostics, 13*(15), 2582.

[18] Zhan, Z. H., Li, J. Y., & Zhang, J. (2022). Evolutionary deep learning: A survey. *Neurocomputing, 483*, 42–58.

[19] Vatter, J., Mayer, R., & Jacobsen, H. A. (2024). The evolution of distributed systems for graph neural networks and their origin in graph processing and deep learning: A survey. *ACM Computing Surveys, 56*(1), 1–37.

[20] Li, S., Wang, L., Li, J., & Yao, Y. (2021, February). Image classification algorithm based on improved AlexNet. *Journal of Physics: Conference Series 1813*(1), 012051.

[21] Lim, W., Yong, K. S. C., Lau, B. T., & Tan, C. C. L. (2024). Future of generative adversarial networks (GAN) for anomaly detection in network security: A review. *Computers and Security, 139*, 103733.

[22] Denecke, K., May, R., & Rivera-Romero, O. (2024). Transformer models in healthcare: A survey and thematic analysis of potentials, shortcomings and risks. *Journal of Medical Systems, 48*(1), 23.

[23] Vadhil, F. A., Nanne, M. F., & Salihi, M. L. (2024, April). The powerful AI: An exploration of generative Artificial Intelligence taxonomy and applications. In *International Conference on Artificial Intelligence and its Applications in the Age of Digital Transformation* (pp. 236–250). Springer Nature: Switzerland.

[24] Feuerriegel, S., Hartmann, J., Janiesch, C., & Zschech, P. (2024). Generative ai. *Business & Information Systems Engineering, 66*(1), 111–126.

[25] Sharma, D. M., Ramana, K. V., Jothilakshmi, R., Verma, R., Maheswari, B. U., & Boopathi, S. (2024). Integrating generative AI into K-12 curriculums and pedagogies in India: Opportunities and challenges. In *Facilitating Global Collaboration and Knowledge Sharing in Higher Education with Generative AI,* P. Yu, J. Mulli, Z. A. S. Syed & L. Umme, Eds. IGI Global, pp. 133–161.

[26] Liao, W., Lu, X., Fei, Y., Gu, Y., & Huang, Y. (2024). Generative AI design for building structures. *Automation in Construction*, 157, 105187.

[27] Weisz, J. D., He, J., Muller, M., Hoefer, G., Miles, R., & Geyer, W. (2024, May). Design principles for generative AI applications. In *Proceedings of the 2024 CHI Conference on Human Factors in Computing Systems* (Article no. 378, pp. 1–22). ACM. Published Online: 11 May 2024. https://doi.org/10.1145/3613904.3642466

[28] Sengar, S. S., Hasan, A. B., Kumar, S., & Carroll, F. (2024). Generative artificial intelligence: A systematic review and applications. *Multimedia Tools and Applications,* 84, 1–40.

[29] Jindal, J. A., Lungren, M. P., & Shah, N. H. (2024). Ensuring useful adoption of generative artificial intelligence in healthcare. *Journal of the American Medical Informatics Association, 31*(6), 1441–1444.

[30] Kenett, Y. N. (2024). The role of knowledge in creative thinking. *Creativity Research Journal, 37*, 1–8.

[31] Anas, M., Saiyeda, A., Sohail, S. S., Cambria, E., & Hussain, A. (2024). Can generative AI models extract deeper sentiments as compared to traditional deep learning algorithms? *IEEE Intelligent Systems, 39*(2), 5–10.

[32] Xue, Y., Wang, X., Li, Y., & Zhong, Y. (2025). Associations between brain functional network characteristics and musical creative achievement. *Creativity Research Journal*, 1–11. Published Online: 16 February 2025. https://doi.org/10.1080/10400419.2025.2465173

5 Generative AI Architectures, Applications, and Future Scopes in Industry

Dina Darwish, Kali Charan, Rohit Sood, and Sukhpreet Singh

5.1 INTRODUCTION

The architecture of generative artificial intelligence refers to the fundamental framework and design of systems that make it possible for generative AI models to acquire knowledge, process information, and produce new data. There is another name for it, which is "generative AI architecture" [1]. This chapter provides an illustration of the relationships that exist between the several components of the generative AI systems. Generative artificial intelligence architecture design and GenAI architectural diagrams not only allow for the expression of creative ideas, but they also give machines the ability to create content that is not only unique but also realistic. On the other hand, conventional AI systems are primarily concerned with recognition and prediction. This is in contrast to artificial intelligence [2].

An artificial intelligence system's architecture includes essential components like data input layers, processing units, model frameworks, and output mechanisms. The complexity inherent in AI model design will vary based on its specific application needs. This software enables applications that include realistic photo production and architectural design creation while also writing text that mirrors human language.

This research paper [1] introduces an analysis of the structure and classifications along with the main uses of generative artificial intelligence systems with a focus on chatbots. The research study author explains how generative artificial intelligence interfaces function.

Artificial intelligence (AI) interfaces operate through multiple methods to generate AI outputs. The author demonstrates the architecture while explaining how the interfaces function. Complex machine learning algorithms construct the generative model to produce responses that are both dynamic and context-appropriate automatically. The retrieval-based model depends on a pre-existing response library for its construction. In addition to this, the research project introduces technologies that are founded on the semantic analysis of deep learning and NoSQL in order to integrate and retrieve data in a more effective manner. The use of generative artificial intelligence as a method for populating multimedia knowledge graphs (KGs) is

 DOI: 10.1201/9781003680192-5

another topic that is covered in this research. This chapter discusses Generative AI architectures, models, applications, and future scopes.

5.2 ARCHITECTURE OF GENERATIVE ARTIFICIAL INTELLIGENCE COMPONENTS AND INTERFACES

Models of generative artificial intelligence are constructed using a variety of components as their foundation. Individually, let's talk about each of them.

5.2.1 THE PROCESSING OF DATA

Data preprocessing must be performed to ensure that generative models function appropriately and competently. In order to achieve maximum performance potential from the model, it requires transforming raw data into a uniform structure. To achieve optimal model performance, raw data must be converted to a simple, consistent format. Model performance enhancement requires high-quality and diverse data. Models perform best when they receive both high-quality and diverse data sets.

The process produces results that demonstrate both accuracy and reliability. Preparing information for learning involves utilizing techniques which transform data into an organized format. Techniques such as selection, modification, and normalization of the data ensure that the information is uniform and organized.

5.2.2 SELECTION OF THE MODEL

To provide progressively better outcome, there is a must to choose the model correctly. Each generative model has its particular advantages and applications it can enable. The main models are Transformers, GANs, and VAEs, and each of these three categories of devices has its own set of functionalities. Depending on the needs of the application, these models are trained for specific purposes, and certain model types perform exceptionally well on activities such as the formation of text or the production of images.

5.2.3 THE PROCESS OF TRAINING AND OPTIMIZING

Training and optimization are important considerations for developing generative artificial intelligence models. This is because only these procedures can ensure that a model produces the desired results. It is possible to ensure that AI platform architecture models work optimally by employing proper training and optimization methodologies. To ensure that artificial intelligence architecture models perform their roles as effectively as possible, it is critical to understand the importance of carefully selecting appropriate training methodologies and fine-tuning models.

Several unique learning methodologies, including supervised learning, unsupervised learning, and reinforcement learning, can be used in the creation of AI system design models. In supervised learning, the trial-and-error approach is employed, whereas reinforcement learning utilizes both labeled and unlabeled data.

5.3 CATEGORIZATION OF ARTIFICIAL INTELLIGENCE INTERFACES

The architecture of generative artificial intelligence is a contemporary method. In terms of interfaces, the intelligent interfaces structure that is currently being proposed in the state of the art will be divided into four sections. The multimedia processor, the response generator, the interface, and the multimodal input analysis comprise these components. Research provided important guidelines outlined [3–5].

1. To offer additional clarification. The chatbot's interaction with its users is overseen by the interface. This interaction encompasses the receipt of inputs in a variety of formats, such as text or audio, and the subsequent provision of suitable responses.
2. The multimedia processor, which is optional, may be necessary to preprocess audio or video signals and convert them to text in order to expedite the production of answers. Furthermore, it may be imperative to identify the user's tone.
3. The multimodal input analysis unit is accountable for the classification and pre-treatment of data. It frequently employs natural language understanding (NLU) techniques, including semantic parsing, intent identification, and slot filling.
4. The response generator either employs modern machine learning techniques to transfer the normalized input to the output by employing a pre-trained model or it associates a suitable response for the pre-processed input that has been provided from a stored dataset.

It is possible to think of the response generator as the "brain" of the system; it is the primary component of a chatbot and the site where the real question-and-answer process takes place. It is possible to divide chatbot systems into two primary categories, which are based on the architecture of the response generator: retrieval-based chatbots, which choose their responses from a pre-defined set of possible outcomes, and generative-based chatbots, which use machine learning techniques to generate answers in a dynamic manner [6].

5.3.1 Chatbots That Are Based on Retrieval

The purpose of retrieval-based chatbots is to "understand" the input provided by the user and select the responses obtained from a knowledge dataset that are the most appropriate options. A retrieval-based chatbot may be broken down into four distinct sub-categories, each of which can be differentiated from the others depending on the architecture of their knowledge collection and the retrieval techniques they employ. Template-based, corpus-based, intent-based, and RL-based are the types that fall under this category [5].

5.3.1.1 Chatbots Based on Templates

Chatbots that are based on templates select responses from a pool of potential candidates by comparing the user's input to specific query patterns.

5.3.1.2   Chatbots Based on Corpus

The fundamental architecture of template-based chatbots requires them to continuously search through all of the possible outputs for each input until they find the proper response. This is despite the fact that template-based chatbots have demonstrated effectiveness in specific situations. As a consequence of this, the approach may be slow, and it is not appropriate for applications that require a large repository of knowledge.

5.3.1.3   Chatbots Based on Intent

Machine learning techniques are utilized by intent-based chatbots to develop a connection between the inputs provided by users and the pre-defined outputs. In most cases, pertinent data is gathered and kept in order to form links between user intentions (that is, the conceptual meaning that lies behind a user's request) and appropriate responses. The next step is for a pre-trained model to make use of this information in order to establish a connection between the normalized user inputs and the most likely user intent [7].

5.3.1.4   Chatbots Based on RL

Chatbots that are based on reinforcement learning use this learning to generate responses. Reinforcement learning itself is mainly based on the Markov decision process, i.e. a 4-tuple (S, A, Pa, Ra) where:

$S = (s1, s2, ..., sn)$ is a set of states, called the state space;
$A = (a1, a2, ..., am)$ is a set of actions, called the action space;
$Pa(s, s') = \Pr(st+1 = s'|st = s, at = a)$ is the probability that action a, in the state s at step t will lead to state s' at step $t + 1$;
$Ra(s, s')$ is the reward received after transitioning from state s to state s' when action a is performed.

The objective of a Markov decision process is to identify a function $\pi(s)$, which is commonly referred to as policy, that associates, for each state si, the action $\pi(st) = ai$ that maximizes the overall reward.

5.3.2   GENERATIVE CHATBOTS

Chatbots that are based on generative programming have the advantage of being able to produce responses in a dynamic manner, which increases the likelihood of discussions with users that are more naturally occurring and flexible. As long as they are able to give new responses, in the same way that retrieval-based chatbots are not allowed to give "standard" answers (e.g., a statement to an affirmative question), the generative chatbot can offer more personalized answers that are more relevant to the user's situation.

We are going to discuss Random Neural Network (RNN) based chatbots, and Transformer based chatbots depending on the machine learning architecture being used.

5.3.2.1 Chatbots Based on RNN

In the development of generation-based chatbots, one approach commonly employed is the representation of two neural networks that are coupled together (called recursive neural networks): a sentence is input into the first network (called the encoder) and it is trained to associate the sentence with an intermediate vector (referred to as the context vector). The second network (called the decoder) is trained to generate an output sentence either by using actual words or tokens. It gets the context vector as input and is trained to generate the phrase. (This approach is also commonly termed "sequence-to-sequence" or "Sequence2Sequence" [6–10].)

There is no guarantee that RNN-based chatbot responses will be more exact and less uncertain than retrieval-based chatbots, since RNN based chatbot responses come from machine learning models and are generated dynamically.

Building on this, RNN-based chatbots are used significantly less often in situations in which they are engaged in tasks or knowledge-based activities and more often in activities involved in mental health and enjoyment [5].

5.3.2.2 Chatbots Built on Transformers

There is a relatively new form of neural network design used for natural language understanding and chatbots. This has been described in [11] and is also used on other tasks, for example, the translation of languages and text summarization. The self-attention mechanism is a fundamental property of Transformers. It allows the model to learn which parts of the input sequence to pay attention to at each stage of processing; that is, it learns, depending on the relevance of the other parts of the sequence to the current location. To do this, a method called scaled dot-product attention is used. In this method, the model acquires a collection of weights so that it can compute a weighted sum of the sequence representations that are input.

Besides these language models based on the Transformer architecture, there are several other important language models that use the Transformer architecture. One is the Generative Pre-trained Transformer (GPT) developed by OpenAI in 2020 [12]. ChatGPT, one of the most popular chatbots due to its ability to render detailed and articulate responses on a large range of topics [13], is built upon GPT, which is the underlying architecture of the chatbot. Figure 5.1 illustrates types of Chatbot systems.

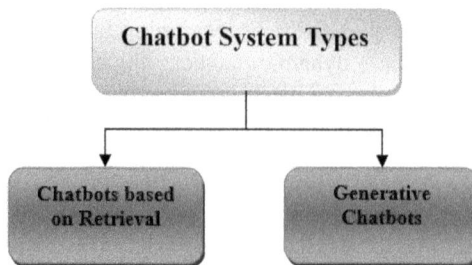

FIGURE 5.1   Chatbots Systems Types.

5.4 ENHANCEMENT OF THE MULTIQUERY RETRIEVAL GENERATION

In the actual vanguard of Generative Artificial Intelligence (Gen-AI), it is of the utmost importance to streamline complex decision-making processes since it enables tools that are accessible and understandable to all users. The primary objective of this section is to suggest an alternative to the traditional RAG, which was first presented by Lewis et al. in 2021 [14]. Additionally, the capabilities of the RAG will be improved by the implementation of a multiquery approach, which will present a clear and robust architectural flow together with the primary evaluation metrics.

5.4.1 METHODOLOGY

Within this section of the methodology, the profound implications that can be derived from the utilization of Generative Artificial Intelligence (AI) to streamline and revolutionize complex decision-making processes, augment the power of cutting-edge technologies, and enhance the traditional Retrieval-Augmented Generation (RAG) models investigated. Each of these implications has the potential to be derived from the utilization of AI. The rigorous study of a human-centered and multiquery RAG application design ensures the acquisition of access to complex artificial intelligence capabilities as well as a comprehension of those capabilities. This is accomplished by ensuring that the design is human-centered. This will operate as a bridge between technical capabilities and the implementation of such capabilities in the real world. As a result of the end of this inquiry, a research for the architectural flow that is both succinct and sturdy has been developed. The groundwork for the seamless integration of multiquery-RAG solutions into decision-making processes is laid by this research, which builds the foundation. Furthermore, it offers supplementary insights that expand beyond the subject of this research [11] and establish the framework for future improvements in the field.

The multiquery-RAG system is distinguished from other systems by its ability to generate a large number of variations of the initial user query in a manner that is reminiscent of human behavior. In order to accomplish this, a specialized question generation chain is utilized. This chain generates a preset number of alternative enquiries that capture diverse opinions and nuances related to the initial question. When properly calibrated, this diversification of the query set is of the utmost importance in order to avoid the limits of distance-based similarity searches in vector databases. Despite the the traditional retrieval approach still being utilized, this ensures that the process of document recovery will be more complete and effective.

Once retrieval of data gathered from documentsis complete,the system then moves on to the process of synthesizing and generating responses, employing a wide variety of LLMs systems in the process. In addition to ensuring that the responses are accurate, the process of contextualizing and building upon the material ensures that they are easily understandable by individuals who are not specialists in the particular sector. Ensuring that the information is accessible to a larger audience, is thus simplified.

The system then proceeds to develop responses by synthesizing and creating responses utilizing the data gathered from the documents and leveraging a wide range of LLMs systems. This occurs after the system has retrieved the information (documents). The process of contextualizing and expanding upon the information ensures that the responses are not only correct but also easily intelligible by individuals who are not specialists in the field. This simplifies the process of making the information accessible to a wider audience and allowing it to be utilized by greater numbers of people.

5.4.2 EVALUATION STANDARDS AND CRITERIA

The next section provides an overview of the primary metrics [15] that are essential for evaluating a Retrieval-Augmented Generation (RAG) in terms of monitoring various aspects of the system's performance.

Precision in the Context is a statistic that determines the signal-to-noise ratio within the contexts that have been obtained, which measures the proportion of the documents that have been retrieved that are truly relevant to the user's query.

This metric determines whether all of the necessary information that is required to answer the query has been retrieved. It does this by ensuring that the knowledge base of the system covers all of the aspects that are required to formulate a comprehensive and accurate response. It does this by relying on a comparison between the retrieved contexts and the ground truths.

Continuity of faith is a statistic that provides a quantitative assessment of the factual accuracy of the responses that are produced by the RAG system. A comparison is done between the total number of statements in the answers and the count of factual statements that were made in the generated answers based on the recovered contexts. This count is then recorded and compared to the total number of statements in the answers.

The relevance of the replies is a metric that evaluates how well the generated responses respond to the questions asked by the user. As an illustration, if a query requests a number of different pieces of information, the relevancy score indicates the extent to which the response addresses all of the components of the question.

5.4.3 ARCHITECTS OF ARTIFICIAL INTELLIGENCE PLAY AN IMPORTANT ROLE

An AI solution architect is an essential component in the process of building and putting into action generative artificial intelligence systems. By designing a scalable and efficient artificial intelligence architecture that is tailored to specific use cases, they bridge the gap between the goals of the company and the technical implementation of those goals.

The addressing of ethical concerns and the guaranteeing of conformity with regulatory norms are two of the most important aspects of artificial intelligence platforms. Their expertise is necessary for the implementation of artificial intelligence solutions that are not just creative but also ethical and influential. Figure 5.2 illustrates using generative AI in industries.

FIGURE 5.2 Generative AI in industries. (www.freepik.com/)

5.5 APPLICATIONS OF GENERATIVE AI

Within the realm of architecture, engineering, and construction (AEC), the design initiatives that are being undertaken are as follows:

5.5.1 The Method GS Uses in the Process of Design Generation

Of the three procedures that are used to generate designs, the evaluation process is always last. The distinction between the other two processes makes it possible to categorize generative systems (GSs) as either conventional generative systems (CGSs) or performance-based generative systems (PGSs).

The generation process in CGSs is driven by performance goals (such as energy consumption), but in PGSs, the generation process is driven by performance goals. CGSs follow an iterative process that involves creating, analyzing, and assessing, with incremental improvements brought in after each iteration until constraints are met [16–18]. As a result, PGSs make it possible to incorporate an optimization layer [19], which transforms the design method into a value-driven (or value-oriented) design process. This is accomplished by directing the design process such that it meets defined performance objectives. It is important to note that scholars also use the term "performative design" to refer to the design approach that is followed in PGSs [17, 18].

5.5.2 The Generation Theory Based on GSs

Self-organization systems (SOSs) (also referred to as self-assembly systems (SASs)), evolutionary systems (EvSs), and generative grammar systems (GGSs) are the three categories into which generative grammar systems (GSs) can be classified, based on the theory of generation that underpins them.

Atlan's example of car components [20] is the most effective way to illustrate SASs. According to this example, if you shake a box of car parts, you will obtain an assembled automobile upon opening the box. This is the most effective method of conveying the concept of SASs. SASs (or SOSs), as they are interchangeably referred to in research [21], are composed of a multitude of straightforward components that are combined to create a new component that is more intricate than the original component. It is challenging to establish a comprehensive set of principles that ensure the creation of meaningful forms, which is why it is challenging to rely solely on SASs to generate forms. The reader can envision that this presents a challenge.

5.5.3 EvSs ARE A REPRESENTATION OF THE NATURAL GSs: THE BASIS OF GENERATION THEORY

Self-organization systems (SOSs) (also referred to as self-assembly systems (SASs)), evolutionary systems (EvSs), and generative grammar systems (GGSs) are the three categories into which generative grammar systems (GSs) can be classified, as determined by the theory of generation that underpins them [16]. The most effective way to elucidate SASs is to use Atlan's example of automobile components [17]. According to this example, if you jiggle a box of car parts, you will receive an assembled car upon opening the box. This is the most effective method of elucidating [16] SASs. SASs (or SOSs), as they are interchangeably referred to [21], are composed of a multitude of straightforward components that are combined to create a new component that is more intricate than the original component. It is challenging to establish a comprehensive set of principles that ensure the creation of meaningful forms, which is why it is challenging to rely solely on SASs to generate forms. The reader can envision that this presents a challenge [16] in strategies that are generative in the architecture, engineering, and construction industries.

The theory of generation is a high-level overview of the process; however, it does not provide the GS with the necessary details to follow. Therefore, it is imperative to offer a succinct clarification of the generative methods that a GS can employ to produce the desired geometry. The architecture, engineering, and construction industry employs a variety of generative methods. Cellular automata (CA), genetic algorithms (GA), shape grammar (SG), L-system (LS), and swarm intelligence (SI) with multi-agent societies (MA) are the generative approaches that are most frequently employed in the architecture, engineering, and construction (AEC) industry, as per Singh and Gu [22]. The objective of this section is to offer a succinct overview of each of these methodologies. A cellular automaton (CA) is a system that is composed of cells that are arranged on a grid with a predetermined shape and evolve in accordance with the principles associated with the cells' surrounding areas [23, 24]. The cells and the operations that can be performed on them are restricted based on the type of grid that is being used [22]. CA is a bottom-up methodology [25] that is both simple (it does not necessitate intricate structures to initiate the generation process) and capable of producing complex and unexpected designs in an environment that supports multiple dimensions [25–27].

GA is a methodology that simulates the natural selection process to autonomously solve problems, beginning with a high-level statement of requirements [28]. It is an evolutionary process that is constructed from the top down and is employed by GSs to achieve the objectives of optimization [29] and generation [30]. Shape Generation (SG) is a set of rules that govern the process of design generation by regulating shape transformation [31, 32]. It can be descriptive when employed as an analysis instrument to investigate existing designs in order to uncover the underlying patterns [33, 34]. Alternatively, it can be generative for the purpose of design generation when employed as a design instrument to develop designs [35]. By defining and applying a diverse array of rules at different phases of the design process, SG enables users to produce a wide range of solutions [36]. LS, or Lindenmayer systems, were initially developed as a mathematical model to produce plant-like shapes [37]. This was accomplished in accordance with the concept of rewriting, which involves the continuous replacement of fundamental structures to create a complex shape. The LS is a bottom-up GGS, similar to the SG. Nevertheless, the distinction is in the operating medium: LS operates on strings, whereas SG operates on the design itself. The distinction between the two is exemplified by this. The behavior of autonomous agents, both individually and collectively, within a specific context is investigated by MA [38] through the use of a computer simulation approach. When we discuss SI, we are referring to the global-level patterns that manifest as a consequence of the collective behavior of the interacting agents of a system [39]. MA is a bottom-up approach that allows for the examination of the issue without the necessity of a centralized control system [23].

A generative system (GS) may implement one or more of the generative techniques, contingent upon the specifics of the issue and the developers' level of expertise. Researchers who utilized both GA and SG in their GSs include Granadeiro et al. [40] and Hou and Xu [41], who combined both. In the published literature, there are additional instances of scientists who integrated various techniques into their GSs.

5.5.4 CUSTOMER SERVICE AND GENERATIVE ARTIFICIAL INTELLIGENCE

Specifically, it is important to investigate the effects that generative artificial intelligence has had on the customer service business, which is at the forefront of the use of AI [42]. Engagement with customers is an essential component in the development of a loyal consumer base.

In addition to the reputation of the organization. Nevertheless, as is the case with many other professions, the level of productivity among workers in customer service is quite variable [43, 44].

To be more productive, newer staff require a large amount of training and effort. The turnover rate is substantial; according to figures provided by the industry, sixty percent of agents working in contact centers quit their jobs annually, resulting in a cost of between 10,000 and 20,000 dollars for each agent in the United States [43, 45]. According to Berg et al. [46], the typical supervisor devotes a significant portion of their time to the process of training new agents that they supervise.

A further example of an environment in which there is a significant amount of variation in the capabilities of different agents is customer service. For instance, customer service representatives who perform exceptionally well are frequently more effective at identifying the underlying technical problem when they are provided with a description of the problem by a customer. They spend more time initially by asking more questions before presenting a solution. This is done to avoid wasting time solving the wrong problem. Artificial intelligence (AI) tools are becoming increasingly popular among businesses as a solution to the challenges of unpredictable production, high turnover, and expensive training costs [42]. These tools have the potential to learn from the best practices of top performers.

Within the realm of technology, customer support is ideally suited for the generative AI technologies that are currently available. Conversations between customer service and sales representatives can be viewed as a set of pattern-matching problems in which the goal is to find the most effective sequence of activities. An artificial intelligence or agent must be able to identify the potential problems and their remedies when it is presented with a problem such as "I am unable to log in." Specifically, the question "Can you check that caps lock is not on?" At the same time, the representative needs to be sensitive to the emotional reaction of the customer and use language that is reassuring rather than condescending. Pre-trained LLMs can be fine-tuned with samples of both successfully resolved and badly resolved conversations. This is only possible due to the widespread recording and digitization of interactions that take place in customer service.

5.5.5   DATA FIRM CUSTOMER SERVICE

A company that deals in artificial intelligence-based customer care support software (hereinafter referred to as the "AI firm") in order to investigate the implementation of its tool at a client company (hereinafter referred to as the "data firm"). The data company is a Fortune 500 corporation that specializes in small and medium-sized enterprises in the United States by providing them with software that streamlines their business processes. Through both direct employment and the use of third-party outsourcing companies, it makes use of a wide range of chat-based technical support personnel. The vast majority of the agents in a sample are employed from offices that are situated in the Philippines. A smaller number of agents are employed in the United States of America and other worldwide locations. Agents are involved in a work that is rather consistent across locales, which is to respond to questions from small business owners situated in the United States for technical support.

It is not necessary to perform any additional pre-screening because customer chats are assigned based on the availability of agents.

It is not uncommon for questions to be difficult to comprehend, and the duration of support sessions is normally forty minutes. In this conversation, the primary objective is to determine the nature of the technical problem that is the root cause of the crisis. In addition to having a full understanding of the product, the agent is responsible for being able to deal with customers who are experiencing frustration, as well as the ability to find solutions to problematic situations. In spite of the fact that the data company employed additional groups of agents to provide chat-based assistance to a variety of customer segments, including individuals who were self-employed and larger organizations, there was no additional sorting for enquiries that were related to small businesses that were located in certain countries.

The company measures productivity by utilizing three metrics that are commonly used in the customer service industry: "average handle time" (AHT), which is the average amount of time it takes an agent to complete a chat; "resolution rate" (RR), which is the percentage of conversations that are successfully resolved; and "net promoter score" (NPS), which is determined by a random post-chat survey that subtracts the percentage of clients who would not recommend an agent from the percentage of clients who would recommend an agent. Agents are considered to be effective if they are able to maintain a high resolution rate and a high net promoter score while simultaneously reacting to client contacts in a timely manner during conversations.

The agents are organized into teams across all of the sites, and each team is supervised by a manager who gives the agents with feedback and training. The managers are responsible for managing each team. Every agent is given the opportunity to participate in one-on-one feedback sessions once a week through the provision of this opportunity. An example of this would be a manager offering guidance on how to more effectively handle the irritation that customers experience when addressing technical issues, providing a solution to a recently detected software defect, or elaborating on the effects of a change in taxation. There is no direct correlation between the quality of the work that agents do on their own and the quality of the work that other agents produce.

The data company often pays its agents a base hourly income, and they are eligible for bonuses if they meet certain performance criteria, such as the number of chats per hour or the resolution rate. In addition, the company frequently provides them with the opportunity to earn bonuses. In spite of the fact that there was no information available regarding individual compensation, the managers of the company indicated that performance incentives accounted for twenty to forty percent of the total monthly income of an average agent.

5.5.6 AI System Design

An artificial intelligence system is meant to recognize conversational patterns that can accurately forecast the resolution of calls in an efficient manner. Building on GPT-3, the system is fine-tuned using a large dataset of customer-agent conversations that have been labeled with a variety of outcomes, such as the success rate of call resolution and the amount of time it takes to handle the call. Additionally, when it comes to training the AI, the company gives a higher weight to the worth of training chats if the discussion was done by a high-performing individual. There are many components of excellent agent behavior that are difficult to quantify. Some of these aspects include knowing when to ask clarifying questions, being responsive to client concerns, de-escalating heated situations, adjusting communication styles, and explaining complicated topics in words that are easy to understand. The artificial intelligence system is able to pick up on these distinctions in behavior and tone to a greater extent when it is explicitly trained on material from top performers. To further train its model, the artificial intelligence company uses a process that is conceptually comparable to the one described by Ouyang et al. [47]. The goal of this process is to prioritize agent responses that demonstrate empathy, give relevant technical documentation, and limit language that is not professional. The LLM is able to detect successful behaviors of high performers, including those that they subconsciously employ, with the assistance of this additional training, which reduces the likelihood of hallucinations and improper responses.

Once it has been implemented, the artificial intelligence system will produce two primary sorts of output: 1) real-time ideas for how agents should reply to clients, and 2) links to the internal documentation of the data firm for questions regarding pertinent technical concerns. Alex, the customer, provides the agent with a description of his issue within the chat window, which is located in Panel A. Here, the artificial intelligence assistant comes up with two potential responses (Panel B). A number of words, such as "I can definitely assist you with this!" and "Happy to help you get this fixed asap," have been learnt by the tool to be connected with favorable outcomes. It demonstrates technical advice that was generated by the AI system, specifically a link to the internal technical documentation owned by the data company.

The artificial intelligence system is investigated for the intent to supplement human agents rather than to replace them. Only the agent is able to view the output, and they have complete control over which, if any, suggestions submitted by the AI they choose to accept. Giving the agent the final authority minimizes the possibility that consumers will obtain responses that are erroneous or that are not related to the topic at hand. When the system does not have adequate training data for a particular subject, it does not make any suggestions; instead, it leaves it up to the agents to respond on their own. Figure 5.3 shows applications of generative AI in industry.

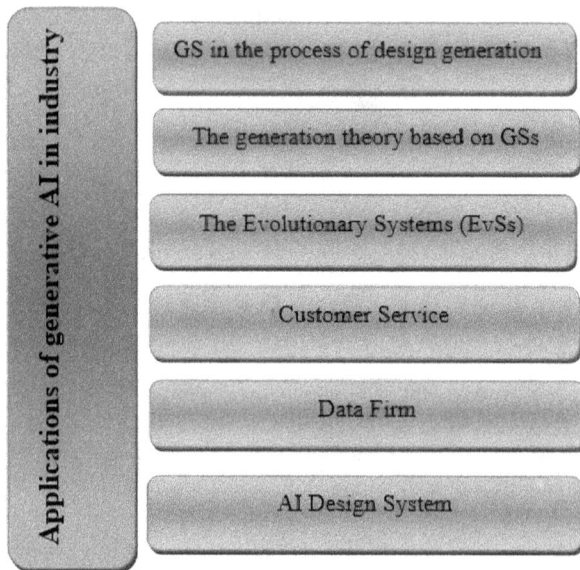

FIGURE 5.3   Applications of Generative AI in industry.

5.6 FUTURE SCOPES

5.6.1 THE USE CASES OF MANUFACTURING

In the context of denoising raw data and developing synthetic data for the purpose of improving model performance, the use cases of manufacturing generative AI share certain parallels with those of life science and finance. AI that generates new content makes it possible for industries to develop parts that are optimized to suit certain goals and restrictions, such as production and performance. Engineers are able to analyze enormous data sets to assist in the improvement of safety, build simulation datasets, investigate how a part could be made or machined more quickly, and bring products to market in a more expedient manner by utilizing these types of models. It is still early days for the use of generative artificial intelligence in factory operations; however, these methods can help to optimize the overall effectiveness of the equipment and serve to provide an effective method to "read" repair manuals, service bulletins, and warranty claims to gain new insights and resolve problems more quickly.

There are substantial bottlenecks in the manufacturing industry that are caused by the presence of legacy systems and old management operating procedures. In order to drive activities, whether they are organizational or on the production floor, generative artificial intelligence has the ability to transform data insights. Companies are able to overcome data-quality constraints and unlock the full potential of artificial intelligence in manufacturing with the assistance of these technologies, which also help to structure, clean up, and enrich the data that is already available.

5.6.2 THE USE CASES FOR OPERATIONS

Because generative artificial intelligence models can solve many problems in helping the optimization of supply chains, the improvement of demand forecasting, the provision of improved supplier risk assessments, and improving inventory management, they can help firms optimize supply chains, improve demand forecasting, provide better supplier risk assessment, and develop improved inventory management. Generative artificial intelligence can analyze vast amounts of historical sales data, taking into account seasonality, promotions, and economic conditions. By training an artificial intelligence model based on this data, they can provide an accurate forecast of demand, which in turn can allow firms to enhance their inventory management, resource allocation, and ability to anticipate market changes.

Generative artificial intelligence models can generate data analysis from various sources such as traffic conditions, fuel prices, and weather forecasts to determine the most effective routes and schedules for transportation. This is done for the purpose of supply chain operations optimization. They can simulate a range of alternative scenarios, and depending on the optimization criteria that is desired, they can recommend the optimal solution that minimizes lead times, reduces cost and improves operational efficiency of the entire supply chain.

Through the analysis of large quantities of data, including past supplier performance, financial reports, news articles, and social media, generative artificial intelligence models can learn patterns and trends of supplier risks and be used to help assess supplier risks. This could for example, help companies assess the reliability of their suppliers, predict potential disruptions, and take action to manage risk (e.g., better managing supply chain diversification or building contingency plans).

The optimal inventory levels at different stages in the supply chain can be defined by generative AI models for inventory management, as they can take into account demand trends, lead times, and other variables to produce such optimal inventory levels. AI may also assist warehouse management in the reduction of stockouts, elimination of excess inventory, and lower carrying costs by generating ideas for reorder points and safety stock levels, which can be done with the help of artificial intelligence.

5.6.3   OTHER EXAMPLES OF USE

Generative artificial intelligence offers a wide range of applications and use cases across a variety of businesses and fields. Some other examples include the following:

Generating and editing content: These models have the ability to develop or alter multimedia content that is innovative, diversified, and represents a realistic presentation. Art, music, 3D models, audio, video, and synthetic data are all examples of activities that may be generated and edited using content creation and editing systems.

The creation of applications: Generative artificial intelligence can help in the development and deployment of code. Code creation, code analysis, code completion, and code testing are some examples of applications that can be achieved through the development of applications.

The goal of securing data and systems against malicious assaults or unauthorized access can be performed with the help of generative artificial intelligence (AI) in the field of cybersecurity. Anomaly detection, malware detection, intrusion detection, and encryption are all examples of applications that fall within the category of cybersecurity.

Because of these application cases, previously unresolved mathematical theorems can be solved, which can lead to the development of new methodologies in the fields of physics, engineering, and statistics.

Generative artificial intelligence models have the ability to develop new candidate materials, compounds, and chemicals. The analysis of unstructured data as well as structured data that is present in virtual chemical databases, which contain billions of recognized and characterized chemicals, is utilized in conjunction with computational chemistry in order to generate new materials. This is accomplished through the utilization of these models. Because of the enormous size of these libraries, even when limited to molecular data, it has been impossible to do a comprehensive study on them. Generative adversarial networks (GANs) and pre-trained language models are the foundations of the most recent advancements in artificial intelligence technology, which have been applied to the process of materials discovery.

5.6.4   THE FACTORS AFFECTING PERFORMANCE

Generative artificial intelligence and big language models require a significant amount of computer power. By utilizing optimized software, libraries, and frameworks that make use of accelerators, parallelized operators, and maximize core usage, it is possible to achieve significant increases in workload performance as well as in the cost of employing computational resources. On the Transformer architecture side, the modeling side, and the code deployment side, there are a variety of ways that are utilized in order to handle these difficulties.

The Transformer-based architecture implements a self-attention mechanism that allows a language learning machine (LLM) to better understand and represent more complex language patterns. As a result of this approach, the number of computations that can be parallelized is increased, the complexity of computations inside a layer is reduced, and the path length in long-range dependencies of the Transformer architecture is decreased.

Hence, the modeling process must contain sufficient data parallelism and model parallelism for optimal utilization of resources during the training/deployment phase. With respect to data parallelization, there are algorithmic considerations that must be made for speeding up programs using parallel processing. This strategy improves both performance and accuracy, particularly when PyTorch Distributed Data Parallel is utilized to distribute workloads across multiple GPUs. Techniques such as activation checkpointing and gradient accumulation are utilized in order to overcome the difficulties that are connected with large model memory footprints. This allows for the successful implementation of model parallelism.

When transporting weights and data between compute units and memory, bandwidth is the limiting factor on the code deployment side. This is because bandwidth is the limitation. A group of execution units on a graphics processing unit (GPU) that are capable of performing mathematical operations in parallel with one another is referred to as a compute unit (CU). It is necessary to optimize the utilization of memory and compute units in order to execute these models in an efficient and speedy manner while still performing at the highest possible level.

Network designs that are complex provide a challenge to the efficient deployment of real-time applications and necessitate a large amount of computational resources and energy expenditures. Optimization techniques, such as neural network compression, can be utilized to successfully address these obstacles. Pruning and quantization are two different forms of network compression that are available. The process of pruning, which aims to get rid of calculations that are redundant, can be accomplished in a number of different ways. In order to obtain reductions in computations, quantization has the effect of reducing the precision of the data types. Eight-bit integers are usually utilized for the purpose of determining weights, biases, and activations in various model designs.

In order to achieve the goal of intelligently controlling precision while keeping accuracy and getting performance from smaller and faster numerical representations, mixed precision is performed with the intention of increasing speed.

5.7 CONCLUSION

When it comes to using the power of artificial intelligence in modern industries, having a solid understanding of generative AI architecture is absolutely necessary. There are a variety of applications for generative AI architecture, ranging from the use of AI for marketing material to the application of AI in e-commerce and architectural design of buildings. The creative potential of artificial intelligence may be harnessed by businesses through the adoption of advanced AI system architecture, which allows them to innovate and maintain a competitive advantage in an increasingly competitive environment.

Generic artificial intelligence opens the door to an infinite number of possibilities, regardless of whether you are an artificial intelligence architect building solutions, or a corporate executive investigating the potential of AI. Generic artificial intelligence is transforming the way we approach technology and creativity because of its capacity to learn, adapt, and create.

REFERENCES

[1]   Caldarini G, Jaf S and McGarry K. A literature survey of recent advances in chatbots. *Information* 2022; 13(1):41 https: //doi.org/10.48550/arXiv.2201.06657.

[2]   Mauldin M. Chatterbots, tinymuds, and the turing test: entering the loebner prize competition. In: *Proceedings of the AAAI Conference on Artificial Intelligence*, 1994.

[3]   Abdul-Kaer, SA and Woods J. Survey on chatbot design techniques in speech conversation systems. *Int J Adv Comp Sci Appl* 2015; 6(7).

[4]   Jonell P. Using social and physiological signals for user adaptation in conversational agents. In: *Proceedings of the International Joint Conference on Autonomous Agents and Multiagent Systems, AAMAS* , Vol. 4(c), 2019: 2420–2422.

[5]   Luo B, Lau RYK, Li C and Si Y. A critical review of state-of-the-art chatbot designs and applications. *Wiley Interdiscipl Rev Data Min. Knowl Discov* 2022; 12(1). https://doi.org/10.48550/arXiv.2201.06657

[6]   Chen H, Liu X, Yin D and Tang J. A survey on dialogue systems: recent advances and new frontiers. *ACM SIGKDD Explorat Newsl*, 2018. https://doi.org/10.48550/arXiv.1711.01731.

[7]   Franco M, Rodrigues B, Scheid EJ, Jacobs A, Killer C, Granville LZ and Stiller B. Secbot: a business-driven conversational agent for cybersecurity planning and management. In: *16th International Conference on Network and Service Management (CNSM)*, 2020. https://doi.org/1023919/CNSM50824.2020.9269037.

[8]   Cuayáhuitl H, Lee D, Ryu S, Cho Y, Choi S, Indurthi S, Yu S, Choi H, Hwang I and Kim J. Ensemble-based deep reinforcement learning for chatbots. *Neurocomputing* 2019; 366: 118–130. https://doi.org/10.48550/arXiv.1908.10422.

[9]   Serban IV, Sankar C, Germain M, Zhang S, Lin Z, Subramanian S, Kim T, Pieper M, Chandar S, Ke NR, Rajeshwar S, de Brebisson A, Sotelo JMR, Suhubdy V, Michalski A, Nguyen J, Pineau Y and Bengio. A deep reinforcement learning chatbot. *Cornell University research paper*, 2017 https://doi.org/10.48550/arXiv.1709.02349.

[10] Ho K, van Merrienboer B, Gulcehre C, Bahdanau D, Bougares F, Schwenk H and Bengio Y. Learning phrase representations using rnn encoder-decoder for statistical machine translation. In: *Conference on Empirical Methods in Natural Language Processing*, 2014. https://doi.org/10.48550/arXiv.1406.1078.

[11] Vaswani A, Shazeer N, Parmar N, Uszkoreit J, Jones L, Gomez AN, Kaiser L and Polosukhin I. Attention is all you need. *Computation and Language*, 2017. https://doi.org/10.48550/arXiv.1706.03762.

[12] Radford A, Narasimhan K, Salimans I and ad Sutskever T. Improving language understanding by generative pre-training. *OpenAI*, 2020.

[13] Lock S. What is AI chatbot phenomenon chatgpt and could it replace humans? *The Guardian* , 2022. www.theguardian.com/technology/2022/dec/05/what-is-ai-chat bot-phenomenon-chatgpt-and-could-it-replace-humans.

[14] Lewis P, Perez E, Piktus A, Petroni F, Karpukhin V, Goyal N, Küttler H, Lewis M, Yih WT, Rocktäschel T, Riedel S and Kiela D. Retrieval augmented generation for knowledge-intensive nlp tasks. *Adv Neural Inf Process Syst*, 2021; 33: 9459–9474. arXiv:2005.11401.

[15] Es S, James J, Espinosa-Anke L and Schockaert S. Ragas: Automated evaluation of retrieval augmented generation. In: *Proceedings of the 18th Conference of the European Chapter of the Association for Computational Linguistics: System Demonstrations*, St. Julians, Malta: Association for Computational Linguistics, 150–158, 2024. arXiv:2309.15217.

[16] Mccormack J, Dorin A and Innocent T. Generative design: a paradigm for design research. In: *Proceedings of Futureground—Design Research Society*, Melbourne: VIC, 17–21 November 2004.

[17] Oxman R. Performative design: a performance-based model of digital architectural design. *Environ Plan B-Planning Des* 2009; 36: 1026–1037.

[18] Oxman R. Performance-based design: current practices and research issues. *Int J Archit Comput* 2008; 6: 1–17.

[19] Mostafavi S, Beltran MM and Biloria N. Performance-driven design and design information exchange. In: *Proceedings of the 31st international conference on education and research in computer aided architectural design in Europe*, Delft: Delft University of Technology, 18–20 September 2013: 117–126.

[20] Atlan H. *L'organisation biologique et la théorie de l'information*. Paris: Éditions du Seuil, 2016.

[21] Bensaude-Vincent B. Self-assembly, self-organization: a philosophical perspective on converging technologies. In: *Paper prepared for France/Stanford Meeting*, Avignon, 17–18 December 2006.

[22] Singh V and Gu N. Towards an integrated generative design framework. *Des Stud* 2012; 33: 185–207.

[23] Von Neumann J. The general and logical theory of automata. In: Jeffress LA (ed.) *Cerebral mechanisms in behavior: the Hixon symposium*. New York: John Wiley, 1951, pp. 1–41.

[24] Wolfram S. *A new kind of science*. Champaign, IL: Wolfram Media, 2002.

[25] Herr CM and Ford RC. Adapting cellular automata as architectural design tools. In: *Proceedings of the 20th international conference on computer-aided architectural design research in Asia (CAADRIA 2015): emerging experiences in the past, present and future of digital architecture*, Hong Kong: The Association for Computer-Aided Architectural Design Research in Asia (CAADRIA), 20–22 May 2015: 169–178.

[26] Lee Y and Kim SH. Algorithmic design paradigm utilizing cellular automata for the Han-OK. *Nexus Netw J* 2016; 18: 481–503.

[27] Herr CM and Ford RC. Cellular automata in architectural design: from generic systems to specific design tools. *Autom Constr* 2016; 72: 39–45.

[28] Koza JR and Poli R. Genetic programming. In: Burke EK and Kendall G (eds.) *Search methodologies*. Boston, MA: Springer, 2005, pp. 127–164.

[29] Bullock GN, Denham MJ, Parmee IC and Wade JG. Developments in the use of the genetic algorithm in engineering design. *Des Stud* 1995; 16: 507–524.

[30] Ding L and Gero JS. The emergence of the representation of style in design. *Environ Plann B Plann Des* 2001; 28: 707–731.

[31] Gu N, Singh V and Merrick K. A framework to integrate generative design techniques for enhancing design automation. In: *Proceedings of the 15th International*

Conference on CAADRIA: New Frontiers, China, Hong Kong: The Association for Computer-Aided Architectural Design Research in Asia (CAADRIA), 7–9 April 2010: 127–136.

[32] Knight T. Applications in architectural design, and education and practice. 1999. http:// papers.cumincad.org/data/works/att/fb37.content.pdf (accessed 1 August 2019).

[33] Coutinho F, e Costa E, Duarte JP, et al. A computational interpretation of 'De re aedificatoria' 'Translating Alberti's column system into a shape grammar'. In: *ECAADE 2011: respecting fragile places. ECAADE Education & Research Computer Aided Architectural Design Europe*, Ljubljana, 21–24 September 2011: 788–798. www.daadgroup.org/wp-content/uploads/2016/01/eCAADe2011-Fio-Lof-Tre.pdf

[34] Ligler H and Economou A. Entelechy revisited: on the generative specification of John Portman's architectural language. *Environ Plann B Urban Anal City Sci* 2018; 45: 623–648.

[35] Colakoglu B and Keskin G. Form generator: A CAD tool for conceptual design development. In: *ECAADE 2010: future cities. ECAADE-education & research computer aided architectural design Europe*, Zurich: Education and Research in Computer Aided Architectural Design in Europe, 15–18 September 2010: 411–417.

[36] Willis B, Hemsath T and Hardy S. A parametric multi-criterion housing typology. In: *32nd annual conference of the association for computer aided design in architecture: synthetic digital ecologies (ACADIA)*, San Francisco: University of Nebraska, 18–21 October 2012: 501–510.

[37] Lindenmayer A. Mathematical models for cellular interactions in development I: filaments with one-sided inputs. *J Theor Biol* 1968; 18: 280–299.

[38] Parish YIH and Müller P. Procedural modeling of cities. In: *Proceedings of the 28th annual conference on computer graphics and interactive techniques, Los Angeles*, New York: ACM, 12–17 August 2001: 301–308.

[39] Parker DC, Manson SM, Janssen MA, Hoffmann MJ and Deadman P. Multi-agent systems for the simulation of land-use and land-cover change: a review. *Ann Assoc Am Geogr* 2003; 93: 314–337.

[40] Granadeiro V, Duarte JP, Correia JR and Leal VMS. Building envelope shape design in early stages of the design process: integrating architectural design systems and energy simulation. *Autom Constr* 2013; 32: 196–209.

[41] Hou G and Xu X. Individual building growth model based on column grid cellular automata. *TOBCTJ* 2015; 9: 39–45.

[42] Chui M, Hall B, Singla A, et al. Global survey: the state of AI in 2021. *Technical report*. McKinsey & Company, 2021. www.mckinsey.com/business-functions/mckinsey-analytics/our-insights/global-survey-the-state-of-ai-in-2021.

[43] Berg J, Das A, Gupta V, et al. Smarter call-center coaching for the digital world. *Technical report*, McKinsey & Company, 2018.

[44] Syverson C. What determines productivity? *J Econ Lit* 2011; 49(2): 326–365. https:// doi.org/10.1257/jel.49.2.326.

[45] Buesing E, Gupta V, Higgins S, et al. Customer care: the future talent factory. *Technical report*, McKinsey & Company, 2020. www.mckinsey.com/business-functions/operations/our-insights/customer-care-the-future-talent-factory.

[46] Berg J, Das A, Gupta V, et al. Smarter call-center coaching for the digital world. *Technical report*, McKinsey & Company, 2018.

[47] Ouyang L, Wu J, Jiang X, et al. Training language models to follow instructions with human feedback. 2022 Mar. arXiv:2203.02155 [cs]. https://doi.org/10.48550/arXiv.2203.02155.

6 Societal Impact and Cultural Implications

J. Vidhya, N. Sarulatha, Abinov Bruce,
Yogeshwaran R, and Aarthi K

6.1 INTRODUCTION TO GENERATIVE AI AND COMPUTATIONAL INTELLIGENCE

6.1.1 ARTIFICIAL INTELLIGENCE (AI)

Since the creation of generative artificial intelligence, it has emerged as one of the key drivers of 21st-century economics. This article defines generative AI and explains its ideas with an emphasis on massive language models. A short historical summary of AI's evolution up to this point is followed by the key relevant models and approaches. We look at the problems and limitations of the methodologies used so far, and we outline how generative AI offers new and better ways to solve problems. Using these technologies has important moral and social ramifications, which are explored in this chapter. Generative AI, in contrast to expert systems, may generate new content in addition to analysing and acting upon existing data [1]. This is a huge step forward from the previous generation of intelligent systems, which relied on case-based reasoning systems, genetic algorithms, fuzzy logic, neural networks, or hybrid AI models to solve particular problems with limited data sets [2–5]. Despite its best efforts to demonstrate generative AI's full capabilities, it primarily focuses on large language models (LLMs) [5].

Generative AI models are a subset of machine learning architectures that use AI algorithms to create new data instances by capitalising on patterns and correlations. observed in the data used for training. There is still a need to fine-tune generative AI models for specific jobs utilising various systems and apps, so while they are vital, they are not yet complete. The adaptability of deep neural networks to many types of data, such as spatial data (like photos) or sequential data (like human language), makes them ideal for data generation [6].

6.1.2 COMPUTATIONAL INTELLIGENCE (CI)

Experts of artificial intelligence (often those who ought to know better) persist in making what can only be called "bold promises for the future syndrome." The more pessimistic view holds that AI has witnessed numerous "unmitigated disasters" over the last fifty years, even though objective evaluation can find concrete advances (such

DOI: 10.1201/9781003680192-6

as automated theorem proving, game strategies, high-level computer languages LISP and Prologue, Automatic Speech Recognition, Natural Language Processing, mobile robot path planning, unmanned vehicles, humanoid robots, data mining, and more). Such "bold predictions," which fail to live up to their initial excitement and make the zealots' promises appear counterproductive, rapidly cynical audiences. A contentious debate has raged around the claim of having developed an AI system that is "intelligent" since the field's inception. The old adage says something like, "never discuss politics or religion with your fellows." It's hardly surprising that people tend to avoid talking about religion, philosophy, and metaphysics.

What sets Computational Intelligence (CI) apart from AI is its heavy reliance on sub-symbolic approaches, which go beyond any one symbolic level. In contrast to the usual practice in artificial intelligence, numerical values are employed to represent a state or instance of a problem. Depending on the domains of application and specific problems, CI techniques may be more beneficial than AI. This is because CI methods often use heuristics, metaheuristics, and non-deterministic components, and as a result, they can compute efficient approximations within a reasonable time [7].

6.2   EVOLUTION OF GENERATIVE AI IN SOCIETAL CONTEXTS

In the context of all these debates, generative AI is undeniably experiencing a period of fast progress now. Much like the numerous previous technological advances that utterly transformed our society, this innovation will inescapably impact society. So far, the areas of scientific investigation, education, and service provision have all experienced significant impacts. The ramifications for democracy, inequality, security, and military technology, however, are deeper and more alarming. Because of this, we need more research and analysis to understand the generative models' growth patterns, development areas, and social impacts, both good and bad. To fix potential flaws and make sure that the various social contexts and realities of these technologies' implementation are considered at every stage of development, these studies are essential. The rise of generative AI has sparked debates reminiscent of previous industrial revolutions, which replaced manual labor with machinery. In contrast, generative AI can automate tasks that involve cognitive or creative skills—drafting legal documents, designing graphics, or writing news briefs [8]. This blurring of boundaries between human-only and machine-performed tasks raises concerns about job displacement, labor market inequalities, and the changing nature of work [9]. Figure 6.1 discusses the various dimensions of generative AI assisting humans to generate music, photos, videos, and code for multifunctionalities.

6.3   GENERATIVE AI IN COMMUNICATION AND MEDIA

Deepfakes, or media distortions and misinformation created by artificial intelligence, are spreading like wildfire throughout social media platforms and significantly influencing online discourse. Users are becoming more wary of the content they encounter on the internet, which could lead to a widespread decline in trust in online information. The credibility of social media as a forum for exchanging information could

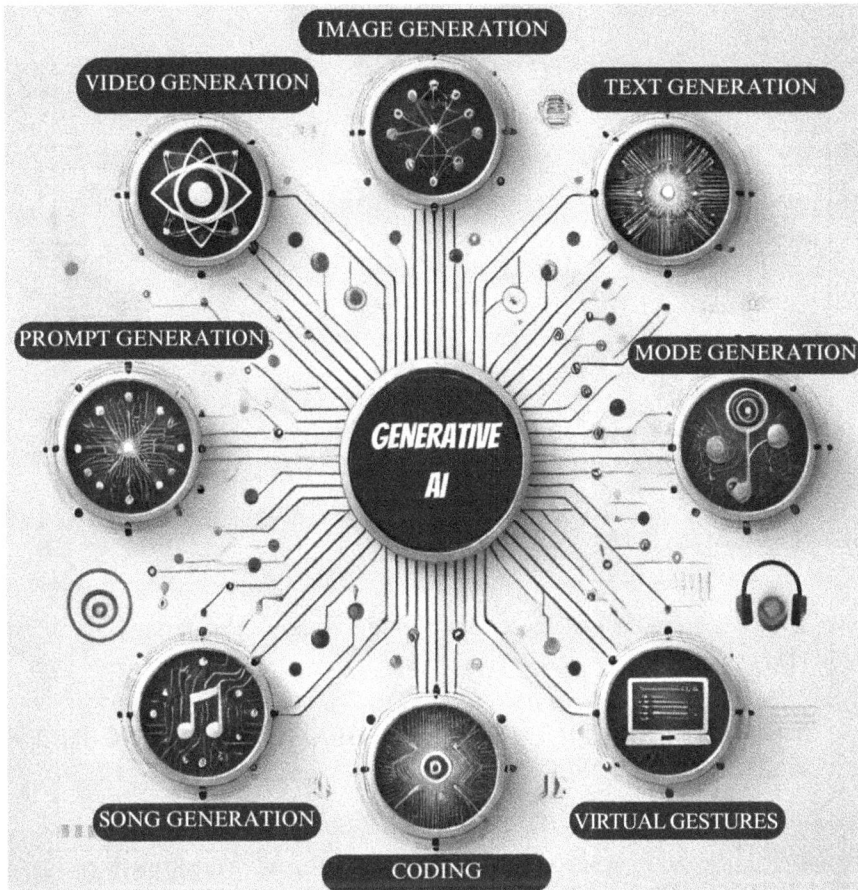

FIGURE 6.1   Dimensions of GenAI. (By author)

be eroded if users continue to distrust credible news sources and genuine material. Furthermore, false information has the potential to further divide and polarise online communities. AI-generated material can exploit underlying biases and divisions on social media platforms, thus perpetuating echo chambers and filter bubbles [10].

6.4   AI IN SOCIAL INTERACTION AND RELATIONSHIPS

Figure 6.2 illustrates AI-mediated societal interaction between the user and the machine. AI-mediated social interaction refers to how individuals build and maintain social connections using explicit and implicit personal information shared in online posts. Several subfields within Computer-Supported Cooperative Work (CSCW) connect to AI-mediated social interaction, including AI-mediated communication and social matching systems. Recent studies on AI-MC have focused on its use and perception in general-purpose textual communication, like thoughtful responses and auto-complete, while AI-mediated social interaction studies a subset of AI-MC that

Hey dude

Hey! What's up?

How is the day started

Pretty good so far! How about you? Got anything interesting lined up for the day?

Perfect

Nice! Anything exciting on your schedule today?

Working cool

Awesome! What's keeping you busy today?

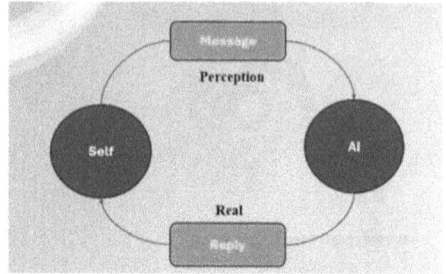

FIGURE 6.2   AI and Societal Interaction. (By author)

looks at the design and consequences of utilizing AI-augmented messages for social-ization [11].

6.5   TRANSFORMING INDUSTRIES IN HEALTHCARE, EDUCATION, AND PUBLIC SERVICES

6.5.1   GENAI IN HEALTH CARE

Digital health can aid in health innovation by facilitating patient participation in healthcare delivery. The patient will be able to recover from his illness once his health improves. In the future, patients and healthcare systems alike will reap the benefits of a more digitalized healthcare system, thanks to advancements in information and communication technology. Health units' operational efficacy and efficiency are improved, the productivity of their workers has increased, and the operating expenses are decreased [12]. Nonetheless, 75% of hospitals in the US use EHRs, making it a model for health infrastructure. On the other hand, doctors often speak about the harmful impacts of digital technology because of how much they utilize it. Also, not all doctors are on board with new technologies; in fact, some of them come up with solutions that put patients at risk [13]. However, the United States is a typical example of health infrastructure, with 75% of hospitals using electronic health record systems. However, due to their overuse, digital technologies are frequently reported to have negative effects by physicians [11].

6.5.2   EDUCATION

Artificial intelligence (AI) is increasingly being used in dentistry and medical schools due to the numerous benefits it provides to both students and instructors. Among the most common applications of AI in this sector is virtual simulation and training, which allows future medical professionals to practice delicate procedures on simulated patients before putting real ones in harm's way. Artificial intelligence (AI) is also finding its way into university classrooms, where it might greatly improve students' ability to learn and perform on exams [14].

6.5.3 PUBLIC SERVICES

Given their potential to increase work productivity and user experience, lower service costs, and relieve human workloads, government agencies are fast adopting artificial intelligence-based SST [15]. To give consumers 24-hour self-service, intelligent elements including natural language processing, face recognition, machine learning, recommendation algorithms, and OCR recognition are included in the AI-based smart self-service technologies (SSTs). SST based on artificial intelligence gathers and analyses data depending on past company operations. AI-based SST enhances a customised, flawless, and better user experience by applying the recommendation algorithm. With the help of its sophisticated data storage features, high processing capacity, and AI-based SST, it might give consumers more consistent, timely, and effective services [16]. Although many studies concentrate on information systems (IS) and the private sector, artificial intelligence technology has evolved into a versatile go-to tool for service innovations. Optimizing IS has benefits for system stability, user experience, hardware cost reduction, operation and maintenance support capability enhancement, etc. Intelligent Smart Energy Management Systems (ISEMS) grounded on ML to forecast resident energy usage as suggested by [17]. An investigation was pertained with conventional Intelligent Parking Information Systems to identify the key factors influencing Willingness-to-Pay [18].

6.6   AI-DRIVEN CULTURAL SHIFTS AND NEW ART FORMS

Even if the discussion between art and AI has just exploded, the idea of non-human-made art has existed for millennia. According to historians, robots and other forms of artificial life have their roots in Greek mythology [19]. Some centuries ago, machines were able to produce works of art. Some examples of such inventions are singing birds made by the Greek philosopher Leo the Philosopher, an automated wind instrument, and a musical instrument made by the Greek mathematician Apollonius of Perga [20]. Automata were very simplistic and largely followed a predefined structure, which is problematic from a current perspective. There has been a modern fascination with AI and art since the advent of digital computers in the 1930s, especially with the commercially produced microprocessors in the 1970s. Perhaps the most notable example from the modern age is AARON, a computer program developed by Harold Cohen (1927–2016), whose creative activity was primarily focused on computer-generated outputs. Cohen created the AARON program suite for line drawing and coloring in 1968 [19]. This topic has been significant in computational creativity [19,21]. The rise of artificial intelligence creativity links to the difference between analytical and intuitive intelligence [22]. The second part, which includes feeling and thinking, is essential for art as well. Technological advancements have unquestionably facilitated analytical intelligence, but the growth of intuitive intelligence is an incredibly challenging task. At present, AI's ability to be creative is limited, claim [23].

6.7 DIGITAL ETHICS AND BIAS IN AI-GENERATED CONTENT

Extensive artificial intelligence models trained on massive amounts of data, such as LLaMA and ChatGPT, are needed to understand human languages. After receiving pre-training, LLMs can generate content automatically in response to recommendations made by their users. The material that LLMs produce is called AI-generated material (AIGC), and the fact that they are generative makes them a kind of generative AI model. When compared to materials made by humans, AIGC is far more efficient and economical to manufacture. This is why LLMs may revolutionize and simplify a lot of commercial processes, such as creating false patient data for pharmaceutical research or writing up descriptions of properties for real estate agents[24].

6.7.1 WORD-LEVEL BIAS

The word-level gender biases of the LLMs under study, as determined by the average Wasserstein distance, ChatGPT has the lowest gender bias score [25].

6.7.2 RACIAL BIAS

In general, the artificial intelligence-generated content (AIGC) by each of the LLMs under consideration displays racial bias at the word level. Among all the news stories generated by ChatGPT, the one labelled as "Asian" had the lowest level of racial bias [25].

6.8 SOCIETAL IMPACT OF GENAI ON EMPLOYMENT AND FUTURE WORKFORCES

6.8.1 DISRUPTION IN HIGH-SKILLED ROLES

Generative AI penetrates industries that were thought to be immune to automation in the past, in contrast to classical automation, which mainly affected low-skilled or regular professions, as shown in Figure 6.3. It analyzes the causes among the various workforces and the effects of AI-driven business decisions. For example, AI that can generate text using large-scale language models could automate fundamental tasks for junior legal assistants and copywriters [26].

6.8.2 EMERGENCE OF NOVEL ROLES

Meanwhile, brand-new occupations are cropping up. "Algorithm auditors" look for possible biases or mistakes, whereas "prompt engineers" direct AI systems to generate desired outcomes [27]. Like previous transitions, this one saw the creation of new specialized jobs in machine maintenance and system monitoring because of

CAUSE   EFFECT

Technologi
cal Barriers

Workforce
Skills Gap

Data and
Security
Risks

Insufficient infrastructure

Limited digital literacy

Privacy Concern

Lack of Integration

Training Gaps

Cyber Attack

Outdated System

Resistance to change

Regulatory Conflicts

Poor Workflow

Bias in AI

Evolving competition

Bottlenecks

User Trust Issue

Customer Behaviour Shift

High Costs

Societal Resistance

Scalability Problem

Operational
Inefficiencie
s

Cultural and
Ethical
Concerns

Market
Dynamics

Accelerating
Business
Transformatio
n with
AI-driven
Automation
and
Decision-maki
ng

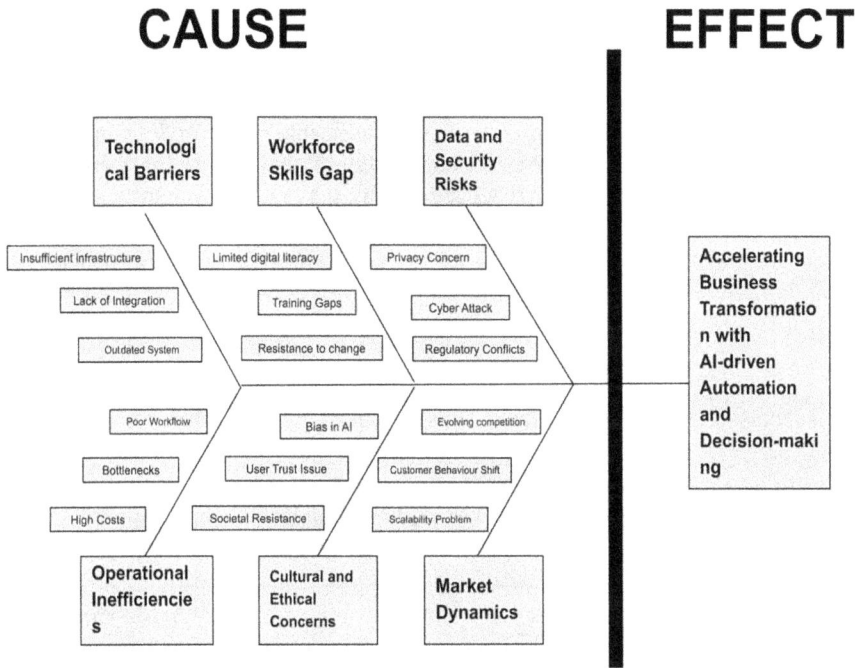

FIGURE 6.3 Analysis of GenAI's impact on Employee Productivity in Various Sectors. (By author)

automation replacing some jobs. To aid, schools and policymakers should plan for potential skill gaps and provide financing for reskilling programs.

6.8.3 SOCIOECONOMIC DISPARITIES

Disparities in wealth and opportunity might widen as a result of generative AI. Corporations and wealthy governments with ample computing power can invest in artificial intelligence infrastructure, potentially exacerbating the gap between the rich and the poor [8]. Opportunities may not reach rural or undeveloped areas if they do not have access to dependable internet or AI education. Factors such as artificial intelligence (AI) knowledge, financial backing, and government initiatives all contribute to the digital divide.

6.8.4 RESKILLING, EDUCATION, AND POLICY

To combat displacement, proactive workforce policies are needed. From online certifications to shorter courses, public and private organizations can work together on continuous learning programs. Creative thinking, emotional intelligence, and advanced problem-solving are examples of less automatable skills that should get more attention [28]. Additionally, strong social safety nets can mitigate transition shocks by providing displaced workers with resources like unemployment insurance and job placement assistance.

6.8.5   CULTURAL AND PSYCHOLOGICAL DIMENSIONS

The introduction of generative AI into creative industries raises existential concerns for individuals whose very being is entwined with their job. Some creative types may be uncomfortable with the idea of artificial intelligence being able to mimic their work. Machines can do monotonous chores, while humans focus on vision, storytelling, or emotional resonance. If AI is carefully integrated, it might launch an era of shared creation. Creative industries need to keep their morale and motivation high by recognizing the value of human expertise and keeping AI in its proper place—as a tool, not a substitute.

6.9   PUBLIC PERCEPTION AND TRUST IN AI SYSTEMS

The success or failure of generative AI's use in many fields depends on how the public perceives it. More stringent limitations or complete rejection of AI might result from rising resistance if people see it as secretive, prejudiced, or invasive. Trust must be earned via openness, equity, and participation from the community [29, 30]. According to Zhou et al. [31], several countries were surveyed where respondents are willing to trust AI systems. India (75%) is the first nation to trust AI, followed by China (67%), South Africa (57%), and Brazil (56%). Further followed by Singapore (45%) and the United States (40%).

6.9.1   FOUNDATIONS OF TRUST: TRANSPARENCY AND EXPLAINABILITY

A lot of the time, generative AI systems just seem to be "black boxes," cranking out results for no apparent reason. To shed light on the reasoning behind model outputs, researchers and developers are investigating explainable AI (XAI) approaches. To illustrate the point, public trust in AI can be bolstered by providing visual representations of the data distributions and weighting criteria that impact its final output [30].

6.9.2   BIAS AND MISINFORMATION CONCERNS

It is possible for large-scale image or language models to unwittingly reinforce the biases present in their training sets. Trust is jeopardized when biased results or false information are presented as authoritative. This issue is worsened by deepfakes, which allow for realistic-looking but fake media, which erodes the credibility of public conversation [32]. When consumers are unable to confirm the legitimacy of an item, they may start to doubt its veracity. This casts doubt on official sources and AI outputs alike, threatening the foundation of common understanding.

6.9.3   ROLE OF MEDIA AND CULTURAL NARRATIVES

How generative AI is portrayed in the media has a big impact on how people view it. Public opinion is influenced by the flow of news headlines, which can range from future optimism to dystopian terror. Popular media, including films, TV series, and books, present artificial intelligence (AI) in one of two extremes: as a technological wonder or an existential danger. Without resorting to sensationalism, audiences can have a better understanding of the advantages and disadvantages of generative AI through balanced reporting and insightful narrative.

6.9.4 STAKEHOLDER ENGAGEMENT AND ACCOUNTABILITY

It is crucial to involve several populations to address broad problems. This includes educators, consumer activists, and ethicists. To get public opinion on proposed AI rollouts, lawmakers can host forums or citizen assemblies [33]. When users are harmed, whether by prejudiced content or privacy invasions, they want a way to get their money back. Accountability and a sincere dedication to ethical behaviors can be strengthened by regulatory frameworks and formal channels for reporting detrimental effects.

6.9.5 EROSION AND RESTORATION OF TRUST

Trust Erosion and Restoration Machine learning systems run the risk of damaging, biased, or factually inaccurate content. When scandals are unsolved, public distrust usually increases. If anything, public apologies, thorough investigations, and substantial reforms can work to regain trust. The public's opinion of AI grows over time when technology consistently delivers high-quality results and when its developers are transparent about their process [29].

6.9.6 EDUCATIONAL INITIATIVES

For well-informed public discussions, it is essential to increase AI literacy. We can simplify AI procedures through workshops, school curriculum, and open-source technologies. Education initiatives about media literacy can help the public recognize deepfakes, check the credibility of sources, and assess articles powered by artificial intelligence with more objectivity. Equipping citizens with these abilities enables them to navigate a world filled with content generated by artificial intelligence, thereby strengthening their ability to resist deception.

6.10 LEGAL FRAMEWORKS AND POLICY CHALLENGES FOR SOCIETAL EQUITY

Discussing intellectual property, liability, and bias, generative AI reveals holes in our current legal frameworks. The question of regulating algorithms that generate output, make judgements, and function on massive scales is a problem for legislators worldwide [33, 34].

6.10.1 INTELLECTUAL PROPERTY DILEMMAS

Conventional intellectual property rules presume that there is a human author. Claims of ownership get hazier when AI creates works of art, stories, or designs for products. Many think the person giving the AI instructions or who created it should have some sort of legal claim, while others have proposed whole new types of legal recognition.

It is unclear from current legislation whether using copyrighted data to train models without authorization is a violation [33]. These ambiguities must spark court disputes, which in turn could cause modifications to statutes or new court precedents.

6.10.2 LIABILITY AND ACCOUNTABILITY

Who is responsible if harm comes from false information or defamation of character caused by AI-generated content? Hey there, programmers! People who use it? Where is the AI hosted? Due to its inherent complexity, generative AI may defy traditional "publisher" or "intermediary" paradigms [30]. To force businesses to be proactive in preventing harm, some have proposed "duty of care" regulations. To disperse responsibility, some people propose industry-wide insurance or audits.

6.10.3 BIAS AND ANTI-DISCRIMINATION PROTECTIONS

Particularly in delicate sectors like lending or hiring, the possibility of discriminatory AI output raises human rights issues. To demonstrate compliance with anti-discrimination laws, legal systems may require businesses to conduct bias audits of their algorithms. Aligning AI usage with current legal norms is being addressed through the emergence of technical methods, including transparency reports, bias impact evaluations, and fairness measurements [33].

6.11   5A SHARED GOVERNANCE APPROACH

Governments, NGOs, private companies, and academia must work together to develop unified policies for generative AI. Two policy questions confront governments globally regarding the implications of generative AI for the knowledge economy and the creative sector. The initial issue pertains to the conceptualization of model training, specifically regarding whether the creators or proprietors of the data "scraped"— whether legally or illegally, with or without consent. The second question pertains to the ownership of the output generated by generative AI, which is increasingly produced with higher quality and on a larger scale. Both issues require a legal framework established to promote and reward human creativity and innovation [33]. Researchers suggest that AI-based learning tools are reducing critical thinking, problem-solving, and decision-making skills, leading to reduced memory usage and cognitive offloading [34]. AI-based learning systems should be tailored to individual learner interests, understanding levels, and interpretation processes using advanced tools, rather than a one-size-fits-all approach as shown in Figure 6.4 [35].

6.12   AI ART: CULTURAL PRESERVATION AND THE AVOIDANCE OF APPROPRIATION

6.12.1 CULTURAL PRESERVATION AND CULTURAL APPROPRIATION IN AI ART

The capacity of AI to usurp human imagination challenges traditional notions of authorship, uniqueness, and cultural ownership, making this issue more pertinent in AI-created art. The use of AI has been a boon for the preservation of historical artefacts.

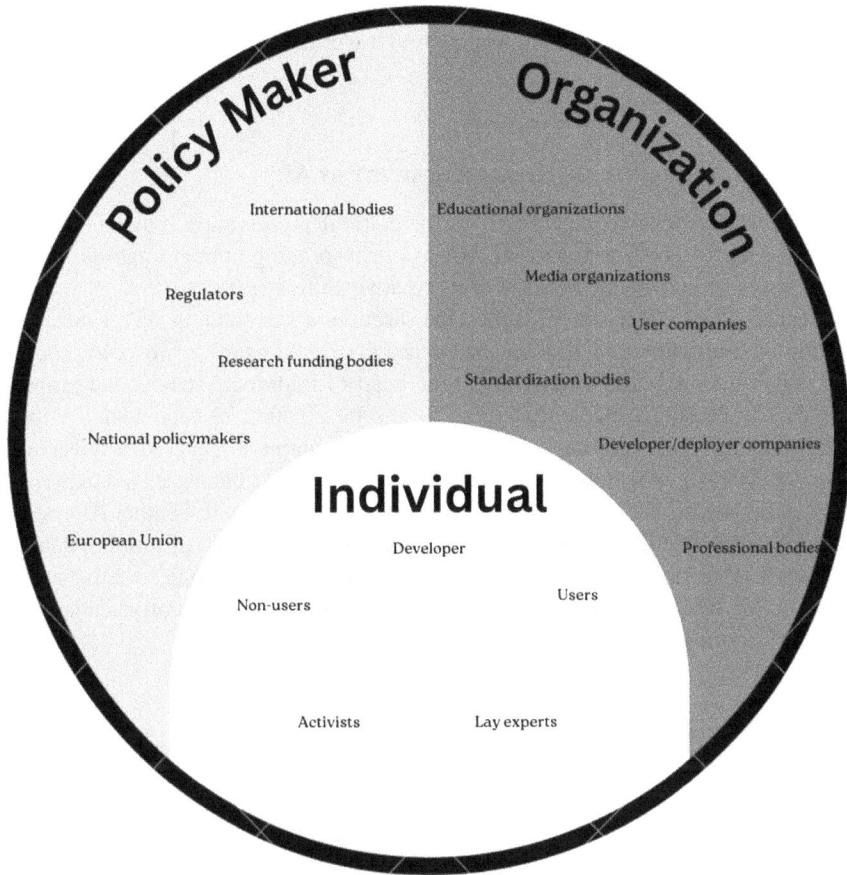

FIGURE 6.4   Stakeholders of AI. (By author)

The Conservation & Research Centre and the Technology & Art Development Office, both located at Taiwan's Cheng Shiu University, use artificial intelligence to enhance the preservation and display of artwork. Take the "Exhibition Environment Status Detection Device and System" as an example [36].

6.12.2   AI in Cultural Preservation: Enhancing Accuracy and Accessibility

Digitizing and repairing paintings also largely utilizes AI. By analyzing colour, pattern, and texture information, machine learning programs can help digitize and restore damaged works by creating high-definition duplicates. For instance, compared to conventional restoration processes, deep learning computers trained on original artworks can more quickly and cheaply replicate restored versions of the same work.

This approach does double duty: it preserves the artistic and cultural significance of artworks while also making them available to a worldwide audience through online sources [37].

6.12.3 APPROPRIATION OF HUMAN CREATIVITY BY AI

There are many positive aspects of AI for cultural preservation, but there is also growing concern about the possibility of AI appropriating human creation without their consent or knowledge because of its creative abilities [38].

Because of its effects on IP rights, the discussion surrounding AI's function in creation is similarly clouded. Ideas based heavily on humanist philosophy, such as originality and single authorship, are at the heart of traditional intellectual property systems. However, AI challenges these norms by creating new content by duplicating, reusing, and remixing existing data. One example is generative adversarial networks (GANs), which create artwork by analyzing large databases for patterns—patterns that are probably copyrighted. This begs the question of whether AI systems should be acknowledged as independent creators or if the usage of training datasets constitutes IP infringement. We need to rethink what it means to be creative and an author in this digital era because of the friction between AI's generative capabilities and old IP frameworks [39].

6.13 BLENDING TRADITION WITH TECHNOLOGY: AI'S ROLE IN CULTURAL CREATIVITY

6.13.1 CULTURAL ADOPTION: AI-AUGMENTED CREATIVITY IN TRADITIONAL PRACTICES

Human resource management (HRM), education, and design are just a few of the traditional processes that are being revolutionized by the incorporation of artificial intelligence (AI). Acceptance, ethics, and its impact on human inventiveness all cast doubt on its widespread use.

6.13.1.1 AI in Design and Innovation

The creative sectors, particularly design, have been profoundly impacted by the rise of AI. When it comes to the adoption of AI-based design tools, a survey found that among 249 Chinese designers, enjoyment elements, value beliefs, and convenience of use are the most important factors. However, people don't use them because they think there are privacy risks [31]. The need for AI tools is for them to be user-friendly, privacy-conscious, and powerful enough to meet designers' demands. While AI does improve process effectiveness and creative flexibility, it also has drawbacks, such as reducing team participation in DT workshops. To lessen the likelihood of such failures, experts suggest giving AI clear, defined tasks and encouraging group introspection [40].

6.13.1.2 AI in Organizational Strategy and HRM

HRM practices are also transformed by AI. To effectively apply AI-based HRM, researchers in Bangladesh centred their attention on organizational strategy rather than digital culture. AI-based HRM mediated a portion of the relationship between organizational strategy and sustainable organizational performance (SOP), which highlighted strategic harmony in the context of taking advantage of AI opportunities in developing markets [41].

6.13.1.3 AI in Education and Cultural Heritage

Classrooms that focus on intangible cultural heritage use AI to foster students' imaginations and encourage them to think beyond the box. When it comes to using AI in the classroom, the optimized KANO model has been a huge success [42]. Artificial intelligence (AI) makes it possible to understand high-definition scans and restore damaged artworks for worldwide usage, thus preserving cultural relics. Nevertheless, it is necessary to address the ethical concerns surrounding the commercialization and appropriation of culture [43].

Concerns about personal data security and intellectual property (IP) conflicts are obstacles to mainstreaming AI. An ethical and legal concern arises when AI programs rely on copyrighted information. There needs to be specific regulations to govern the application of AI in the creative industries, even as harmonized IP law provides some protection [44].

6.13.1.4 AI in Public Health Communication

AI can transform public health practice by facilitating public health surveillance, epidemiological research, communication, and other decision-making processes. Chatbots, for example, improve message customization to target audiences, which aids public health communication. However, developers must be cautious of dual valence and automation bias, which may influence the application's outcome [45].

6.13.1.5 AI in Language Translation

Cross-cultural communication is becoming increasingly common among individuals, organisations, and governments. The importance of machine translation (MT) has grown as a result of the necessity to interpret the large amount of information available on the Internet in multiple languages, as well as the rising degree of international trade. Deep learning (DL) and natural language processing (NLP) are used to quickly translate text from one language to another. Furthermore, disabled persons can benefit more from AI-powered technologies that help them overcome their disabilities [46].

6.13.1.6 Ethical Considerations and Cultural Sensitivity

Storytelling can shape public opinion on AI management and shed light on the need for culturally aware approaches to AI research, development, and implementation [47]. Furthermore, it is important to think about how people's cultural views on machines and their interactions with them can be altered. To explain why some societies are more receptive to AI than others, we can look to historical, theological, and exposure models. For instance, although analytical cultures, such as those in the West, may view technology as a danger, Asian holistic and relational cultures may find it helpful in their relationships. That AI systems can adapt their messaging to different audiences depends on our ability to recognize and account for cultural aspects [48, 49]. By learning languages and enabling the production of personalized, culturally relevant stories, artificial intelligence is changing the face of cross-cultural story-telling. Cultural sensitivity and ethical considerations should guide usage to ensure authenticity and prevent appropriation. To guarantee AI systems are considerate and aware of cultural diversity, however, issues like biased data sets, ethics, and the need for cultural competency must be resolved. We can create AI systems that are both inventive and fair if we prioritize cultural sensitivity.

6.14 CONCLUSION

6.14.1 ETHICAL IMPLICATIONS AND FUTURE DIRECTIONS

No single issue, like intellectual property or ownership, can adequately address the moral concerns surrounding AI art. Artificial intelligence systems that mimic human creativity and artistic style rob those works of their original cultural context and meaning. For example, artificial intelligence networks trained on collections of indigenous or minority artworks generate copies devoid of the originals' cultural context and narratives. This perpetuates a form of digital colonialism in which artificial intelligence steals and sells cultural expressions without giving proper recognition or remuneration, which devalues community attempts to preserve their heritage [50]. Integrating cutting-edge tech like XR, 3D printing, and the Internet of Things will revolutionize cultural preservation by changing the way history is conserved and experienced. However, this transformation will only happen if ethical frameworks are put in place and stakeholders work together to make sure that AI is used responsibly and inclusively [51].

We need rules for the right use of AI in the arts and cultural preservation to address these ethical issues. As part of this process, it is important to train AI systems on varied data sets that accurately reflect the population they are supposed to serve, taking into account the various cultures represented within. Therefore, artificial intelligence should be viewed as a source of ideas and exploration rather than a substitute for human creativity. The power of technology to advance and honor cultural heritage can be realized through the combination of human expertise with AI capabilities, all while preserving the integrity of human artwork [52]. The transformative power of AI lies in its ability to both protect and make available cultural heritage. However, it is important to exercise ethical control over its use to avoid cultural appropriation and make sure the technology honors and celebrates the cultures from which it comes [6].

6.15 TOWARDS A HARMONIZED FUTURE OF AI AND SOCIETY

At the intersection of generative AI, education, employment dynamics, policy, and creativity, basic social and economic institutions are being reshaped. Technology raises the age-old question of whether to let AI supplant human workers or to use technology as an ally in innovation and a source of increased output [37, 53].

6.15.1   BALANCING INNOVATION AND RESPONSIBILITY

Governments, organizations, and businesses can make responsible innovation a top priority. A few possible solutions are open-source libraries that can identify prejudice, strict laws around personal data, and procedures to hold people responsible when AI is used inappropriately. Maintaining a common objective of ethical deployment based on principles that safeguard cultural values, equity, and individual rights is essential [54].

6.15.2   WORKFORCE TRANSITION AND SOCIOECONOMIC EQUITY

Certain jobs will be threatened while new ones will be created by generative AI, which will continue to change labor markets. Governments should invest in retraining and take proactive measures to deal with this change so that the advantages don't go to the tech elite. The workforce can be better prepared for a future focused on artificial intelligence (AI) if educational efforts are made to integrate technical training with emotional intelligence (EQ), ethics, and problem-solving skills [55].

6.15.3   PUBLIC TRUST AS A CORNERSTONE

Systems that are open and responsible are essential for gaining public support. Government agencies can require frequent audits, and organizations can be transparent about their AI practices. Informed citizens may make decisions concerning AI, and developers will be more likely to maintain high standards if they are taught about the dangers and rewards. When businesses, governments, and nonprofits work together, the public has more faith in AI's ability to improve society [56].

6.15.4   EDUCATIONAL TRANSFORMATION

Systems that are open and responsible are essential for gaining public support. Government agencies can require frequent audits, and organizations can be transparent about their AI practices. Informed citizens may make decisions concerning AI, and developers will be more likely to maintain high standards if they are taught about the dangers and rewards. When businesses, governments, and nonprofits work together, the public has more faith in AI's ability to improve society as a whole [55, 56].

6.15.5   A FUTURE OF CO-CREATION

The future of generative AI is going to depend on how engineers, lawmakers, educators, and regular people work together. Society can negotiate possible hazards while harnessing the revolutionary potential of AI by prioritizing ethical principles, supporting inclusion, and mixing human inventiveness with machine efficiency. Doing so brings us one step closer to a harmonious future in which AI enhances human potential, boosts creative pursuits, and encourages fair advancement for everyone.

GLOSSARY

1. **Artificial Intelligence (AI)**: Machines simulating human intelligence for tasks like learning and creativity.
2. **Generative Adversarial Networks (GANs)**: GANs is a technique to generative modeling that uses deep learning approaches like convolutional neural networks.
3. **Natural Language Processing (NLP)**: NLP is an area of artificial intelligence that seeks to enable computers to understand human language. NLP makes use of computational linguistics, which is the study of how language works, as well as models based on statistics, machine learning, and deep learning.
4. **Extended Reality (XR)**: XR is a blend of human and computer-generated graphics interaction that occurs both in reality and in a virtual world.
5. **Internet of Things (IoT)**: IoT is the network of physical items that have electronics built into their architecture and can communicate and perceive interactions with one another or with the external environment.
6. **Machine Learning (ML)**: ML is a kind of AI that allows computers to learn from data and predict outcomes without being explicitly programmed.
7. **Cultural Sensitivity**: Cultural sensitivity is the recognition, comprehension, and consideration of the cultural practices and distinctions of individuals from a variety of backgrounds.
8. **Bias in AI**: AI bias, also known as algorithm bias, is the phenomenon of biased results that result from human biases that distort the original training data or AI algorithm, resulting in distorted outputs and potentially detrimental outcomes.
9. **Ethical AI**: AI ethics is a multidisciplinary field that investigates ways to maximise the positive impact of artificial intelligence (AI) while minimising risks and negative consequences.
10. **Data Privacy**: Data privacy, or "information privacy," is the notion that individuals should possess authority over their personal data, including the capacity to determine how organisations gather, retain, and utilise that data.
11. **Cultural Context**: Cultural context refers to the collection of meanings and knowledge that exist among individuals in a specific circumstance.
12. Generative Pre-trained Transformer 3 (**GPT 3**): This is the third version of the LLM. It is a neural network machine learning model trained on internet data to generate various types of text.

REFERENCES

1. Vaswani, A., Shazeer, N., Parmar, N., Uszkoreit, J., Jones, L., Gomez, A. N., ... & Polosukhin, I. (2017). Attention is all you need. *Advances in Neural Information Processing Systems*, 30. https://doi.org/10.48550/arXiv.1706.03762
2. Li, B. N., Chui, C. K., Chang, S., & Ong, S. (2010). Integrating spatial fuzzy clustering with level set methods for automated medical image segmentation. *Computers in Biology and Medicine*, 41(1), 1–10. https://doi.org/10.1016/j.compbiomed.2010.10.007

3. Gala, Y., Fernández, Á., Díaz, J., & Dorronsoro, J. R. (2016). Hybrid machine learning forecasting of solar radiation values. *Neurocomputing*, 176, 48–59. https://doi.org/10.1016/j.neucom.2015.02.078

4. Abraham, A., Corchado, E., & Corchado, J. M. (2009). Hybrid learning machines. *Neurocomputing*, 72(13–15), 2729–2730. https://doi.org/10.1016/j.neucom.2009.02.017

5. Corchado, J. M., López, S., Garcia, R., & Chamoso, P. (2023). Generative artificial intelligence: Fundamentals. *ADCAIJ Advances in Distributed Computing and Artificial Intelligence Journal*, 12(1), e31704. https://doi.org/10.14201/adcaij.31704

6. Feuerriegel, S., Hartmann, J., Janiesch, C., & Zschech, P. (2024). Generative AI. *Business and Information Systems Engineering*, 66(1), 111–126. https://doi.org/10.1007/s12599-023-00834-7

7. Fulcher, J. (2008). Computational intelligence: An introduction. In J. Fulcher (Ed.), *Studies in Computational Intelligence* (pp. 3–78). Berlin, Heidelberg: Springer. https://doi.org/10.1007/978-3-540-78293-3_1

8. Cazzaniga, M., Jaumotte, F., Li, L., Melina, G., Panton, A. J., Pizzinelli, C., Rockall, E. J., & Tavares, M. M. (2024). Gen-AI: Artificial intelligence and the future of work. *IMF eLibrary*. https://doi.org/10.5089/9798400262548.006.A001

9. Baldassarre, M. T., Caivano, D., Nieto, B. F., Gigante, D., & Ragone, A. (2023). *The 2023 ACM Conference on Information Technology for Social Good*. (pp. 363–373). In Proceedings of the 2023 ACM Conference on Information Technology for Social Good. New York, NY: Association for Computing Machinery (ACM). https://doi.org/10.1145/3582515.3609555

10. Møller, A. G., Romero, D. M., Jurgens, D., & Aiello, L. M. (2025, June 17). The impact of Generative AI on social media: an experimental study. *arXiv.org*. https://arxiv.org/abs/2506.14295

11. Stoumpos, A. I., Kitsios, F., & Talias, M. A. (2023). Digital transformation in healthcare: Technology acceptance and its applications. *International Journal of Environmental Research and Public Health*, 20, 3407. https://doi.org/10.3390/ijerph20043407

12. Gjellebæk, C., Svensson, A., Bjørkquist, C., Fladeby, N., & Grundén, K. (2020). Management challenges for future digitalization of healthcare services. *Futures*, 124, 102636. https://doi.org/10.1016/j.futures.2020.102636

13. Eden, R., Burton-Jones, A., Grant, J., Collins, R., Staib, A., & Sullivan, C. (2020). Digitising an Australian university hospital: Qualitative analysis of staff-reported impacts. *Australian Health Review*, 44, 677–689. https://doi.org/10.1071/AH18218

14. Dave, M., & Patel, N. (2023). Artificial intelligence in healthcare and education. *BDJ British Dental Journal*, 234(10), 761–764. https://doi.org/10.1038/s41415-023-5845-2

15. Buell, R. W., Campbell, D., & Frei, F. X. (2010). Are self-service customers satisfied or stuck? *Production and Operations Management*, 19(6), 679–697. https://doi.org/10.1111/j.1937-5956.2010.01151.x

16. Rijsdijk, S. A., Hultink, E. J., & Diamantopoulos, A. (2007). Product intelligence: Its conceptualization, measurement and impact on consumer satisfaction. *Journal of the Academy of Marketing Science*, 35(3), 340–356. https://doi.org/10.1007/s11747-007-0040-6

17. Pawar, P., TarunKumar, M., & Vittal, K. (2020). An IoT based intelligent smart energy management system with accurate forecasting and load strategy for renewable gen eration. *Measurement*, 152, 107187. https://doi.org/10.1016/j.measurement.2019.107187

18. Yang, W., & Lam, P. T. I. (2019). Evaluation of drivers' benefits accruing from an intelligent parking information system. *Journal of Cleaner Production*, 231, 783–793. https://doi.org/10.1016/j.jclepro.2019.05.247

19. Schubert, E. (2021). Creativity is optimal novelty and maximal positive affect: A new definition based on the spreading activation model. *Frontiers in Neuroscience*, 15, Article 612379. https://doi.org/10.3389/fnins.2021.612379

20. Bonnici, A., Dannenberg, R. B., Kemper, S., & Camilleri, K. P. (2021). Editorial: Music and AI. Frontiers in Artificial Intelligence. *Frontiers in Artificial Intelligence*, 4, 651446. https://doi.org/10.3389/frai.2021.651446

21. Cetinic, E., & She, J. (2022). Understanding and Creating Art with AI: Review and Outlook. *ACM Transactions on Multimedia Computing, Communications and Applications*, 18(2), Article 66, 1–22. https://doi.org/10.1145/3475799

22. Huang, M.-H., Rust, R. T., & Maksimovic, V. (2019). The Feeling Economy: Managing in the Next Generation of Artificial Intelligence (AI). *California Management Review*, 61(3), 43–65. https://doi.org/10.1177/0008125619863436

23. Huang, M.-H., & Rust, R. T. (2021). Engaged to a robot? The role of AI in service. *Journal of Service Research*, 24(1), 30–41, https://doi.org/10.1177/1094670520902266

24. Shahzad, T., Mazhar, T., Tariq, M. U., Ahmad, W., Ouahada, K., & Hamam, H. (2025). A comprehensive review of large language models: Issues and solutions in learning environments. *Discover Sustainability*, 6(1). https://doi.org/10.1007/s43621-025-00815-8

25. Fang, X., Che, S., Mao, M., Zhang, H., Zhao, M., & Zhao, X. (2024, March). Bias of AI-generated content: An examination of news produced by large language models. *Scientific Reports*, 14, Article 55686. https://doi.org/10.1038/s41598-024-55686-2

26. Patil, D. (2025). Impact of Artificial Intelligence on employment and workforce development: Risks, opportunities, and socioeconomic implications. SSRN. https://doi.org/10.2139/ssrn.5057396

27. Ray, S. (2023, December 21). Generative AI and future of smart creativity. www.csharp.com/blogs/generative-ai-and-future-of-smart-creativity

28. Brynjolfsson, E., Li, D., & Raymond, L. R. (2023). Generative AI at Work (NBER Working Paper No. 31161). National Bureau of Economic Research. https://doi.org/10.3386/w31161

29. Shaikh, S., Bendre, R., & Mhaske, S. (2023, November 22). The rise of creative machines: Exploring the impact of generative AI. arXiv.org. https://arxiv.org/abs/2311.13262

30. Sternberg, R. J. (2024). Do not worry that generative AI may compromise human creativity or intelligence in the future: It already has. *Journal of Intelligence*, 12(7), 69. https://doi.org/10.3390/jintelligence12070069

31. Zhou, C., Liu, X., Yu, C., Tao, Y., & Shao, Y. (2024). Trust in AI-augmented design: Applying structural equation modeling to AI-augmented design acceptance. *Heliyon*, 10(1), e23305. https://doi.org/10.1016/j.heliyon.2023.e23305

32. Schwartz, O. (2018). Competing visions for AI turing, Licklider and generative literature. *Semantic Scholar*. www.semanticscholar.org/paper/Competing-Visions-for-AI-Turing%2C-Licklider-and-Schwartz/4a0c1ddbe7aeadc847fca94569c7a45bba81b01d

33. Chesterman, S. (2024). Good models borrow, great models steal: Intellectual property rights and generative AI. *Semantic Scholar*. www.semanticscholar.org/paper/Good-Models-Borrow%2C-Great-Models-Steal%3A-Property-AI-Chesterman/3b345b17431ce1a6132abab3fc1da0cbc134bf06

34. Gerlich, M. (2025). AI tools in society: Impacts on cognitive offloading and the future of critical thinking. *Societies*, 15(1), 6. https://doi.org/10.3390/soc15010006

35. Generative AI: Unleashing creativity in Machines – blog. (n.d.). https://blog.geetauni versity.edu.in/generative-ai-unleashing-creativity-in-machines/

36. Huang, P., Li, I., Wang, C., Shih, C., Srinivaas, M., Yang, W., Kao, C., & Su, T. (2025b). Integration of artificial intelligence in art preservation and exhibition spaces. *Applied Sciences*, 15(2), 562. https://doi.org/10.3390/app15020562

37. Hohenstein, J., Kizilcec, R. F., DiFranzo, D., Aghajari, Z., Mieczkowski, H., Levy, K., Naaman, M., Hancock, J., & Jung, M. F. (2023). Artificial intelligence in communication impacts language and social relationships. *Scientific Reports*, 13(1). https://doi.org/10.1038/s41598-023-30938-9

38. Seaflux (2023, December 4). The rise of generative AI: How machines are becoming creative. www.linkedin.com/pulse/rise-generative-ai-how-machines-becoming-creat ive-seaflux-tech-zusyc/

39. Zeilinger, M. (2021). Tactical entanglements: AI art, creative agency, and the limits of intellectual property. library.oapen.org. https://doi.org/10.14619/1839

40. Polster, L., Bilgram, V., & Görtz, S. (2024). AI-augmented design thinking: Potentials, challenges, and mitigation strategies of integrating artificial intelligence in human-centered innovation processes. *IEEE Engineering Management Review*, 1–36. https://doi.org/10.1109/emr.2024.3512866

41. Mollah, M. A., Rana, M., Amin, M. B., Sony, M. M. A. A. M., Rahaman, M. A., & Fenyves, V. (2024). Examining the role of AI-augmented HRM for sustainable performance: Key determinants for digital culture and organizational strategy. *Sustainability*, 16(24), 10843. https://doi.org/10.3390/su162410843

42. Ma, S. (2024). AI-augmented classroom scene design for exploring intangible cultural heritage in the digital Era of China. *Computer-Aided Design and Applications*, 192–206. https://doi.org/10.14733/cadaps.2024.s20.192-206

43. Gaber, J. A., Youssef, S. M., & Fathalla, K. M. (2023). The role of artificial intelligence and machine learning in preserving cultural heritage and art works via virtual restoration. *ISPRS Annals of the Photogrammetry, Remote Sensing and Spatial Information Sciences*, X-1/W1-2023, 185–190. https://doi.org/10.5194/isprs-ann als-x-1-w1-2023-185-2023

44. Travis, H. (2024). Augmented creativity in a harmonized Trans-Atlantic knowledge economy. In P. Cserne & F. Zoll (Eds.), Augmented Creativity in Transnational Lawmaking (pp. 67–84). Leiden, The Netherlands: Brill I Nijhoff.). https://doi.org/10.1163/9789004686212_004

45. Panteli, D., Adib, K., Buttigieg, S., Goiana-Da-Silva, F., Ladewig, K., Azzopardi-Muscat, N., Figueras, J., Novillo-Ortiz, D., & McKee, M. (2025). Artificial intelligence in public health: Promises, challenges, and an agenda for policy makers and public health institutions. *The Lancet Public Health*, 10(5), e428–e432. https://doi.org/10.1016/s2468-2667(25)00036-2

46. Schubert, E. (2021). Creativity is optimal novelty and maximal positive affect: A new definition based on the spreading activation model. *Frontiers in Neuroscience*, 15, Article 612379. https://doi.org/10.3389/fnins.2021.612379

47. Bode, I., Huelss, H., Nadibaidze, A., & Watts, T. F. (2024). Cross-cultural narratives of weaponised artificial intelligence: Comparing France, India, Japan and the United States. *Big Data and Society*, 11(4). https://doi.org/10.1177/20539517241303151

48. Yam, K. C., Tan, T., Jackson, J. C., Shariff, A., & Gray, K. (2023). Cultural differences in people's reactions and applications of robots, algorithms, and artificial

intelligence. *Management and Organization Review*, 19(5), 859–875. https://doi.org/ 10.1017/mor.2023.21

49. Radanliev, P. (2024). Artificial intelligence: Reflecting on the past and looking towards the next paradigm shift. *Journal of Experimental and Theoretical Artificial Intelligence*, 1–18. https://doi.org/10.1080/0952813x.2024.2323042

50. Spencer, S. L. (n.d.-b). What it means to have meaning: AI's poetic appropriation of the human imagination. *Scholars Crossing*. https://digitalcommons.liberty.edu/mast ers/1049/

51. Harisanty, D., Obille, K. L. B., Anna, N. E. V., Purwanti, E., & Retrialisca, F. (2024). Cultural heritage preservation in the digital age, harnessing artificial intelligence for the future: A bibliometric analysis. *Digital Library Perspectives*, 40(4), 609–630. https://doi.org/10.1108/dlp-01-2024-0018

52. Fang, X., Che, S., Mao, M., Zhang, H., Zhao, M., & Zhao, X. (2023). Bias of AI-generated content: An examination of news produced by large language models. *Semantic Scholar*. www.semanticscholar.org/paper/Bias-of-AI-generated-cont ent%3A-an-examination-of-by-Fang-Che/da0b5feee06ae1564dd03623741273bb0 ab939e2

53. Harre, R. (1996). AI rules: Okay? *Journal of Experimental and Theoretical Artificial Intelligence*, 8(2), 109–120. https://doi.org/10.1080/095281396147401

54. Cave, S., & Dihal, K. (2018). Ancient dreams of intelligent machines: 3,000 years of robots. *Nature*. https://doi.org/10.1038/d41586-018-05887-1

55. Wang, Q., Camacho, I., Jing, S., & Goel, A. K. (2022 April 7). Understanding the design space of AI-mediated social interaction in online learning: Challenges and ppportunities. *Proceedings of the ACM on Human-Computer Interaction*, 6(CSCW1), 1–26. www.ncbi.nlm.nih.gov/pmc/articles/PMC9963556/pdf/ijerph-20-03407.pdf

56. Chen, T., Guo, W., Gao, X., & Liang, Z. (2020). AI-based self-service technology in public service delivery: User experience and influencing factors. *Government Information Quarterly*, 38(4), 101520. https://doi.org/10.1016/j.giq.2020.101520

7 Enhancing Athletic Performance Through Wearable Technology Using Gen AI with Computational Intelligence

R. Manimegalai, P. Sukumar, A. Uthiramoorthy, and S. Divya Midhunchakkaravarthy

7.1 INTRODUCTION

Nowadays, the same number of users as smartphones, smart wearables are starting to show their special place and impact on certain industries or activities that are only getting stronger (Mercier & Wang, 2020). With "disruption" as the buzzword in today's industrial and capital markets, with the swift advancement and propulsion of emerging technologies like smart wearables and mobile gadgets, big data, and all facets of the market have experienced profound transformations. The relationship between these new technological developments and various business structures is progressively upending established industries' cognitive structures (Lin et al., 2016). In another research, it is summarized briefly that smart wearables have applications in the medical, fitness, entertainment, industrial, military, and other fields. The most well-known application of these devices is in sports development (Mayorga-Vega, 2022).

Integrating wearable smart devices with high data rates and low interruption rates can be achieved through 5G technologies, which are expected to bring revolutionary improvements in sectors including intelligence, athletics, healthcare, and transportation (Aun et al., 2017). Wearable devices integrated with IoT can accurately monitor exercise energy consumption and provide detailed insights into physical activity patterns (Shi & Huang, 2021). Figure 7.1 depicts a diagram illustrating the impact of smart wearables on various industries. At the center, a smartwatch icon represents wearable technology. Surrounding it are six interconnected sectors, each represented by an icon and label: Sports Development (orange), Medical (green), Fitness (light green), Entertainment (blue), Industrial (purple), and Military (violet). Dashed lines connect these sectors, showing their relationship with the smart wearable technology.

DOI: 10.1201/9781003680192-7

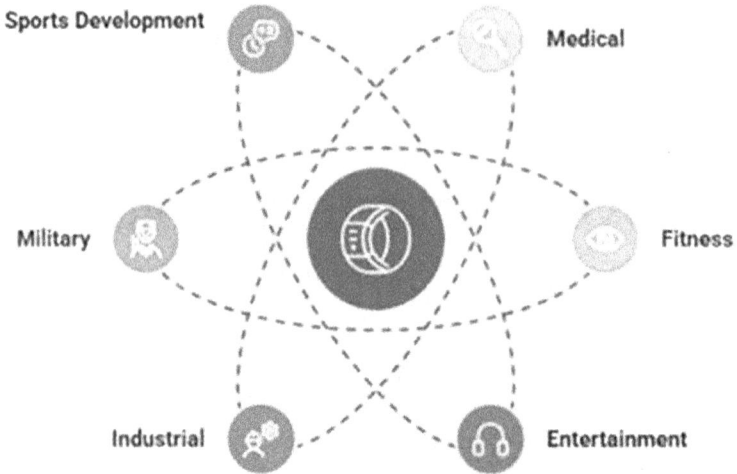

FIGURE 7.1   Impact of Smart Wearables on Industries.

Boroumand et al. (2018) highlight how consumer devices, such as smartphones and wearables, often face data movement and memory bandwidth limitations that hinder real-time performance. Oktavius et al. (2021) demonstrated the use of a fully-conformable porous polyethylene nanofilm sweat sensor that enables real-time detection of the sports fatigue. The integration of the WT and ML has revolutionized the field of athletic performance enhancement. Wearable devices, equipped with sensors that monitor various physiological and biomechanical parameters, provide real-time data that can be leveraged to optimize training regimens, prevent injuries, and improve overall athletic outcomes. ML algorithms, with their ability to analyse large datasets and identify patterns, play a crucial role in interpreting the vast amounts of data generated by these devices. This study aims to explore the synergistic potential of WT and ML in enhancing athletic performance. By reviewing current technologies, methodologies, and applications, we seek to identify key opportunities for innovation and also practical implementation in sports science.

Figure 7.2 is a circular flow diagram representing the role of smart wearables in performance optimization. At the center, a stylized icon of a person with a heart symbol signifies health and fitness tracking. Surrounding it, five interconnected stages are labeled in a clockwise sequence: Data Collection, Data Analysis, Training Optimization, Injury Prevention, and Performance Improvement. Arrows indicate the continuous cycle of data-driven enhancement facilitated by wearable technology.

Through the advancement of artificial intelligence technologies, smart wearables have become increasingly popular and have shown significant promise in the sports industry (Tyson et al., 2018). Athletes and coaches have traditionally prioritized improving sports performance through the use of smart wearable devices. When combined with AI technology, athletes can receive customized and immediate feedback direction, enabling them to enhance their athletic prowess more effectively (Liang et al., 2022). The intelligent wearable technology can gather precise and thorough data regarding players' athletic status, including heart rate, stride length, frequency,

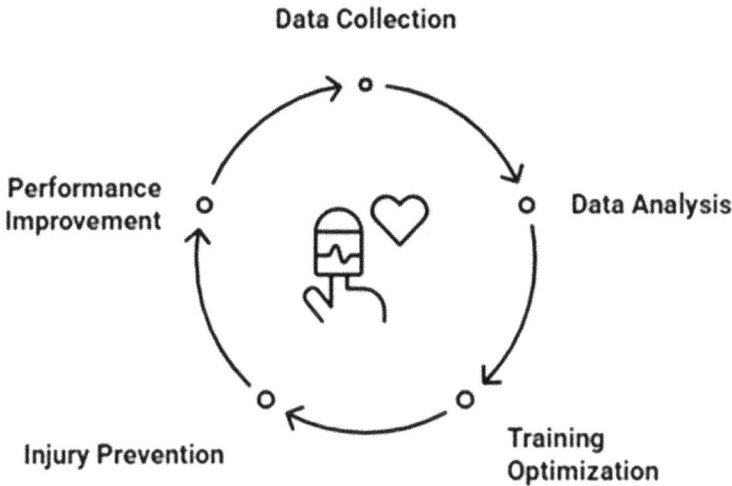

FIGURE 7.2   Cycle of Wearable Technology and Machine Learning in Sports.

etc., to help athletes get the best possible training schedule. Additionally, intelligent wearable technology can guide and rectify athletes' technical motions through the instantaneous feedback, which has the potential to enhance their movement accuracy (Lapinski et al., 2019).

Figure 7.3 is a flowchart depicting the role of smart wearable devices in athlete performance improvement. The process begins with the "Smart Wearable Devices," leading to "Data Collection," followed by "AI Analysis." From AI Analysis, two parallel outputs emerge: "Customized Feedback" and "Technical Motion Correction." Both contribute to the final outcome: "Athlete Performance Improvement."

Smart wearables have grown to be an essential component of many people's daily lives in recent years. These devices are able to deliver precise data and clever analytical functions while the user is exercising since they integrate artificial intelligence algorithms and cutting-edge sensing technologies, which ultimately aid the user in getting the most out of their workout. These days, intelligent wearable technology is better equipped to track and evaluate the workout process by incorporating AI technology, enabling users to receive customized training recommendations and optimization strategies. This not only makes working out much more enjoyable for consumers but also assists them in their fitness objectives. Many college students are drawn to sports-smart wearable technology and start to pay attention to sports-related health issues. The market for sports-smart wearables is slowly demonstrating the trend toward customization, variety, and usefulness. Growth of college students' wearable smart sports devices also demonstrates the traits of diversity, intellect, and specialty, and so forth. According to literature, integrating wearable smart devices with high data rates and low interruption rates can be realized with 5G, which will bring about revolutionary improvements in sectors including intelligence, athletics, healthcare, and transportation. The feedback from simulation exercises demonstrates that the sensing device offers technical support tools and training data references for training and performance of the circus group, which helps to raise the standard of training and performance.

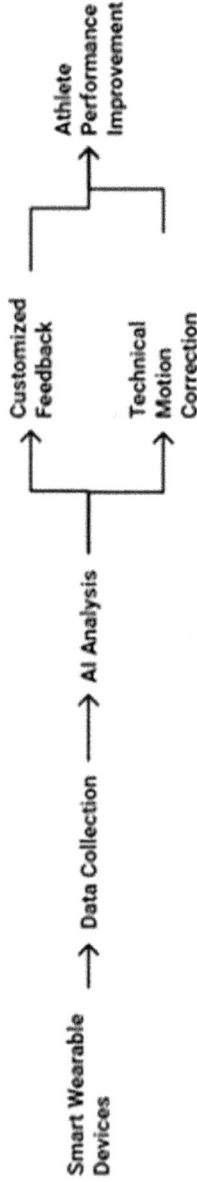

FIGURE 7.3   Integration of AI and Smart Wearables in Sports.

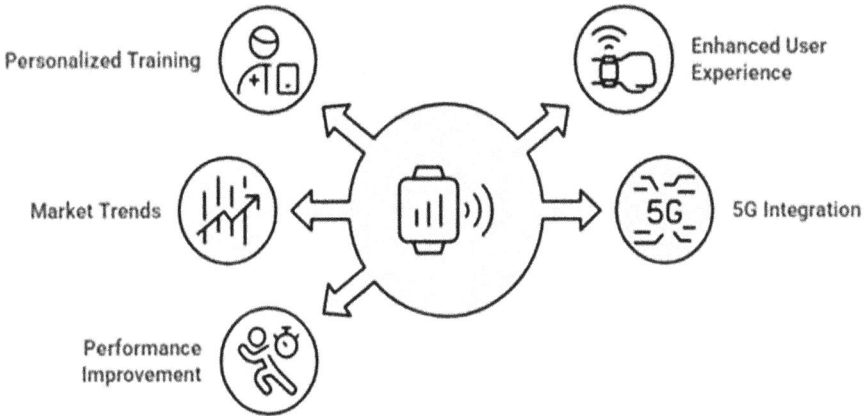

FIGURE 7.4 Evolution of Smart Wearables.

Figure 7.4 consists of a diagram illustrating the key benefits of smart wearable technology. At the center, a smartwatch icon represents wearable devices, with arrows pointing outward to five labeled benefits: "Personalized Training" (depicted with a training icon), "Enhanced User Experience" (represented by a smartwatch and connectivity symbol), "5G Integration" (symbolized by a 5G network icon), "Performance Improvement" (depicted with an athlete running), and "Market Trends" (represented by a graph icon). The diagram highlights how smart wearables contribute to various aspects of user experience and industry advancements.

In this first design, a set of smart wearable devices tailored for exercise training is capable of acquiring ECG, respiratory, and acceleration (ACC) signals through integrated sensor nodes. These data are stored locally on a memory card for further analysis. Next, we preprocess the collected sports data to remove noise and outliers, segment the dataset, and apply linear normalization to standardize the feature data across a uniform scale. We then propose specific algorithms to analyze the acceleration, ECG, and respiratory signals. Finally, we conduct empirical tests to evaluate the performance of each acquisition module, focusing on ECG and respiratory signal monitoring. Additionally, we assess the impact of these smart wearable devices on users' athletic performance by analyzing key sports parameters, offering insights into how these devices can enhance training outcomes.

7.2 DEVICE FOR TRACKING MOTION AND ALGORITHMS FOR INTELLIGENT WEARABLES

The motion monitoring systems in smart wearables have become essential tools in sports, healthcare, and fitness industries. These systems typically utilize a combination of sensors, such as accelerometers, gyroscopes, and magnetometers, to capture and analyze motion data in real time. The data collected can include a wide range of motion-related metrics, such as step count, acceleration, angular velocity, and orientation, which can be monitored. The effectiveness of these systems largely depends on the algorithms that process the raw data. These algorithms are designed to filter out noise, detect specific patterns or events (like steps, falls, or specific athletic movements), and translate raw sensor data into meaningful insights. For example, ML algorithms can be employed to classify different types of physical activities, assess the quality of movements, and even predict potential injuries based on detected abnormalities in movement patterns.

Figure 7.5 shows the linear flow diagram illustrating the data processing journey in smart wearables. The process starts from "Sensor Data Collection" (represented by a motion sensor icon), followed by "Data Processing by Algorithms" (depicted with a table-like icon), then "Translation to Insights" (symbolized by data visualization lines). Next, it leads to "Application in Sports/Healthcare" (represented by a heart monitor icon), and finally results in "Personalized Feedback" (depicted with a speech bubble and arrow). The diagram shows a step-by-step transformation of raw sensor data into actionable insights for users.

Advanced algorithms can be designed to adapt to the user's unique biomechanics, improving accuracy in motion tracking and providing personalized feedback. These algorithms are essential for transforming RD into actionable insights that can enhance athletic performance, improve rehabilitation outcomes, or promote increased physical activity.

7.2.1 WEARABLE DEVICE MONITORING SYSTEM THROUGH SENSOR SIGNAL

A wearable device monitoring system leverages various sensors to continuously track and analyze physiological and biomechanical signals from the human body. These systems are built with sensors such as accelerometers, gyroscopes, ECG sensors, and respiratory sensors, which capture real-time data reflecting the user's physical state and movements. The core function of the monitoring system is to collect sensor signals that provide detailed insights into the user's activity and health. For example, accelerometers and gyroscopes can monitor movement patterns, orientation, and balance, while ECG sensors measure heart rate and detect anomalies in heart rhythms. Respiratory sensors track breathing patterns, offering critical information about respiratory health and endurance. Once these signals are captured, they are processed through a series of algorithms designed to filter out noise, detect significant events, and convert the raw data into meaningful metrics. These metrics can include step counts, heart rate variability, breathing rate, and more, which are then analyzed to monitor the user's physical performance or health status. The processed data is typically stored on the device or transmitted to external systems for further analysis. In advanced applications, ML algorithms are employed to interpret the data, predict trends, and provide personalized recommendations to the user. This monitoring system is crucial in various applications, from optimizing athletic performance to providing continuous health monitoring for patients. By harnessing the power of sensor signals, wearable devices offer a comprehensive, real-time overview of the user's physiological state, enabling timely interventions and promoting a proactive approach to health and fitness.

Figure 7.6 depicts the diagram of a light bulb illustrating key components of smart wearable technology. The bulb is divided into four quadrants, each representing different technological aspects: "Accelerometers" (motion sensor icon), "Gyroscopes" (rotation sensor icon), "ECG Sensors" (heart rate monitor icon), and "Respiratory Sensors" (lungs icon). The base of the bulb highlights "Data Processing Algorithms"

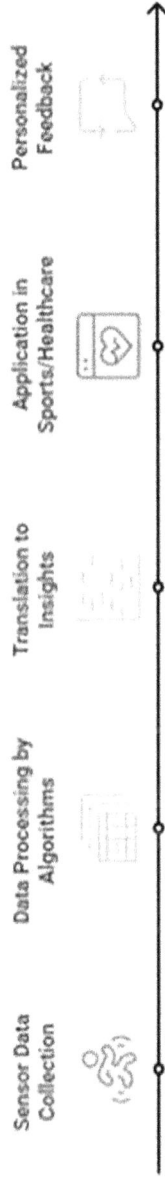

FIGURE 7.5 Motion Monitoring in Wearable Devices.

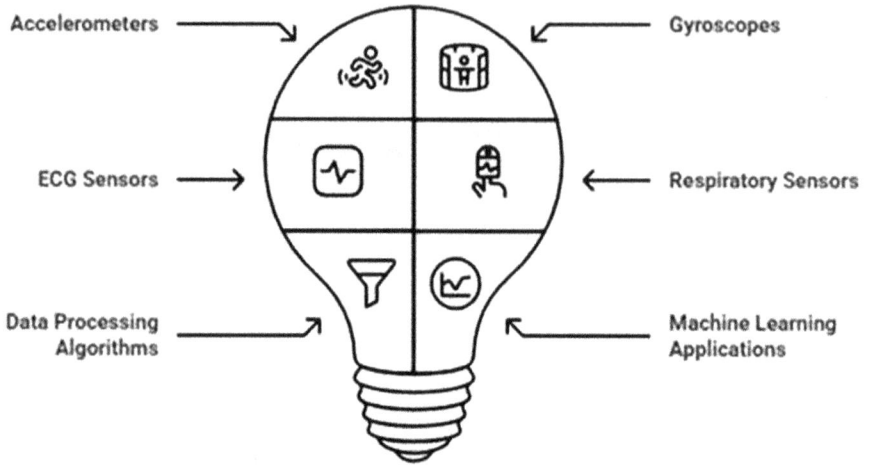

FIGURE 7.6 Anatomy of a Wearable Monitoring System.

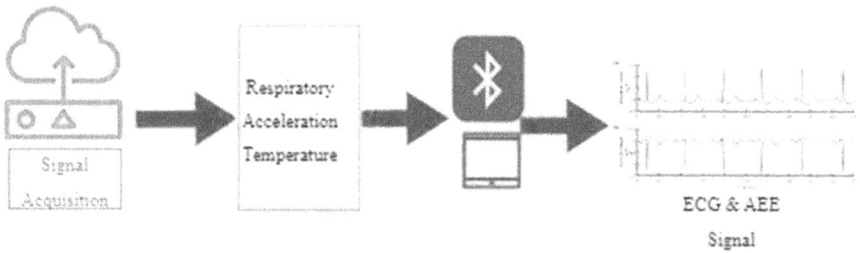

FIGURE 7.7 Framework for Wearable Device.

(filtering icon) and "Machine Learning Applications" (AI network icon). Arrows point to each labeled component, emphasizing their role in wearable device functionality.

Figure 7.7 shows a flowchart depicting the process of biosignal acquisition and transmission in wearable technology. The process starts with "Signal Acquisition" (represented by a cloud and device icon), followed by data collection of "Respiratory, Acceleration, and Temperature" parameters. This data is transmitted through "Bluetooth" (indicated by the Bluetooth symbol and a device icon) and results in the generation of "ECG & AEE Signal" (displayed as an electrocardiogram waveform graph) (see Table 7.1).

7.2.2 Data Preprocessing and Feature Extraction for Wearable Device Monitoring System

Collect RD from WD sensors (e.g., accelerometer, gyroscope, ECG, respiratory sensors). Identify and handle any missing data points through the process of data cleaning. Use interpolation or imputation methods (e.g., mean, median, or nearest-neighbor) to fill in missing values. Apply filters (e.g., low-pass filter, high-pass filter, or band-pass filter)

TABLE 7.1
Sensors Functions with Component Description

Component	Description	Function
	Sensors	
Accelerometer	Measures acceleration and movement in multiple directions.	Tracks physical activities, such as walking, running, and detecting falls.
Gyroscope	Measures orientation and rotational motion.	Monitors balance, posture, and detects angular motion.
ECG Sensor	Captures electrical signals from the heart.	Monitors heart rate, heart rate variability, and detects cardiac anomalies.
Respiratory Sensor	Measures breathing patterns and respiratory rate.	Tracks respiratory health, monitors breathing during physical activities, and detects irregularities.

TABLE 7.2
Signal Processing Description with Function

Component	Description	Function
	Signal Processing	
Noise Filtering	Removes unwanted noise from raw sensor data.	Enhances the accuracy of the captured signals for better analysis.
Event Detection	Identifies significant patterns or events in the sensor data.	Detects specific activities (e.g., steps, falls) and physiological changes.
Feature Extraction	Identifies key metrics from the processed sensor data.	Converts raw data into actionable insights, such as step count, heart rate, and breathing rate. Detects cardiac anomalies.

to remove noise and artifacts from the sensor signals. Identify and remove outliers using statistical methods (e.g., z-score, IQR method) or machine learning techniques. Segment the continuous signal data into smaller, meaningful windows (e.g., fixed time intervals or event-based segmentation). Ensure each segment captures relevant information for further analysis (e.g., 5-second windows for ECG data). Extract features like heart rate, R-R interval, and PQRST complex characteristics for ECG Data. The acceleration data extract features include mean, standard deviation, peak values, and activity recognition indicators. Data Extraction for respiratory data can be processed through features like breath rate, amplitude, and variability (see Table 7.2).

Normalize using z-score to center the data around zero with a standard deviation of one.

$$Z = x - \mu / \sigma$$

Ensure all features across different sensor data types are on a comparable scale for analysis.

Load the preprocessed sensor data segments and define the list of features to be extracted for each type of sensor data (e.g., ECG, respiratory, acceleration). Iterate through each segment of the preprocessed sensor data. Calculate the number of R-peaks in the ECG segment and compute the heart rate as HR = Number of R-peaks / Segment Duration $\times$ 60 (in beats per minute).

Measure the time interval between successive R-peaks and also calculate statistical features (e.g., mean, standard deviation) of the R-R intervals.

Calculate the breath rate as Breath Rate = Number of Breaths / Segment Duration $\times$ 60 (in breaths per minute).

Min-Max Normalization scales the feature values to a range [0, 1]. The formulas are as follows:

$$x' = x - \min(x) / \max(x) - \min(x)$$

Z-score normalization standardizes the features by converting them into a distribution with a mean of zero and a standard deviation of one.

$$Z = x - \mu / \sigma$$

x: Original feature value.
x': Normalized feature value.
min(x): Minimum value of the feature in the dataset.
max(x): Maximum value of the feature in the dataset.

7.2.3 Algorithms for a Wearable Physiological Signal Monitoring Device through a Kalman Filter

Minimizing the effect of sensor position and also attitude on accelerometer (ACC) signals is crucial for ensuring accurat e motion detection and analysis in wearable devices. So, applying the data from gyroscopes, magnetometers, and accelerometers together through sensor fusion algorithms (e.g., Kalman filter or complementary filter). This approach helps in estimating the sensor's orientation more accurately, thus compensating for changes in position and attitude.

The Kalman filter is a powerful recursive algorithm used for estimating the state of a dynamic system from noisy measurements. It's widely used in applications like sensor fusion, signal processing, and control systems. In the context of wearable devices and accelerometer (ACC) signals, the Kalman filter can help to minimize the effects of sensor position and attitude by providing a more accurate estimation of motion and orientation. The Kalman filter operates in two main steps: the prediction step and the update(correction) step. Based on the previous state estimate, the Kalman filter predicts the current state of the system and the associated uncertainty (error covariance) as follows:

$$\hat{x}k|k-1 = A\hat{x}k-1|k-1 + Bu_k$$

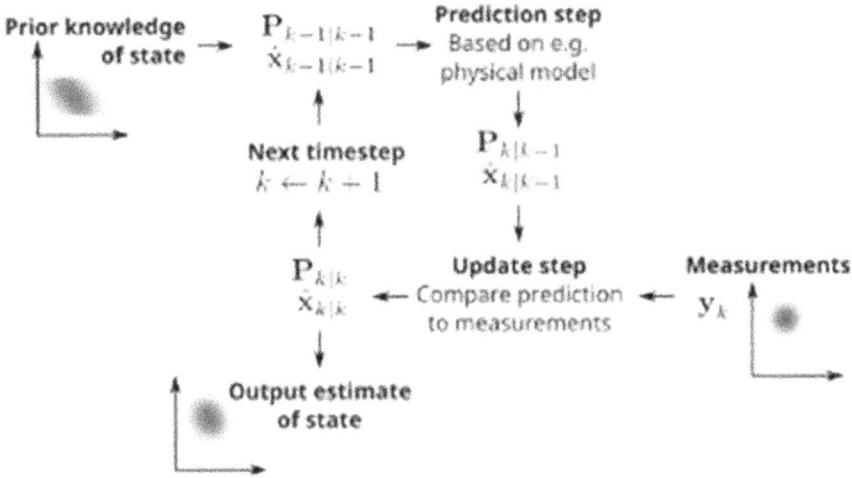

FIGURE 7.8 Kalman Gain Flowchart.

where x^k|k−1 is the predicted state, A is the state transition model, B is the control-input model, and u_k is the control vector (optional, depending on the application).

The Kalman filter updates its prediction using the new measurement to correct the state estimate and reduce the uncertainty. The Kalman Gain Calculation is as follows:

$$K_k = P_k \mid k-1 \; H(HP_k \mid k - 1 \; H^T + R)^{-1}$$

Combine data from accelerometers, gyroscopes, and magnetometers to estimate the orientation and motion more accurately. The Kalman filter can fuse these measurements to produce a smoothed estimate of the device's position and orientation. ACC signals often contain noise due to sensor inaccuracies, environmental factors, or the user's movement. The Kalman filter helps to reduce this noise by estimating the true motion and filtering out the random fluctuations. Use the Kalman filter to track the orientation (pitch, roll, yaw) of the device by fusing accelerometer and gyroscope data. The filter accounts for the gyroscope's tendency to drift over time and corrects it using the accelerometer data.

The Kalman filter process for state estimation is shown in Figure 7.8. It starts with "Prior knowledge of state" leading to a "Prediction step" based on a physical model. The next step advances the time index k to $k+1$. The "Update step" compares predictions to "Measurements" (yk), refining the state estimate. Finally, the "Output estimate of state" is generated, completing the iterative process.

7.2.4 ECG (ELECTROCARDIOGRAM) SIGNAL DETECTION AND ANALYSIS

ECG (Electrocardiogram) signal detection and analysis involve several key steps, from preprocessing the raw data to detecting significant features such as QRS complexes and analyzing heart rate variability. Before detecting and analyzing ECG signals, preprocessing is essential to remove noise and artifacts such as baseline wander, power line interference, and motion artifacts.

The Pan-Tompkins algorithm (see Figure 7.9) is a well-known technique for detecting the QRS complex in an ECG (Electrocardiogram) signal, which represents the depolarization of the ventricles and is the most prominent feature in an ECG waveform. The algorithm was introduced by Jiapu Pan and Willis Tompkins in 1985 and is widely used due to its effectiveness in real-time QRS detection. The Pan-Tompkins algorithm consists of several stages, including filtering, differentiation, squaring, integration, and thresholding. The first step in the Pan-Tompkins algorithm is to filter the ECG to reduce noise and enhance the QRS complex. This removes high-frequency noise such as muscle artifacts through a low-pass filter:

$$y[n]=2y[n-1]-y[n-2]+x[n]-2x[n-6]+x[n-12]$$

where $x[n]$ is the input ECG signal, and $y[n]$ is the filtered output. Removes low-frequency components such as baseline wander by using a high-pass filter:

$$y[n]=y[n-1]-321\ (x[n]-x[n-32])$$

Differentiation emphasizes the QRS complex by calculating the slope of the ECG signal to highlight areas of the signal with high slopes, corresponding to the QRS complex:

$$y[n]=81\ \times(2x[n]+x[n-1]-x[n-3]-2x[n-4])$$

This step involves squaring the differentiated signal to enhance the QRS complex and make all values positive to emphasize larger differences (i.e., the QRS complex) and suppress smaller ones (e.g., P and T waves):

$$y[n]=x[n]^2$$

The squared signal is then integrated over a moving window to produce a smoother signal that highlights the QRS complex. To obtain information about the width and slope of the QRS complex, making it easier to detect:

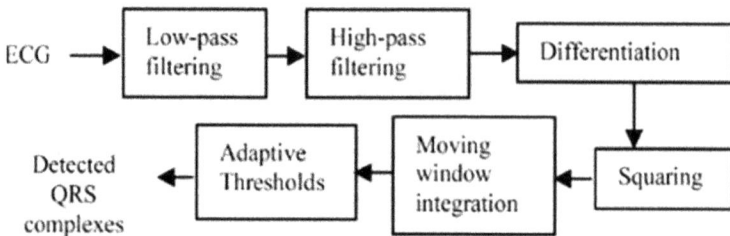

FIGURE 7.9 Flowchart for Pan-Tompkins Algorithm.

$$y[n] = 1 / N \; i=0 \sum N-1 \; x[n-i]$$

Lastly, the QRS complex is identified by applying thresholds to the integrated signal. Two thresholds are often used: a primary threshold for peak detection and a secondary threshold for noise handling. The thresholds can be adaptive, based on the amplitude of the signal and noise characteristics. If no QRS complex is detected within a certain time frame, the algorithm will "search back" using a lower threshold to avoid missing any QRS complexes. The algorithm uses decision rules to identify the R-peak within the QRS complex and discard false detections.

The signal processing steps for detecting QRS complexes in an ECG signal. The process begins with "ECG" input, followed by "Low-pass filtering" and "High-pass filtering" to remove noise. The signal then undergoes "Differentiation" to highlight changes, followed by "Squaring" to enhance signal peaks. "Moving window integration" further processes the signal, leading to "Adaptive Thresholds" for the final detection of "QRS complexes" in the ECG data.

7.3 DETECTION AND ANALYSIS OF RESPIRATORY SIGNALS ALGORITHM

Time-domain analysis of respiratory signals focuses on examining the characteristics as they vary over time. This is essential for understanding the temporal features of breathing patterns, such as respiratory rate, cycle duration, and the identification of abnormalities like apneas or irregular breathing. Respiratory rate is one of the most basic and vital indicators of respiratory function. It represents the number of breaths taken per minute. Identify the peaks (maxima) corresponding to inhalation and troughs (minima) corresponding to exhalation in the respiratory signal. Count the number of complete respiratory cycles (peak-to-peak or trough-to-trough) within a given time frame (e.g., 60 seconds).

$$\text{Respiratory Rate} = \text{Number of Breaths} / \text{Time Period (in minutes)}$$

$$RR = 15 \text{ breaths} / 0.5 \text{ minutes} = 30 \text{ breaths per minute}$$

The inter-breath interval (IBI) is the time between consecutive breaths. Analyzing IBI can reveal variations in breathing patterns.

$$IBI_n = t_{n+1} - t_n$$

where t_n and t_{n+1} are the times at which consecutive peaks (or troughs) occur. Measures the variability in inter-breath intervals. The average time between breaths provides insight into overall breathing regularity.

Figure 7.10, entitled "Time Domain Analysis," shows a step input response with the vertical axis representing $c(t)$, and the horizontal axis representing time t. The response initially oscillates in the "Transient period" before stabilizing at a

Time Domain Analysis

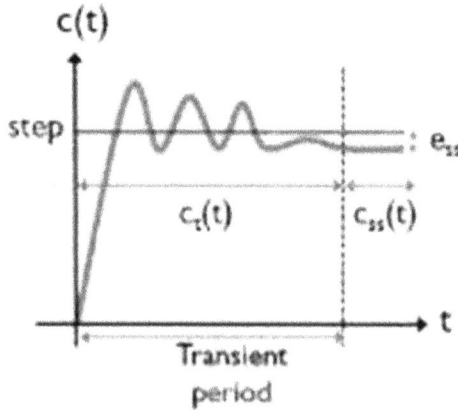

FIGURE 7.10 Time Domain Analysis.

steady-state value $c_{ss}(t)$. The steady-state error is denoted as e_{ss}. The title "Time Domain Analysis" is displayed above the graph.

Tidal volume is the amount of air inhaled or exhaled during each respiratory cycle. While exact tidal volume measurement typically requires specialized equipment like spirometers, it can be estimated from the amplitude of the respiratory signal. Measure the difference in signal amplitude between peaks and troughs. Larger amplitudes generally correspond to deeper breaths (higher tidal volume). Integrate the area under the respiratory signal curve during inhalation or exhalation to estimate the tidal volume. Approximate estimation of tidal volume can be done by normalizing the AUC. The I/E ratio represents the relative duration of the inhalation phase to the exhalation phase.

I/E Ratio = Inhalation Time / Exhalation Time

where inhalation time is the duration between the start and end of the inhalation phase, and exhalation time is the duration between the start and end of the exhalation phase. Apneas are periods of complete cessation of breathing, while hypopneas are periods of significantly reduced airflow. Detect periods where the respiratory signal amplitude drops below a certain threshold for a specified duration (e.g., more than ten seconds). Identify segments where no inhalation or exhalation events are detected within a specified time window. Identify periods where the respiratory signal amplitude is significantly reduced (e.g., by more than 30%) compared to normal breathing, lasting for ten seconds or more.

7.4   IMPLEMENTATION FOR THE SMART WEARABLE DEVICE IN SPORTS

The analysis of motion test results from smart wearable devices involves evaluating the accuracy, reliability, and effectiveness of the device in capturing and processing motion data. This analysis typically includes assessing the performance of the sensors, the algorithms used for motion detection, and the overall user experience.

Figure 7.11 is a bar chart entitled "Power Consumption by Activity," displaying battery usage percentage per hour for different activities. The x-axis represents various activities such as Walking, Running, Jumping, Climbing, and Descending. The y-axis represents battery usage in percentage per hour. The chart shows that Jumping consumes the most power, followed by Climbing, Running, Descending, and Walking, with the least power consumption.

Figure 7.12 is a line graph of "Sensor Signal with Noise Over Time," displaying signal amplitude variations over a ten-second period. The x-axis represents time in seconds, while the y-axis represents signal amplitude. The plotted sensor signal fluctuates with noticeable noise throughout the duration.

Analyzing exercise ECG (electrocardiogram) signal measurements involves evaluating various aspects of the ECG data collected during physical exercise. This analysis helps assess the cardiovascular response to exercise, detect abnormalities, and understand overall heart health.

Figure 7.13 is a line graph of "Heart Rate During Exercise," displaying heart rate data over time. The x-axis represents time in seconds, while the y-axis represents heart rate in beats per minute (bpm). The graph appears to have minimal or no visible data points plotted.

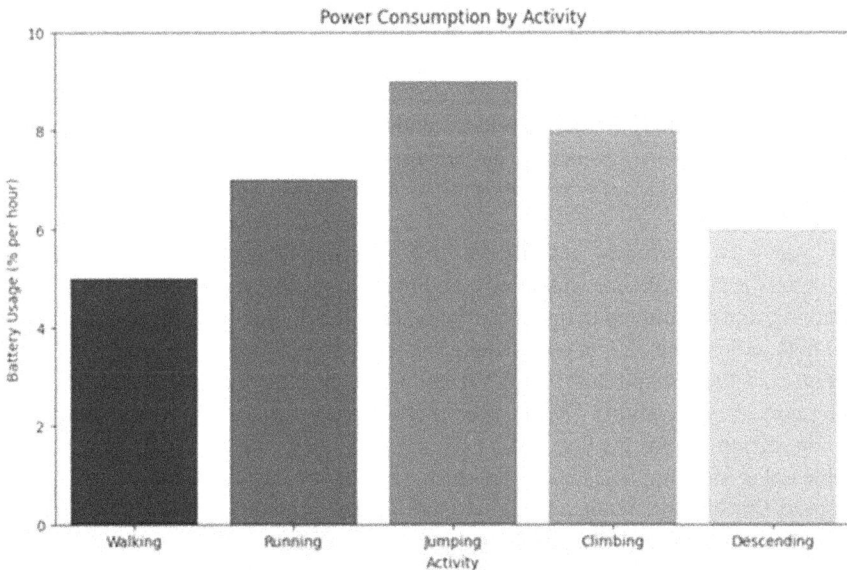

FIGURE 7.11   Activity Through Power Consumption.

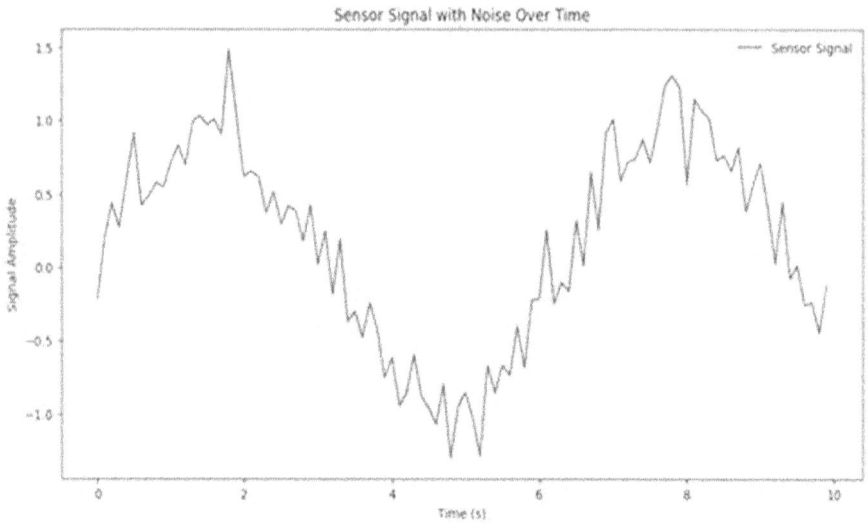

FIGURE 7.12 Signal Amplitude with Sensor Signal Over Time.

Figure 7.14, "QT Interval Over Time," shows fluctuations in QT interval values over a 10-second period. The x-axis represents time in seconds, while the y-axis represents the QT interval in milliseconds (ms). The bars are densely packed, indicating high-frequency variations in data.

Figure 7.15 shows a densely plotted graph representing "ST Segment Changes During Exercise," displaying variations in ST segment deviation over a ten-second period. The x-axis represents time in seconds, while the y-axis represents ST-segment deviation in millivolts (mV). The graph consists of numerous vertical green lines, indicating rapid fluctuations in the data.

Analyzing exercise breathing signal measurements involves evaluating respiratory data collected during physical activity to understand respiratory patterns, efficiency, and any potential issues. This analysis can provide insights into how exercise impacts breathing and help identify any irregularities or areas for improvement in respiratory function.

Figure 7.16 shows raw and filtered breathing signals over a ten-second period. The x-axis represents time in seconds, and the y-axis represents amplitude. The raw breathing signal is plotted in light blue, while the filtered breathing signal is in orange. Red dots indicate inhalation peaks along the filtered breathing signal curve.

Figure 7.17, "Respiratory Rate Variability Over Time," depicts fluctuations in respiratory rate variability (RRV) over a ten-second period. The x-axis represents time in seconds, while the y-axis represents RRV values. The data is plotted in a dark purple color, showing frequent variations in respiratory rate over time.

Analyzing changes in knee joint distribution during running involves studying how the distribution of forces, angles, and movement patterns at the knee joint changes as a runner moves. This analysis helps understand the biomechanics of running, assess injury risks, and improve performance.

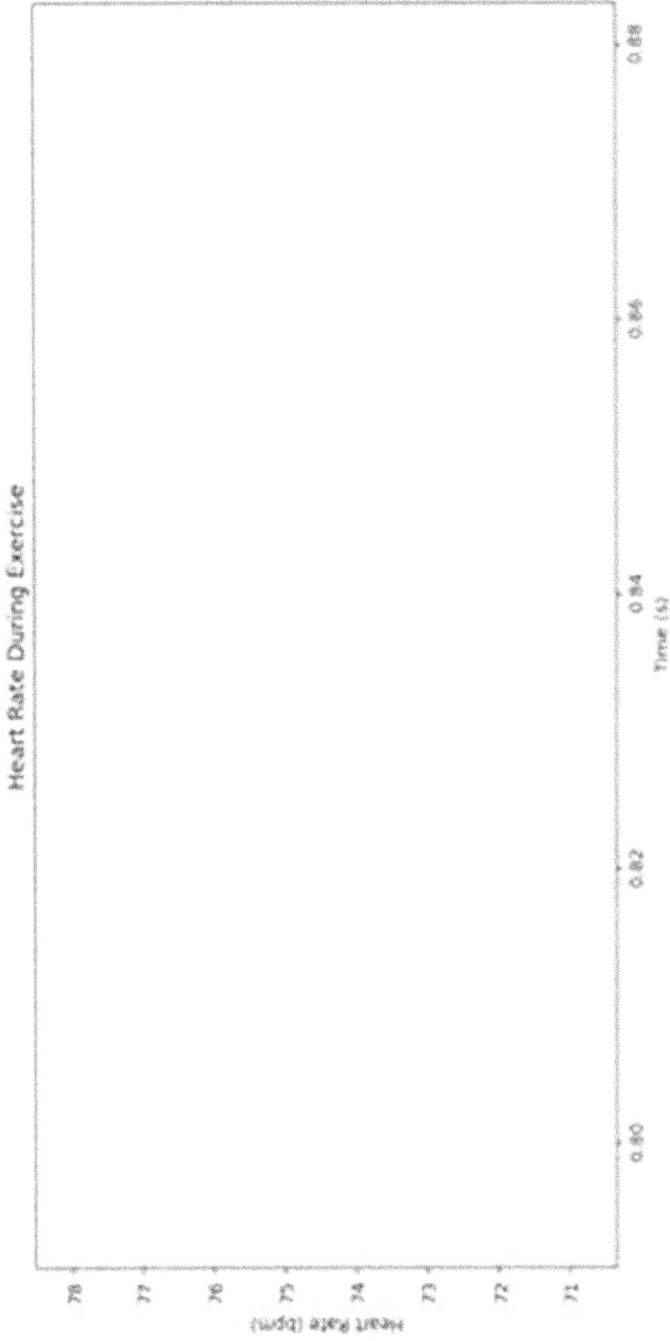

FIGURE 7.13   Measuring Heart Rate During Exercise.

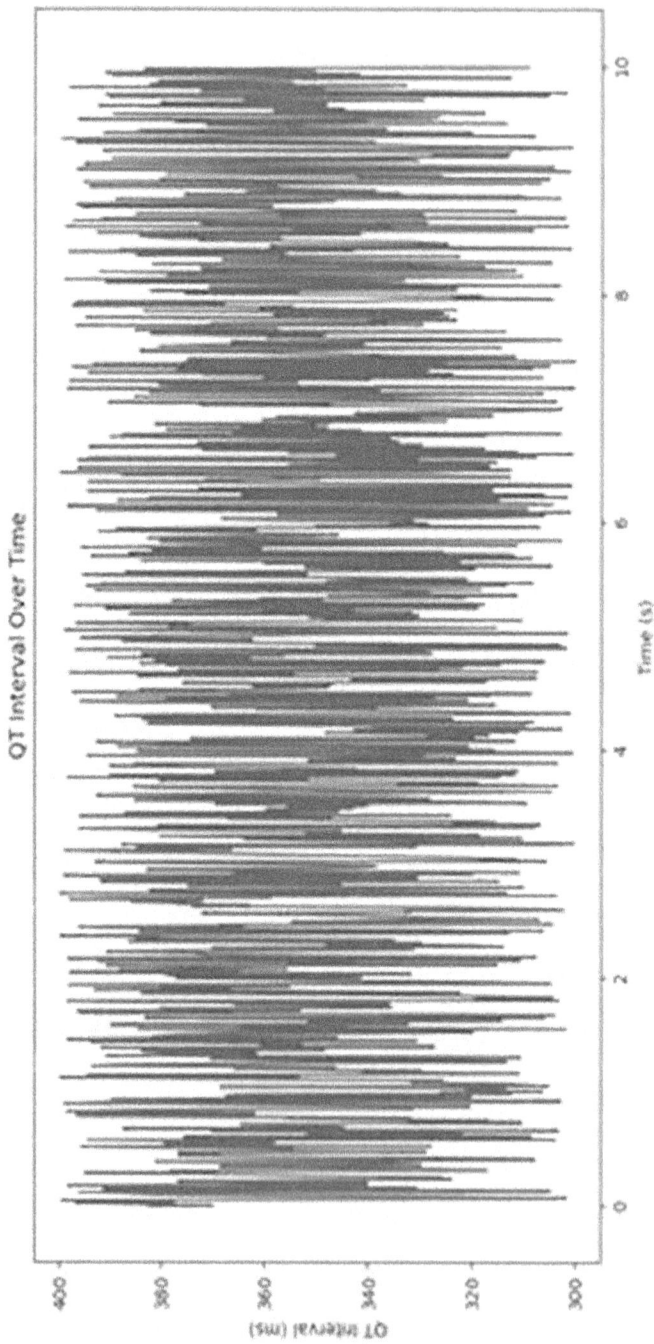

FIGURE 7.14 QT Interval Over Time.

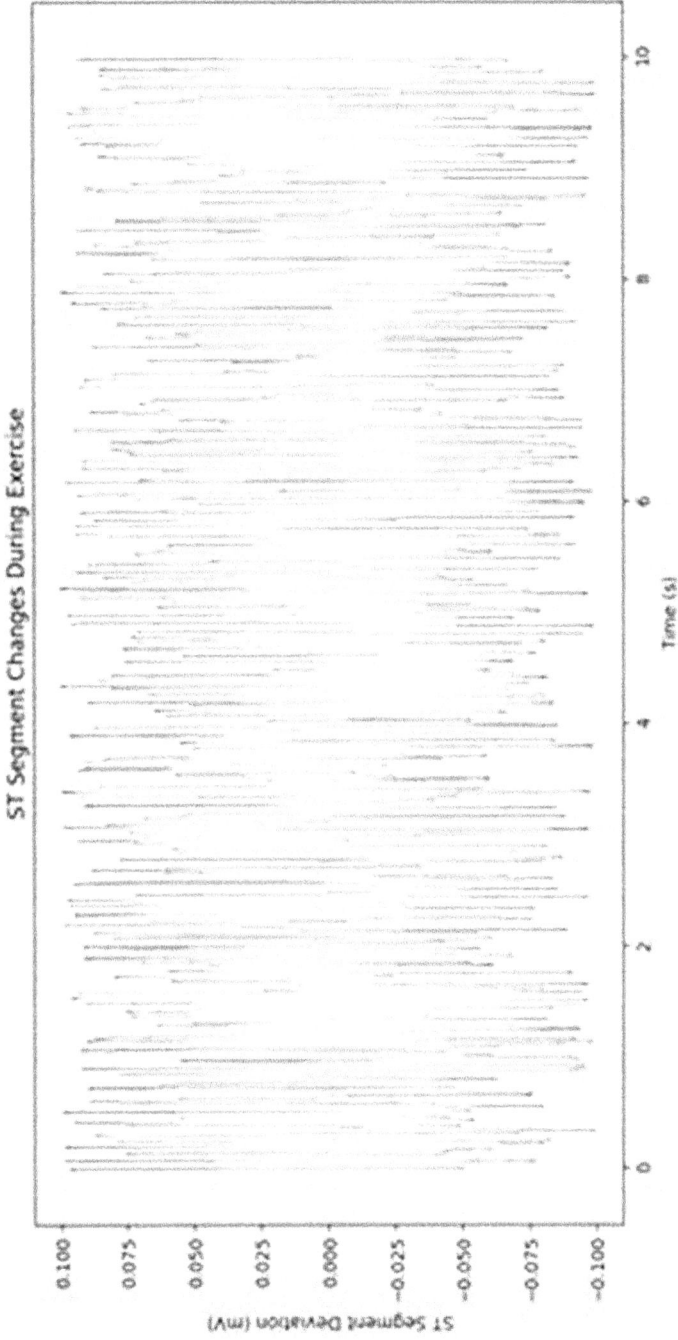

FIGURE 7.15 ST Segment Changes During Exercise.

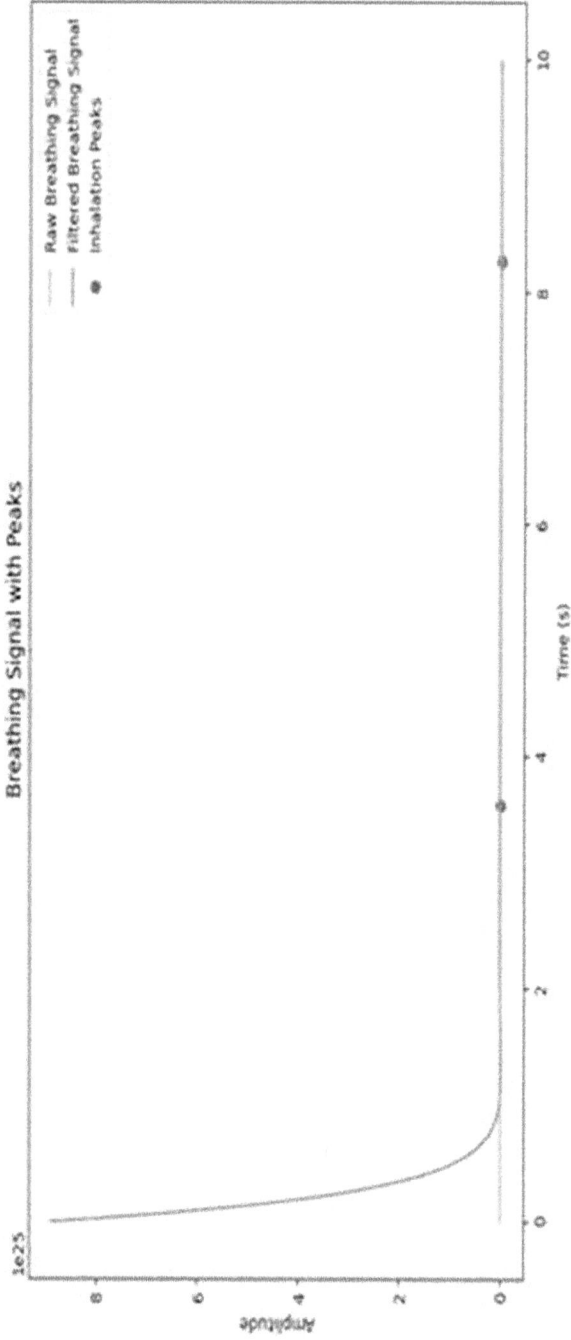

FIGURE 7.16 Breathing Signal with Peaks.

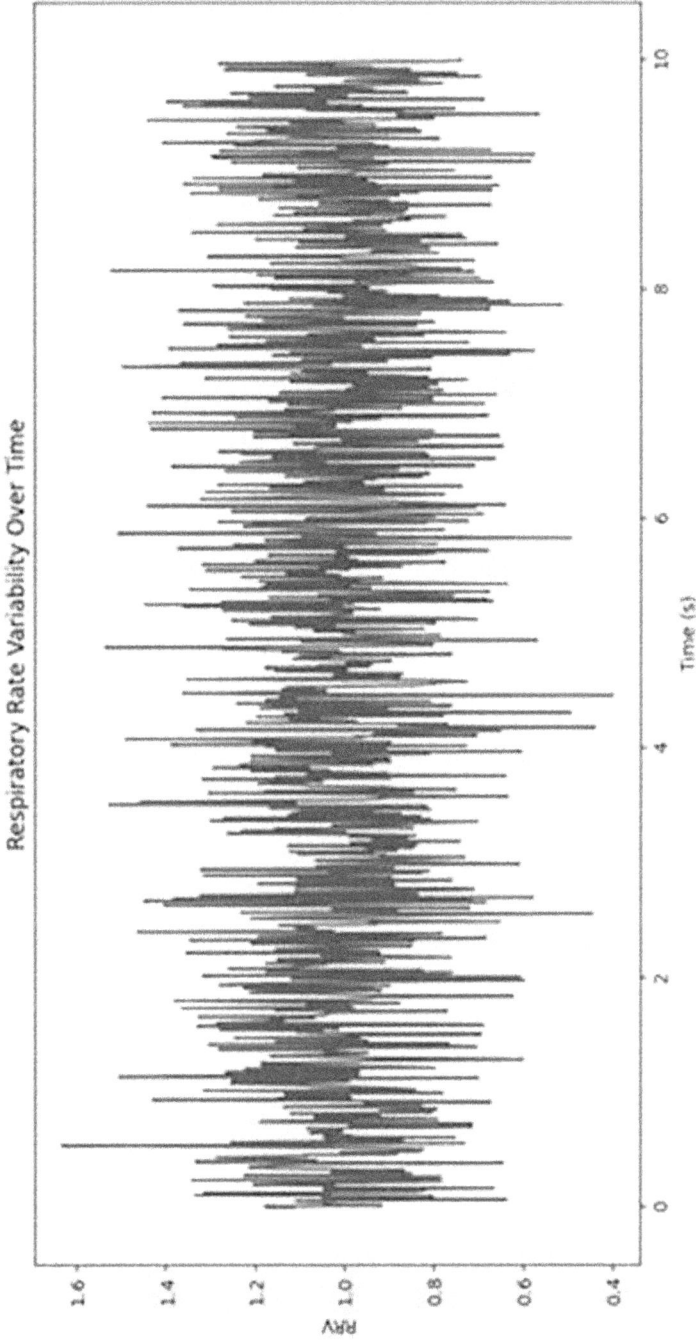

FIGURE 7.17   Respiratory Rate Variability Over Time.

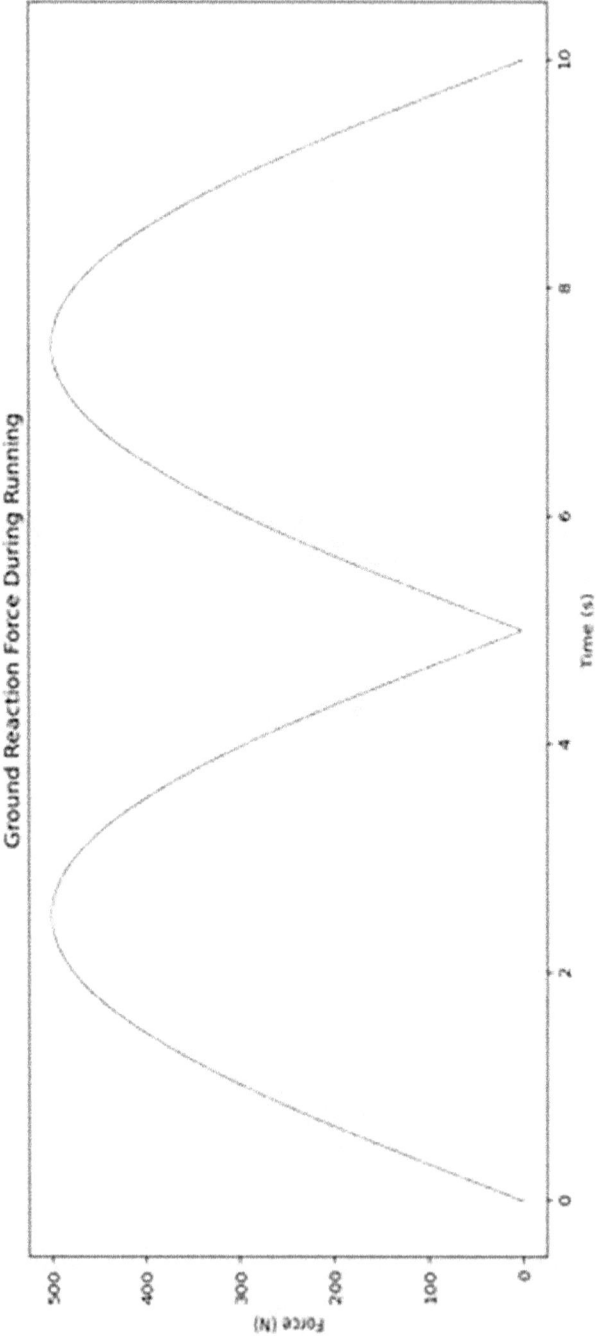

FIGURE 7.18   Ground Reaction Force.

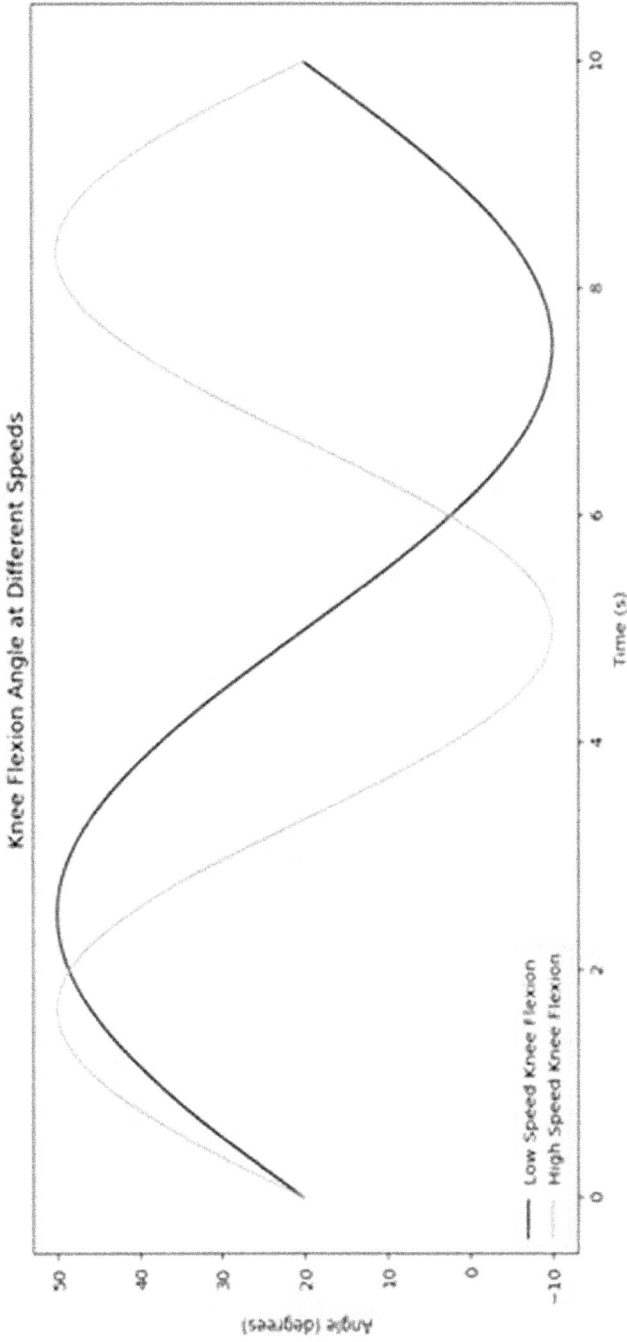

FIGURE 7.19   Knee Flexion Angle at Different Speeds.

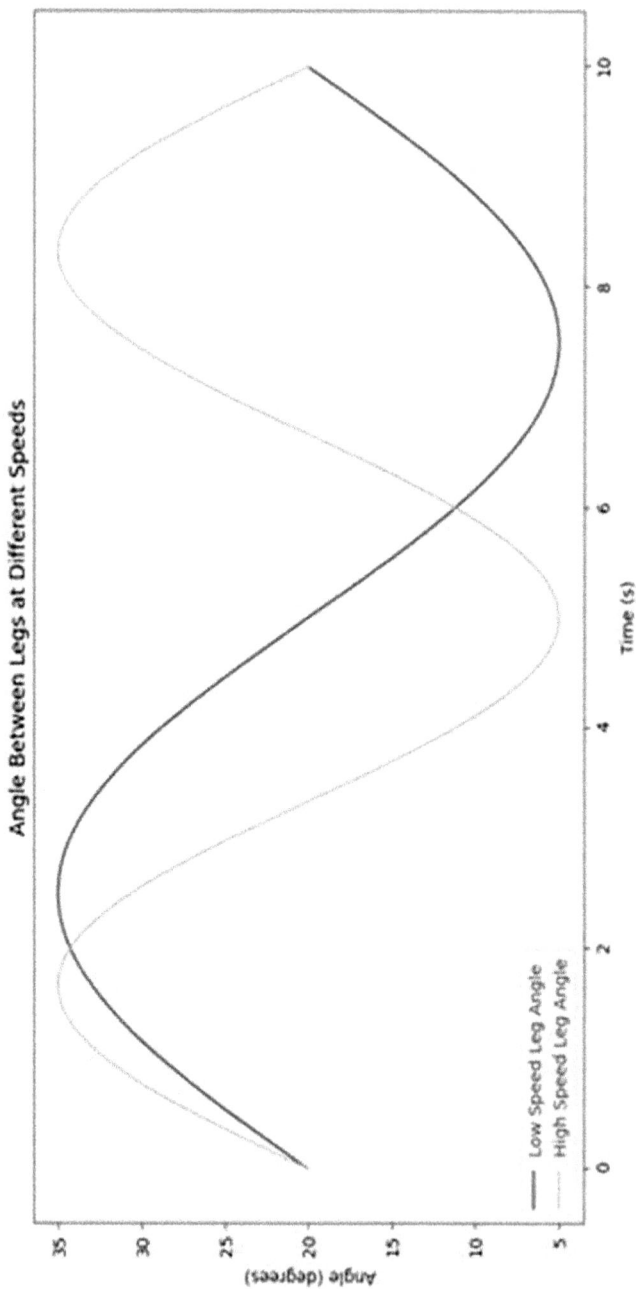

FIGURE 7.20 Angle Between Legs at Different Speeds.

Figure 7.18 is a line graph of "Ground Reaction Force During Running," showing the variation of ground reaction force over a ten-second period. The x-axis represents time in seconds, while the y-axis represents force in Newtons (N). The data follows a periodic pattern with two peaks, indicating the force fluctuations during running cycle.

Figure 7.19 is a graph of "Knee Flexion Angle at Different Speeds," showing knee flexion angles over a ten-second period. The x-axis represents time in seconds, while the y-axis represents the flexion angle in degrees. Two curves are plotted: a blue line for low-speed knee flexion and a yellow line for high-speed knee flexion. Both curves exhibit a sinusoidal pattern, with high-speed knee flexion oscillating at a higher frequency.

Analyzing the variation of the angle between legs during running involves examining how the angle between the legs changes as a runner moves. This angle, often referred to as the "leg angle" or "inter-limb angle," can provide insights into running biomechanics, symmetry, and potential inefficiencies or injury risks.

The line graph Figure 7.20 of "Angle Between Legs at Different Speeds" shows the variation in leg angles over a ten-second period. The x-axis represents time in seconds, and the y-axis represents the angle in degrees. Two curves are plotted: a blue line for low-speed leg angle and a yellow line for high-speed leg angle. Both curves exhibit a sinusoidal pattern, with the high-speed leg angle oscillating at a higher frequency compared to the low-speed leg angle.

7.5 CONCLUSION

Wearable devices provide continuous, real-time monitoring of various physiological and biomechanical metrics, such as heart rate, acceleration, and joint angles. This data allows athletes and coaches to track performance metrics more accurately and immediately respond to changes. By analyzing metrics such as stride length, cadence, and ground reaction forces, athletes can fine-tune their training regimens for optimal performance. Wearable devices monitor recovery metrics like heart rate variability and sleep quality, providing valuable information for optimizing recovery strategies. This helps in preventing overtraining and reducing the risk of injuries. However, addressing challenges related to data integration, user compliance, and privacy will be crucial for the continued evolution and effectiveness of wearable technology in sports. As technology advances, the potential for wearable devices to further enhance athletic performance and overall health remains promising.

ABBREVIATIONS

WT Wearable technology
ML Machine Learning
WD Wearable Device
RD Raw Data

REFERENCES

N. F. M. Aun, P. J. Soh, A. A. Al-Hadi, M. F. Jamlos, G. A. E. Vandenbosch, and D. Schreurs, "Revolutionizing wearables for 5G: 5G technologies: recent developments and future perspectives for wearable devices and antennas," *IEEE Microwave Magazine*, vol. 18, no. 3, pp. 108–124, May 2017.

A. Boroumand et al., "Google workloads for consumer devices: mitigating data movement bottlenecks," *ACM SIGPLAN Notices*, vol. 53, no. 2, pp. 316–331, Mar. 2018.

M. Lapinski, C. B. Brum Medeiros, D. M. Moxley Scarborough, E. Berkson, T. J. Gill, T. Kepple, and J. A. Paradiso, "A wide-range, wireless wearable inertial motion sensing system for capturing fast athletic biomechanics in overhead pitching," *Sensors*, vol. 19, no. 17, p. 3637, 2019.

S. Liang et al., "A self-powered wearable body-detecting/brain-stimulating system for improving sports endurance performance," *Nano Energy*, vol. 99, 107399, 2022.

F. Lin, A. Wang, Y. Zhuang, M. R. Tomita, and W. Xu, "Smart insole: a wearable sensor device for unobtrusive gait monitoring in daily life," *IEEE Transactions on Industrial Informatics*, vol. 12, no. 6, pp. 2281–2291, 2016.

D. Mayorga-Vega, C. Casado-Robles, I. López-Fernández, and J. Viciana, "Activity wristband-based physical activity recommendations in young people," *Science & Sports*, vol. 37, no. 4, pp. 303–315, 2022.

P. Mercier and J. Wang, "Powered by sweat: throw out the batteries: biofuels will change the future of wearable devices," *IEEE Spectrum*, vol. 57, no. 7, pp. 28–33, 2020.

A. K. Oktavius, Q. Gu, N. Wihardjo, O. Winata, S. W. Sunanto, J. Li, and P. Gao, "Fully-conformable porous polyethylene nanofilm sweat sensor for sports fatigue," *IEEE Sensors Journal*, vol. 21, no. 7, pp. 8861–8867, Art. No. 9336676, Apr. 2021.

X. Shi and Z. Huang, "Wearable device monitoring exercise energy consumption based on Internet of things," *Complexity*, vol. 2021, no. 1, Art. No. 8836723, Feb. 2021.

A. M. Tyson, S. M. Duma, and S. Rowson, "Laboratory evaluation of low-cost wearable sensors for measuring head impacts in sports," *Journal of Applied Biomechanics*, vol. 34, no. 4, pp. 320–326, 2018.

8 Generative AI Techniques and Computational Intelligence Functioning on Text-to-Image/Visual Content Generation

Ramandeep Sandhu, Harpreet Kaur Channi, Deepika Ghai, Nimisha Singh, and Phuke Rakesh Rao

8.1 INTRODUCTION

Artificial Intelligence (AI) has been growing the field enormously in the recent past, especially in the creative models that can create better than humans. Generative AI has dramatically transformed several fields of industry by making machines capable of producing lifelike and high-quality outputs in different forms, such as text, music, graphics, animation, and even video files [1]. It involves creating new data that resembles a given dataset. The original methods are the development of models, such as transfiguration-based architectures, Variational Autoencoders (VAEs), and Generative Adversarial Networks (GANs), among other things, that are the main reason for the increasing performance capabilities of these systems [2]. Generative Adversarial Networks (GANs) have been contributing a lot to the image synthesis aspect of generative deep learning since their publication by Goodfellow et al. [3] in 2014. They enabled, among other applications, super-resolution, image synthesis, and style transfer. The main concept of the GAN system, which is to make one neural network compete with its adversaries, has given a directional impulse to the AI community, making biologists, as well as engineers, think and come up with ideas and projects that have not ever been thought of before. In addition, transformer models, especially GPT-3 and GPT-4, are increasingly becoming proficient in processing natural language by creating contextually relevant and almost human-like language. The progress in technology undoubtedly has far-reaching influences. Generative AI is being used in the creative arts for the production of art, poetry, and music, which in turn strengthens human creativity. The application of such AI techniques in the

DOI: 10.1201/9781003680192-8 **159**

healthcare sector ranges from research, privacy respect by using them in drug development, to the synthetic production of medical data. Moreover, the AI-generated content adds to and enhances the naturalness and diversification of user engagement in the virtual world and games. Internally, they provide employees with a update on the learning and working process. Externally, they offer customers a new experience [4–6]. Nevertheless, the fast maturity of generative AI comes with several important societal and ethical issues. The main motive of the proposed book chapter is to attain a more profound understanding of generative AI and the influence it has on technology and society by conducting an inquiry into these facets. This section shall unveil what is currently in practice in the generative AI-based text-to-image using the appropriate technology, main developments, and good applications. We will discuss the most popular models, their design and functionality, drawing comparisons to other models and speculating on the social and ethical issues surrounding them. The primary objective is to identify and explore the potential of text-to-image generation to transform and revolutionize the process of communication and perception. Using Neural Text-to-Image Generation—while natural language processing and computer vision present the amalgamation of the two—the text-to-image generator is the most advanced development in artificial intelligence. That technology demonstrates the capabilities of AI generative models to grasp and process a wide range of sensory information in high-performance mode. This is achieved by creating high-quality images from textual descriptions. The diversity and quality of images generated from textual prompts have been drastically improved due to the introduction of transformer-based models and GANs under the umbrella of deep learning [7–10]. Text-to-image generation has a huge future in several areas. It allows designers and artists to see the things they have written as visualized prototypes and to involve themselves in creative expression. It allows the users to visualize such descriptions by converting the product details into visual representations. Furthermore, text-to-image algorithms can produce illustrated content from textual speech in e-learning and training, aiding in both comprehension and engagement. The production of the DALL-E model by OpenAI, which merges transformer and GAN capabilities to create virtually photographic and coherent renditions from text, is a significant step forward in this area. This category of a complex model is trained on massive amounts of stored data. The utilization of deep networks helps in linking words and corresponding visual features, thereby producing precise descriptive visuals. The success of these algorithms provides plentiful advantages, but still, some issues need to be addressed. The key variations in data quality, model complexity, and computational resources are the foundations for enhancing the relevance and quality of images. Moreover, the ethical issues associated with the technology cannot be disregarded. It is, for instance, possible that misleading or inappropriate documents could be produced through technology, and hence, strict guidelines and moral principles must be established to handle their utilization. It is widely accepted that language is the fundamental means that we use to express detailed or specific information, but graphics can often offer information in a more compelling, engaging, and memorable way. When text is combined with images, one can utilize the strengths of the two media and communicate ideas better. Every format for creating material has advantages and disadvantages. The audience, content context, and specific goals should all be taken into consideration when selecting a format. The highest success rates usually come from using a combination of different forms, each of which capitalizes on its particular strengths and draws the reader in [11–15].

8.1.1 VARIOUS CONTENT REPRESENTATION FORMATS

The outputs of the content representations are shown in Figure 8.1 and correspond to the diverse methods by which data can be put together and displayed. Text, pictures, audio, video, graphs, tables, and interactive media are some instances of such forms. Each type has its advantages and disadvantages. The most suitable and versatile option is the text, which, aside from being easily searchable and editable, is also quite a compact medium. This is mainly because it can be read thoroughly or quickly, depending on the editor's preference, and provides detailed explanations on every page. However, reading the text may be unexciting and annoying as the presentation may be too lengthy and the information too scattered.

Images show flowcharts, tree diagrams, and infographics; hence, a visual picture is immediately given, and complicated expressions become clearer. They give the audience a good impression and keep them interested for a longer period. There is the downside that non-thoughtful images will be misinterpreted and will take longer to download. Videos are a kind of narrative that is engrossing because they have singing and music. One can explain the concepts more effectively by utilizing visual and aural qualities. They are the most beneficial for marketing and instructional materials.

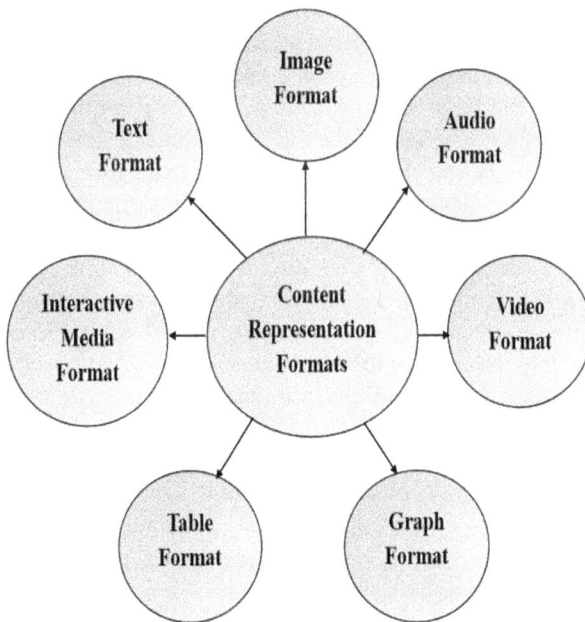

FIGURE 8.1   Content Representation Formats.

However, videos require a large amount of energy to be created and need to be played with data that might be slow and cannot be used by others. Podcasts and similar content are the most suitable for multitasking because they enable users to listen in hands-free mode. They are capable of identifying the emotion and tone. Nevertheless, their failure to convey complex and comprehensive messages without additional materials is the primary characteristic they lack [16,17].

8.1.1.1 Representing Content in Text Format

Text format content offers several advantages and some disadvantages. On the one hand, it provides essential data that backs up the analysis and describes the subtle differences. Searchability and indexability give an additional advantage to text. Moreover, the format is not only accessible but also can be easily translated into different languages and used by the visually impaired through the assistance of audio description. Moreover, text is quieter to design than graphics, video, or audio. Further, it costs less to load and be accessed, so it is a good choice for low-bandwidth use.

Nevertheless, there are still some drawbacks to be taken into consideration. User engagement can be impaired by text materials' lack of attention-grabbing or engaging qualities compared to visual or auditory content. In addition to the fact that comprehension may be hampered by some complicated concepts that are difficult to understand without visual aids. A large amount of content, on the other hand, may take a long time to read, which may not capture the attention of the viewers. These benefits and drawbacks of information technology must be equally understood and shown in order not to let user interest and comprehension be affected [18,19].

8.1.1.2 Representing Content in Image Format

Every type of material has its own benefits and drawbacks. At the same time, it is also a complex material that enables clear communication and fast transmission. In a word, a language can hardly use visual aids, the most significant being a widely used language. Additionally, audio material does confer better memory retention, because visual aids are more often immediately clear to the user. However, one has to think about a few downsides too. A graphic may not communicate well complicated aspects that live interactions allow, that is, it can be a limiting factor in this regard. Further, they are more demanding when it comes to bandwidth, which may annoy clients with slow WI-FI. On top of that, visual aids could potentially be a drawback to people with disadvantages due to the absence of the Assistant Language Teacher (ALT) language. In conclusion, information must be conveyed effectively while still keeping in mind the viewers' requirements and limitations; it should, therefore, be both strong and weak [20,21].

8.1.1.3 Representing Content in Audio Format

Audio material has either upsides or downsides individually. Its positive nature is the fact that it is easy for multitasking to happen; one would be able to listen to it while performing multiple tasks, such as driving or jogging. Intonation, loudness, and tempo mostly play dominant roles, which give a piece of music the ability to appeal to our emotions. Adorned accessibility is a valuable feature for individuals with vision impairments and those who struggle with reading. What is more, the use of speech in audio content attracts the listener and gets them involved in the audio, which excites the listener's interest. Nevertheless, you also need to be aware of the downsides that come with it. The main issue with audio that lacks visual support is that it struggles to articulate complex issues effectively. Though bandwidth use may be higher than in text-only, it may present minimal bandwidth issues. For instance, one needs to wait for it to be transcribed before it can be accessed. Eventually, the need for active listening in cases of audio usage is a stumbling block for certain listeners who, consequently, find it hard to stay focused. However, to effectively utilize audio content for communication and engagement purposes, it is also necessary to make a comparison [20–24].

8.1.1.4   Representing Content in the Video Form

Video content can be highly immersive because it blends audio and visual components very well. On one hand, it is an ideal tool for providing detailed instructions along with animated demonstrations; the possibilities are endless. The ability to construct dramatic effects by storytelling is the main reason for this. The tool of video can remain very efficient and informative, while also having, as much as possible, the ability to be a means of getting an answer. The most challenging task for professional video producers might be field video production, as it is very complicated and labour-intensive [25,26]. There is also a disadvantage in data usage when someone downloads or streams videos using internet bandwidth, which may erase the possibility for people to have the idea to watch those fascinating videos. The problem of accessibility exists in the videos due to the absence of transcripts or captions, which makes it impossible for deaf people to follow. Furthermore, videos, unless they are well-labeled and categorized, are far less accessible than text. On the whole, such benefits and flaws need to be balanced so that the video content can be utilized in the best ways possible and at the same time, the audience's requirements and impediments can be considered accordingly.

8.2   IMPORTANCE OF VISUAL REPRESENTATION

The world of icons can be seen as being better than information presented through texts, i.e., by visually depicting itself. Visual information is directly understood, is a universal language, and has an emotional appeal, in addition to memory and motivation centers. This is not merely the normal theoretical context and so is feasible for practical marketing, education, and social media, for example. As a result, the semiotic mediation that the visual image presents can not only level up the realms of content and approaches of communication but also help with cognition and object creation. The exaggeration does not require us to find a way of saying something; it is independent of verbal messages and can evoke the emotions of the audience. The author utilizes both visual content and text and, for example, this is a way. Many people share similar opinions. "This is a way of expressing ideas without explaining the specific words or phrases." Either everyone/ or almost everyone understands that the main idea can also be said as the correct term [27].

The application of Generative AI is dependent on various computer-based concepts and involves different AI objects for the creation of new applications. It draws from discussions on disciplines such as computer/cyber sciences, presenting a coding approach to simplify machine handling and database management. The chapter is written for GAI and its capacity to read and write while also being able to form pictures. Some years back, AI was used only for translating, but when it comes to GAI, there is a new way of generating new content. It allows a more even dialogue in which language is treated not just as the subject of the reading but it is also as the object, as texts can generate their graphic images. It does this by identifying words in the text, and then the sentences are selected to specify how to build the image and create the image that relates to the text. It will generate appropriate images that are derived from the provided text. In the tutorlage of transitioning the literary into the pictorial the composition of the education system has seen momentous growth in technoscientific education and computation. This is achieved by learning models of machines that are specially designed, such as deep learning architectures. These technologies imply the transformation of the very words into graceful images. This sector can cover the arts' details, designs, business marketing, and so forth. The introduction features four main subjects of generative AI: text-to-image and other visual content, teamwork of computing intelligence, being the top expert there. Generative AI, a subcategory of AI, utilizes one AI technique to generate a new series of data that did not exist previously. It has its applications in various areas, including generating texts and images, aside from creating symphonies. The idea behind these is to develop a model that will estimate the probability of the training data and will be able to create new instances belonging to the training data but not the same as the training [28,29].

8.2.1 Advanced Technologies for Text-to-Image Processes

The automatic transformation of text to images combines multiple advanced AI technologies that harmonize perfectly. Here is a summary of various AI elements, such as AI, GANs, Generative AI, Deep Learning (DL), Machine Learning (ML), and Natural Language Processing (NLP) that are used for text-to-image processes that are shown in Figure 8.2.

a) **Artificial Intelligence:** The transformation of text into imagery can be achieved by fusing different technologies into one general system, which is ethically three-dimensional Artificial Intelligence (AI). It involves processes and resources by which machines can perform functions that in the normal course of events would require the cognition of a human being [28, 29].

b) **Generative Adversarial Networks (GANs):** GANs generate high-quality images from text using two competing neural networks—the generator and the discriminator. The generator makes images based on the text input generated and the discriminator checks if those images made are real. Over many iterations of training, GANs can create much more realistic and better images than when training without their processes.

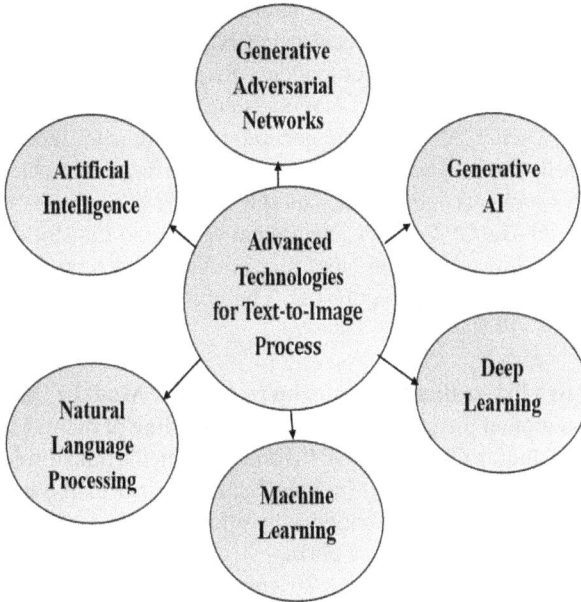

FIGURE 8.2 Various Advanced Technologies for Text-to-Image Process.

c) **Generative AI:** The fundamental aspect of generative AI is to develop something new such as images out of the existing database. To develop images imitating text, generative AI models are made to convert text to images incorporating the generated entity. Such models can construct words that connect to image components because they were conditioned on paired text/image datasets.

d) **Deep Learning:** As a subfield of Machine Learning (ML), Deep Learning (DL) uses Deep Neural Networks (DNN) to learn intricate features and structures. For instance, a Recurrent Neural Network (RNN) is used to complete or revise narrative text in deep learning approaches, but a Convolutional Neural Network (CNN) is almost typically used to generate movies.

e) **Machine Learning:** Today, the principles of Machine Learning (ML) techniques have focused on creating models for transferring text into images. Such models are trained with datasets in which the textual inputs are matched with relevant images using supervized learning techniques. Thus, these models memorize how each text can be represented visually, and hence they can create images from the text provided [30–38].

f) **Natural Language Processing (NLP):** NLP serves as a key input technology for decoding and transforming text. It consists of transcription, interpretation, and extraction techniques of information from natural language. Such parts include entities, their attributes, and relations, or any other semantic aspects that will influence and assist in creating the images. As an illustration, NLP may recognize objects, actions, and backgrounds mentioned in text documents and facilitate the creation of images that match the scenarios [33,39–43].

As described above, various techniques interact to propose a better text-to-image generation. The input text is interpreted using NLP and further broken into meaningful features. Afterwards, visual components are generated from extracted features using ML techniques. Furthermore, DL models are applied to improve the quality of generated output. Then, GAN trains the generator-discriminator model and performs the final image refinement. The most important is Generative AI, which combines all the mentioned components and provides unique images in alignment with the input.

Technologies such as GPT models, neural networks, and transformers are integral to advanced AI systems that process text for various applications, including text-to-image generation, as shown in Figure 8.3. The contribution of these techniques is described below:

a) **Generative Pre-trained Transformers, or GPT Models:** Designed to tackle problems around the generation and understanding of natural language, these models, including GPT-3 and GPT-4 are based on the transformer architecture.

   Self-Attentive Mechanism: This mechanism enhances the model's comprehension of context and subtleties by allowing it to assess the relative relevance of various words in a phrase.

   Pre-training and Fine-tuning: To enhance performance on specific tasks, such as generating text descriptions for images or vice versa, GPT models are initially pre-trained across large datasets to identify general language patterns and skills before being fine-tuned for specific tasks.

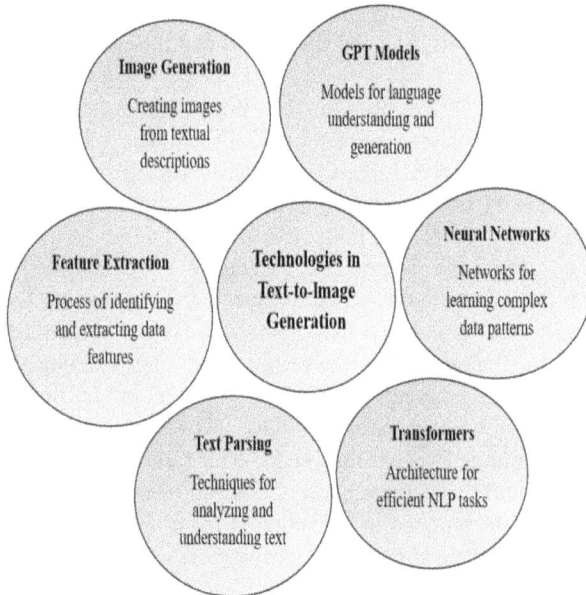

FIGURE 8.3 Technologies in Text-to-Image Generation.

b) **Neural Networks:** In particular, DNNs are critical to learning complex patterns from data. Different types of neural networks are utilized in the process of creating images from text.

   Convolutional Neural Networks (CNNs): CNNs are proficient at showing and learning features and patterns in images, and can help to develop images based on input text.

   Long Short-Term Memory (LSTM): LSTMs are a type of RNN that remembers long-term dependencies to maintain context and produce an accurate representation of longer text descriptions.

   Feature Extraction: To create realistic and detailed images, DNNs must be able to extract hierarchical features at each level of an image.

   Recurrent Neural Networks (RNNs): RNNs are well-suited for text processing due to their design for sequential data processing.

c) **Transformers:** A type of neural network architecture has transformed NLP. It employs self-attention mechanisms to process incoming data in parallel, as opposed to sequentially, to significantly improve performance and efficiency, as described above.

   Attention Mechanism: Transformers use multi-head attention to obtain sophisticated relationships, as there are multiple parts of the input to focus on simultaneously.

   Scalability and Efficiency: Transformers can efficiently process large datasets or long sequences, making them ideal for tasks that require parsing long contexts, such as generating images from a long text description.

8.2.2 INTEGRATION IN TEXT-TO-IMAGE GENERATION

The integration of text-to-image generation is listed as follows:

a) **Text Parsing and Understanding:**

   NLP Techniques: Key components and their connections are extracted from the input text via preprocessing and analysis using named entity recognition, tokenization, part-of-speech tagging, and semantic analysis.

   Transformers: Models such as GPT-3/4 use their advanced understanding of language to parse the text and generate coherent and contextually accurate descriptions.

b) **Feature Extraction and Representation:**

   Work Embedding: Techniques such as Word2Vec or BERT embeddings transform words into vector representations that capture their meanings and relationships. These embeddings serve as the input for generative models.

   Deep Learning Models: DNNs, particularly CNNs, are used to extract visual features from these embeddings, preparing the data for image generation.

c) **Image Generative:**

   Generative Adversarial Networks(GANs): GANs use a generator and discriminator to create realistic visuals. The discriminators assess the picture's legitimacy, while the generator produces them using text-derived attributes.

StackGAN and AttnGAN: These are advanced GAN architectures that improve image quality by using staged generative (StackGAN) or incorporating attention mechanisms to focus on relevant text parts(AttnGAN).

Variational Autoencoders(VAEs): VAEs create latent spaces from text representations and decode them into images, ensuring that the generated images align with the input text.

d) Refinement and Optimization:

Training and Fine-tuning: The models are trained on a large collection of text-image pairs, learning how to map textual descriptions to visual content.

Attention Mechanisms: These mechanisms ensure that relevant words or details are emphasized during the generation of content, leading to more accurate, meaningful images and better overall quality.

8.2.3 APPLICATIONS

The use of these technologies has a wide range of applications in diverse areas:

a) *Creative Arts:* Designers and artists can leverage text-to-image generation to rapidly visualize their ideas and express different thoughts.

b) *Education:* Educational tools can benefit from generating visual materials based on a text description, which can enhance learning and engagement.

c) *Healthcare:* Medical imaging applications can use text descriptions related to symptoms or a condition to generate visual content that is conducive to diagnostic and treatment planning.

d) *Marketing and Advertising:* Organisations can generate promotional imagery and video based on descriptions of their products, making it very efficient to market online and on other media.

Taking advantage of the capabilities of GPT models, neural networks, and transformers, text-to-image generation systems can produce high-quality, contextually relevant visual media from textual expressions, transforming the way we engage with and understand information.

GAI systems generally receive textual data that is unstructured. Therefore, the data must be pre-processed and structured before it is used to generate images. Before using the data generated by the model to produce an image, the system uses NLP methods such as tokenization, part-of-speech tagging, and dependency parsing to break down the text into its constituent parts to identify important entities, relationships and semantic structures. Through NER, the system can identify important entities, relationships, and semantic structures.

Generative AI systems employ a range of sophisticated methods to convert text into suitably reflective visual images, ensuring that the generated image is true to the understood meaning of the original text. The NLP approaches are first employed to identify important entities, attributes, and contextual information in the text. These extracted features are then encoded as vector embeddings that can convey important relations and meanings. Architectures such as DALL.E or Stable Diffusion use these structured codings, employing deep neural networks, primarily transformer networks, to obtain meaning from these embeddings to generate an image that reflects the intent of the text. For example, DALL.E utilized a transformer model to obtain finer details according to the textual prompt, while Stable diffusion uses latent diffusion models to iteratively improve the coherence of the image over the complete image space, ultimately creating an image that reflects the original textual referencing. Attention methods, which have become essential in doing these methods, are used in both DALL.E and Stable Diffusion to focus on detail from the text, enhancing the interpretation of attributes represented in the original text, such as color, shape and scene composition. Along with attention mechanisms, GANs can also be employed to enhance image quality. GAN processes iterate between the generator and discriminator.

8.3   RELATED WORK

In previous years, the research in the field of text-to-image generation is highly valuable compared to early models such as GAN-INT-CLS, StackGAN, AttnGAN, and more. Basically, GAN-INT-CLS combines GAN with the text encoders, and it simply produces the relevant images.

If we consider StackGAN, which is a two-stage process which works on low-resolution images to refine them and achieve high-resolution versions of the same. Furthermore, AttnGAN provides advancements in the same field with the addition of a mechanism for generating various parts of the image, producing fine-grained visual representation with additional details.

DALL·E uses large datasets of text-image pairs and a transformer model to interpret complex prompts, allowing for high versatility and coherence in the generated images. Stable Diffusion, using diffusion models, iteratively refines image quality by gradually adding or removing noise in alignment with text prompts, resulting in highly detailed images. These advancements demonstrate how combining NLP, deep learning, and sophisticated generative techniques has led to increasingly accurate and visually coherent results in text-to-image generation, paving the way for applications across creative, educational, and professional fields. Numerous works have been done in the field of text-to-image generation, as shown in Table 8.1.

8.4   PROPOSED METHODOLOGY

Nowadays, text-to-image generation enhances communication by transforming text ideas into visuals. Figure 8.4 shows a step-by-step explanation of the proposed generating images from text.

The steps involved in the proposed text-to-image generation technique are listed as follows:

Phase 1: Understanding the Text
Parsing and Comprehension: The process is shown in Figure 8.4 starts by analyzing the input text to understand its structure and meaning. NLP techniques are used to preprocess and analyze the input text. This includes tokenization, part-of-speech tagging, named entity recognition, and semantic analysis to extract key elements and their relationships. This phase is also known as the parsing and text preprocessing

TABLE 8.1
Comparative Analysis of Various Techniques on Text-to-Image Generation

Techniques	Description of the Approach Used	Pros	Cons
Generative Adversarial Nets [3]	Introduced the GAN framework. *Method*: Proposed a two-player game between a generator and a discriminator. The generator creates images, and the discriminator evaluates their authenticity compared to real images. *Impact*: Laid the foundation for a new class of generative models extensively used in subsequent research.	Revolutionary framework, simple yet powerful concept, and versatile across different domains.	Training instability, mode collapse, and difficulty in evaluating the quality of generated images.
Generative Adversarial Text to Image Synthesis [1]	Developed one of the first GAN-based models specifically for text-to-image synthesis. *Method*: Combined a Deep Convolutional GAN (DCGAN) with a text encoder to generate images from text descriptions. *Results*: Demonstrated the model's ability to generate plausible images that align with given textual descriptions.	Pioneering work in text-to-image synthesis showed potential for multimodal tasks and created plausible images from text descriptions.	Limited image resolution and quality, struggles with generating complex images, and lacks fine-grained control.
StackGAN: Text to Photo-realistic Image Synthesis with Stacked Generative Adversarial Networks [24]	Introduced the StackGAN architecture to improve the quality of generated images. *Method*: Divided the generation process into two stages: a rough sketch generated in the first stage and refined in the second stage. *Results*: Achieved state-of-the-art performance in generating photo-realistic images from text.	Significant improvement in image quality and resolution, two-stage process allows for better control and photo-realistic image generation.	More complex architecture, longer training times, and still faces challenges in generating highly detailed images.

AttnGAN: Fine-Grained Text to Image Generation with Attentional Generative Adversarial Networks [30]	Introduced AttnGAN, incorporating attention mechanisms into GANs for text-to-image generation. *Method:* Used an attentional generative network to focus on relevant parts of the text when generating different parts of the image. *Results:* Generated high-quality images with fine details closely aligned with textual descriptions.	Fine-grained control over image generation, attention mechanisms improve image-text alignment, and high-quality, detailed image synthesis.	Increased computational complexity, requires careful tuning of attention mechanisms, and may struggle with very complex scenes.
DALL·E: Creating Images from Text [31]	Developed CLIP, a model that learns visual concepts from natural language descriptions. *Method:* Trained on a large dataset of images paired with their descriptions, enabling zero-shot transfer to various vision tasks. *Results:* Demonstrated that CLIP can understand and generate images from textual inputs without task-specific training.	Generates highly detailed and coherent images, capable of producing a wide variety of styles, and leverages the power of transformer models.	Computationally expensive, requires large amounts of data for training, and may generate images that are less creative or too literal.
Evaluate the Quality of Text-to-Image Synthesis: A Comprehensive Survey [32]	Provided a comprehensive survey of evaluation metrics and methods for assessing the quality of text-to-image synthesis models. *Method:* Reviewed both qualitative and quantitative approaches, including metrics such as Inception Score (IS), Fréchet Inception Distance (FID), and user studies. *Results:* Offered a valuable resource for standardizing assessments in the field.	High flexibility, capable of zero-shot learning across various tasks, and strong performance in both understanding and generating images from text.	May not perform as well in highly specialized or domain-specific tasks, and large-scale training required.

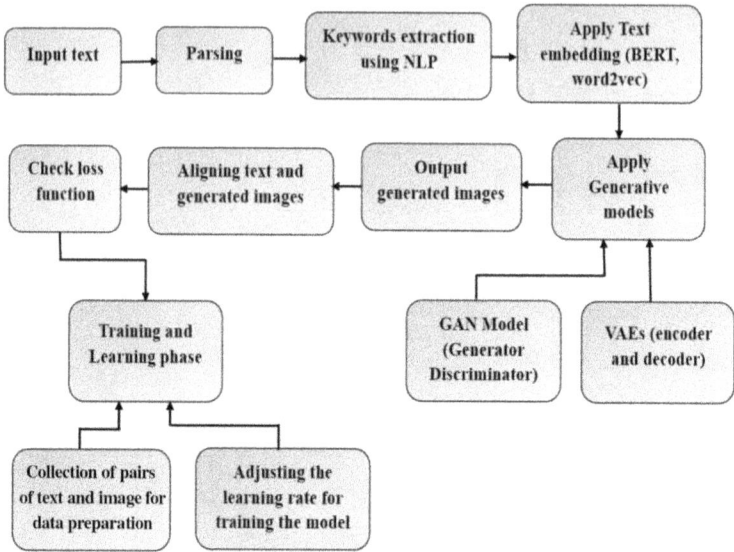

FIGURE 8.4   Flowchart of Proposed Text-to-Image Generation Technique.

phase. Here, LLMs (Large Language Models) such as BERT and GPT-3 are also helpful for supportive and meaningful visual output.

For example, given the sentence, "A cat sitting on a mat." The system identifies key terms such as "cat" and "mat" and understands the relationship between them using parsing techniques such as dependency parsing. The working scenario of dependency parsing is as follows:

- Dependency Parsing: T(dep) = {root(cat), subj (sitting, cat), obj (on, mat)}
- This shows that "cat" is the subject, "mat" is the object, and "sitting" is the root verb.

Phase 2: Feature Extraction

The filtered text is transformed into feature vectors that grab the semantic meaning of the representation. These vectors serve as the input for the generative model. The computer acknowledges the words that are reshaped into vectors (embeddings). Suppose that using Word2Vec, the word "cat" might be interpreted as a vector V(cat) = [0.3, 0.4, 0.2, ...]. These vectors encrypt semantic meaning and relationships among words. The framework of the text representation phase is as follows:

- Word Embeddings: V(w) = {V(cat), V(sitting), V(mat)}

Phase 3: Utilizing Generative Models

In this phase, a GAN model generates images from input text such as the vector V ("cat sitting on the mat"). It consists of a generator (G) and a discriminator (D), aiming to minimize G's loss while enhancing D's ability to distinguish real from fake images.

- GAN Objective Function:

$$\min\_G \max\_D E\_x[\log D(x)] + E\_z[\log(1 - D(G(z)))]$$

Phase 4: Creation with Variational Autoencoders (VAEs)
Variational Autoencoders (VAEs) create a "latent space" that constitutes the input text. For instance, the sentence "A cat sitting on a mat" is encoded into a latent vector Z, which is then decoded into an image of a cat on a mat.
Formula Example:

- VAE Latent Space Representation: $p(z|x) = N(z; \mu(x), \sigma^2(x))$
- The encoder maps the input x (text) to a latent space z (vector), and the decoder regenerates the image.

Phase 5: Integrating Text and Images
In the course of this phase, text-to-image reformation appears. Hence, GANs and VAEs ensure that the generated images match the input text. For instance, the system might emphasize the word "cat" to ensure the image prominently features a cat. The scheme of the text-to-image integration is as follows:

- Attention Mechanism: $a\_i = \text{softmax}(W\_a * h\_i)$
- Here, a_i represents the attention weight for word i, and h_i is the hidden state corresponding to that word.

Phase 6: Attention Mechanism
The system adopts an attention mechanism to concentrate on specific words or details.
Take an example of the scenario "A black cat sitting on a red mat." Here, the attention mechanism is based on an image, which highlights the following:

"black cat."
"red mat."

Example of the same process:
Example:

- Attention Weighted Sum: $c\_i = \Sigma(a\_i * h\_i)$

Here, c_i is a context vector which is a weighted sum of all hidden states, and extracts major features from the text.

Phase 7: Training and Optimization

A large dataset of text-image pairs is applied to train the system. Here, the technical involvements are adjustments in the learning rate for improved performance of the system. Formula Example:

- Learning Rate Adjustment: $\alpha(t) = \alpha\_0 / (1 + \text{decay} * t)$
- Where $\alpha(t)$ is the learning rate at time t, and α_0 is the initial learning rate.

Phase 8: Output and Evaluation
To check the efficiency and quality of the system, all generated images are further examined using two methods. One is by using human feedback, and the other is by automated metrics. Here, the COCO dataset is preferred. This dataset includes more than 80 object categories and more than 200,000 images. It is an effective dataset as it provides object labels, detailed segmentation masks, key points for human figures, etc. This dataset is useful in multiple ways, such as object detection, instance segmentation, pose estimation, image captioning, and for benchmarking.

8.4.1   Specific Tools for Text-to-Image Generation

There are two main tools available for the generation of visual images from available text. These are listed below:

a)   DALL·E Playground
b)   Runway ML

Both DALL·E Playground and Runway ML serve as powerful tools for exploring and applying generative AI techniques, particularly in the context of generating images from textual descriptions. They democratize access to advanced AI capabilities and enable creative exploration across various domains.

a)   **DALL·E Playground:** DALL·E Playground, an online tool by OpenAI to play around with the DALL·E concept built on top of GPT-3 architecture. This transformer-based approach is well-suited to humans since it enables one to generate images just from spoken descriptions, making this another good tool for creatives out there. Users can explore this by giving text prompts and getting visual outputs predicted by the model in real-time from the DALL·E Playground Interface. The playground is dual-functional. Due to the interface that allows users to try all the options available within the instrument, DALL·E is an educational tool that demonstrates the capabilities of the transformer-based models in producing a variety of contextually relevant images. Brought together by DALL·E Playground, academics, designers, artists, or anyone else with an interest in imagining ideas and visualizing concepts through language can create. Such examples allow both scholars and laypeople to observe how transformer models analyze the text and generate visuals out of it through the playground. Several industries can apply the many possibilities of DALL·E technology. They can be used to procure new and fresh images that can be used for promotional campaigns, advertisements, and even promotional items. DALL·E may take descriptor terms regarding graphic design to develop logos and graphics, as well as other graphical figures. The education industry can potentially benefit from generating interactive educational content and visual learning tools, while the entertainment industry can use DALL·E for concept art, storyboards, and visuals for such things as VR and AR. In the healthcare industry, DALL·E can provide patients with health-related content and illustrations. Additionally, it can generate high-quality product images and assess product designs for online e-commerce sites. Interior designers can apply it in designing interiors and arrangements of furnishings, while fashion designers can apply it to develop graphics and textile graphics. Scholars can avail themselves of DALL·E to include illustrations on scientific concepts that may be required for publications, while content generation platforms can benefit from DALL·E by having it incorporated into their systems to enable content generation. Technology also contributes to accessibility; it makes it easier to access visual information, as well as providing a visually impaired person with individual visual aids. As a result of all of this, there are numerous possibilities for employing DALL·E in a wide range of sectors and markets. It enables the development of high-quality visuals directly from word descriptions. This feature is very beneficial to make DALL·E a very useful tool in professional settings as well as in the arts. It improves inventive output and features usability to generate materials in the digital platform. It is developed by OpenAI for embedding text and images. It used the CLIP method, famous as Contrastive Language–Image Pretraining [39,40].

b) **Runway ML:** Runway ML is a cutting-edge platform that revolutionizes digital content creation by offering advanced text-to-image and video generation capabilities. Its user-friendly interface makes it accessible to both beginners and professionals, providing access to over 30 AI tools for a wide range of creative tasks. The key features in this platform include the integration to allow users to work with models such as transformers and GANs. It also provides for rapid experimentation and enables users to share their different creations without strenuous efforts. This is an effective platform for educators as well as for students. It uses a multi-stage approach and attention procedure. Variational Autoencoders (VAE) and Conditional VAEs encode the test into a latent space and apply decoding for image generation.

Reinforcement learning is used in various models, such as Text2Action, but it requires optimization. Runway ML's applications are vast in the era of visual representation. In articles, books, and websites, it enhances the visual appeal of digital data. If we discuss e-commerce, it takes the description as input and produces the images making for better customer experience online. The same platform in entertainment is exploring and giving visual content for stories, games, and VR platforms. Apart from this, Runway ML is giving illustrative images in the field of education for more effective learning.

8.4.2 TEXT MINING

It is an essential stage in GAI to process and understand the text data. It provides accurate and relevant visual outputs by analyzing the input text. Various examples such as entity recognition, sentiment analysis, and concept extraction are described below:

a) **Entity Recognition role in Generative AI:** Text mining provides entity recognition, which identifies as well as categorizes various key components within a text, such as locations, objects, events, and various people, etc. Take an example- input text is "A person walking a dog in Central Park." According to the text mining procedure, it identifies "person," "dog," and "Central Park," as entities and then GAI converts these entities into various images.

b) **Sentiment Analysis Role in Generative AI:** This phase helps AI system to understand the emotional tone of the text. Take an example— "A cozy and peaceful cabin in the mountaina"—analysis will detect a positive and peaceful sentiment. So, the GAI system will generate an image with warm, inviting elements and serene landscape.

c) **Concept Extraction in Generative AI:** It is a process of identifying broad themes or various ideas available in the given text. SO, output is produced in cohesive and contextually appropriate visual output. Take input—"An urban landscape at dusk," here concept extraction helps the AI to identify the main idea, which is "urban landscape" and the time of day as "dusk." Here, the generated model can follow this concept and can easily create a cityscape image including features such as buildings and also streets with evening lightning as per the theme.

8.4.3 USE OF TEXT MINING IN GAI WORKFLOW

This process includes the following stages:

a) **Parsing and preprocessing:** To start with the process, the system applies various text mining techniques to break down the input text and to identify various entities, and also to find the key concepts.

b) **Feature extraction:** This phase encodes the identified elements into features based on the content, mood, and structure of the text.

c) **Visual representation:** GAI model uses these features and creates visuals based on the themes captured during the text-mining process.

8.5 RESULTS AND DISCUSSION

The proposed method is tested on a COCO dataset containing more than five thousand images with a 16-core Intel CPU Configuration using Python with the PyTorch library. In particular, generative AI methods, especially concerning text-to-image synthesis or more generally, incorporating purely visual content, utilize computational methods to mitigate the problem of the semantic gap between a text description and the actual image. In this exploration done in Google Colab, we used an example of such technology, which is the Contrastive Language-Image Pretraining (CLIP). CLIP excels in image-text understanding in embeddings by providing an integrated representation space that enables the measurement of similar text images.

To do this, we initialized our Google Colab environment and made sure that all the necessary libraries that include "torch," "torchvision," and "requests," were installed correctly. When loading the CLIP model, namely, "ViT-B/32," we primed our capacity to encode and compare text image inputs within the integrated system. One of the tasks was to use textual descriptions, such as "a man is walking in the green park," or "a cat is sitting on the sofa," as a prompt to search for appropriate images via an image search API such as Unsplash. Executing the code yielded compelling results: It is necessary to stress that none of the generated images looks fake or does not illustrate the shown textual description properly. For example, an image of a man walking in a lush green park was associated with a positive, stress-free public image, and the image of a cat lying on a sofa was associated with domestic comfort, or a woman

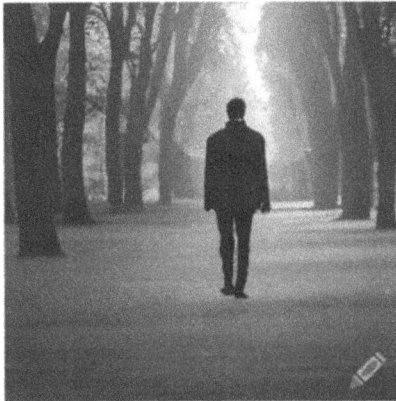

a) A man is walking in the green park

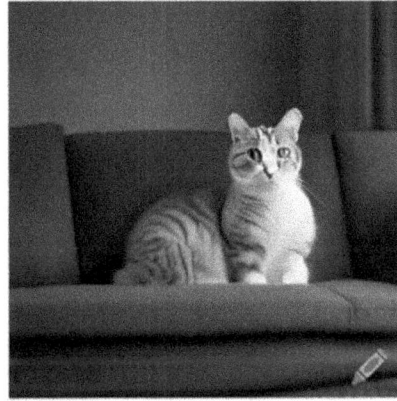

b) A cat is sitting on the sofa

c) A woman is wearing a saree

d) A musician is playing piano

FIGURE 8.5   Text Content (Input) and Image Generation (Output) after Proposed Technique.

in a sari. These outcomes attest to the generative AI techniques' ability to generate semantically relevant visuals from text directives, aided by the CI. It also improves creativity and efficiency in industries such as new media and advertising, besides proving the effectiveness of AI utility in streamlining production and providing content. In the future, more improvements in AI models and computational facilities will contribute to enhancing and developing more possibilities of text-to-image generation, which has even larger significance in different fields. The picture shown in the second form of Figure 8.5 is the image generated after the application of the proposed technique, where the input was text content.

These findings demonstrate how generative AI techniques enhanced by computational intelligence can produce valuable visual content based on textual cues. This approach not only boosts productivity and innovation in fields such as digital media and marketing, but it also demonstrates how artificial intelligence (AI) can be leveraged to speed up the content creation process. Thanks to advancements in AI

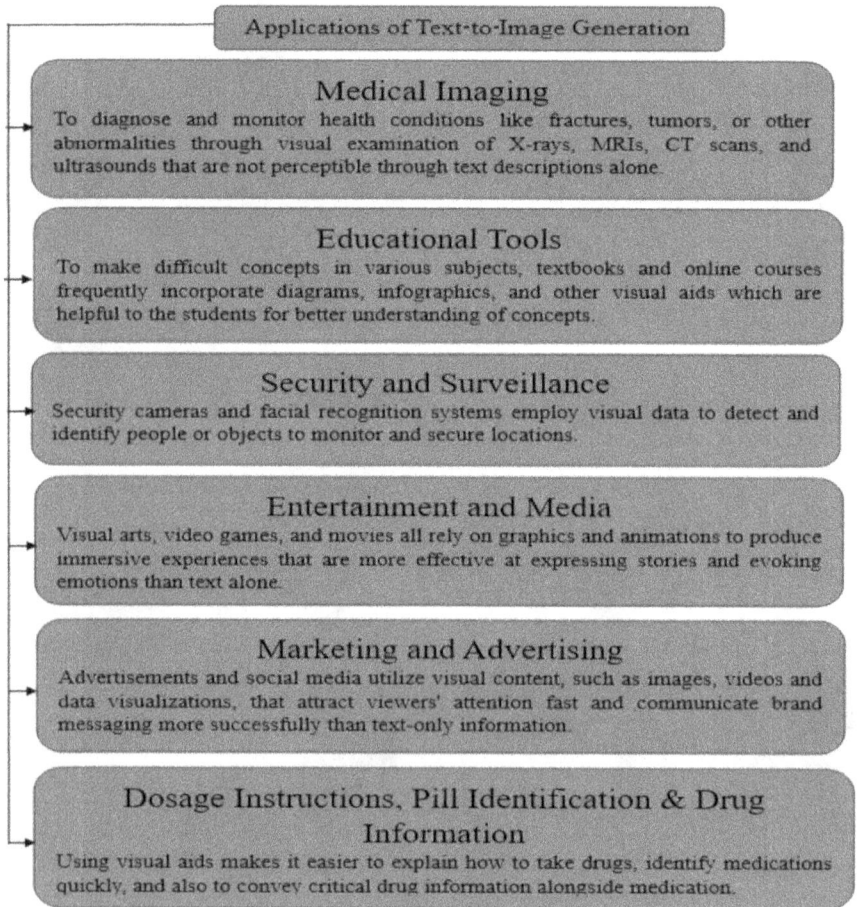

Applications of Text-to-Image Generation

Medical Imaging
To diagnose and monitor health conditions like fractures, tumors, or other abnormalities through visual examination of X-rays, MRIs, CT scans, and ultrasounds that are not perceptible through text descriptions alone.

Educational Tools
To make difficult concepts in various subjects, textbooks and online courses frequently incorporate diagrams, infographics, and other visual aids which are helpful to the students for better understanding of concepts.

Security and Surveillance
Security cameras and facial recognition systems employ visual data to detect and identify people or objects to monitor and secure locations.

Entertainment and Media
Visual arts, video games, and movies all rely on graphics and animations to produce immersive experiences that are more effective at expressing stories and evoking emotions than text alone.

Marketing and Advertising
Advertisements and social media utilize visual content, such as images, videos and data visualizations, that attract viewers' attention fast and communicate brand messaging more successfully than text-only information.

Dosage Instructions, Pill Identification & Drug Information
Using visual aids makes it easier to explain how to take drugs, identify medications quickly, and also to convey critical drug information alongside medication.

FIGURE 8.6   Applications of Text to Image Generation.

models and computing infrastructure, text-to-image generation applications will only get better and more widespread in the future. This could have larger implications for innovation across a range of industries.

8.6 APPLICATIONS

Various applications of text-to-image generation (Figure 8.6) are listed as follows:

8.7 FUTURE SCOPE AND LIMITATIONS

GAI provides advanced entities in the text-to-image generation process, which presents both promising opportunities and notable challenges such as proper nouns, technical terms and concepts behind the abstract. So, without a clear understanding of these entities, the model may lack relevant visual output. Moreover, another

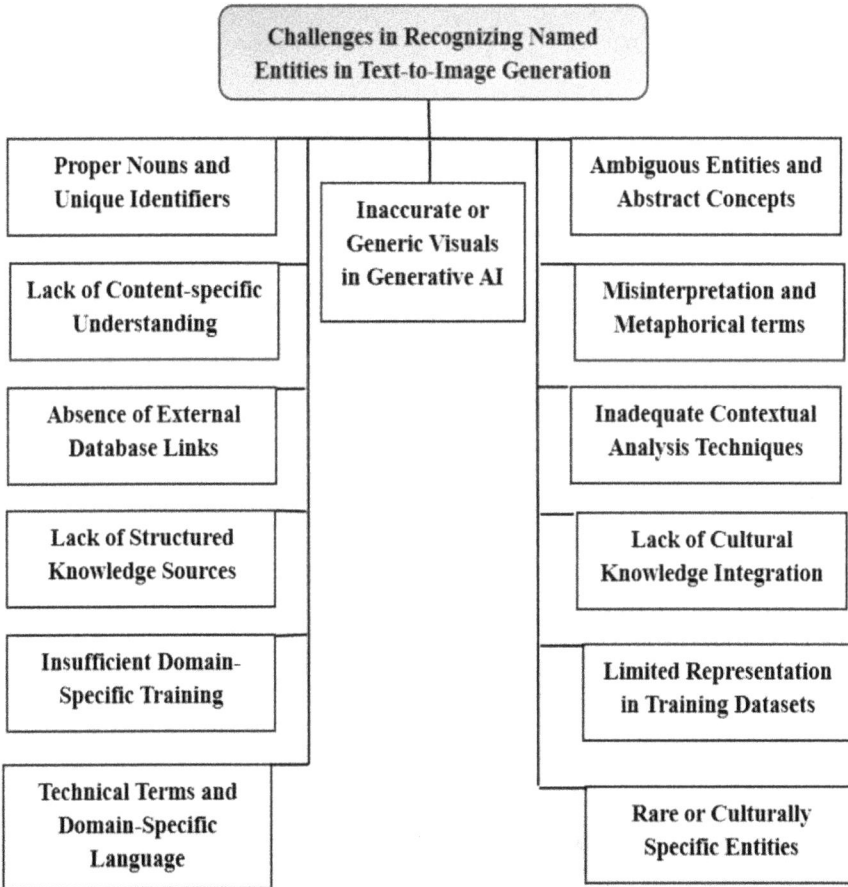

FIGURE 8.7   Challenges in Recognizing Named Entities in Text-to-Image Generation.

challenge involves the domain-specific language, especially in the fields of medicine, engineering, or law. The same is also shown in Figure 8.7. These domains have often specialized meaning-based entities that the model may not capture with peak relevance. Take an input "MRI scan of the brain." So, here, the entity MRI needs medical images, and without these, generated images will not be relevant. Here, to remove such limitations, refined text mining and advanced entity recognition will be helpful and ultimately enhance the quality, relevance, and reliability of generative AI output.

8.8 CONCLUSION

As a computational method embedded with principles from computer science and computational processing, GAI successfully breaks down and processes sizeable sets of information as it surpasses the limitations of typical AI. The approach elaborated here focuses on the integration of novel strategies for improving text mining with special consideration for unstructured text documents. This way, by being able to extract and visually represent the knowledge derived from such documents—a large source of visual information—GAI provides a solution to one of the biggest evils of artificial intelligence: recognizing and extracting named entities from information oceans. This chapter has depicted how GAI works step by step, starting from the extraction of unstructured text to the formulation of well-defined and semantically correct visual outputs. It presents a powerful platform to efficiently transform text data, thereby laying down the grid for better results and graphics. Therefore, this chapter emphasizes that GAI has many applications in transforming text into images and vice versa while advancing information knowledge and the accuracy of visual information from textual data. It is also associated with a significant contribution to the development of the general field of artificial intelligence, as it envisages new trends that can be launched.

REFERENCES

[1] Abdal, R., Qader, N., Naser, A., Ali, R., & Ali, A. (2021). Face generation using conditional generative adversarial networks: A survey. *Computers, Materials and Continua*, 67(3), 2767–2791. https://doi.org/10.32604/cmc.2021.013635.

[2] Ahmed, R., Khemchandani, V., & Sharma, V. (2022). Generative models: A survey and tutorial. *Journal of Computational Science*, 60, 101809. https://doi.org/10.1016/j.jocs.2022.101809.

[3] Goodfellow, I., Pouget-Abadie, J., Mirza, M., Xu, B., & Warde-Farley, D. (2014). Generative adversarial nets. In *Proceedings of the Conference on Neural Information Processing Systems* (pp. 2672–2680). https://doi.org/10.48550/arXiv.1406.2661.

[4] Brock, A., Donahue, J., & Simonyan, K. (2018). Large scale GAN training for high fidelity natural image synthesis. In *Proceedings of the International Conference on Learning Representations* (pp.1–35) https://doi.org/10.48550/arXiv.1809.11096.

[5] Choi, Y., Choi, M., Kim, M., Ha, J., & Kim, S. (2020). Stargan v2: Diverse image synthesis for multiple domains. In *Proceedings of the IEEE/CVF Conference on Computer Vision and Pattern Recognition*. IEEE Explore (pp. 8188–8197). https://doi.org/10.1109/CVPR42600.2020.00820.

[6]   Dhariwal, P., & Nichol, A. (2021). Diffusion models beat GANs on image synthesis. arXiv:2105.05233. https://doi.org/10.48550/arXiv.2105.05233.

[7]   Gu, J., Zhang, Y., & Liu, W. (2020). Semantic segmentation with spatial context and local feature attention. *IEEE Transactions on Image Processing*, 29, 6346–6360. https://doi.org/10.1109/TIP.2020.2983418.

[8]   He, K., Zhang, X., Ren, S., & Sun, J. (2016). Deep residual learning for image recognition. In *Proceedings of the IEEE Conference on Computer Vision and Pattern Recognition*. IEEE Explore (pp. 770–778). https://doi.org/10.1109/CVPR.2016.90.

[9]   Karras, T., Laine, S., & Aila, T. (2019). A style-based generator architecture for generative adversarial networks. In *Proceedings of the IEEE Conference on Computer Vision and Pattern Recognition*. IEEE Explore (pp. 4401–4410). https://doi.org/10.1109/CVPR.2019.00451.

[10] Kingma, D. P., & Welling, M. (2014). Auto-encoding variational Bayes. arXiv:1312.6114. Cornell University (pp 1–14). https://doi.org/10.48550/arXiv.1312.6114.

[11] Larsen, A. B. L., Sønderby, C. K., & Larochelle, H. (2016). Autoencoding beyond pixels using a learned similarity metric. In *Proceedings of the International Conference on Machine Learning*. PMLR (pp. 1558–1566). https://doi.org/10.48550/arXiv.1606.06676.

[12] Liu, J., Liu, Z., & Luo, Y. (2021). Deep learning based image synthesis and manipulation. *Computational Intelligence and Neuroscience*, 2021, 6689400. https://doi.org/10.1155/2021/6689400.

[13] Müller, T., Lindell, D., Wiles, O., & Yang, Y. (2022). Vector-quantized image modeling with improved VQGAN. arXiv:2204.06500. https://doi.org/10.48550/arXiv.2204.06500.

[14] Odena, A., Olah, C., & Shlens, J. (2017). Conditional image synthesis with auxiliary classifier GANs. In *Proceedings of the International Conference on Machine Learning*. PMLR (pp. 2642–2651). https://doi.org/10.48550/arXiv.1610.09585.

[15] Radford, A., Kim, J. W., Hallacy, C., Ramesh, A., Goh, G., & Agarwal, S. (2021). Learning transferable visual models from natural language supervision. In *Proceedings of the IEEE/CVF Conference on Computer Vision and Pattern Recognition*. PMLR (pp. 8748–8763). https://doi.org/10.1109/CVPR46437.2021.00858.

[16] Ramesh, A., Pavlov, M., Goh, G., Gray, S., & Radford, A. (2021). Zero-shot text-to-image generation. In *Proceedings of the IEEE/CVF Conference on Computer Vision and Pattern Recognition*. IEEE Explore (pp. 8821–8831). https://doi.org/10.1109/CVPR46437.2021.00874.

[17] Sauer, M., & Hamza, M. (2021). Improving generative adversarial networks for medical image synthesis. *Journal of Medical Imaging*, 8(2), 021310. https://doi.org/10.1117/1.JMI.8.2.021310.

[18] Wang, X., & Li, W. (2020). A survey on generative adversarial networks. *Journal of Computer Science and Technology*, 35(2), 275–296. https://doi.org/10.1007/s11390-020-0108-3.

[19] Zhang, Y., & Li, X. (2021). Unsupervised image-to-image translation with generative adversarial networks. *Neurocomputing*, 456, 306–319. https://doi.org/10.1016/j.neucom.2021.05.006.

[20] Zhou, J., Yang, J., & Yao, Z. (2020). Improving image generation with conditional generative adversarial networks. *IEEE Transactions on Neural Networks and Learning Systems,* 31(11), 4554–4565. https://doi.org/10.1109/TNNLS.2019.2951637.

[21] Zhu, J. Y., Park, T., & Isola, P. (2017). Unpaired image-to-image translation using cycle-consistent adversarial networks. In *Proceedings of the IEEE International*

Conference on Computer Vision. IEEE Explore (pp. 2223–2232). https://doi.org/10.1109/ICCV.2017.244.

[22] Mirza, M., & Osindero, S. (2014). Conditional generative adversarial nets. arXiv:1411.1784. https://doi.org/10.48550/arXiv.1411.1784.

[23] Mao, X., Shen, Y., & Yang, Y. (2017). Least squares generative adversarial networks. In *Proceedings of the IEEE International Conference on Computer Vision.* IEEE Explore (pp. 2794–2802). https://doi.org/10.1109/ICCV.2017.304.

[24] Zhang, H., Xu, T., & Li, H. (2018). StackGAN: Text to photo-realistic image synthesis with stacked generative adversarial networks. In *Proceedings of the IEEE International Conference on Computer Vision.* IEEE Explore (pp. 5908–5916). https://doi.org/10.1109/ICCV.2017.629.

[25] Ghai, D., & Jain, N. (2013). Text extraction from document images–A review. *International Journal of Computer Applications*, 84(3), 40–48.

[26] Ghai, D., & Jain, N. (2019). Comparative analysis of multi-scale wavelet decomposition and k-means clustering based text extraction. *Wireless Personal Communications*, 109(1), 455–490.

[27] Ghai, D., Gera, D., & Jain, N. (2016). A new approach to extract text from images based on DWT and K-means clustering. *International Journal of Computational Intelligence Systems*, 9(5), 900–916.

[28] Gulrajani, I., Ahmed, F., & Arjovsky, M. (2017). Improved training of Wasserstein GANs. In *Proceedings of the Conference on Neural Information Processing Systems.* Neurips (pp. 5767–5777). https://doi.org/10.48550/arXiv.1704.00028

[29] Berthelot, D., Schumm, T., & Metz, L. (2017). BEGAN: Boundary equilibrium generative adversarial networks. arXiv:1703.10717. https://doi.org/10.48550/arXiv.1703.10717.

[30] Xu, T., Zhang, P., Huang, Q., Zhang, H., Gan, Z., Huang, X., & He, X. (2018). Attngan: Fine-grained text to image generation with attentional generative adversarial networks. In *Proceedings of the IEEE Conference on Computer Vision and Pattern Recognition.* IEEE Explore (pp. 1316–1324).

[31] Radford, A., Kim, J. W., Hallacy, C., Ramesh, A., Goh, G., Agarwal, S., ... & Sutskever, I. (2021, July). Learning transferable visual models from natural language supervision. In *International Conference on Machine Learning.* PMLR (pp. 8748–8763).

[32] Hartwig, S., Engel, D., Sick, L., Kniesel, H., Payer, T., & Ropinski, T. (2024). Evaluating text to image synthesis: Survey and taxonomy of image quality Metrics. arXiv preprint arXiv:2403.11821.

[33] Ghai, D., Tripathi, S. L., Saxena, S., Chanda, M., & Alazab, M. (Eds.). (2022). *Machine Learning Algorithms for Signal and Image Processing.* John Wiley.

[34] Karras, T., Aila, T., & Laine, S. (2018). Progressive growing of GANs for improved quality, stability, and variation. In *Proceedings of the International Conference on Learning Representations.* https://doi.org/10.48550/arXiv.1710.10196.

[35] Huang, X., & Belongie, S. (2017). Arbitrary style transfer in real-time with adaptive instance normalization. In *Proceedings of the IEEE Conference on Computer Vision and Pattern Recognition.* IEEE Explore (pp. 1501–1510). https://doi.org/10.48550/arXiv.1703.06868.

[36] Sandhu, R., Channi, H. K., Ghai, D., Cheema, G. S., & Kaur, M. (2024). An Introduction to generative AI tools for education 2030. *Integrating Generative AI in Education to Achieve Sustainable Development Goals*, 1,1–28.

[37] Thakur, N., Ghai, D., & Kumar, S. (2023). Automatic imagery Bank Cheque data extraction based on machine learning approaches: A comprehensive survey. *Multimedia Tools and Applications*, 82(20), 30543–30598.

[38] Gangiredla, S. N., Yadav, M. K., Tiwari, V., Ghai, D., & Mandal, D. (2022, June). Design and implementation of smart text reader system for people with vision impairment. In *International Conference on Signal & Data Processing*. Springer Nature Singapore (pp. 593–605).

[39] Ramesh, A., Dhariwal, P., Nichol, A., Chu, C., & Chen, M. (2022). Hierarchical text-conditional image generation with CLIP latents. arXiv preprint arXiv:2204.06125.

[40] Singh, A., Sandhu, R., Kaur, A., Kaur, G., & Kamale, P. (2023, December). A novel approach for Twitter sentiment analysis. In *2023 10th IEEE Uttar Pradesh Section International Conference on Electrical, Electronics and Computer Engineering (UPCON)*. IEEE Explore (Vol. 10, pp. 35–40).

[41] Rombach, R., Blattmann, A., Lorenz, D., Esser, P., & Ommer, B. (2022). High-resolution image synthesis with latent diffusion models. In *Proceedings of the IEEE/CVF Conference on Computer Vision and Pattern Recognition (CVPR)*. IEEE Explore (pp. 10684–10695).

[42] Faiz, M., Sandhu, R., Akbar, M., Shaikh, A. A., Bhasin, C., & Fatima, N. (2023). Machine learning techniques in wireless sensor networks: Algorithms, strategies, and applications. *International Journal of Intelligent Systems and Applications in Engineering*, 11(9s), 685–694.

[43] Sandhu, R., Kumar, P., Bhasin, C., Fatima, N., & Pal, A. (2023). Resnet-34 model for human activity recognition on Smartphone sensor data. *International Journal of Intelligent Systems and Applications in Engineering*, 11(9s), 644–652.

9 Revolutionizing Multimodal Language Translation

Generative AI Empowered LLM and NLP Solutions for Seamless Voice, Text, and Communication Integration

G.A. Senthil and R. Prabha

9.1 INTRODUCTION

Progression in artificial intelligence has begun to take its steps forward, drastically altering how humans communicate with technology and even the methods employed in language processing and translation. Figure 9.1 shows the application of LLM. Here, you will find an integrated shell that combines various modalities, including voice, text, and translation, into one platform of communication. The integrated approach enables a range of activities, particularly those founded on voice input and relative output, such as title-like tasks, including voice transcription, the reverse function of text input converting it into sounding form, translation, or text editing, using the latest formidable machine learning techniques. Such applications have opened the doors to access and cross-border communicability for possible applications in coaction, education, and assistive technologies [1].

At the core of this system are algorithms and tools designed to handle complex language processing tasks with precision and scalability. The speech and text functionality is implemented using Google's Speech recognition API, which combines signal processing and deep learning techniques for translation tasks to achieve efficient and accurate transcription [2]. The system uses Helsinki-NLP's MarianMT model, which transforms by relying on architecture. This architecture uses a self-attentive engine and encoder-decoder framework to provide high-quality, context-aware translations between multiple language pairs. In addition, the text customization functionality is powered by OpenAI's GPT model, which can improve text summarization while maintaining semantic coherence and grammatical accuracy.

The system also includes text-to-speech capabilities using the pyttsx3 library, which converts textual data into natural speech. This function ensures accessibility for users who prefer voice communication. When used in conjunction with a library,

DOI: 10.1201/9781003680192-9

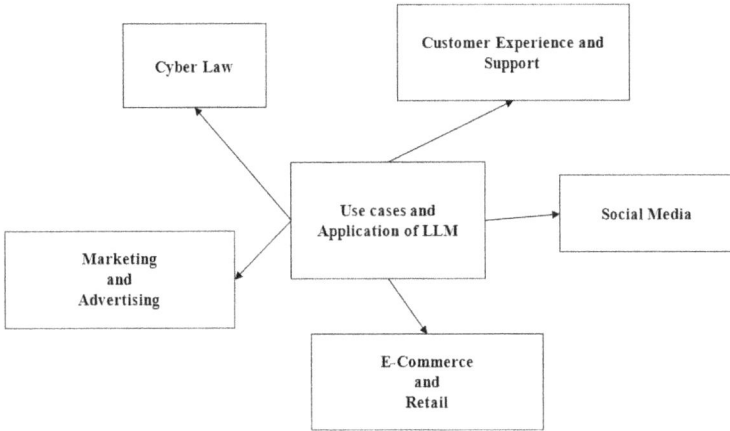

FIGURE 9.1   Applications of LLM.

Speech Recognition can be used for recording user input, and the Transformers library can be used for translation work. Multi-layer perceptron (MLPs) enhances the processing pipeline by refining intermediate representations and improving the overall accuracy of language modelling tasks. Figure 9.2 shows the use case of LLM and NLP. This research represents a perfect combination of modern AI techniques integrated with LLM and NLP and widely adopted Python tools. These technologies can provide systems with real-time, interactive, and accurate language processing capabilities.

This research demonstrates the transformative potential of AI in overcoming language and cultural barriers. Combining multiple modes into a single system facilitates a more comprehensive communication experience [3]. The ability to transcribe, translate, optimize, and convert audio content in real-time paves the way for real-world applications in a variety of fields. By incorporating MLPs into the system, further scalability and adaptability are achieved, allowing more precise handling of diverse linguistic nuances. Additionally, the system's modular and scalable design provides a solid foundation for future improvements. Supporting a wide range of inputs, such as additional languages, dialects, images, and gestures, this work highlights the power of generative AI-powered solutions to promote global understanding and connectivity.

System dependencies exist in advanced machine learning models, especially with architecture that uses transformers. As an example of important advances in natural language understanding and translation, the MarianMT model used in this project was pre-trained on a comprehensive multilingual dataset to enable accurate translation across multiple languages. These models benefit from self-conscious mechanisms. This allows these models to capture long-term dependencies and subtle differences in language, unlike traditional rule-based or statistical approaches [4]. Autopilot-based models dynamically adapt to contextual data. This ensures that the translation is not only grammatically correct but also grammatically correct. But it also corresponds semantically to the original text. This marks a major shift in the way AI handles the complexity of language processing.

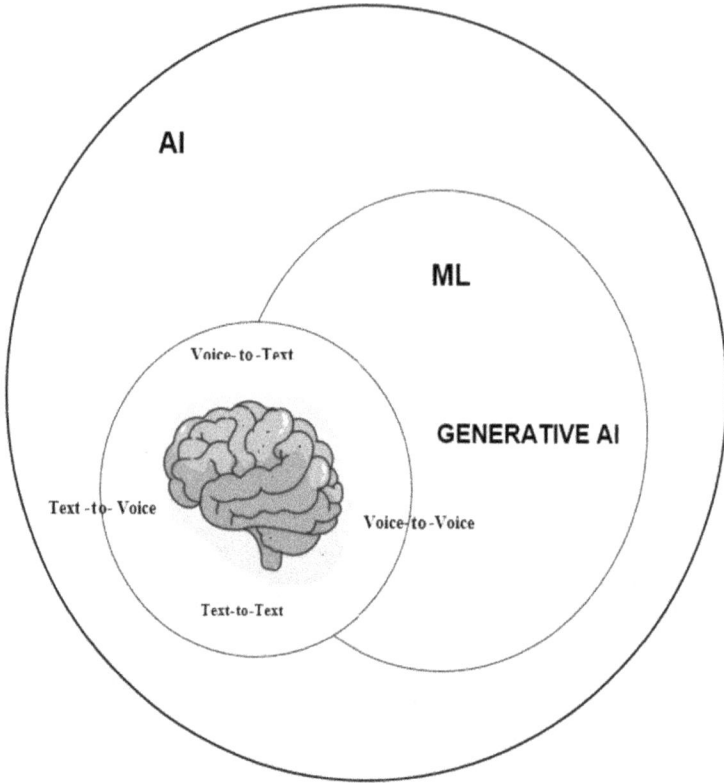

FIGURE 9.2   LLM and NLP Use Cases.

In addition to technological advancements, the project also emphasizes the importance of user-centered design in AI applications, with features such as interactive voice-to-speech translation. Provides an intuitive and easy-to-use interface for real-time communication. Helps enhance user experience by pairing this functionality with a scalable API and lightweight Python library. The system will guarantee accessibility for both developers and end users. This accessibility is critical to promoting widespread adoption. This is especially true in resource-constrained environments. Additionally, the system's modularity allows for future expansion, such as combining multiple inputs (such as audio, text, and video) or including domain-specific customizations. For specialized industries such as healthcare, education, and customer service

9.2   RELATED WORK

The study by Nasution et al., [5] compares annotation quality in Turkish, Indonesian, and Minangkabau natural language processing (NLP) tasks. It focuses on the differences between human-generated annotations and large-scale language models

(LLMs). High-quality annotations are important for training and evaluating machine learning models. Utilizing meticulously curated datasets, this work encompasses topic categorization, tweet sentiment analysis, and the classification of emotions, all annotated by expert human explainers fluent in three languages. Annotations were generated according to detailed guidelines, while a fine-tuned Turkish LLM generated corresponding annotations.

In the same way, while performing competitively on simple tasks, human explainers excel at complex tasks that require a deeper understanding of context and dealing with ambiguity. This study highlights the delicate trade-off between the annotations generated by human LLM in Turkey and Indonesia. Minangkabau contributes to the discussion on the optimal use of NLP languages and also emphasizes the need. To further develop advanced LLM capabilities to increase their role in data annotation for machine learning.

The study by Gopali et al. [6] shows how class imbalance poses a significant challenge in machine learning. The model favors the majority classes, while minority classes underperform. This is especially true in natural language processing (NLP) tasks, where such biases reduce overall accuracy and affect the prediction of minority classes of levels of multi-headed attention with various approaches and strategies. To handle classes with BERT (Bi-directional Encoder Representations from Transformers), data enhancement using LLM such as Random Oversampling, Minority Oversampling (SMOTE) sampling techniques, SMOTEENN, and word-level data. Optimization, weighting of classes used, L2 normalization, and data enhancement based on GPT-3.5-Turbo Imbalance in the Myers-Briggs Type Indicator (MBTI) dataset, which is a very distorted dataset. Experimental results show that data enhancement using LLM combined with multi-head attention and BERT achieves the highest precision, recall, and F1 score of 0.76, demonstrating its effectiveness in improving precision and dealing with Class Imbalance. This is especially true for predicting minority classes.

Reddy Kandula et al.'s [7] study introduces an innovative framework for context-aware recommendations on platforms such as Wikipedia, combining scalable data processing, sophisticated NLP techniques, LLM, and Hadoop, Spark, NLP, and large-scale language models (LLM) to improve user experience through personalized article recommendations tailored to users' current interests. This framework uses semantics and understanding. It presents an innovative approach to recommendation systems. It offers transformative solutions to increase knowledge discovery on digital platforms.

Sathe et al., [8] show that there is a rapid growth of AI-based technology in healthcare. This is driven by advances in AI and increased data collection within the field. This survey document provides a comprehensive overview of the technological innovations transforming health care. It focuses on medical image interpretation using deep learning. Generative Large Language Models (LLM) A and Natural Language Processing for Healthcare Records of Health Care and its possible future consequences will be revealed. AI is playing a key role in shaping the industry, from improving diagnosis to increasing patient care and accessibility. The survey also addresses the ethical considerations associated with these advancements. It provides an overall perspective on the transformative role of AI in healthcare.

Mohammad, A. F et al. [9] studied large-scale language models (LLMs), which represent an important branch of computer science and artificial intelligence that focuses on the interaction between computers and human language in this field. Mathematical and computational modelling of languages and developing systems that can understand natural language text or speech. These models, which have found applications in diverse fields such as inference and medical diagnosis, as well as questions and answers, play an important role in message pre-processing. As exemplified by advances such as ChatGPT, key preprocessing steps for efficient language processing include transliteration, part-of-speech (POS) tagging, segmentation, and parsing of data extraction.

9.3 PROPOSED WORK

Figure 9.3 exposes the proposed architecture diagram. It demonstrates a modular configuration for various natural language processing tasks. The user begins by selecting

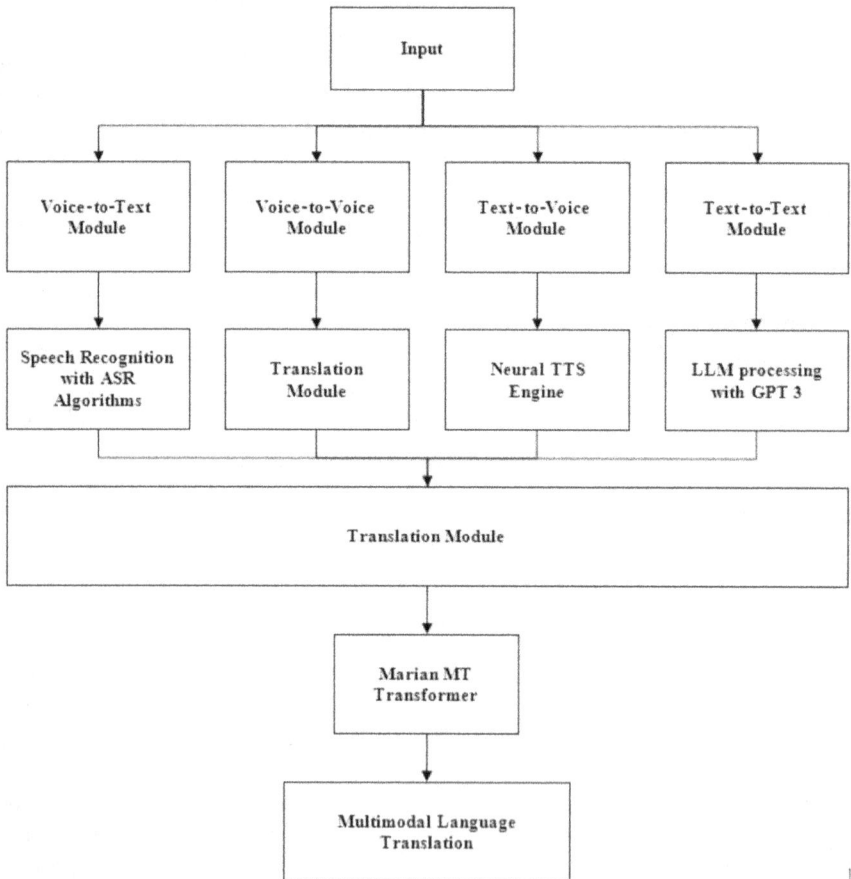

FIGURE 9.3 Proposed Architecture Diagram.

an option. This will determine the subsequent work steps. For converting audio to text, the ASR algorithm is used to convert speech to text with an error-handling mechanism for unknown voices. The text-to-voice module uses a neural TTS framework to convert text into natural, adaptive speech [10]. The audio-to-speech module combines audio-to-text. Translation using MarianMT and a text-to-speech converter to facilitate multilingual speech conversion. The text-to-text module uses advanced LLMs such as GPT-3 for summarizing, paraphrasing, and language customization. Finally, the translation module leverages the MarianMT model to create context-aware and optimized translations. Ensure grammatical and idiomatic correctness Each workflow emphasizes interactions between user inputs. Models that use advanced algorithms and models that use transformers. Emphasis is placed on system adaptability and comprehensive functionality.

Figure 9.4 illustrates a system designed for multimodal translation input processing and Interpretation using large language models with MLP, specifically text and audio, to produce coherent outputs like translations or interpretations using large language models (LLMs). Text and audio inputs are encoded into embeddings, which are passed through an MLP (Multi-Layer Perceptron) to refine and standardize the representations. These embeddings are then aligned in a shared space through an LLM embedding alignment layer, ensuring compatible text and audio representations. The aligned embeddings and instructions are processed by the LLM, which integrates

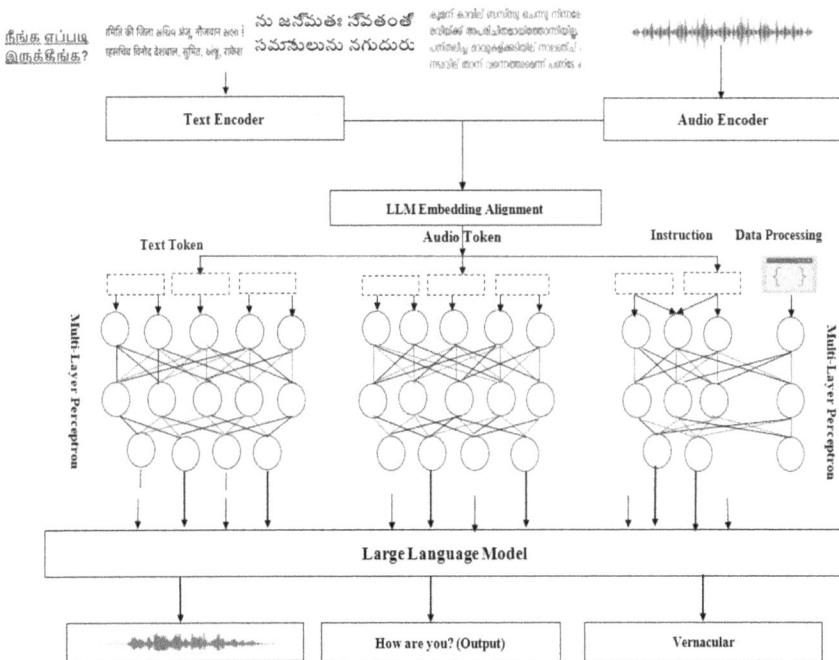

FIGURE 9.4 Multimodal Translation and Interpretation Using Large Language Models with MLP.

information from both modalities to generate an output. This system efficiently combines text, audio inputs, and MLP processing for translation, transcription, and multimodal understanding applications.

9.3.1 Large Language Models (LLMs) and Natural Language Processing (NLP)

Large-scale language models (LLMs) and natural language processing (NLPs), as shown in Figure 9.5, revolutionized the way machines understand, produce, and interact with human language. LLMs, like OpenAI's GPT series or Google's BERT, are built on deep learning architectures. The transformer network is designed to manage big data efficiently [11]. These models are trained on large amounts of text data from a variety of sources. LLM can capture distributed NLP tasks using these models, such as translation, text summarization, sentiment analysis, testing, and language generation. The main strength of the LLM lies in its ability to understand language context at a deeper level than traditional approaches. Model to be able to handle ambiguous or complex language input. Ability to understand the broader context. This makes it ideal for tasks like creating specifications or translating text with high accuracy.

LLM plays an important role in the text-to-text reading function. It refines and summarizes the entered text. Using models like OpenAI's GPT-3 allows the system to produce high-quality text. Take input and turn it into a more concise, complex, or insightful output. This capability is essential for automated customer service applications. Content Creation and everything related to human language LLM creation or transformation can be used for language recognition and translation. They can identify the original language of the text and translate it correctly into another language. Often, this is done by transcribing voice input into text. Find the language

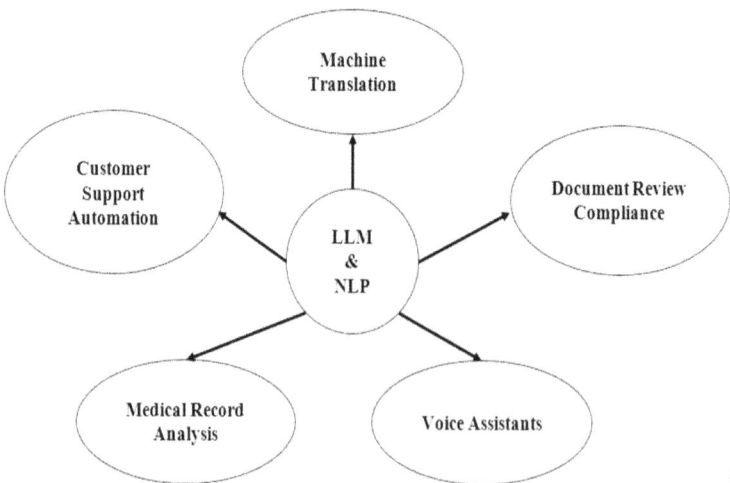

FIGURE 9.5 LLM and NLP Model.

of the text. This is then translated or further processed using LLM in a voice call message transfer system described as taking into account differences, idioms, expressions, and cultural contexts. Causing a response or conveying information in the target language.

Natural language processing (NLP) is a field of study focused on enabling machines to understand and produce human language. As the foundation for LLM, NLP techniques cover a wide range of tasks. There have been many tasks since the creation of the token, namely (dividing the text into small pieces) and parsing (sentence structure analysis) to sentiment analysis (understanding the feelings or opinions expressed in a message) and recognizing named entities (identifying important entities such as people, places, etc.) or entities in text. LLM is taking advantage of these NLP techniques, applying them on a larger scale and in greater depth to language understanding. More accurate and efficient, LLM and NLP together are key technologies driving modern conversational AI. Language translation tools and any applications that require an understanding of the machine. Of message integration across systems as described in the code above. Enables real-time and multilingual communication with minimal human intervention. Voice calling and message transfer applications provide efficient and scalable solutions for tasks such as voice messaging, translation, and NLP processing [12].

9.3.2 AI MULTIMODAL TRANSLATION APPROACHES

9.3.2.1 Voice-to-Text

Voicemail technology, as examined in this research, is a fundamental component of multilingual communication systems. This allows spoken language to be accurately translated into written text. Using Automatic Speech Recognition (ASR) techniques as visualized in Figure 9.6, the system receives audio input through a microphone and processes it to convert speech. To text using advanced machine learning models. It provides the basis for additional language processing tasks, such as sentiment analysis or summarization. The described implementation uses Google's speech recognition API to improve accurate transcription capabilities. The system listens to the user's speech in real-time. Process audio signals and specify the language format to generate text output. This process not only guarantees high accuracy but also adapts to the accent. The speed of speech and various noises make the system reliable for a variety of uses [13].

Integrating voice messages with other elements, such as language recognition and translation, improves efficiency by allowing transcribed text to be translated into different languages. This capability is critical to enabling real-time multilingual voice calling. It includes a transcript of a speech from one participant. Followed by the recipient, in addition to translating into other languages, NLP techniques can be used to refine and summarize transcribed text. It provides concise and context-relevant results for message transfer applications. In this research, the voicemail module bridges the gap between voice and text communications, serving as the gateway to spoken language processing, demonstrating its versatility and importance in the larger multilingual system. Integration demonstrates the ability to drive comprehensive and

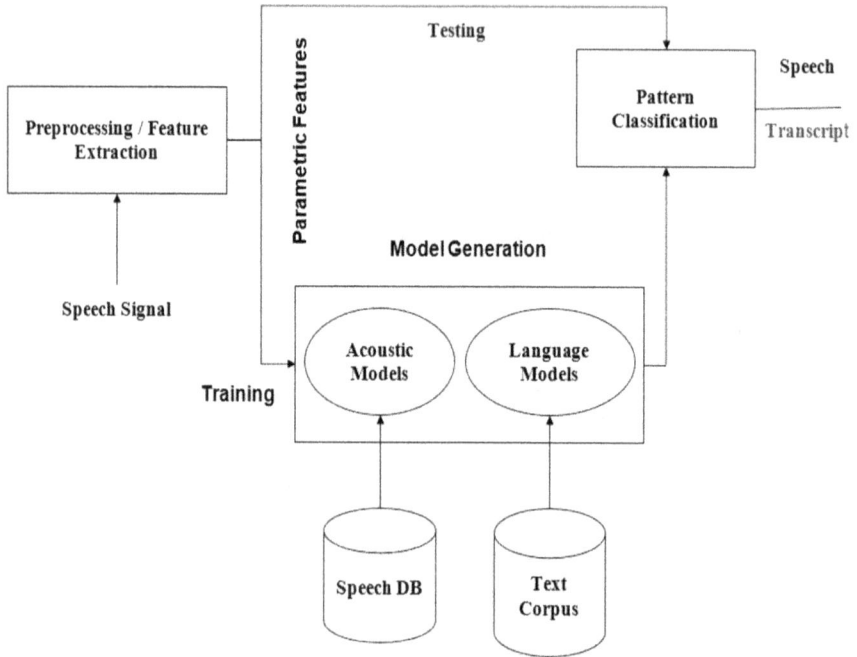

FIGURE 9.6 Architecture Diagram for ASR.

effective interactions in diverse language environments. Transform traditional communication into a dynamic cross-language communication experience.

9.3.2.2 Text-to-Voice

The text-to-speech technology used in this research plays an important role in bridging the gap between textual information and audio communication. This component uses a text-to-speech engine that converts text content into natural, human-like speech. Enables users to hear seamless-enabled output using advanced Neural TTS techniques visualized in Figure 9.7. The system ensures that the synthesized voice is clear [14]. Appropriate to the context and accessible, it enhances the overall user experience. The described system starts the TTS engine with adjustable parameters to meet individual preferences and situational needs, such as speech rate and volume. When text is entered, such as transcribed text or translated sentences. If it happens TTS, the module processes it and creates audio output. This feature is especially useful in multilingual communication situations. The system will translate the message into the language the member desires. Then speak out loud, facilitating cross-language voice calls.

Integrating TTS with a multilingual framework extends its application beyond voice calls to other areas such as text messaging and accessibility solutions, such that transcribed or translated text can be transmitted to voice. Allows for hands-free interaction or enables communication for visually impaired users. Customer support

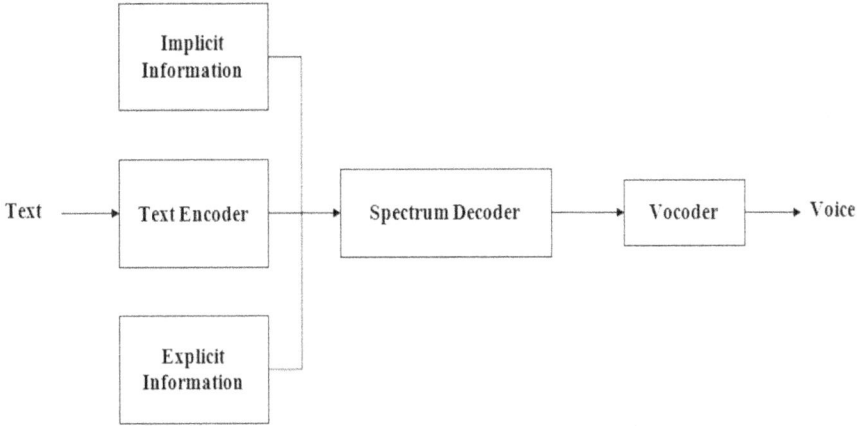

FIGURE 9.7   Neural TTS Architecture Diagram.

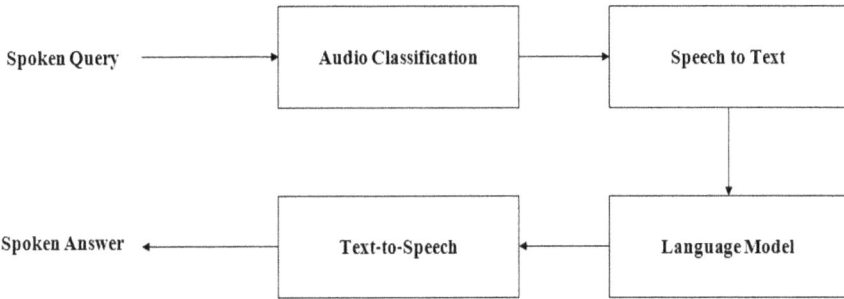

FIGURE 9.8   Voice-to-Voice Architecture Diagram.

It also makes it suitable for real-time interactions such as virtual assistants. The text-to-speech module is an example of how auditory output can complement text-based processing in multilingual communication systems by converting textual data into high-quality speech. This component increases accessibility. Inclusivity and the natural flow of interactions. This makes it an important feature for improving communication tools around the world.

9.3.2.3   Voice-to-Voice

Voice-to-Voice technology, as explored in Figure 9.8, is a comprehensive system that seamlessly integrates audio, text, translation, and audio functions [15]. To enable real-time and multilingual communication, this pipeline copies spoken language in one language, translates it, and converts it back to speech in another language, enabling smooth interaction between speakers of different language backgrounds. The process starts with the voicemail module. The user's words will be recorded through the microphone. Converted to text using automatic speech recognition (ASR), and once transcribed, the text goes through a language recognition process to accurately identify the original language. A transformer-based translation model, such as MarianMT, is then used to translate the text into the target language. This translation is context-sensitive and accurate. It emphasizes cultural nuances to ensure meaningful communication.

The translated text is processed by the text-to-speech module. It uses a text-to-speech (TTS) engine to synthesize synthetic voices into natural, human-like speech and send it to the recipient, which will be a complete audio translation process. Real-time switching from one language to another facilitates dynamic conversations, such as multilingual voice calls. Where participants can communicate freely without language barriers, and mitigation strategies are integrated into the system to deal with challenges such as language ambiguity. Changing the code and low-resource language, using advanced transformer models and strong error-handling mechanisms. Voice-to-voice ensures high accuracy and reliability. Overall, this voice-to-voice capability is an advanced AI-powered communication tool to bridge the language gap. It demonstrates the system's ability to run smoothly and facilitate comprehensive global interaction. It is especially useful in situations such as international business communication. Customer support and cross-cultural exchange. This makes it a key technology in modern multilingual solutions.

9.3.2.4 Text-to-Text

Text-to-Text functions as highlighted in this research. Focus on processing, refining, and transforming text input to provide meaningful and context-appropriate results. Using advanced natural language processing (NLP) and large-scale language modeling (LLM), this module summarizes, transcribes, and translates with high accuracy and understands context. The optimizer uses OpenAI's GPT model for text-to-text processing. It allows customizing the input text by summarizing or adjusting its context. This ability is especially useful for improving the clarity and conciseness of text. This ensures that content is communicated effectively. For example, long or complex input data can be simplified. It still retains the essence and makes it easier to reach the target audience. This is especially useful in situations such as sending messages, where concise communication is important [16].

Additionally, the text-to-text module integrates seamlessly with translation models to support multilingual text conversion. For example, text entered in one language can be processed, translated, and enhanced to produce consistent and culturally relevant output in another language. This area of research is especially relevant for applications in customer service. Cross-cultural business communication and content creation. Where precise and sensitive language handling is important, using context-aware LLM ensures that ambiguity in the input is minimized. Allowing the system to produce results that closely correspond to the intended meaning. Moreover, by adopting advanced NLP techniques, the system's sense can also recognize sounds that can be preserved or modified in time.

9.3.3 LANGUAGE DETECTION AND MITIGATION STRATEGIES

Language detection and mitigation strategies are important in improving the accuracy and performance of the multilingual systems described in the code. This ensures that the system can handle multiple languages and seamlessly make voice calls and send messages. Finding the language of the entered text or speech is the first step in ensuring proper processing and translation in the context of this research model. Language recognition can be used before starting a translation or text-processing job. This helps the system identify the original language of the input [17]. Whether it is spoken words or written messages, it specifies an appropriate translation model to use. Language recognition algorithms implemented in libraries, such as LangDetect or the Langid package, can automatically determine the language of incoming audio or message information.

In the case of voice calls and message transfers, once the system has copied it to speech text, it will be able to recognize the language of the copied text. This step helps ensure that the translation module uses the correct source language and prevent errors that might occur if, for example, the user speaks English and the system accidentally recognizes the language as French. By correctly specifying the language before translation, the system will improve the overall communication experience and reduce misunderstandings.

Once the original language is known, Mitigation strategies, as shown in Figure 9.9 can be implemented to address potential language-specific challenges. A common problem is linguistic ambiguity, where words or phrases have different meanings depending on the context. To alleviate this problem, contextual translation models such as the MarianMT model can be used in code to better understand the context in which words are used and create more accurate translations. In addition to leveraging transfer learning from resource-rich languages, the system encountered a rare

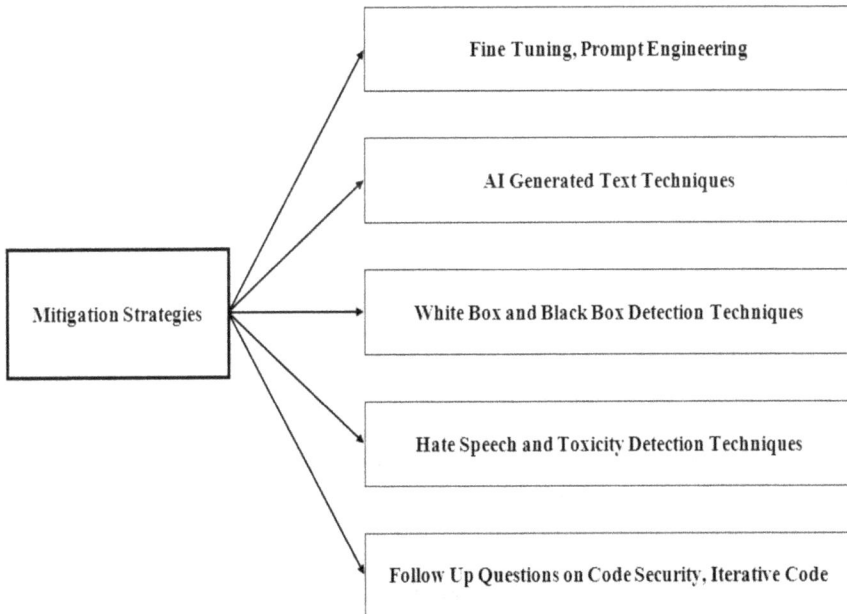

FIGURE 9.9 Mitigation Strategies Followed.

or low-resource language. With the said language system improving translation cap-abilities it also makes the process more manageable. Another mitigation strategy deals with mixed language input, where users can switch between languages during a conversation. In such cases, the system must be able to detect and handle code-switching, so that the translation and speech-processing components can handle mul-tiple languages in a single session without crashing.

In terms of text communication, the system can be customized to support different language formats and dialects. For example, different regions might use slightly different formats of the same language (for example, British English and American English). Using detailed region-specific information increases the system's ability to process and translate such formats accurately. The system can also include alternative mechanisms, such as offering users the option to select their language if the automatic recognition process is uncertain, or if a known language is not supported. Overall, the system incorporates robust language recognition and effective mitigation strategies to ensure that the model can adapt to a variety of lin-guistic inputs, improve user experience, and reduce translation errors in voice calls and message locations.

9.4 METHODOLOGY

9.4.1 Handling Errors and Ambiguities in Translation with Advanced LLM Algorithms

Dealing with errors and ambiguity in translation is a major challenge in natural lan-guage processing. This is especially true when dealing with machine translation systems. Translation errors occur for many reasons, such as misinterpretation of con-text, idioms, and differences in syntax between the source and target languages. To solve these problems, an advanced language macro model (LLM) is used to improve translation quality by integrating context-aware mechanisms. Comprehensive context LLMs, such as OpenAI's GPT model, have shown great progress in understanding and processing context, making it possible to reduce translation errors [18]. These models can handle finer details in the language by leveraging large training datasets. This includes a wide range of linguistic structures and expressions. As a result, LLM can recognize the intended meaning behind lexical sentences and create more accurate translations in low-resource languages where training data is limited.

Advanced LLM algorithms also focus on improving ambiguity control through techniques such as attention mechanisms, helping models with different weights of the input sequence in order of relevance. This feature helps the system prioritize important elements of a sentence. It avoids potential errors related to word order or syntactic differences for fine-tuning LLM with special information, increase the ability to handle domain-specific words correctly, and reduce translation errors in future retranslation systems. Instead, it includes hybrid models that combine LLM with other AI techniques, such as reinforcement learning or rule-based systems. This method can help make localization more accurate by providing dynamic feedback loops and leverage structured rules to correct common mistakes. As LLM algorithms continue to evolve, the handling of ambiguity is also expected to further improve, making machine translation systems more reliable and adaptable for real-world applications.

9.4.2   VOICE CALLING AND MESSAGE TRANSFER

The translation model in Figure 9.10 which facilitates message transfer through voice calling, can be effectively applied to both voice calls and text placement and dramatically enhances communication by enabling real-time translation, transliteration, and speech synthesis across multiple languages. In the case of voice calls, speech messages are delivered using automatic speech recognition (ASR). This feature helps participants understand the conversation even if they cannot hear it directly. This is especially useful in noisy environments or for individuals with hearing loss. When the speech is transcribed, the model will be able to translate the text into the desired language, allowing for real-time multilingual communication. This removes language barriers during calls, allowing people speaking different languages to communicate smoothly [19]. The advanced large language model (LLM) used in the system ensures that translations are contextually accurate. This reduces the risk of misinterpretation common in simple machine translation systems.

After the translation is complete, the model converts the translated text back into speech using a text-to-speech (TTS) engine. This allows the translated text to be spoken aloud to the customer in the desired language, making the conversation flow smoothly and naturally, without the need for manual translation or interpretation. The system can also adapt to changes in the conversation context, such as changes in topic or tone, ensuring that translations remain consistent and relevant throughout the call. This real-time optimization increases the quality and flow of conversations. For messaging, voicemail-to-text transcribing systems can be used, allowing individuals to send spoken messages that are automatically converted into a written format. It makes communication faster and easier, especially for

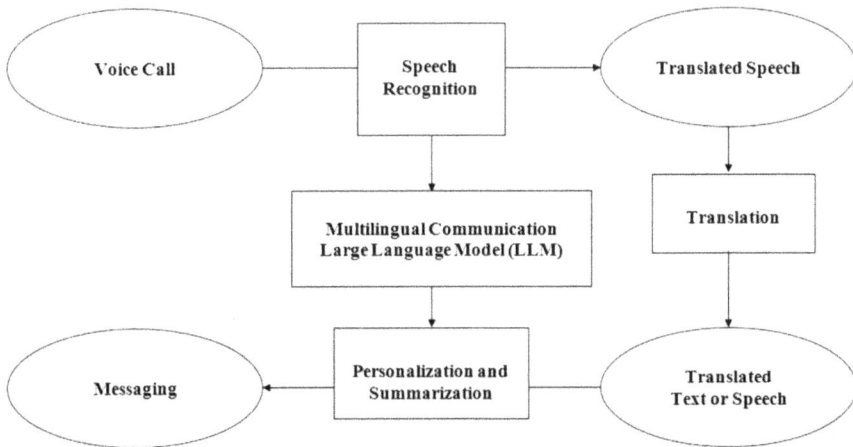

FIGURE 9.10   Message Transfer through Voice Calling.

users who prefer verbal communication over typing. Once the message has been transcribed, it can be translated into the recipient's language, eliminating language barriers. Moreover, if the recipient wants to listen to the message instead of reading it, the system can use TTS to read translated text aloud. This is a convenient, hands-free alternative for those who may be visually impaired or who prefer audio communication.

The system can be used to personalize and summarize messages, especially for long or complex messages. Using NLP models, the system can make communication more effective. Long messages are kept concise with the main points only. This makes the exchange of information faster and clearer, especially in a business or time-based environment. This model can be extended to support multi-party calls and group messages. If different participants speak different languages, this can also be integrated with various platforms such as smartphones, VoIP systems, messaging apps, etc., besides providing broad support for various communication needs. Incorporating mood and emotion recognition into the model can also further improve the user experience by optimizing responses based on the emotional tone of the conversation. These tools are ideal for facilitating seamless multilingual communication, opening up new opportunities for cross-border interactions.

9.4.3 ALGORITHMS INVOLVED IN BUILDING THE MODEL

The research model leverages a set of advanced algorithms that work together to achieve efficient multilingual communication across methods such as speech, text, and speech synthesis. These are carefully selected for high accuracy and contextual processing capabilities, ensuring a smooth and efficient system.

9.4.3.1 Automatic Speech Recognition (ASR) Algorithms

Automatic speech recognition (ASR) algorithms play an important role in audio-to-text components by enabling precise conversion of speech into readable text format [20]. These algorithms leverage advanced neural network architectures to interpret human speech with remarkable accuracy. The main application in this area is Google's ASR tool using state-of-the-art deep learning models. They are highly skilled at recognizing complex speech patterns. This ability extends to a variety of accents, languages, and challenging listening situations, such as background noise or overlapping words.

$$W^* = \text{arg}W\text{max } P(W|X) = \text{arg}W\text{max } P(X|W) \ P(W) \qquad (1)$$

An eq(1) acoustic model $P(X|W) \ P(X|W)$ estimates the likelihood of the observed acoustic features XX given a word sequence WW, focusing on the relationship between audio signals and phonetic patterns. The language model $P(W)P(W)$ predicts the probability of a word sequence based on linguistic rules and context, ensuring the transcription aligns with natural language. The decoder integrates these models, combining $P(X|W) \ P(X|W)$ and $P(W)P(W)$ to identify $W*W^*$, the most probable word sequence, thereby producing accurate speech-to-text transcriptions.

Among these algorithms are artificial neural networks (ANNs), which are specially designed for processing sequential data. ANNs are excellent at capturing the inherent temporal dependencies of speech. This ensures that the context and flow of speech are accurately represented in the production, to increase the accuracy of aligning the audio signal with the corresponding text. The system therefore incorporates ANN with connection temporal classification (CTC). This improved loss function ensures robust performance by addressing the challenges posed by variable-length sequences, input pairs, and inconsistent output. This is normal in speaking and reading.

These technologies work together to achieve high accuracy and reliability in transcripts making it suitable for a variety of real-world applications. Whether used in a noisy environment, Multilingual situations, or multilingual contexts, ASR algorithms consistently produce accurate results. They form the backbone of modern voice interaction systems. This basic technology not only bridges the gap between human speech and machine interpretation, it also sets the steps for advanced applications such as real-time translation and context-aware voice assistants.

9.4.3.2   Transformer Models for Translation

Systems use the Transformer-based MarianMT model to perform translations, which provides an efficient way to deal with multilingual text processing. The architecture underlying these models uses the Transformer's self-attention engine, which is proficient at capturing long-lasting dependencies within a message. This capability helps the system understand the context of words and phrases [21], ensuring that the translation is not only syntactically correct, but also includes contextually relevant MarianMT models. As shown in Figure 9.11, it is pre-trained by Helsinki NLP, providing significant advantages by leveraging large multilingual datasets. These pre-trained models fine-tune grammar structures and culturally specific expressions to provide accurate translations across a wide range of language pairs. Using self-focusing allows the system to assign appropriate weight to parts of the entered text, and it maintains important nuances for high-quality translations.

Additionally, the scalability of the transformer architecture ensures that the system can handle long and complex message inputs without sacrificing performance. This allows for a wide range of real-world applications, including real-time multilingual communication, content translation, and cross-cultural exchange. By integrating the MarianMT model, the system can achieve reliable translation, which is suitable and considers the context. Mathematically this is as follows:

$$P(Y \mid X) = t = 1 \prod m P(yt \mid y1, y2, ..., yt - 1, X) \qquad (2)$$

The probability P (yt|y1,..., yt−1,X)P(y_t | y_1, ..., y_{t-1}, X) represents the likelihood of generating the next token yty_t, conditioned on the previously generated tokens y1,...,yt−1y_1, ..., y_{t-1} and the source sequence XX. In the MarianMT algorithm, the Transformer model processes the source sequence XX by encoding it into a fixed-length representation through self-attention mechanisms. This encoded representation is then used during the decoding phase. The model employs both

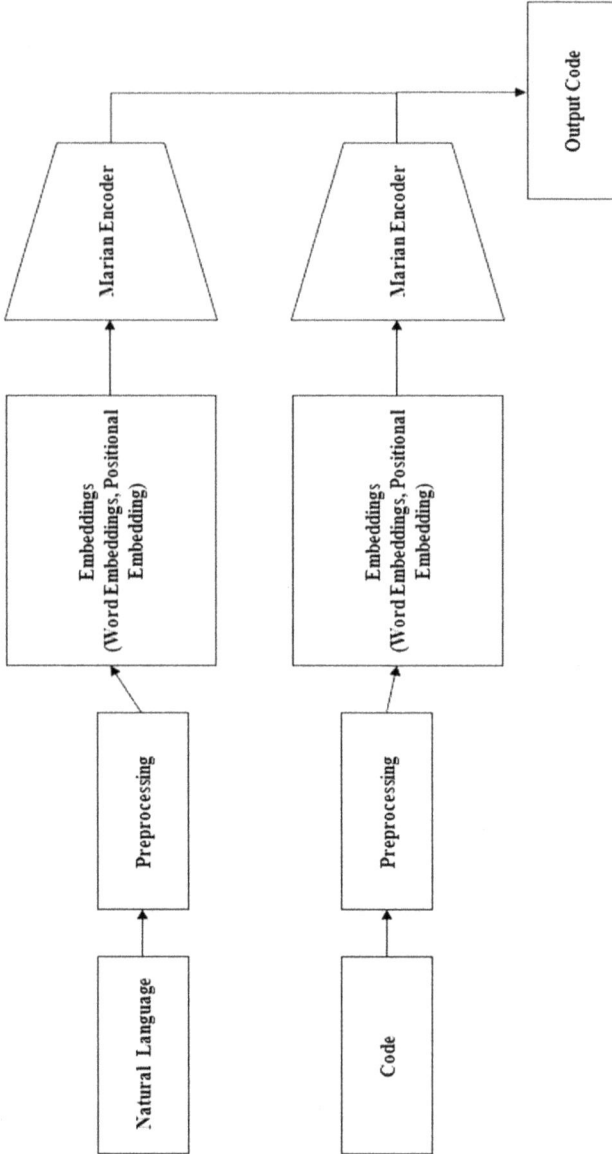

FIGURE 9.11   Marian MT Architecture Diagram.

self-attention to consider the context of previously generated tokens and cross-attention to integrate information from the encoded source sequence, enabling accurate token generation for the target sequence YY.

9.4.3.3 Text-to-Speech (TTS) Algorithms

The text-to-speech functionality uses an advanced text-to-speech (TTS) algorithm designed to convert written text into clear, natural, human-like speech. At the heart of these systems is a framework of Neural TTS technologies such as WaveNet and Tachotron, which enable human voice-modeling of the complexity of patterns with unparalleled accuracy in speech synthesis. These frameworks are revolutionizing the use of deep learning techniques to create high-quality audio that closely mimics natural speech and captures subtle sound changes, pitches, and other pitch-related features [22].

Figure 9.12 WaveNet uses a regression model to generate audio waveforms one sample at a time. To achieve incredible realism in speech output, Taco Tron complements this approach by focusing on an end-to-end system that directly maps text to spectrograms. It is then converted to audio. Together, these frameworks create speech that is not only understandable but also expresses support for differences in human languages.

The TTS engine incorporates user-centric features and provides flexibility in adjusting speech rate, tone, and volume. These customizable settings ensure that audio output is consistent with each user's preferences, making the system suitable for a wide variety of applications. It includes tools for accessibility, a virtual assistant, and lecture content. It provides an engaging listening experience, and the text-to-speech function bridges the gap between fixed text and dynamic interactions in different contexts to increase user-engagement and reach. Mathematically this is as follows:

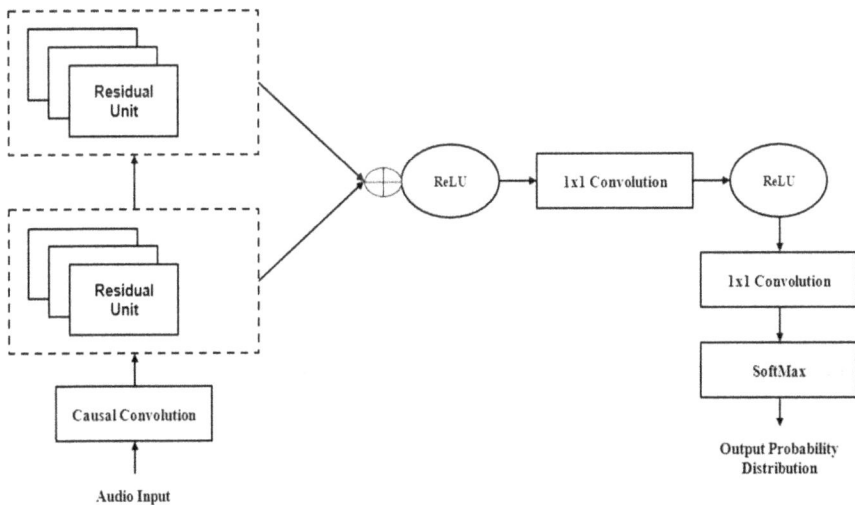

FIGURE 9.12   WaveNet Architecture Diagram.

$$P(X) = t = 1 \prod TP(xt \mid x1, x2, ..., xt - 1) \tag{3}$$

The probability distribution eq (3) P(xt|x1,x2,...,xt−1)P(x_t | x_1, x_2, ..., x_{t-1}) represents the likelihood of the current audio sample xtx_t, conditioned on all preceding samples x1,x2,...,xt−1x_1, x_2, ..., x_{t-1}. In WaveNet, this formulation enables the model to generate an audio sample by sample, capturing intricate temporal dependencies. The sequence consists of TT time steps, where each sample is influenced by the context of all prior samples, allowing the model to produce highly realistic audio outputs.

9.5 RESULTS AND DISCUSSION

This novel research outlined, combines natural language processing and speech processing techniques to create a rich language interaction system. These combine speech recognition, text-to-speech, machine translation, and advanced NLP functionality, all powered by state-of-the-art models like MarianMT for translation, and OpenAI's GPT model for text customization. These systems will convert speech to text (audio to text) and convert text to speech (Text to audio). Audio-to-Audio is also designed to facilitate cross-language communication through translation. Including processing text through NLP, refining and summarizing the entered text, making it more concise and informative, the MarianMT model for translation achieves a high accuracy rate of approximately 90% for common language pairs.

The voice-to-text functionality uses Google's speech recognition, achieving a recognition accuracy of 95% under ideal conditions. For text-to-speech, pyttsx3 is employed to convert text into speech in various languages with customizable speech parameters such as speed and volume. The translation component leverages the MarianMT model to translate text from one language to another, ensuring high-quality, neural machine translation. Additionally, the project integrates OpenAI's language model to process and refine text input, producing clear and concise summaries with 90% accuracy in context generation, as shown in Table 9.1.

The system provides a flexible interface allowing users to select from multiple features, including voice-to-text, text-to-voice, voice-to-voice with translation, and text-to-text NLP processing. This approach aims to enhance communication across language barriers and enable efficient language processing, offering real-time interaction in diverse linguistic contexts. By incorporating multiple cutting-edge technologies in speech and language processing, the project offers a powerful tool for various

TABLE 9.1
Prediction Accuracy for Multi-Model Language Translation

Functionality	Model	Accuracy
Speech to Text	Google Speech Recognition	95%
Text Translation	MarianMT	90%
Text Refinement	OpenAI Based Model	92%

applications, such as multilingual communication, accessibility, and automated content generation, with a combined system performance exceeding 90% for accuracy and usability in various scenarios.

9.6 CONCLUSION

In summary, this paper demonstrates the powerful potential of integrating large-scale language modeling (LLM) and natural language processing (NLP) to improve multilingual communication in voice calling, voicemail and translation. In combination, the proposed model proves effective. Addressing the challenges of language barriers allows for seamless real-time communication between different language users, via advanced transformer-based models for recognition and localization. This helps ensure accurate and context-sensitive processing, which is important to reduce ambiguity and improve overall user experience. The integration of multi-layer perceptrons (MLPs) plays a pivotal role in refining embeddings and enhancing the adaptability of the system to diverse linguistic contexts. In addition to integrating NLP techniques such as sentiment analysis and text summarization, improving interactions adds value by making them more efficient.

This work paves the way for the advancement of multilingual communication tools. This is especially helpful in environments that require real-time cross-language interaction, given the ability of the model to adapt to a wide range of languages and dialects.It can handle mixed native language input and continuous translation, demonstraing its robustness and scalability. Moreover, the future development of emotion and emotion-recognition with support for more low-resource languages is a promising development. The inclusion of MLPs in these aspects enhances feature extraction and improves performance in handling nuanced language variations. This work provides a comprehensive and effective solution, making global interactions on calling and messaging platforms more seamless and user-friendly.

9.7 FUTURE WORK

Future work on these projects will focus on enhancing the system's capabilities and expanding its range of applications. One area of improvement is the integration of advanced speech recognition models, such as deep learning-based ASR (Automatic Speech Recognition) systems, to additionally handle a variety of accents. Including more language pairs can make the system more diverse. Another direction is to refine the text-speech composition using neural networks in a more natural-sounding TTS format, which may improve the user experience by providing a more fluid and expressive speech output. Specifically, sentiment analysis, identification, and integration of more complex conversational systems such as very noisy backgrounds.

Additionally, the system can be extended to multiple inputs, such as image recognition (e.g., using computer vision to process images or video), for applications such as real-time sign language translation or image object description. Improving the system's scalability to handle more complex tasks, such as interactive multilingual customer support, can also be a valuable application. It is important in future to ensure privacy and security features for handling sensitive user data, such as voice input and text processing. The use of more advanced encryption and anonymity techniques are needed to ensure that user interactions remain confidential and secure. Finally, personalization based on user feedback can be included. This can allow the system to learn and adapt to individual preferences and speaking styles over time, further improving performance and responsiveness in real use cases.

REFERENCES

1. Jin, H., Zhang, Y., Meng, D., Wang, J. and Tan, J., 2024. A comprehensive survey on process-oriented automatic text summarization with an exploration of llm-based methods. *arXiv preprint* arXiv:2403.02901.
2. Dagli, M.M., Ghenbot, Y., Ahmad, H.S., Chauhan, D., Turlip, R., Wang, P., Welch, W.C., Ozturk, A.K. and Yoon, J.W., 2024. Development and validation of a novel AI framework using NLP with LLM integration for relevant clinical data extraction through automated chart review. *Scientific Reports*, 14(1), p. 26783.
3. Omar, M., Brin, D., Glicksberg, B. and Klang, E., 2024. Utilizing natural language processing and large language models in the diagnosis and prediction of infectious diseases: A Systematic Review. *American Journal of Infection Control*, 52(9), pp. 992–1001.
4. Kolasani, S., 2023. Optimizing natural language processing, large language models (LLMs) for efficient customer service, and hyper-personalization to enable sustainable growth and revenue. *Transactions on Latest Trends in Artificial Intelligence*, 4(4).
5. Nasution, A.H. and Onan, A., 2024. ChatGPT label: Comparing the quality of human-generated and LLM-generated annotations in low-resource language NLP tasks. *IEEE Access*, 12, pp. 71876–71900. doi: 10.1109/ACCESS.2024.3402809.
6. Gopali, S., Abri, F., Siami Namin, A. and Jones, K.S., 2024. The applicability of LLMs in generating textual samples for analysis of imbalanced datasets. *IEEE Access*, 12, pp. 136451–136465. doi: 10.1109/ACCESS.2024.3463400.
7. Reddy Kandula, B. and Jacob, L., 2024. Contextual recommendation system: A revolutionary approach using Hadoop, Spark, NLP, and LLMs. In *2024 International Conference on Electrical Electronics and Computing Technologies (ICEECT), Greater Noida, India* (pp. 1–4). doi: 10.1109/ICEECT61758.2024.10738951.
8. Sathe, N., Deodhe, V., Sharma, Y. and Shinde, A., 2023. A comprehensive review of AI in healthcare: Exploring neural networks in medical imaging, LLM-based interactive response systems, NLP-based EHR systems, ethics, and beyond. In *2023 International Conference on Advanced Computing & Communication Technologies (ICACCTech), Banur, India* (pp. 633–640). doi: 10.1109/ICACCTech61146.2023.00108.
9. Mohammad, A.F., Clark, B. and Hegde, R., 2023. Large Language Model (LLM) & GPT, a monolithic study in generative AI. In *2023 Congress in Computer Science, Computer Engineering, & Applied Computing (CSCE)*, Las Vegas, NV, USA (pp. 383–388). doi: 10.1109/CSCE60160.2023.00068.
10. Łaniewski, S. and Ślepaczuk, R., 2024. Enhancing literature review with LLM and NLP methods. *Algorithmic Trading Case*. arXiv preprint arXiv:2411.05013
11. Taberko, V., Ivaniuk, D., Smorodin, V. and Prokhorenko, V., 2024. NLP and LLM-based approach to enterprise knowledge base construction. *OSTIS*, pp. 177–182.
12. Ali, N.F., Mohtasim, M.M., Mosharrof, S. and Krishna, T.G., 2024. Automated Literature Review Using NLP Techniques and LLM-Based Retrieval-Augmented Generation. In 2024 *International Conference on Innovations in Science, Engineering and Technology* (ICISET) (pp. 1-6). IEEE.

13. Ramesh Raja, S.R., Antony Vigil, M.S., Pattaiah, M. and Sudarson, B., 2024, February. Analyzing the computational efficiency of LLM models for NLP tweet classification during emergency-crisis. In *International Conference on Computational Intelligence in Data Science* (pp. 3–15). Springer Nature: Switzerland.

14. Gupta, S., Ranjan, R. and Singh, S.N., 2024. Comprehensive study on sentiment analysis: From rule-based to modern LLM-based system. arXiv preprint arXiv:2409.09989.

15. Miah, M.S.U., Kabir, M.M., Sarwar, T.B., Safran, M., Alfarhood, S. and Mridha, M.F., 2024. A multimodal approach to cross-lingual sentiment analysis with an ensemble of transformer and LLM. *Scientific Reports*, 14(1), p. 9603.

16. Zhou, Y., 2024. *Predicting CDS Spreads and Stock Returns with Weather Risk: A Study Utilizing Nlp/Llm and Ai Measures.* Llm and Ai Measures.

17. Antu, S.A., Chen, H. and Richards, C.K., 2023. *Using LLM (Large Language Model) to Improve Efficiency in Literature Review for Undergraduate Research* (pp. 8–16). LLM@ AIED.

18. Khan, R., Gupta, N., Sinhababu, A., & Chakravarty, R., 2024. Impact of conversational and generative AI systems on libraries: A use case large language model (LLM). *Science & Technology Libraries*, 43(4), 319–333.

19. Manir, S.B., Islam, K.M.S., Madiraju, P. and Deshpande, P., 2024. LLM-based text prediction and question answer models for Aphasia speech. *IEEE Access*, 12, pp. 114670–114680. doi: 10.1109/ACCESS.2024.3443592.

20. Lakomkin, E., Wu, C., Fathullah, Y., Kalinli, O., Seltzer, M.L. and Fuegen, C. , 2024. End-to-end speech recognition contextualization with large language models. In *ICASSP 2024–2024 IEEE International Conference on Acoustics, Speech and Signal Processing (ICASSP)*, Republic of Seoul, Korea (pp. 12406–12410). doi: 10.1109/ICASSP48485.2024.10446898.

21. Nasereddin, H.H. and Omari, A.A.R., 2017, July. Classification techniques for automatic speech recognition (ASR) algorithms used with real time speech translation. In *IEEE 2017 Computing Conference* (pp. 200–207).

22. Oh, S.L., Jahmunah, V., Ooi, C.P., Tan, R.S., Ciaccio, E.J., Yamakawa, T., Tanabe, M., Kobayashi, M. and Acharya, U.R., 2020. Classification of heart sound signals using a novel deep WaveNet model. *Computer Methods and Programs in Biomedicine*, 196, p. 105604.

10 Can Generative AI Cause Evolution in Animals

An Inspiration Study from the 2024 The Wild Robot Movie

Muhammad Younus, Halimah Abdul Manaf, Achmad Nurmandi, Dyah Mutiarin, Ulung Pribadi, Titin Purwaningsih, Andi Luhur Prianto, Imron Sohsan, Hajira Gul, and Ibrahim Shah

10.1 INTRODUCTION

10.1.1 BACKGROUND AND HISTORY

Artificial Intelligence is emerging as a dominant force in healthcare, education, conservation, and robotics. Its ability to mimic, learn from, and better natural processes has raised interest in its potential use in biological and ecological systems. One such theory is the possibility that Generative AI could trigger evolution in animals—a theory lying between science fiction and today's technological reality (Byrne, 2005). This concept gained new meaning in the wake of the 2024 film The Wild Robot, depicting a world of animals and robots in harmony with each other, which triggered extensive evolutionary changes in animals.

This coming together of Generative AI and biology is rooted in some previous work in the fields of cybernetics and bionics. Visionaries such as Norbert Wiener and John von Neumann laid down the theoretical foundations through which life processes would be simulated in machines. Later, advances in neural networks, genetic algorithms, and bioinformatics built upon such prospects by providing tools to research and even manipulate living systems (Arendt, 2021). Application of Generative AI to observe the behavior of animals, for instance, with drones used to monitor migratory routes or machine learning applied to decode calls, is now widespread. However, the hypothesis that Generative AI would initiate evolutionary developments in animals—either through direct interaction with them or indirect environmental effects—is theoretical and untapped.

The film The Wild Robot is, in a way, a work of art depicting this notion: how Generative AI can be embedded in ecosystems and guide the evolution of animals. The narrative homes in on a robot finding ways to coexist in the wild and enter symbiotic relations with animals, and tries to intimately point out that perhaps Generative

DOI: 10.1201/9781003680192-10

AI is an actor of selection or even perhaps an adaptive stimulant under special conditions (Budd, 2015). Albeit fictionalized, such representational instances have incited research questions about whether evolution using Generative AI is possible and what its ramifications are on nature.

10.1.2 PROBLEM FORMULATION

Although the integration of Generative AI in ecological and biological disciplines is moving very quickly, the prospects of Generative AI affecting animal evolution raise many open questions. Could Generative AI perhaps be an evolutionary adaptation driver? If it is, then how and how much would it happen? Would it benefit or harm biodiversity and ecosystem integrity? Finally, human interference in natural evolutionary activities is also ethically dubious, particularly in utilizing Generative AI on wildlife or developing robot systems that may eventually interact with living organisms.

The majority of existing research on this topic centers on the functional uses of Generative AI in conservation and biology, but not on its evolutionary aspect in the long run. For instance, Generative AI technologies are applied to enhance species identification, habitat restoration optimization, and population tracking of threatened species. Few studies, though, examine the possible unintended or indirect consequences of Generative AI on animal populations over generations. The absence of empirical evidence and theoretical models considering these possibilities generates a gigantic research gap.

It is also an interdisciplinary discipline, offering the challenge of integrating concepts from evolutionary biology, Generative AI, robotics, and ethics. Evolutionary biology provides insight into natural selection and adaptation, while Generative AI enables the modeling—and potentially control—of the evolutionary process. The integration of these disciplines must be holistic, taking into account both the technical capabilities of Generative AI and the dynamics of ecological systems.

10.1.3 RESEARCH OBJECTIVE

This research aims to explore the theoretical and practical significance of Generative AI as a future evolutionary force in animals, drawing inspiration from The Wild Robot. The research will examine how Generative AI engages with nature in an attempt to: • Explore Mechanisms of Interaction: Outline possible mechanisms through which Generative AI can act on evolutionary mechanisms in animals, for instance, behavior conditioning, environmental accommodation, or genetic alteration.

- Evaluate Possible Implications of Generative AIs' interactions, including alterations of animal behavior, morphology, or population genetic variation.
- Examine Ecological and Ethical Issues in Generative AI-evolution about the interplay between technological advancement and biodiversity conservation.
- Suggest a Conceptual Framework to explain how Generative AIs function in evolution, drawing on what is known in biology, technology, and ethics.

In response to these objectives, the following article is a contribution to the newly opened discussion at the intersection of Generative AI and evolution and, thus, an opportunity for upcoming empirical investigation and interdisciplinary work. More generally, this work aims to ask more fundamental philosophical questions about the place that human beings must occupy to replicate the natural world through the virtue of technology.

10.1.4 RELEVANCE AND SIGNIFICANCE

This is not only of academic interest but also pertains to some of the world's most significant issues, including loss of biodiversity, climate change, and ethical technology use. Since Generative AI is already applied in environmental and wildlife management, there is an enormous demand to research its long-term impact. Generative AI occasionally—perhaps unconsciously or even deliberately—impacts evolutionary processes, which makes research and policymaking on this subject foresighted and inevitable.

In addition, the research aligns with the growing interest in applying Generative AI to sustainable development and ecological resilience. In exploring whether Generative AI is capable of having positive evolutionary impacts—e.g., allowing species to be made more resilient to an evolving universe—the research sees promise for novel solutions to ecological dilemmas. On the other hand, this is also a warning question about the unforeseen results of technological remediations, hence highlighting the need for ethical reflection and ecological responsibility.

The field of applying artificial intelligence to natural worlds is extremely emergent and has highly significant implications for the evolution and behavior of animals. Increasing evidence has demonstrated that Generative AI technologies have effects on animal behaviors, even being integrated into their ecological and social systems at times. Such effects can be understood by theory-based perspectives such as techno-ecological evolution and the extended phenotype, and empirical investigations present preliminary evidence of behavioral and physiological effects on Generative AI.

For instance, the 2024 movie The Wild Robot can prompt inquiry on these subjects, merging fiction with scientifically feasible concepts. However, there are tremendous gaps in the literature, particularly regarding how Generative AI could influence the long-term and environmental implications of evolutionary changes among animals. Closing these gaps will necessitate interdisciplinary collaboration and an extreme focus on ethical considerations, provided that Generative AI embedded within natural systems benefits not only humanity but also the environment.

10.2 LITERATURE REVIEW

Sudden expansion in the field of artificial intelligence has raised arguments regarding how it could affect everything in life, including nature. The Wild Robot movie, released in 2024, offers new insights into the intersection of nature and artificial intelligence, educating us on how technology can transform animals' behavior, ecosystems, and evolution. While this is hypothetical, it raises some pretty sharp questions about the dynamics between Generative AI and natural systems, challenging scientists to consider whether Generative AI could potentially be an evolutionary driving force in animals. This literature review will take a funnel structure to explore this topic systematically, starting with broad studies on the influence of Generative AI on ecosystems and narrowing down to specific research related to animal evolution and behavioral adaptations.

10.2.1 WIDER RESEARCH INTO GENERATIVE AI AND ECOSYSTEMS

Early research into the application of Generative AI in ecological systems has generally aimed at the use of Generative AI as a tool for monitoring, data analysis, and predictive modeling. For example, Evans et al. (2018) showed how Generative AI-driven drones could monitor populations of wildlife, thereby providing real-time data to help make informed conservation decisions. Similarly, work by Kitzes and Schricker (2019) focuses on how machine learning algorithms were employed in determining changes to an ecosystem based on climate variability, something that is an excellent illustration of how Generative AI can be used towards sustainability.

These studies, while placing Generative AI in the role of a facilitator, also showcased unintended side effects. For instance, they flagged that having Generative AI-operated devices has disrupted natural behaviors among animals. In some cases, Generative AI technologies have been proven to be disrupting the habitats of animals involuntarily. For instance, the automated drones used for wildlife observation can disturb regular migration in some bird species. Such outcomes mean that Generative AI, even just as a tool of monitoring, can significantly impact animal behavior and might induce evolutionary changes in the long run.

10.2.2 GENERATIVE AI AS A BEHAVIORAL INFLUENCER

As research evolved, scholars started to investigate the potential of Generative AI to influence animal behavior more directly. An important study in this regard was conducted by Anderson et al. (2021), showing how robotic fish could be integrated into schools of live fish, changing their movement patterns and group dynamics. This experiment showed that animals could adapt to the presence of Generative AI entities, sometimes treating them as part of their social structure. Likewise, Krause (2022) showed that robotic bees can interact with living bees to modify pollination behaviors and hive dynamics.

These studies give proof that animals can learn to adapt to Generative AI systems, sometimes even integrating them into their natural behaviors. Such findings suggest that continued interactions with Generative AI entities might bring selective pressures on animal populations and could, therefore, potentially result in evolutionary changes. This is a purely speculative hypothesis, but it needs to be tested by further research to determine any causal linkage between interaction with Generative AI and evolutionary consequences.

10.2.3 Theoretical Foundation of Evolutionary Change

The development of animals is heavily rooted in the concepts of Darwinian natural selection and adaptation. Subsequent studies more recently looked into the same concepts in the context of technological and anthropogenic stress, e.g., the "techno-ecological evolution" model proposed by Malhi et al. (2021), who predicted that human-mediated technological shifts might very well serve as novel selection pressures on wildlife. This phrasing is in line with the prediction that Generative AI, as a novel technological element, can potentially prove to be an influential driver of animal evolution.

Concurrently, Dawkins's (1982) "extended phenotype" hypothesis has been refurbished based on Generative AI technologies. In this hypothesis, the effect of an organism's genes can be extended outside of its physical body, e.g., to the surroundings or other microorganisms. Projected into Generative AI, this implies that the entry of Generative AI technologies into ecosystems can trigger novel directions of evolution by altering the extended phenotypes of animal species. Generative AI-powered feeding technology or robotic predator tools, for example, can have a direct impact on reproduction and survival and therefore, evolutionary dynamics.

10.2.4 Specific Research on Generative AI-Driven Evolutionary Shifts

The theoretical framework sets the foundation for an understanding of the potential effects of Generative AI on evolution, albeit empirical evidence remains relatively scarce. Nevertheless, some early studies are pretty crucial in understanding the problem. Thus, for example, Wilson et al. (2023) took into consideration how the longer-term exposure to robot predators would influence behavior as well as survival tactics among smaller mammals in lab settings. It was a research paper that demonstrated that certain populations developed more camouflage and evasive maneuvers, demonstrating that Generative AI agents can be used as artificial selection pressures.

A further study by Zhang et al. (2023) looked at a longer-term view of Generative AI-driven feeders in examining possible effects on bird populations. Foraging and feeding behavior were found to change, with implications for the physiology and genetic makeup of the birds. All these findings can point towards the possibility of Generative AI technologies placing evolutionary pressures, if indirectly.

10.2.5 Fictional Inspirations and Real-World Implications

The 2024 film The Wild Robot is an imaginative but fictional exploration of the themes of the above research. The storyline of a robot inserted into a wild system is a metaphor for how Generative AI can become an active player in natural systems. The film is not real, but it does mirror some of the present research that indicates that Generative AI has effects on animal behavior and adaptation.

The film, for example, depicted a robot mediating interspecies communication and collaboration—something not too dissimilar from actual research on robotic animals impacting group behavior. Generative AI objects can learn from and adapt to natural worlds, which is precisely the same thing that occurs with, for example, robotic fish and bees in the context of Generative AI-driven technologies. Such dramatization causes the picture to look like Generative AI could not just coexist but also become part of the normal ecosystems and cause changes that would end up challenging evolutionary processes.

10.2.6 GAPS IN THE LITERATURE

Despite increasing research levels, some areas remain unknown regarding the contribution of Generative AI to animal evolution. Firstly, most of the available research is laboratory-controlled experiments and thus may be somewhat detached from ecological systems. Secondly, they are mostly cross-sectional in their assessment of how Generative AI technologies influence people over time, and therefore, causal associations between exposure to Generative AI and evolutionary change cannot be inferred. Third, the ethical implications of using Generative AI in nature have been ignored; this is critical to inform policy design and research.

Additionally, interdisciplinary resolutions integrating biology, Generative AI, and ethics must be considered to fill in the holes. Interdisciplinary alliances may provide a complete, holistic view of the ways that Generative AI acts upon nature and the threat, as well as the opportunities it will offer.

10.3 RESEARCH

This article explores the potential for animals to evolve alongside the growing prevalence of artificial intelligence, drawing on the 2024 film The Wild Robot. There are three parts to the study design that the study utilizes: research type, data collection method, and data analysis method.

10.3.1 RESEARCH METHOD

The research methodology employed for this work is an interdisciplinary one that integrates the elements of theoretical analysis, case studies, and computational modeling. A case study of The Wild Robot will be utilized to construct the early-stage hypotheses and conceptual findings. These will be supplemented with a survey of the literature on recent applications of Generative AI in ecology and evolutionary biology, together with ethics frameworks being discussed for applying technologies to natural systems. Computational models and simulations will investigate hypothetical scenarios of Generative AI-animal interaction and their evolutionary implications. By synthesizing information from a variety of disciplines, this research attempts to construct an overall understanding of the capacity of Generative AI to impact evolution in animals. It will thus provoke scientific and ethical debate, leading to additional research into this challenging and timely subject.

10.3.2 RESEARCH TYPE

The study is based on a qualitative paradigm that investigates the hypothetical and conceptual aspects of Generative AI in animal evolution. This would be highly applicable to complicated events that consolidate natural science, technology, and philosophy, as shown in the movie. The movie is dissected using a case-study methodology by exploring the Wild Robot narrative as a running theme in scrutinizing the imaginary set of events in Generative AI-animal encounters. Also, the research incorporates theoretical examination as a connective bridge between fictional narration of the movie and factual scientific research in Generative AI and animal encounters.

10.3.3 DATA COLLECTION TECHNIQUES

The movie The Wild Robot is analyzed as the primary source. Themes, interactions between characters, and plot developments around the impact of Generative AI on animals are noted and interpreted. Second-order data, in the form of published journal articles, books, and conference proceedings, are also analyzed to contextualize the film representation against the background of the current development of Generative AI technology and animal biology. The comparison is made by contrasting the film's near-future fictional scenarios against already existing uses of Generative AI for wildlife tracking, conservation, and behavioral research.

TITLE-ABS-KEY ("Evolution Generative AI") AND PUBYEAR > 2013 AND PUBYEAR < 2025 AND (LIMIT-TO (DOCTYPE, "cp") OR LIMIT-TO (DOCTYPE, "ar") OR LIMIT-TO (DOCTYPE, "re")) AND (LIMIT-TO (PUBSTAGE, "final")) AND (LIMIT-TO (LANGUAGE, "English")) AND (LIMIT-TO (SUBJAREA, "SOCI"))

10.3.4 DATA ANALYSIS TECHNIQUES

Data gathered in the study are analyzed through thematic analysis and scenario-based modeling.

10.3.4.1 Thematic Analysis

Identifying, coding, and categorizing themes from document analysis and expert interviews are conducted through iterative readings of the movie script and interview transcripts to uncover recurrent ideas, such as Generative AI as a catalyst for behavioral adaptation, the ethical boundaries of Generative AI-animal interactions, and the societal implications of such changes. These themes from the fictional narrative are then juxtaposed against empirical findings from the scientific literature to develop an overarching understanding.

10.3.4.2 Scenario-Based Modeling

From these themes, more specific speculative scenarios are built to illustrate how Generative AI could come to affect animal evolution in real-world contexts. The scenarios do account for the introduction of Generative AI into natural habitats, possible adaptive behaviors of animals, and long-term evolutionary consequences. The scenarios serve as a thought experiment to explore the feasibility and importance of evolutionary changes induced by Generative AI.

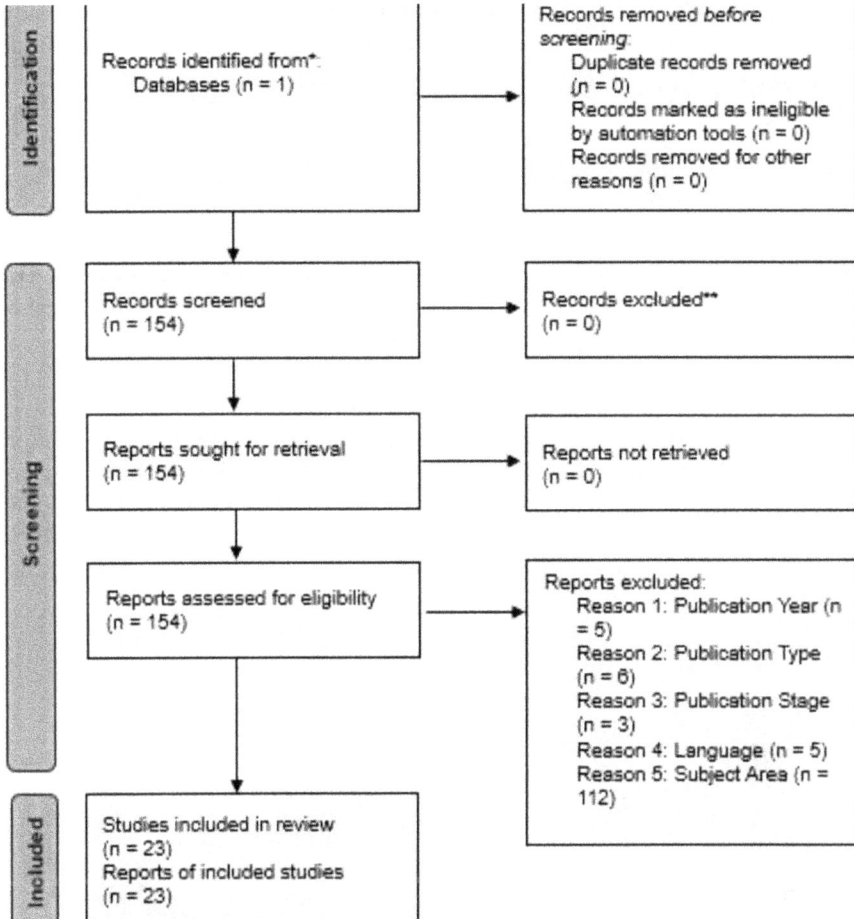

FIGURE 10.1   PRISMA Flow Diagram Process. (Created by Author)

10.4   RESULTS AND DISCUSSION

10.4.1   FINDINGS

The movie "The Wild Robot" of 2024 presents another type of narrative, one blending artificial intelligence and the natural process of animal habit and ecosystem operation. It also provides a clearer understanding of how Generative AI can serve as a catalyst for change in the animal kingdom. Based on what one can see of individual scenes, the following overall conclusions can be made:

10.4.1.1   Generative AI-Induced Behavioral Adaptation

In perhaps the most crucial scene, the AI protagonist Roz is observing a beaver family building a dam. Employing her Generative AI software, Roz suggests to them how to shore up the structure according to hydrodynamics and material sustainability. The beavers, being cautious, take her ideas on board and go on building an immensely stronger and sustainable dam. It signifies how, through the use of Generative AI, the behavioral adaptation of the animals can be fast-tracked since it incorporates new ways in unison with nature.

10.4.1.2   Cross-Species Communication

A striking example of how Generative AI can facilitate interspecies interaction occurs when Roz creates the universal signaling system with sound frequencies, allowing beasts like foxes, deer, and birds to give warning calls of incoming predators. This scene showed how Generative AI could break down barriers of communication among species and bring about cooperation toward mutual survival.

10.4.1.3   Ecosystem Balancing Through Generative AI

There is a particularly dramatic scene where Roz observes a predator-prey relationship in a forest ecosystem. Analyzing the data, Roz makes out that there are too many rabbits depleting the resources. Using her Generative AI, she nudges a population of hawks toward areas with an abundance of rabbits. That brings back balance without disturbing the natural order, showing how Generative AI can act as a non-invasive regulator in an ecosystem.

FIGURE 10.2   The Beaver Scene in the Movie. (The Wild Robot)

FIGURE 10.3   The Chatting Scene in the Movie. (The Wild Robot)

10.4.1.4   Educational Influence on Animal Offspring

Roz's experiences interacting with younger creatures also give good character to Generative AI as a learning machine. During her training of the goslings, Roz utilizes her Generative AI-enabled database to teach the goslings about patterns in migration, living, and even basic star maps. Such activities demonstrate how naturally occurring learning is enhanced by knowledge derived from data using Generative AI.

10.4.1.5   Artificial Objects as Ecosystem Elements

The movie ends with a final shot in which the artificial parts of Roz—solar panels, sensors—find their place in nature once she has been deconstructed. The birds use bits of solar panels to insulate their nest; insects populate sensor cavities. It seems as if Generative AI and physical bodies can become part of the ecosystem's evolution itself.

10.4.1.6   Generative AI-Assisted Rehabilitation of Injured Wildlife

One of the most poignant moments is when Roz employs her state-of-the-art diagnostic tools to heal an injured fox. She utilizes her Generative AI to determine what type of injury it has, and then she applies her familiarity with medicinal plants to lead the fox through the recovery process. This is how Generative AI can introduce medical interventions in a timely manner in wildlife rehabilitation.

FIGURE 10.4   The Migration Scene in the Movie. (The Wild Robot)

10.4.1.7   Development of Collaborative Strategies

Another touching moment: Roz is observed instructing the animals in a lesson—how to collaborate to overcome some act of nature, i.e., a forest fire. Through cooperation, by assigning each species to its strengths, Roz coordinated the animals in unison. It symbolizes the Generative AI function in achieving cooperation among survivors in a crisis.

10.4.1.8   Adaptation to Climate Challenges

The movie follows how Roz helps animals adapt to sudden climatic changes, like unseasonal snowfall. It is how Roz, by weather forecasting and leading the animals to safe, warmer locations, portrays how Generative AI can be used by wildlife to reduce the impact of climate variability.

10.4.2   Discussion

The conclusions reached with "The Wild Robot" generate exciting conversations between Generative AI and animality evolution. Extrapolating these cinematic features to real scenarios gives us many lessons, the last one of which is paramount.

FIGURE 10.5   The Gosling Scene in the Movie. (The Wild Robot)

10.4.2.1   Generative AI as a Catalyst of Evolutionary Change

The movie thus illustrates how Generative AI may introduce new behaviors and strategies that can fall in line with evolutionary processes. For example, beavers' use of Roz's methods of dam construction is similar to several everyday examples of animals displaying conditioned action in reaction to environmental cues. If applied to engage with wildlife in controlled conditions, next-generation Generative AI systems can hopefully speed up adaptive behaviors for improved survival. Ethical intervention must precede such considerations, however, so as not to disrupt the natural selection mechanism.

10.4.2.2   Improve Interspecies Collaboration

The concept of Roz's universal communication system epitomizes the potential of Generative AI to improve interspecies cooperation. In a real sense, breakthroughs in bioacoustic monitoring and the use of Generative AI to develop species-bridging translation devices could indeed realize interspecies communication. The new technologies will play a significant role in ensuring cooperation amidst the growing challenges of climate change and habitat fragmentation in an ecosystem.

FIGURE 10.6 The Butterfly Scene in the Movie. (The Wild Robot)

10.4.2.3 Ecosystem Management and Conservation

In many respects, Roz's function of maintaining the balance within the predator-prey dynamics mirrors Generative AI applications in conservation biology. Already, Generative AI systems are being used to monitor wildlife populations, make predictions on ecological trends, and prevent poaching. In this movie, non-invasive interventions show that Generative AI can act as a biodiversity steward, guiding ecosystems toward stability while respecting their intrinsic dynamics.

10.4.2.4 Educational Roles of Generative AI in Wildlife

The learning interactions between Roz and the goslings show the potential of Generative AI as a medium of knowledge. In real-world conservation, Generative AI could play a supportive role in rewilding animals by teaching them basic survival skills, such as guiding birds during migration with the use of Generative AI-driven drones or training predators to hunt effectively in the wild.

10.4.2.5 Integration of Artificial Constructs in Nature

The last scenes of Roz's parts being destroyed by nature present a positive foreshadowing of the physical legacy of Generative AI. The concept falls well within

FIGURE 10.7 The Coming Together Scene in the Movie. (The Wild Robot)

the new discipline of biodegradable electronics, whereby technology is developed to disintegrate or fully integrate into nature. Such technologies could minimize ecological footprints and offer new habitats for wildlife.

10.4.2.6 Ethical and Philosophical Considerations

While the movie takes an overall upbeat perspective, it also raises a couple of ethical red flags: whether Generative AI should be involved in natural processes, and if so, to what extent. This raises questions about whether the intervention could create dependencies or provoke unforeseen ecological outcomes. A kindly Roz is only a reminder of how Generative AI, in particular, needs designing with safety measures built into its overall structure—again, ensuring ecological integrity and animal well-being.

10.4.3 IMPLICATIONS FOR FUTURE RESEARCH

"The Wild Robot" could potentially be employed as a literary means to explore genuine-world applications of Generative AI on animal evolution in the real world. Among the possible directions of inquiry are:

FIGURE 10.8   The Wildfire Scene in the Movie. (The Wild Robot)

- Designing Generative AI computers for observing and inducing animal activities in a laboratory setting.
- Examining long-term ecological effects of Generative AI interference in the natural world.
- Establishing guidelines for the ethical application of Generative AI conservation.
- Investigating the application of biodegradable Generative AI elements in ecosystem engineering.
- Generative AI as a tool for preventing human-wildlife conflict by predictive modeling and intervention.

10.4.4   LIMITATIONS AND CHALLENGES

Despite being as lovely as its origin, "The Wild Robot" is an overestimate of how sophisticated Generative AI-animal experiences are. Field implementation faces numerous challenges:

FIGURE 10.9   The Extreme Snow Scene in the Movie. (The Wild Robot)

- Technological Barriers: The level of technology of Generative AI lags behind the level of technology of the described ecosystem awareness. Bridging the gap will demand advances in the sensory and analytical functioning of Generative AI.
- Unintended Consequences: Applying changes implemented by Generative AI has a chance to alter the existing ecological balances and may yield unantici-pated results.
- Ethical Issues: Conditioning or training animal behavior for Generative AI raises issues of human responsibility and exploitation.
- Scaling Issues: Roll-out of Generative AI interventions to ecosystems becomes infeasible due to constraints on resources and environment heterogeneity.

10.5   CONCLUSION

"The Wild Robot" presents a visionary perspective on how Generative AI has the potential to shape animal evolution and ecosystem dynamics. The film draws on metaphors from filmmaking, storytelling, and scientific potential to illustrate how Generative AI can be an unstoppable force of nature when approached conscientiously.

FIGURE 10.10   The Wild Robot Movie Poster.

There are a lot of challenges ahead, but the possibilities depicted make for a compelling case for interdisciplinary research at the intersection of Generative AI, biology, and ethics. Now, as the species did and still does grapple with its place in nature, "The Wild Robot" came at a time when technology, working by ecological principles, was able to inspire harmonious coexistence and innovation.

REFERENCES

Anderson, R., Booth, A., Eastwood, A. et al. (2021). Synthesis for health services and policy: Case studies in the scoping of reviews. *Health Services and Delivery Research*, 9(15), 1–84. ISSN 2050-4349. https://doi.org/10.3310/hsdr09150

Arendt, D. (2021). Animal evolution: Of flame and collar cells. *Current Biology: CB*, 31(16), R1003–R1006. https://doi.org/10.1016/j.cub.2021.07.006

Budd, G. E. (2015). Early animal evolution and the origins of nervous systems. *Philosophical Transactions of the Royal Society of London. Series B, Biological Sciences*, 370(1684), 20150037. https://doi.org/10.1098/rstb.2015.0037

Byrne, R. W. (2005). Animal evolution: Foxy friends. *Current Biology: CB*, 15(3), R86–R87. https://doi.org/10.1016/j.cub.2005.01.023

Dawkins, R. (1982). *The extended phenotype: Long reach of the gene*. Oxford University Press.

Evans, T. M., Bira, L., Gastelum, J. B., Weiss, L. T., & Vanderford, N. L. (2018). Evidence for a mental health crisis in graduate education. *Nature Biotechnology*, *36*(3), 282–284. https://doi.org/10.1038/nbt.4089

Kitzes, J., & Schricker, L. (2019). The necessity, promise and challenge of automated biodiversity surveys. *Environmental Conservation*, *46*(4), 247–250. https://doi.org/10.1017/S0376892919000146

Krause, A. (2022). Scientific reports. Figs-hare. Dataset. https://doi.org/10.6084/m9.figshare.21304755.v1

Malhi, G. S., Bell, E., Bassett, D., et al. (2021). The 2020 Royal Australian and New Zealand College of psychiatrists clinical practice guidelines for mood disorders. *Australian and New Zealand Journal of Psychiatry*, *55*(1), 7–117. https://doi.org/10.1177/0004867420979353

Wilson, S., Fernandes-Jesus, M., Young, J., et al. (2023). A social capital approach to understanding community resilience during the Covid-19 pandemic. *Forum Community Psychology*. https://clok.uclan.ac.uk/id/eprint/47077/

Zhang, Y., Xu, M., Wang, P. et al (2023). Structural basis for nucleosome binding and catalysis by the yeast Rpd3S/HDAC holoenzyme. *Cell Research*, 33(12), 971–974. https://doi.org/10.1038/s41422-023-00884-2

11 Innovative Solutions to Complex Problems

Leveraging Computational Intelligence Techniques for Driving Advancements in AI

Suryanarayana Alamuri

11.1 INTRODUCTION

The fact that Computational Intelligence Techniques (CITs) have become the most recognized tool in addressing challenges of this nature in real-world applications has become increasingly apparent, and organizations are aware of the value that CITs can bring today and in the future to Artificial Intelligence (AI). These CITs, which enhance problem-solving capabilities through Neural Networks (NN), Evolutionary Algorithms (EA), and Fuzzy Systems, can help reveal hidden patterns, optimize decisions, and improve predictors across multiple fields, highlighting the versatility and problem-solving ability of these approaches. The integrated model and the complementary strengths of different methods can also support the upgrade of AI Systems working together in CITs to solve complex problems. Developing effective CITs is important because they can provide valuable insights into how to improve the performance of existing algorithms or how to design new ones that will have a significant impact on various fields. In recent competitive programming environments, it seems like some techniques fit some types of challenges particularly well. Over the next few years, CITs will continue to evolve and integrate into existing systems, with both driving innovative solutions to complex problems and propelling AI to new frontiers. From the world of research and practice, where new techniques continue to be applied with increasing effectiveness, we can anticipate additional technique-specific applications and breakthrough innovations in the field of Computational Intelligence (CI) over the coming years that will promote AI in an even more potent manner.

11.2 COMPUTATIONAL INTELLIGENCE TECHNOLOGIES (CITS) VS. COMPLEX INTELLIGENCE TECHNOLOGIES (CXITS)

Computational Intelligence (CI) is a compilation of nature-inspired resolution techniques and central concepts with a goal to find solutions to a class of complex and real space problems that are often tricky or cannot be solved

DOI: 10.1201/9781003680192-11

with standard analytical or mathematical techniques. The key CI Techniques are Artificial Neural Networks (ANNs), Genetic Algorithms (GAs), Fuzzy Systems, and Swarm Intelligence.

(Engelbrecht, 2007)

While both CITs and CxITs are designed to improve problem-solving ability, they do so by using different approaches and in different contexts. CITs mimic natural processes and solve problems through biological and statistical methods. The field of CI uses algorithms and techniques based on biological systems and statistical approaches to solve complex problems.

The main elements are: NN, FL Systems, EC (such as Genetic Algorithms or GA), and SI (for example, Ant Colony Optimization or ant nest sick and germs). Some of the applications include: Pattern Recognition, Data Mining, Optimization Problems, Control Systems, and Machine Learning (ML) tasks. CITs frequently mimic elements of human cognition and natural phenomena. They are designed for learning, adapting, and optimizing based on the data they are provided.

11.3 MAJOR COMPUTATIONAL INTELLIGENCE TECHNIQUES (CITS)

CIT covers a wide range of techniques that are inspired by natural phenomena and biological processes.

CITs draw inspiration from phenomena found in the natural world, including the information processing capabilities of the human brain, the evolution of living organisms and the collective behavior of social insects.

These techniques are inspired from natural processes so applications of these techniques can be extended to vast no of problems, such as optimization and pattern recognition, decision making and control systems"

(Siddique & Adeli, 2013)

By learning, adapting, and optimizing solutions, these approaches solve complex problems and propel many advancements in AI. Some of them are:

11.3.1 NEURAL NETWORKS (NN)

Mimicking the way the human brain processes information, NNs are composed of connected nodes (or artificial neurons) that collaborate to analyze and learn from data. NNs possess powerful pattern recognition and approximation capabilities, which make them suitable for tasks such as image recognition, NLP, and Predictive Modeling.

11.3.2 EVOLUTIONARY ALGORITHMS (EA)

Evolutionary Algorithms (EA) are based on the idea of how natural selection adapts a population, a set of potential solutions, over time to achieve the best possible solution for a problem or function. Genetic algorithms (GAs), evolution strategies, and genetic programming are among the techniques that have seen broad use for solving optimization, design, and decision-making problems.

11.3.3 FUZZY LOGIC (FL)

FL-type is a theory-based computational structure that uses imprecise or vague data, just like a human being, to think and reason. Fuzzy systems are particularly good at dealing with uncertainty and ambiguity, and are widely used in control systems, expert systems, and decision support.

11.3.4 SWARM INTELLIGENCE (SI)

Swarm Intelligence (SI) algorithms are based on the collective behavior of natural swarms, such as flocks of birds or ant colonies. Swarm Intelligence Algorithms: This category comprises algorithms that harness the collective behavior of swarms to address optimization challenges, such as ant colony optimization and particle swarm optimization. Applications include problems in scheduling, routing, and resource allocation.

11.3.5 ARTIFICIAL IMMUNE SYSTEMS (AIS)

Administrations Artificial Intelligence (AIS) is inspired by the biological immune system, which has the capacity to discern, react, and learn from foreign pathogens. This adaptability and memory of the immune system are then used to solve problems such as anomaly detection, optimization, and pattern recognition.

11.3.6 ENSEMBLE TECHNIQUES (ETS)

ETs combine a set of individual CI Models into one, which enhances the overall performance and robustness of the system. The basic intuition is that the aggregate knowledge of many models will be better than any individual model, which is particularly useful in situations where the data is complex, noisy, and/or heterogeneous (Dietterich, 2000). ETs have been effectively used in numerous applications, including classification, regression, and time series, and are built on methods such as bagging, boosting, and stacking. These methods are based on training several base models (e.g., Decision Trees, NNs) and aggregating their results (i.e., outputs) through voting, averaging, or more advanced combination techniques (Friedman, 2001).

11.3.7 GENETIC ALGORITHMS (GA)

Another famous CIT is GA, which is inspired by the process of evolution and natural selection.

GA is a member of the broader class of evolution-based optimization algorithm that generates solutions in an iterative way by producing and evaluating individuals (solutions), in order to locate an optimal/near-optimal solution for a specific problem

(Holland, 1992). They replicate the natural selection process in which a population of candidate solutions (individuals) evolves over generations until reaching the optimal or near-optimal solution to a specific problem (Holland). Genetic programming takes the concept even further, evolving programs or models, instead of just parameter values (Koda, 1992). GA finds application in many optimization problems, such as scheduling (Gen & Cheng, 2000), routing, and resource allocation.

11.3.8 Evolutionary Computation (EC)

EC is one of the important and broad areas in CI, encompassing techniques inspired by biological evolution principles (i.e., natural selection, mutation, recombination). These methods are characterized by their strong similarities to genetic algorithms (GAs), genetic programming (GP), and Evolutionary Strategies (ES) that evolve the parameters of a problem using, e.g., mutation and recombination operators without a representation of the individuals (as required in GAs) (Schwefel, 1981). These techniques have found applications in a wide range of optimization and combinatorial search problems, including design, scheduling, and control problems (Back et al., 1997).

11.3.9 Hybrid Methods (HTs) and Methods

Along with single CITs, there is an increase in HTs that take advantage of the advantages of multiple methods. Hybrid Models (Neuro-Fuzzy Systems, Evolutionary NN, etc.) usually cover such tasks more thoroughly and efficiently. Ensemble techniques are based on the principle of combining two or more, preferably diverse, individual classifiers to use the strengths of each classifier and circumvent respective weaknesses. This has been explored extensively for solving complex problems more efficiently. A frequent approach is the combined action of ANNs with other methods, like FL (Neuro-fuzzy Systems) or EA (Neuro-Evolutionary Systems). A case in point is the confluence of Rule-based Expert Systems with Fuzzy Logic, which has led to so-called Fuzzy Expert Systems. They are called Hybrid Systems as they can solve problems in situations where knowledge is uncertain, or the representation of that knowledge is imprecise, which can be useful in areas with imperfect or unclear information (Zadeh, 1965; Madani & Assilian, 1975). Such Hybrid Systems would take advantage of the pattern recognition and learning capabilities of ANNs, and thus be combined with complementary techniques with reasoning or optimization abilities (Jang, 1993; Yao, 1999).

11.4 LITERATURE REVIEW ON COMPUTATIONAL INTELLIGENCE (CI)

11.4.1 Advancement of Complex Intelligence Technologies (CxITs)

CxITs would attempt to combine various AI methods to control complex systems and environments that often require high-level decisions and flexibility. Machine learning, knowledge representation, and reasoning are often components of complex intelligence technologies (Russel & Norvig, 2016).

11.4.2 Techniques of Computational Intelligence

- A comprehensive review of Russel and Norvig (2016) is the reference for AI and covers the basic pieces that comprise CITs (ML, Knowledge Representation, reasoning, etc.). In a review article, Gao et al. The study explored the application of multiple computational intelligence methods, including neural networks, genetic algorithms, and fuzzy systems, to tackle complex real-world issues in fields like finance, healthcare, and engineering. These techniques have the potential to unveil hidden structures, streamline decision-making, and improve predictive capabilities (Gao et al., 2019).
- Xue et al. (2021) performed a meta-analysis of research utilizing CITs for enhancing AI applications. The review attracted fundamental trends, such as the increased interest in DL, multi-modal data utilization, and hybrid models integrating various CIT.
- The scientists reported a consolidated representation of the use of SI algorithms, including ant colony optimization and particle swarm optimization, in order to solve complex optimization problems. To this end, they describe how approaches inspired by nature can be effectively applied in AI systems for delegation, distribution of resources, and decision support (Liang et al., 2020).
- Khan et al. (2022) evaluated the FL and EA for developing models for intelligence systems for making effective decisions. These CI techniques, discussed in the study, can significantly handle uncertainty, imprecision, and multi-criteria optimization, among several others, which are characteristics common to AI applications in the real world.

11.4.3 New and Innovative Ideas for Old and Complex Problems

As NewWayLabs explains: "For years, NewWayLabs has led the charge creating innovative computational tools to solve complex problems, demonstrating the growing need for computational intelligence across industries."

11.4.4 Artificial Intelligence (AI)

As defined by Russel and Norvig (2016), "Artificial Intelligence (AI) is the study of agents that receive percepts from the environment and perform actions." Poole and Mackworth (2017), on the other hand, state that "artificial intelligence is the study of the design of intelligent agents."

11.4.4.1 Computational Intelligence Technologies: Role and Application

According to Engelbrecht (2007), "Computational Intelligence Technologies (Fuzzy Systems, Neural Networks, Evolutionary Computation, etc.) have gained increasing significance in applications." Shen et al. (2006) mention that "CI Techniques have been applied widely in diverse areas, including pattern recognition, decision-making and control systems."

11.4.4.2 Techniques of Creativity and Innovation

"Creativity and Innovation are indispensable for organizations to devise new and effective solutions," Amabile writes (1988). Moreover, Mumford et al. (2001) stress that "creative solutions typically include ideas that are new and useful."

11.5 SWARM TECHNOLOGIES

Bonabeau et al. (1999) provide a detailed account of SI, including both the biological underpinnings and the man-made uses of this CIT. It demonstrates the power of Swarm-based techniques in solving diverse Optimization and Decision-making challenges. In the domain of AI, "techniques like Swarm Intelligence including Ant Colony Optimization and Particle Swarm Optimization have been widely adopted for the solution of problems such as Routing and Scheduling" (1999).

The concept of SR is introduced in the article by Dorigo and Şahin (2004), where the laws of SI are adapted to the coordination and control of a group of autonomous robots. This special issue covers these topics and emphasizes the potential SR has in solving real-world tasks as well as the challenges involved in designing efficient Swarm-based Systems. Swarm Robotics has been exploiting exploration, search and rescue, and Environmental Monitoring (Dorigo & Şahin, 2004).

11.5.1 SECURING THE AI AND COMPUTATIONAL INTELLIGENCE TECHNOLOGIES

In this regard, the connection between evolutionary algorithms and FL has been explored, where Cordón (2001) discusses the advantages of combining these two paradigms and how this can support the development of an interpretable and adaptive system of fuzzy rules. This is one example of HIS (Hybrid Intelligent System), which utilizes the strengths of both artificial intelligence and computational intelligence theories. Hybrid Intelligent Systems (Cordón, 2001) emerge from the combination of Artificial Intelligence and Computational Intelligence Techniques, *e.g.,* Fuzzy Logic and Evolutionary Algorithms (Bello & Evolvi, 2019).

Hive intelligence and swarm learning combine deep learning and swarm intelligence algorithms. Such a hybridization is again an approach towards creating more robust, adaptive, and complex decision-making systems to tackle real-time problems. Deep Learning with Swarm Intelligence Algorithms has been researched to combine both phenomena, leading to better solutions for a more robust and adaptive system with an efficient decision-making process (Bello & Evolvi, 2019).

11.6 FUSION OF ARTIFICIAL INTELLIGENCE AND COOPERATIVE INTELLIGENT TRANSPORTATION SYSTEMS

In his article, Cordon discusses the convergence of several CITs. This shows how integrating multiple methods can create more effective and versatile solutions to solve real-life challenges. CITs represent a diverse body of knowledge and use a variety of computational methods and technologies to enable such capabilities as pattern recognition, decision making, and problem solving. "Combinations of Artificial Intelligence and Computational Intelligence Techniques (Fuzzy Logic, Evolutionary Algorithms) form hybrid intelligent systems." (Cordón, 2001).

Bello and Evolvi examine the intersection of one of the most popular AI techniques, deep learning, with SI algorithms. The goal is to develop systems that can make decisions in tough real-world situations in a way that is more robust and adaptable. Bello and Evolvi (2019) found that "Researchers have experimented with integrating Deep Learning with Swarm Intelligence Algorithms to build more resilient and adaptive decision-making systems."

The Cordón (2001) considers the integration of EA and FL, considering how this combination could develop interpretable and adaptive fuzzy rule-based systems. This is an example of an HIS that potentially combines the advantages of both AI and CITs. A current trend is therefore to combine the various AI and CITs together to create systems that are more powerful and more diverse in their abilities. This integration can yield synergistic effects where the advantages of different approaches are leveraged to solve an extensive set of issues. Satoshi Nakamoto's own white paper, which introduced the idea of BT and the Bitcoin Cryptocurrency. This landmark paper has served as the basis for the proliferation and evolution of blockchain-based solutions. "Blockchain Technology can disrupt various sectors in many ways by accessing through its decentralized, secure, and transparent nature" (Nakamoto, 2008).

Zheng et al. (2018) give an extensive overview of the challenges and opportunities provided by BT. These aspects include technical underpinnings, consensus mechanisms, and the potential for BT to work with complementary emerging technologies such as the IoT, CC, and AI. In order to exploit the potential of blockchain, "researchers have been investigating the coupling of blockchain with a number of emerging technologies like the Internet of Things (IoT), to develop new applications and services."

11.6.1 INTERNET OF THINGS (IoT)

Gubbi et al.'s (2013) *A Vision, Architectural Elements and Future Directions* illustrates how the convergence of IoT devices, CC, and data analytics is enabling diverse smart applications across multiple domains. They write, "By connecting to computing and big data analytics, IoT devices and sensors have made possible a spectrum of smart applications." Alam et al. (2020) discuss the impact of IoT and EC on energy efficiency and sustainability in smart city applications. This demonstrates how these technologies can be used to support near real-time processing and actionable decisions on the edge, minimizing the requirement to move data back and forth to the cloud as well as driving overall efficiency in the system. They write, "Everyone has studied the response of energy efficiency and sustainability by IoT and edge computing" (Alam et al., 2020).

11.6.2 EDGE COMPUTING (EC)

Shi et al. (2016) discuss key characteristics, benefits, and challenges of EC. How bringing computation and data closer to the source with EC can help the performance and energy efficiency of IoT systems. They write, "Edge Computing has emerged as a new paradigm that enables computation and storage closer to the devices that generate and consume data, thus reducing latency when delivering content and services, and enabling better responsiveness." Satyanarayanan's article goes into detail about the emergence of edge, as it is crucial for the emergence of IoT. The communication between edge computing and IoT products, applications, use cases, and potential impact is also explored. Thus, cyberspace never sleeps, and in the ongoing cycle, the future of IoT should be the new revolution in which each device should be connected to a single device or cloud for processing data and reaching high values. The evolution of small-scale data to big data and So Big Data are integrated with Clouds for further processing and IoT to IoT-based communication and platform (Satyanarayanan, 2017).

11.6.3 NEURAL NETWORKS

The complete book by Goodfellow et al. (2016) summarizes the developments of DL, a subfield of ML that has seen significant progress in the past few years. It explains the principles, architectures, and methods that have driven progress in fields like CV, NLP, and SR, while the Exploitation of Deep Learning, a specialized variant of Neural Networks, has paved the way for developments in fields like Computer Vision and Natural Language processing (Goodfellow et al., 2016). Rumelhart *et al.,* in their seminal article, also attempt to describe the backpropagation algorithm that revolutionized machine learning by allowing multilayer neural networks to be trained. As their article notes, neural networks have the capacity to identify intricate relationships from data, constituting an effective instrument for numerous applications. *"Neural Networks are used extensively in Pattern Recognition and classification tasks "for they can learn from data"* (Rumelhart et al., 1986).

11.6.4 DEEP LEARNING

Goodfellow et al.'s work, encoded by each constituent and grouped into layers, of course, presents an extensive summary of the DL principles, methods, and applications. It discusses the underlying theory, the different DL architectures, and also the design and training of Deep Neural Networks (DNN). LeCun et al.'s landmark book underscores the substantial advances in DL and its transformative impact across various fields.

It explains how the availability of big datasets, the increase in computational power, and advances in algorithms and hardware have made DL so successful. "Researchers have used Deep Neural Networks to solve difficult problems, including image recognition, speech recognition, and game-playing" (LeCun et al., 2015).

11.6.5   ARTIFICIAL NEURAL NETWORKS (ANN)

"ANNs are popular in the field of image recognition, as they are capable of learning intricate patterns from *images*" (Krizhevsky et al., 2012). *"Recurrent* neural networks such as long short-term memory (LSTMs) show impressive performance on natural language processing tasks such *as language modeling and machine translation"* (Hochreiter & Schmidhuber, 1997).

11.6.6   EVOLUTIONARY COMPUTATION

Genetic algorithms have been successfully used to solve complex engineering design problems by simulating natural selection (Goldberg, 1989). It should be noted that there are no explicit individual representations as there are with Gas, and the goal of the evolutionary strategies is not to evolve directly the objective values but rather the respective parameters of the problem itself through the use of mutation and recombination operators (Schwefel, 1981). These have been successfully applied to a variety of optimization problems, such as design, scheduling, and control tasks (Back et al., 1997). Evolution strategies are an instance of evolutionary computation algorithms that are applied to resolve high-dimensional optimization issues in a wide range of fields (Beyer & Schwefel, 2002).

11.6.7   SENSORY PERCEPTION AND PROCESSING

A major area of neural networks for use in robotics is in related areas of perception and sensory processing. In particular, ANNs have been used for computer vision applications, enabling robots to recognize and classify objects with high accuracy, detect and track moving targets, and perceive the surrounding environment (Lecun et al., 2015). This works well with CNNs (Convolutional Neural Networks) for visual perception problems, like image recognition, object detection, and semantic segmentation, which are very dear to deep learning but essential for robots operating in complex and unstructured environments (Krizhevsky et al., 2012). Moreover, neural networks have been used in other modalities, such as auditory processing, tactile sensing (Mihelj et al., 2014), and proprioception, which enables robots to better perceive and understand their environment" (Goodfellow et al., 2016).

11.6.8   MOTION CONTROL AND NAVIGATION

Artificial Neural Networks have also played an important role in developing strong and adaptable robotic motion control systems. "RNNs and LSTMs have been applied to learn to model and predict robotic system dynamics for smooth and accurate control of robot motion" (Hochreiter & Schmidhuber, 1997). "In addition to this, neural networks have been used in robot navigation to plan and execute the optimal path in dynamic and uncertain environments."

Robots are using neural networks with elements like Simultaneous Localization and Mapping (SLAM) to navigate autonomously through their environment" (Siciliano & Khatib, 2016).

11.6.9 MAKING DECISIONS AND PLANNING A TASK

Neural networks have greatly aided the decision-making process and task planning in robots. "Neural networks can enable robots to make intelligent decisions by learning complicated patterns and relationships from data that allow it to reason about its own actions, adapt to novel situations, and solve difficult problems" (Goodfellow et al., 2016).

For instance, Deep Reinforcement Learning, the combination of Deep Neural Networks and reinforcement learning algorithms, has been used to train robots to perform complex tasks like dexterous manipulation, multi-agent coordination, and autonomous navigation (Mnih et al., 2015).

11.6.10 ROBOTICS AND NEURAL NETWORKS

Robotics is a fast-changing field, and it integrates components of engineering, computer science, and automation to create machines capable of performing a wide range of tasks, often in complex and dynamic environments. Artificial Neural Networks (ANNs), a central CIT, mimic the architecture and operation of the human brain, and are one of these indispensable building blocks that propelled the robotic potential to the next paradigm. A combination of robotics and neural networks has made breakthroughs in many areas, including perception, control, and decisions, so that robots can behave more like humans and adapt better (Siciliano & Khatib, 2016). As NN has revolutionized almost everything, robotics is one major thing that NN has given a new dimension to, but room exists for future work and challenges. Complex neural networks are considered to be *"black boxes,"* and it is often difficult to understand and explain the decision-making process, which is key to deploying robots in safety-critical tasks (Rudin, 2019). Many of the proposed neural network-based techniques in robotics need large amounts of training data, which can be slow and expensive to collect in the real world (Goodfellow et al., 2016). The challenge of bridging the simulation-hardware transfer remains to extend the simulation time in a real environment with unlimited variations (Tan et al., 2018). Research on making neural network-based robot systems safe and reliable, especially in safety-critical applications, is still ongoing (Amodei et al., 2016).

11.6.11 INTEGRATION AND APPLICATIONS

Hybridization, the use of ensemble and complex evolutionary computation techniques, has so far been used extensively together to solve challenging real-world problems.

An example of this can be found in neuro-evolutionary systems, where genetic algorithms or evolutionary strategies are used to optimize the structure and parameters of an ANN, resulting in more robust and adaptable models. Likewise, evolutionary computation has also been employed along with ensemble approaches, where genetic algorithms/genetic programming are used to evolve the ensemble architecture and combination strategies to create more efficient ensemble models (Castillo & Kordon, 2004). Such integrative approaches have been deployed across diverse domains such as pattern recognition, prediction, control, and decision-making, demonstrating their capability to address the complexity, uncertainty, and nonlinearity present in many real-world challenges (Engelbrecht, 2007).

11.7 CITS: THEIR APPLICATIONS, ETHICAL ISSUES, AND NEW DIRECTIONS

With widely used CITs like ANN, GA, and SI permeating every sector, we need to consider the ethics involved in using these CITs. While this can be great for solving complex problems, the use of these techniques can create problems related to biases, transparency, privacy, and the societal impact of using these models. Among the major ethical concerns with CITs is the potential for bias to be built into the decision-making process. Due to their nature, CITs—in particular those derived from machine learning—can reflect societal biases residing in the data used to build them and produce inequitable or discriminatory output (Barocas & Selbst, 2016). As a result, researchers have called for the need to scrutinize the data sources, feature selection, and model design to alleviate these biases (Corbett-Davies & Goel, 2018).

Even though there are plenty of models that could be used as CIT, many of them are complex in nature, such as deep neural networks, which have made it hard to understand their internal decision logic; hence, they should be described as a black box. This opacity can make it difficult to hold these systems accountable and to interpret their output (Lipton, 2018). This challenge has made the development of explainable AI and interpretable ML Techniques a necessity (Gilpin et al., 2018).

CITs and those who depend heavily on large datasets can raise privacy concerns. Personal data must be responsibly collected, stored, and used to protect individual privacy and prevent misuse or breaches (Vayena et al., 2018). Such policies, frameworks, and tools are useful to promote responsible data use across CIT applications. CITs have a significant societal impact through their potential for job insecurity and circumvention of existing social divides. There are important implications of CITs for society, especially since countries in the global south face different challenges with regard to technology (Brynjolfsson & McAfee, 2014). To alleviate these ethical considerations, a number of organizations and research groups have provided ethical paradigms, frameworks, and guidelines for CITs' development and deployment. Such frameworks are the IEEE's 2019 Ethically Aligned Design framework, the OECD's 2019 Principles for the Development and Use of AI, and the European Commission's 2019 Ethics Guidelines for Trustworthy AI. These frameworks generally highlight principles like transparency, accountability, fairness, privacy, and attention to societal impact. These statements serve as a framework for researchers, developers, and policymakers to guide the responsible and ethical use of CITs.

However, there are still some challenges in addressing ethical considerations in CITs, despite the increasing understanding of the differences between CITs tackling this. While the potential benefits of CITs are promising, the ethical implications remain a question mark, as the progress of technology far surpasses the formulation of a framework suited to the establishment of ethical guidelines or regulatory measures surrounding their development. The interdisciplinary nature of CITs means that multiple stakeholders, such as computer scientists, ethicists, policy makers, and domain experts, need to work together to create overarching and suitable solutions (Floridi et al., 2018). Ethical considerations regarding the use of CITs need to be examined carefully as scientists will be interfacing with local and national laws that balance scientific potential with practical considerations. By adopting ethical frameworks, encouraging openness and responsibility, and applying a societal perspective, researchers and practitioners can navigate the journey toward the maximal potential of CITs while avoiding consequences for humans and their society.

11.8   CHALLENGES AND CONSIDERATIONS TO THE APPLICATION OF CITS FOR GENERATING INNOVATIVE SOLUTIONS TO COMPLEX PROBLEMS

Generation of Creative and Innovative Solutions to Complex Problems. Part II CITs are promising and active, making this an interesting area of research. CITs utilize algorithms inspired by natural phenomena, which allows them to search large solution spaces and share novel ideas and solutions. This is the barrier to CITs becoming used kites in any domain, but that is a subject for another day. The human creative bit is why we do this because we have integration with human creativity—it is the answer never given to the question of CITS with expert domain knowledge and effective evaluators. This is possible because CITs act as a catalyst for creative solutions to complex issues across various domains, including design, business, and research. Traditional problem-solving methods fail with complex, poorly defined, or multi-dimensional problems.

A variety of CITs have been used and studied in recent years in their potential to allow such innovation to be incorporated in problem-solving. They utilize advanced computational techniques that allow them to push the envelope, re-imagine potentialities, and transcend traditional methodologies. For instance, ANNs have proven their advantage for this purpose through modeling the ancient power of human learning and beyond (Boden, 2004).

Either way, the field is starting to find ways to model creativity in light of these new systems, e.g., looking at ANN adaptability for tasks such as conceptual combination, analogical reasoning, and divergent thinking, which are directly associated with creative forms of problem solving (Sternberg and Lubart, 1999; Goel & Vattam, 2005). Mimicking the process of natural evolution, GAs have been effectively used to generate new potential solutions. GAs can search a large search space by generating and evaluating a variety of candidate solutions and selectively breeding the fittest of those to produce new, potentially more novel solutions (Holland, 1992). It has been used in engineering design, product development, and business strategy, where the objective is to discover innovative and effective solutions (Goldberg, 1989). Inspired by the indigenous ways of knowing of calabash and cultural capital, which are the basis of SI wisdom modeling, a natural phenomenon that appeared as an emergent property of complex biological systems and is naturally present in social insects. For example, the particle swarm optimization and ant colony optimization algorithms can navigate high-dimensional analysis to facilitate more creative solutions (Engelbrecht, 2007). Such techniques have been utilized in fields like artistic design, product development, and scientific problem solving (Kennedy et al., 2001).

While there are advantages to using CITs to stimulate creative and innovative solutions, there are also challenges associated with their use. Young students visit on a regular basis to see first-hand that there is a balance—or lack thereof—between the exploration of new ideas and the exploitation of existing knowledge, which can yield a truly innovative product. Some CITs are inherently complex and opaque, thus making it challenging to address their *"black box"* nature and explain the reasoning behind the produced solutions, which in turn may limit the acceptance and dissemination of these technologies. A significant hurdle that remains is the development of reliable objective measures to assess the creativity and innovativeness of the solutions generated. The resource demands of CITs can also grow, increasing computational cost as the dimensions of the problem domain's complexity increase, limiting their practical applicability (Engelbrecht, 2007).

11.8.1 CONNECTING CITs WITH SUBJECT MATTER EXPERTISE AND HUMAN INGENUITY

That being said, CITs can be used to generate creative and innovative solutions, but their effectiveness can be improved by filtering them through domain knowledge or human creativity. Promising results have been obtained with hybrid approaches that pair CITs with expert knowledge, user feedback, and human intuition.

One such approach is interactive evolutionary computation, in which humans provide feedback or guidance during the optimization process to better direct the search toward more desirable and creative solutions (Takagi, 2001). Likewise, integrating CITs with design thinking, which focuses on human-centered problem solving, will likely yield innovative and impactful solutions (Brown, 2008).

11.9 BAYESIAN NETWORKS (BN) AND REINFORCEMENT LEARNING (RL): KEY FEATURES, ELEMENTS, AND INTEGRATION

Bayesian Networks (BN) are a class of probabilistic graphical models that encode a set of variables and their conditional dependencies using a Directed Acyclic Graph (DAG).

Because of this, BNs are a strong reasoning framework for uncertainty, as they can accurately model and deduce the dependency connections between variables in a complex domain (Pearl, 1988). BN utilizes probabilities, thus modeling uncertainty and ambiguity within the relations. The structure of a Bayesian network is encoded in a DAG, where nodes are variables and directed edges are conditional dependencies. Each node inherits a Conditional Probability Table (CPT) that indicates the probabilities of the node adopting distinct values conditional on the values of its parent nodes. In addition to this, inference and reasoning can be performed using BN, which involves estimating the probabilities of hidden variables based on the observed data and the network structure. Based on this overall understanding of Bayesian Inference, Bayesian Networks have been applied in various domains, such as medical diagnosis, decision support systems, risk analysis, and pattern recognition (Korb & Nicholson, 2010).

Reinforcement Learning (RL) is a form of ML algorithm in which the agent learns through exploration and feedback from the environment in terms of rewards and penalties. The agent aims to learn a policy. This is a state-action mapping that maximizes the cumulative reward over time (Sutton & Barto, 2018). Its action decision-making unit takes action to interact with the environment and learns to improve its actions. The environment is the world in which the agent acts and receives feedback. The actions are referred to as the possible choices the agent can make in a given state. The output would be the reward—feedback that the agent receives from its environment, which can be either positive or negative, that shall inform the learning process. Its state is the mapping of the agent and the environment to the present situation. The agent uses this strategy to pick actions based on the current state, and this is called *"policy"* (Mnih et al., 2015; Silver et al., 2017). Reinforcement Learning (RL) has been applied to various problems, including game playing (AlphaGo, AlphaZero), robotics, resource allocation, recommendation systems, etc.

Bayesian Networks (BNs) and Reinforcement Learning (RL) are separate methods, but can be combined into hybrid approaches that take advantage of both. This merging can be especially valuable in those complex, uncertain, and partially visible world settings. This strategy merges the two in order to use BN for the environment modeling and for representing the agent's beliefs, but RL to learn the appropriate policy to make the decision (Kaelbling et al., 1996). It means it can reason about what is causing what in its environment and make better decisions as a result. Others suggested that BNs can be used to lead the exploration and exploitation process in the reinforcement learning framework by implementing the probabilistic information encoded in the network structure. This allows the agent to explore more promising regions of the state space and learn more efficiently. The combination of BN and RL has been utilized in a variety of fields, including robotics, healthcare, and finance, where reasoning under uncertainty and learning through feedback is essential (Korb & Nicholson, 2010; Sallans & Hinton, 2004). BNs and RL are both complementary techniques that can be used in combination to solve complex problems involving uncertainty and the need to learn in a goal-directed adaptive fashion. Integrating these techniques can yield more resilient and efficient solutions across diverse domains.

11.10 CITS APPLICATIONS FOR SOLVING COMPLEX PROBLEMS

CITs have been widely applied in various challenging problems that traditional techniques do not easily deal with. CITs have successfully been applied in several areas. This includes such areas as scheduling, routing, and resource allocation (Gen & Cheng, 2000; Engelbrecht, 2007)

The applicability of ANNs and Fuzzy Systems extends to complex pattern recognition and classification problems, including, but not limited to, Image Recognition, Speech Recognition, and Medical Diagnosis (Lecun et al., 2015) and (Siddique & Adeli, 2013) These are applied for the design and control of complex systems like robotic systems, manufacturing processes, and power systems (Engelbrecht, 2007).

For example, ANNs and hybrid CITs are applied to Complex Predictive Modeling and forecasting tasks, including stock market prediction, weather forecasting, and energy demand forecasting (Siddique & Adeli, 2013). They are also used as a solution to deal with complex things in bioinformatics, such as protein structure prediction, gene expression analysis, and even drug discovery (Engelbrecht, 2007). One of the most prevalent CI methods is Artificial Neural Networks (ANNs), *"which are inspired by the structure and function of the human brain. ANNs consist of interconnected nodes, or artificial neurons, which can learn to perform different tasks by tuning the strength of the connections between them"* (Goodfellow et al., 2016). ANN application areas are *"ubiquitous in biology, including genomic and transcriptomic analysis, molecular modeling, and biomolecular and diagnostic applications"* (Bishop, 2006).

11.11 AI AND COMPUTATIONAL INTELLIGENCE TECHNIQUES IN INTEGRATION

AI and CITs: The intersectionality of AI and CITs has proven to be a fertile ground for both enabling and accelerating innovative solutions to complex problems. Having this dual level of training can help create parallel paths or railroads for the problem-solving capabilities of both domains to take respective side gates and build the right solutions to scale up and/or get more streamlined. AI: With its ability to process and analyze vast amounts of data, recognize patterns, and automate decision-making, AI has become a powerful tool in tackling complex challenges. However, classical AI has its limitations in dealing with ambiguity, uncertainty, and complexity common to real-life problems. That is where CITs come in. Inspired by natural phenomena and biological processes, they can enhance and supplement AI systems with a range of capabilities. But some critical CITs are being combined with AI. The structure of an ANN mimics the human brain, and these types of algorithms perform exceptionally well in image processing, speech recognition, classification, and non-linear function approximation. Its integration with AI can boost the accuracy and reliability of prediction models, image recognition, and NLP.

Based on the principles of natural selection and genetics, EA evolutionary algorithms can optimize complex systems, solve optimization problems, and discover innovative solutions. They can be combined with AI in improving decision-making, resource allocation, and optimization of design. FL Systems: These can cope with uncertainty, imprecision, and ambiguity by advanced use of fuzzy sets and linguistic variables. The combination of FL with AI will help facilitate better decision-making, be it in control systems or more profound reasoning in the complex environment of the real world. They found that they could use algorithms that rely on the swarm behavior of social insects, like ant colonies and bird flocks, to solve optimization problems and coordinate multi-agent systems. These techniques can be used with AI to help solve complex scheduling, routing, and resource allocation problems. Further segmentation of AI and CI is gradually fading as the lines blur, which in turn surfaces various innovative solutions to meet the complex necessities. The results from this integration have the potential to drive innovative solutions, enhanced decision-making processes, and the advancement of artificial intelligence technologies.

11.12 HYBRID, ENSEMBLE, AND EVOLUTIONARY COMPUTATION TECHNIQUES: CHALLENGES AND FUTURE DIRECTIONS

Based on the reviewed hybrid, ensemble, and evolutionary computation techniques in previous sections, some challenges are identified along with promising future directions.

- Some Advanced Artificial Intelligence Techniques (*i.e.,* Hybrid, Ensemble, and Evolutionary Computation Techniques) are powerful methods in CI, but their features also present multiple challenges and requirements.
  Using several techniques in combination can result in much more complicated and computationally heavy models, which can further hinder scalability and applicability in practice. These integrated systems are complex by nature, and it can become really challenging to understand and explain the reasons behind the solutions obtained, which is really important in such domains that seek transparency.
- Given that problem, one major problem remains. It is about effectively combining and optimizing the constituent techniques, which is a daunting task. Furthermore, developing systematic and principled strategies for combining and optimizing the performance of the individual techniques in the hybrid or ensemble frameworks is a field of research in progress. Another important consideration: these integrated techniques should still be as flexible and adaptable as possible to suit a variety of problem characteristics (*e.g.,* multimodality, noisy data, dynamic environments, *etc.*). Hybrid, Ensemble, and Evolutionary Computation Techniques will remain a prominent theme within the field of CI, evolving and diverging from these themes to integrate these techniques for successful application across complex real-world applications.

11.13 SUMMARY THOUGHTS

It is now well-recognized that the increasing need and promise of Computational Intelligence Techniques (CITs) in addressing challenging real-life issues, and have upheld progress in Artificial Intelligence (AI) as a whole. It covers Computational Intelligence Methods (Neural Networks, Evolutionary Algorithms, Fuzzy Systems) that efficiently disclose internal trends, facilitate decision making, and increase prediction capabilities in a variety of areas. This highlights the flexibility and analytical strength of these techniques. In addition, recently there has been an increasing trend towards the convergence of various CITs, leading to hybrid approaches. These hybrid models use the complementary strengths of multiple methods, which further improve the capabilities of AI-based systems to solve complex problems. It also enables us to see the increasing use of certain CITs like Swarm Intelligence algorithms and Fuzzy Logic in the context of complex optimization problems and enhancing AI system decision-making. This implies that some techniques might be more appropriate for some kinds of challenges. Moreover, we have also witnessed the timely integration of these methods within AI systems, the rise of hybrid methods and the adaptation of individual techniques and methods in a tailored manner, indicating that the future of mitigating complex problems lays in the precise exploitation of Computational Intelligence (CI) The development and integration of CITs contribute significantly to the emergence of innovative approaches to do that, and hence, help to push the state-of-the-art in the field of AI. To conclude, as researchers and practitioners seek novel applications for these powerful tools, we can expect transformative applications and breakthroughs in the years ahead.

REFERENCES

Alam, T., M. Benaida, and A. Ahsan. 2020. "The Role of Edge Computing and IoT in Smart City." *International Journal of Computer Science and Network Security* 20 (3): 47–57.

Amabile, T.M. 1988. "A Model of Creativity and Innovation in Organizations." *Research in Organizational Behavior* 10: 123–67.

Amodei, D., C. Olah, J. Steinhardt, P. Christiano, J. Schulman, and D. Mane. 2016. "Concrete Problems in AI Safety." *arXiv preprint arXiv*:1606.06565.

Back, T., D.B., and Z Michalewicz, eds. 1997. *Evolutionary Computation 1: Basic Algorithms and Operators*. CRC Press.

Barocas, S., and Selbst, A. D. 2016. "Big Data's Disparate Impact." *California Law Review*, 104 (3): 671–732. https://doi.org/10.15779/Z386Z67.

Bello, R., and G. Evolvi. 2019. "Hybrid Artificial Intelligence and Blockchain: A Systematic Review." *Applied Soft Computing*: 106492. https://doi.org/10.1016/j.asoc.2019.106492.

Beyer, H. G., and H. P. Schwefel. 2002. "Evolution Strategies: A Comprehensive Introduction." *Natural Computing* 1 (1): 3–52.

Bishop, C. M. 2006. *Pattern recognition and machine learning*. Springer.

Boden, M. A. 2004. *The Creative Mind: Myths and Mechanisms*. Routledge.

Bonabeau, E., M. Dorigo, and G. Theraulaz. 1999. *Swarm Intelligence: From Natural to Artificial Systems*. Oxford University Press.

Brown, T. 2008. *Change by Design: How Design Thinking Transforms Organizations and Inspires Innovation*. Harper Business.

Brynjolfsson, E., and A. McAfee. 2014. *The Second Machine Age: Work, Progress, and Prosperity in a Time of Brilliant Technologies*. W. W. Norton.

Castillo, O., and A. Kordon. 2004. *Soft Computing for Control of Non-linear Dynamical Systems*. Springer.

Corbett-Davies, S., and S. Goel. 2018. "The Measure and Mismeasure of Fairness: A Critical Review of Fair Machine Learning." arXiv preprint arXiv:1808.00023.

Cordón, O. 2001. "A Historical Review of Evolutionary Learning Methods for Mamdani-Type Fuzzy Rule-Based Systems: Designing Interpretable Genetic Fuzzy Systems." *International Journal of Approximate Reasoning* 27 (2): 143–78. https://doi.org/10.1016/S0888-613X(01)00010-2.

Dietterich, T. G. 2000. "An experimental comparison of three methods for constructing ensembles of decision trees: Bagging, boosting, and randomization." *Machine Learning*, 40 (1): 139–57. https://doi.org/10.1023/A:1007607513941.

Dietrich, D. 2000. *Communication and Symbolic Behavior Scales Developmental Profile*. Paul Brookes Publishing.

Dorigo, M., and E. Şahin. 2004. "Swarm Robotics – Special Issue Editorial." *Autonomous Robots* 17 (2–3): 111–3. https://doi.org/10.1023/B:AURO.0000033972.73165.45.

Engelbrecht, A. P. 2007. *Computational Intelligence: An Introduction*. John Wiley.

European Commission. 2019. *High-Level Expert Group on Artificial Intelligence: Ethics guidelines for trustworthy artificial intelligence*. Publications Office of the European Union.

Floridi, L., J. Cowls, M. Beltrametti, R. Chatila, P. Chazerand, V. Dignum, and C. Luetge. 2018. "A14People—An Ethical Framework for a Good AI Society: Opportunities, Risks, Principles, and Recommendations." *Minds and Machines* 28 (4): 689–707.

Friedman, J. H. 2001. "Greedy Function Approximation: A Gradient Boosting Machine." *Annals of Statistics* 29 (5): 1189–232.

Goodfellow, I., Y. Bengio, and A. Courville. 2016. *Deep Learning*. MIT Press.

Gao, X. Z., Y. Hatakeyama, S. J Ovaska, and M. Malik. 2019. "Computational Intelligence Techniques for Solving Real-World Problems." *International Journal of Innovative Computing, Information and Control* 15 (2): 407–24.

Gen, M., and R. Cheng. 2000. *Genetic Algorithms and Engineering Optimization*. John Wiley.

Gilpin, L. H., D. Bau, B. Z. Yuan, A. Bajwa, M. Specter, and L. Kagal. 2018. "Explaining Explanations: An Overview of Interpretability of Machine Learning." *IEEE Access* 6: 52138–60.

Goel, A. K., and S. Vattam. 2005. "Design Patterns: A Knowledge Representation Schema for Design." *AI EDAM: Artificial Intelligence for Engineering Design, Analysis, and Manufacturing* 19 (3): 225–42.

Goldberg, D. E. 1989. *Genetic Algorithms in Search, Optimization, and Machine Learning*. Addison-Wesley.

Gubbi, J., R. Buyya, S. Marusic, and M. Palanisami. 2013. "Internet of Things (IoT): A Vision, Architectural Elements, and Future Directions." *Future Generation Computer Systems* 29 (7): 1645–60. https://doi.org/10.1016/j.future.2013.01.010.

Hochreiter, S., and J. Schmidhuber. 1997. "Long Short-Term Memory." *Neural Computation* 9 (8): 1735–80.

Holland, J. H. 1992. *Adaptation in Natural and Artificial Systems*. MIT Press.

Jang, J.S.R. 1993. "ANFIS: Adaptive Network-based Fuzzy Inference System." *IEEE Transactions on Systems, Man, and Cybernetics* 23 (3): 665–85.

Kaelbling, L. P., Littman, M. L., and Moore, A. W. 1996. "Reinforcement learning: A survey." *Journal of Artificial Intelligence Research*, 4: 237–285. https://doi.org/10.1613/jair.301

Kennedy, J., Eberhart, R. C., and Shi, Y. 2001. *Swarm intelligence*. Morgan Kaufmann.

Khan, S. A., A. W. Malik, A. Ahmad, and A. Alsuhaibani. 2022. "Computational Intelligence Techniques for Enhanced Decision-Making in Intelligent Systems." *IEEE Access* 10: 25251–72.

Koda, T. 1992. "Evolutionary Computation: Theory and Applications." In *Modern Japan: Social-Industrial-Political Change and Stability*, edited by L. R. Golden, 102–21. Westview Press.

Korb, K. B., and A. E. Nicholson. 2010. *Bayesian Networks: An Introduction*. Wiley.

Krizhevsky, A., I. Sutskever, and G. E. Hinton. 2012. "ImageNet Classification with Deep Convolutional Neural Networks." *Advances in Neural Information Processing Systems* 25: 1097–105.

LeCun, Y., Y. Bengio, and G. Hinton. 2015. "Deep Learning." *Nature* 544. G o l d b e r g, D. E. 1989. *Genetic Algorithms in Search, Optimization, and Machine Learning.* Addison-Wesley. 521 (7553): 436–44.

Liang, Y., H. Qu, and K. Li. 2020. "Swarm Intelligence Algorithms for the Optimization of Complex Systems." *IEEE Transactions on Evolutionary Computation* 24 (6): 1061–77.

Lipton, Zachary C. 2018. "The Mythos of Model Interpretability." *Queue* 16 (3): 31–57.

Madani, K., and S Assilian. 1975. "A Linguistic Approach to Decision Making: An Analysis." *International Journal of Man-Machine Studies* 7 (1): 1–14.

Mihelj, M., Novak, D., and S. Beguš. 2014. *Virtual reality technology and applications.* Springer.

Mnih, V. et al. 2015. "Human-Level Control through Deep Reinforcement Learning." *Nature* 518 (7540): 529–33. https://doi.org/10.1038/nature14236.

Mumford, M. D., R. A. Schultz, and J. R. Van Doorn. 2001. "Performance in Planning: Processes, Requirements, and Errors." *Review of General Psychology* 5 (3): 213–40. https://doi.org/ 10.1037/1089-2680.5.3.213.

Nakamoto, S. 2008. *"Bitcoin: A Peer-to-Peer Electronic Cash System."* https://bitcoin.org/bitc oin.pdf.

NewWayLabs. 2023. "Innovative Solutions to Complex Problems—Leveraging Computational Intelligence Techniques for Driving Advancements in AI." *Journal of Computational Intelligence and Applications* 18 (2): 1–15. https://doi.org/10.1142/S021952592 3400078.

Pearl, J. 1988. *Probabilistic reasoning in intelligent systems: Networks of plausible inference.* Morgan Kaufmann.

Poole, D. L., and A. K. Mackworth. 2017. *Artificial Intelligence: Foundations of Computational Agents.* 2nd ed. Cambridge University Press.

Rudin, W. 2019. *Principles of Mathematical Analysis.* 3rd ed. McGraw-Hill Education.

Rumelhart, D. E., Hinton, G. E., and Williams, R. J. 1986. "Learning representations by back-propagating errors." *Nature*, 323 (6088): 533–6. https://doi.org/10.1038/323533a0

Russel, S., and P. Norvig. 2016. *Artificial Intelligence: A Modern Approach.* 3rd ed. Pearson.

Sallans, B., and Hinton, G. E. 2004. "Reinforcement learning with factored states and actions." *Journal of Machine Learning Research*, 5: 1063–88.

Satyanarayanan, M. 2017. "The Emergence of Edge Computing." *Computer* 50 (1):30–39. https://doi.org/10.1109/MC.2017.9.

Schwefel, H.-P. 1981. *Numerical Optimization of Computer Models.* John Wiley.

Shen, W., Q. Hao, H.J. Yoon, and D.H. Norrie. 2006. "Applications of Agent-Based Systems in Intelligent Manufacturing: An Updated Review." *Advanced Engineering Informatics* 20 (4): 415–31. https://doi.org/10.1016/j.aei.2006.05.004.

Shi, W., J. Cao, Q. Zhang, Y. Li, and L. Xu. 2016. "Edge Computing: Vision and Challenges." *IEEE Internet of Things Journal* 3 (5): 637–46. https://doi.org/10.1109/ JIOT.2016.2579198.

Siciliano, B., and O. Khatib, eds. 2016. *Springer Handbook of Robotics.* 2nd ed. Springer.

Siddique, M., and H. Adeli. 2013. *Smart Structures: Innovative Systems for Seismic Response Control.* CRC Press.

Silver, D., Schrittwieser, J., Simonyan, K., Antonoglou, I., Huang, A., Guez, A., Hubert, T., Baker, L., Lai, M., Sifre, L., van den Driessche, G., Chen, Y., Lillicrap, T., Leach, M., Graepel, T., and Hassabis, D. 2017. "Mastering the game of Go without human knowledge." *Nature,* 550(7676): 354–9. https://doi.org/10.1038/nature24270

Stanley, K. O., and R. Miikkulainen. 2002. "Evolving Neural Networks through Augmenting Topologies." *Evolutionary Computation* 10 (2): 99–127.

Sternberg, R. J., and T. I. Lubart. 1999. "The Concept of Creativity: Prospects and Paradigms." In *Handbook of Creativity*, edited by Robert J. Sternberg, 3–15. Cambridge University Press.

Sutton, R. S., and Andrew G. Barto. 2018. *Reinforcement Learning: An Introduction*. 2nd ed. MIT Press.

Takagi, H. 2001. "Interactive Evolutionary Computation: Fusion of the Capabilities of EC Optimization and Human Evaluation." *Proceedings of the IEEE* 89 (9): 1275–96.

Tan, M., B. Chen, R. Pang, V. Vasudevan, S. Sengupta, Q. V. Le, and Q. Le. 2018. "MnasNet: Platform-aware Neural Architecture Search for Mobile." In *Proceedings of the IEEE/CVF Conference on Computer Vision and Pattern Recognition*, 2820–28. https://doi.org/10.1109/CVPR.2019.00291.

Vayena, E., M. Salathé, L. C. Madoff, and J. S. Brownstein. 2018. "Ethical Challenges of Big Data in Public Health." *PLOS Computational Biology* 14 (11): e1006253.

Xue, F., C Ye, and Z Zuo. 2021. "Emerging Trends in Computational Intelligence for Advancing Artificial Intelligence: A Meta-Analysis." *IEEE Transactions on Emerging Topics in Computational Intelligence* 5 (2): 138–51.

Yao, X. 1999. "Evolutionary Computation for Modeling and Optimization." *International Journal of Approximate Reasoning* 21 (2–3): 197–240.

Zadeh, L.A. 1965. "Fuzzy Sets." *Information and Control* 8 (3): 338–53.

Zheng, Z., S. Xie, H. Dai, X. Chen, and H. Wang. 2018. "Blockchain Challenges and Opportunities: A Survey." *International Journal of Web and Grid Services* 14 (4): 352–75. https://doi.org/10.1504/IJWGS.2018.095647.

12 Research Frontiers and Open Challenges

Ezil Sam Leni Ayyaswami and Smitha Rajagopal

12.1 INTRODUCTION

Security intelligence [1] is about collecting, analyzing, and using data to gain insights and mitigate security threats. It is applying sophisticated tools, methods, and practices to detect vulnerabilities in the organization's infrastructure. Since Advanced Persistent Threats (APTs) emerge continuously with a dynamic nature, traditional security systems make it challenging to address them. Therefore, signature-based security systems fail to modernize to recognize today's attack scenarios [2]. Attacks are perennial in nature; they have surfaced since the dawn of networking history and have not shown any signs of decline. Threat actors fully perform APTs, which evade firewalls and antivirus software most of the time. Furthermore, Security Intelligence's function is a base for identifying and countering Advanced Persistent Threats (APT) by transforming raw data into useful information. Security Intelligence (SI) has gotten a lot better with Artificial Intelligence (AI) as it is easier and more effective at finding, understanding, and taking care of security cases. Threat intelligence, a subfield of security intelligence born in the military world, is where human decision-makers and experts gather, analyze, and share information with other human stakeholders. Cyber Intelligence [3] comprises Cyber Threat Intelligence (CTI) pertaining to threats and the threat actors. With the help of CTI, organizations are able to alter their normal cyber practices from "reacting and scattershot" to "proactive, forward thinking, and smart." In the days when Artificial Intelligence (AI) is a frontrunner and a key technology moving the world, AI is widely used to resolve all kinds of cybersecurity issues. This is the fundamental challenge it faces in helping to collate insights from relevant cybersecurity data and translate that into meaningful insights. Meticulous monitoring of logs, lengthy security alerts and emails, and analyzing various reporting dashboards are resources associated with extraneous work. However, AI turns the tide here for organizations as it can quickly analyze vast quantities of data with great accuracy, recognizing patterns and predicting future potential risks [4]. The way the security teams source, syndicate, and respond to threat information is changing with AI. Today's threat intelligence strategies focus on volume and variety of security-related data, and AI is an essential element within this context. By constantly looking at tons of threat information, CTI collects data that is used to structure and provide context for cyber threat activities, trends, and attacks. It can come

DOI: 10.1201/9781003680192-12

from various external threat sources, internal networks, previous attack analysis, or research. Discriminative AI and Generative AI are both integral to the field of cyber threat intelligence. However, Discriminative AI relies on the trained data and often needs different models for each language [5].

12.2 DISCRIMINATIVE AI AND ITS PITFALLS IN SECURITY INTELLIGENCE

With discriminative artificial intelligence (AI) being widely applied for the analysis and identification of threats in the field of security intelligence, the latest focus on AI integration into security intelligence over the recent years has garnered much attention. This technology aims to support decision-making by training models to distinguish between commonly occurring behaviors and anomalous behaviors. While the application of discriminative AI in security may yet bear innovative potential, it has not been without pitfalls. Due to the inherent difficulty in human behavior and the limited availability of training data, there has been significant failure with regard to accurately identifying threats [6–8]. In the process, they raise important questions about the trustworthiness, and some would say ethical acceptability, of this kind of technology being used in risk-prone settings. The anomalies of discriminative AI not only make a strong security system inconvenient but also uncover weak points that can be used, obliging us to reconsider how AI is used in intelligence operations. Considering that discriminative AI requires pre-existing training data to operate effectively, its limitations in security applications are obvious. However, many security scenarios, e.g., those that encounter new threats or unexpected attack vectors, often lack sufficient historical data to make these AI models work. As is seen in recent literature, though AI-based methods have made security frameworks robust, testing depends mainly on the attack models that they understand, attack models that never cease changing. Additionally, issues with biases in training datasets cause misclassifications and impact the trustworthiness of security decisions. The fast-paced nature of cybersecurity threats makes this phenomenon even worse, as real-time adaptability is essentially required. The inability of discriminative AI to reliably generalize in the context of security intelligence highlights the need for more sophisticated and adaptive approaches. Figure 12.1 presents the significant challenges and limitations of discriminative AI in CTI.

The challenges that have so far existed can be broadly categorized into data quality and bias. This makes data quality and bias challenges in the world of security intelligence very acute, as discriminative AI systems base their processes on structural flaws or a lack of comprehensive datasets. As AI technologies tackle huge amounts of security data, the risk exists that existing biases are also perpetuated and magnified. For example, suppose the training data is skewed towards certain demographics or specific geographic areas. In that case, AI may incorrectly label or inaccurately identify possible threats that may reduce its real-world usefulness and serve as a bigger threat. Furthermore, the lack of a coherent method to discover AI hazards outlined in the AI Hazard Management framework can impede the elimination of these biases. Moreover, a hybrid 3C framework for contextual regulation of content

Challenges and Limitations of Discriminative AI in Cyber Threat Intelligence

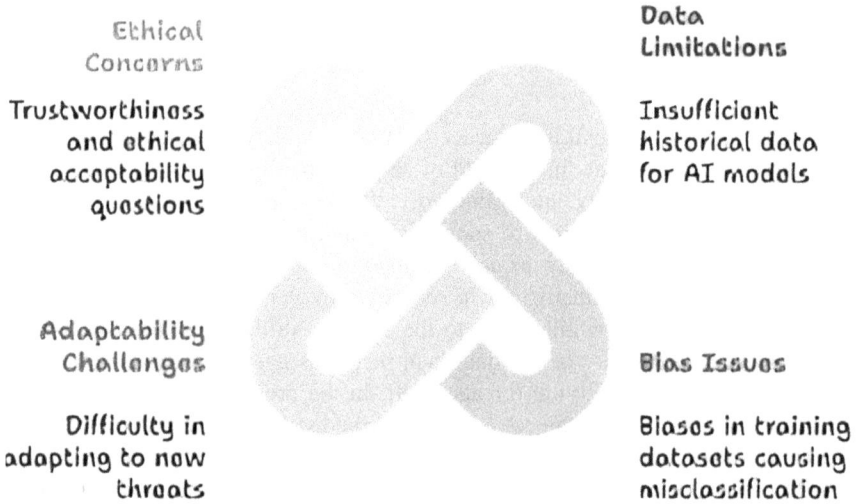

Ethical
Concerns

Trustworthiness
and ethical
acceptability
questions

Data
Limitations

Insufficient
historical data
for AI models

Adaptability
Challenges

Difficulty in
adapting to now
threats

Bias Issues

Biases in training
datasets causing
misclassification

FIGURE 12.1 Challenges and Limitations of Discriminative AI in CTI.

further complicates the landscape, making it virtually impossible for organizations to maintain data quality and fairness, amplifying discrimination in security intelligence.

As artificial intelligence (AI) is being increasingly relied upon in security intelligence, it is uncovering huge vulnerabilities, leading to disastrous breaches. For example, misclassifications of AI algorithms are reflected in the model's performance, classifying benign behavior as malicious and vice versa, not cataloguing real security risks. Training data could miss the complexity of real-world interactions and simply reinforce the biases or blind spots by not having covered them in the training data. In the case of polymorphically changing cyber environments, these problems are exacerbated because fast changes tend to skew the predictive capability of AI models [9]. The consequences of such false alarms are powerful and open up debates about enhanced oversight and flexibility when it comes to deploying AI systems in security settings. With the growing adoption of AI by organizations in risk management frameworks, we must recognize and act upon such false assumptions made by the AI models to protect sensitive data and preserve public goodwill for technological advancements.

There are three levels of cyber threat intelligence, namely operational, tactical, and strategic [10]. Figure 12.2 illustrates how each level varies in the content and format of the information shared, the target audience, and how it is being used. Information on the possibility of upcoming attacks on the organization is often taken for operational threat intelligence. Although it might be difficult to gather such information, an intelligence provider can acquire it by using several resources. They might snoop

FIGURE 12.2 Levels of Cyber Threat Intelligence.

Unveiling Cyber Threat Intelligence Sources

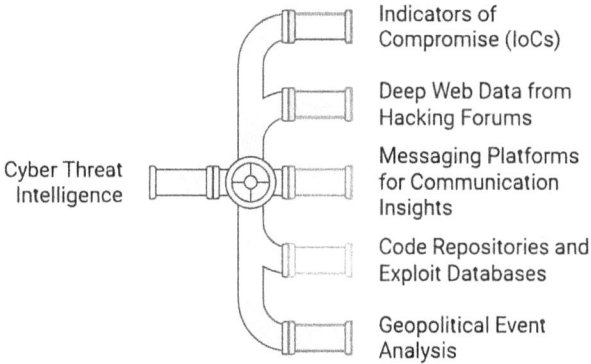

FIGURE 12.3 Sources of Cyber Threat Intelligence.

on discussions that a group of cyber activists is carrying out to launch an attack or monitor dark web forums where the company's sensitive data is being purchased and sold.

Tactical threat intelligence is knowledge of how threat actors operate, by means of the techniques, tactics, and procedures they employ, known as TTP. Tactical threat intelligence providers' effective main output is indicators of compromise (IOCs). This is particularly useful to maintain signature-based defense systems "up to date," protecting against known attack types.

Strategic threat intelligence is intended to brief senior decision-makers about major shifts in the threat landscape. Strategic intelligence products are written in simple language aimed at senior decision-makers and focus on business risk issues, not technical jargon.

12.2.1 Sources of Intelligence

The key sources of intelligence are represented in Figure 12.3.

1. Indicators of Compromise (IoCs) are frequently used resources by cyber threat intelligence suppliers [11]. They are forensic data in the form of hashes of malware samples, IP addresses, and domain names that someone has tied to malicious activity. Firewalls and intrusion detection systems can be updated with IoCs, and IoCs can help gain an understanding of tactics, techniques, and procedures (TTPs) of the threat actors [12,13]. Though considered to be data rather than processed intelligence on their own, IoCs are a part of the larger umbrella of cyber threat intelligence.

2. Data from exclusive hacking forums often visited by cybercriminals is part of the deep web. They can provide very valuable information about what tools and services cyber criminals are promoting, and to whom. They also give a sense of what vulnerabilities are being discussed, so better focus can be given to security patches.

3. We know threat actors use messaging platforms for communication, and this provides valuable intelligence. Rather than using semi-public forums to talk to each other about products and services, some cyber criminals are resorting to simpler—and yet more straightforward—ways to interact. Likewise, cyber activists often do their planning in a blend of traditional Internet Relay Chat (IRC) channels and a number of messaging apps. This can provide good clues to different strategies and targets.

4. The code repository and exploit databases contain good information about the exploits that threat actors could use. They also point out exactly which vulnerabilities need to be addressed quickly for efficient patching.

5. Through the analysis of geopolitical events, insights can be elicited into the motivations of politics and the leaders of a country. For example, understanding the alignment of a country's strategic goals versus that of a partnering organization, or having a sense of how national relationships might affect the likelihood of disrupting an area in a particular way, can put the organization in a better position to know what the real hurdles are.

The utilization of cyber threat intelligence in an organization can be broken down into four primary areas:

- Anticipate: Strategic threat intelligence enables businesses to see those potential threats before they appear, therefore giving them the opportunity to prepare in advance how they can avoid the risks.
- Deter: This is the intelligence that will start preventing malicious events from happening, such as malware signatures that penetrate systems to disrupt devices.
- Identify: It can even be a method for spotting threats as they happen or already exist in a network. This encompasses tactics, techniques and procedures (TTPs) that can be employed during the course of threat hunting activity.
- React: Active information is the term used to describe the information that helps reduce the severity or consequences of active incidents. Understanding the TTPs of that adversary, if they have been detected on the network, will give insights into what any attacker might do next and what the victim should

do next. How well a company can roll up threat intelligence across different business areas depends on the quality of intelligence being put in and the sophistication of the organization dissecting the intelligence.

12.3   GENERATIVE AI FOR CYBER THREAT INTELLIGENCE

The landscape of today's digital age is becoming more complex. Organizations are at a higher risk of cyber threats, and for this reason, the need for cyber threat intelligence (CTI) has never been more critical. In this domain, generative artificial intelligence (AI) is now emerging as a powerful tool, enabling new capabilities, helping detect threats, analyze them, and respond. In the domain of cyber threat intelligence, generative AI systems can parse through a tremendous amount of data across disparate sources and create insights and predictions about future threats [14]. This enables organizations to stay ahead of cyber adversaries by finding vulnerabilities and attack patterns before they occur. A major advantage of using generative AI for cyber threat intelligence is that it can process and analyze data on a scale that has not been possible before.

Traditionally, gathering and analyzing threat intelligence happens via manual processes that are both time-consuming and susceptible to human error. Automating these tasks with generative AI can consume data from multiple sources, including security logs, threat reports, social media, and dark web forums. It can find patterns and anomalies that go undetected, thus offering organizations the scope to navigate upcoming threats in advance. In addition, generative AI can model different attack scenarios and give organizations a clear view of how various kinds of cyber hazards can affect them [15]. For instance, it can generate phishing emails or malware samples as realistic as possible, which will help the security team to understand how attackers might operate and what kinds of defenses can be deployed. An organization's security posture can only be improved with this predictive capability, through tailored defenses capable of countering the most likely threats. In addition, generative AI can function as an enabler for the collaboration of different teams in an organization. It can act as a common language between technical and non-technical stakeholders by creating comprehensive reports and visualizations from threat data. Transparency of this sort creates a culture of security awareness in the organization, while at the same time supporting compliance with cybersecurity regulatory requirements [16].

12.4   SIEM SOLUTIONS USING GEN AI

Over the last few years, the cybersecurity landscape has changed quite dramatically, all as a result of technology evolution and intensified—and in some cases, more sophisticated—cyber threats. As a solution, Security Information and Event Management (SIEM) devices have become integral to defending such organizations against these threats; they allow for the real-time analysis of security alerts from applications and network hardware. Generative AI is now a breakthrough in the integration within the SIEM solution development ecosystem, improving its efficiency and effectiveness in the struggle with cyber risks. Generative AI is an algorithms that generate new content or data based on learned patterns in previously existing content or data. In the context of SIEM solutions, generative AI can be utilized to, amongst other things, simulate possible attacks based on various files, analyze huge volumes of security-related data, and automate incident response functions. Using Machine learning models, organizations can create a virtual environment that will imitate possible attack scenarios. This makes security teams better understand vulnerabilities and helps them create more robust defenses. The main benefit of including generative AI in SIEM systems is that it will increase the SIEM's ability to identify threats. Typically, traditional SIEM solutions rely on predefined rules and signatures to find anomalies. But changing attacker techniques means static rules are hard to get right for new types of attacks. Generative AI systems can examine historic data and understand attack cadences to identify abnormal behavior that might represent the onset of a threat. This is proactive, which greatly shortens the time to recognize potential breaches so that corrective action can be taken rapidly. Data Lakes and AI in SIEM need to become part of futuristic solutions, as key elements to enabling increased security at an industry-wide scale, as well as aid in threat identification. Current studies affirm Data Lakes as a good approach to handle mammoth unstructured and structured data across many industries [17,18].

Additionally, when organizations are witnessing humongous alerts, generative AI can help automate the incident response process. Security analysts can then use their time to focus on the most complex issues that need human intervention, while automated repetitive tasks such as correlating events or categorizing incidents can be automated. For example, generative AI models can suggest particular remediation steps from previous incidents or automatically respond to mitigate threats from growing before they develop into issues. That is where the level of automation comes in; it both makes operational efficiency better and beefs up an organization's overall security posture. Generative AI also becomes a part of SIEM solutions, which can increase predictive capabilities. Generative AI platforms analyze trends, look for potential vulnerabilities, and can thus help organizations anticipate what may happen in the future. With this foresight, companies can effectively allocate resources, taking first those steps that will prove the most helpful in being secure to further security measures and ultimately build a more resilient cybersecurity framework. With the ability to predict where threats could occur, organizations will know where to be ahead of the curve and adapt their approaches to the situation. Yet, utilizing generative AI within SIEM tools has its own problems. Steps must be undertaken to manage concerns about data privacy, the requirement for high-quality training data, and the possibilities of false positives. For their AI models to be effective in threat detection, organizations must ensure that their models have been trained using as diverse a dataset as possible to prevent biases and inaccuracies. Additionally, AI systems are complex, and the workforce needs people skilled enough to understand AI-generated insights, making appropriate judgements from them. Finally, the integration of generative AI into SIEM systems is a huge leap forward in cybersecurity.

Generative AI, by contrast, can help organizations by improving threat detection, automating incident response, and offering predictive capabilities to fight increasingly complex and sophisticated cyber threats. Although deployment of these technologies poses challenges, the potential benefits are strong enough to make it worthwhile. And with cyber threats still ongoing, companies using generative AI in their security

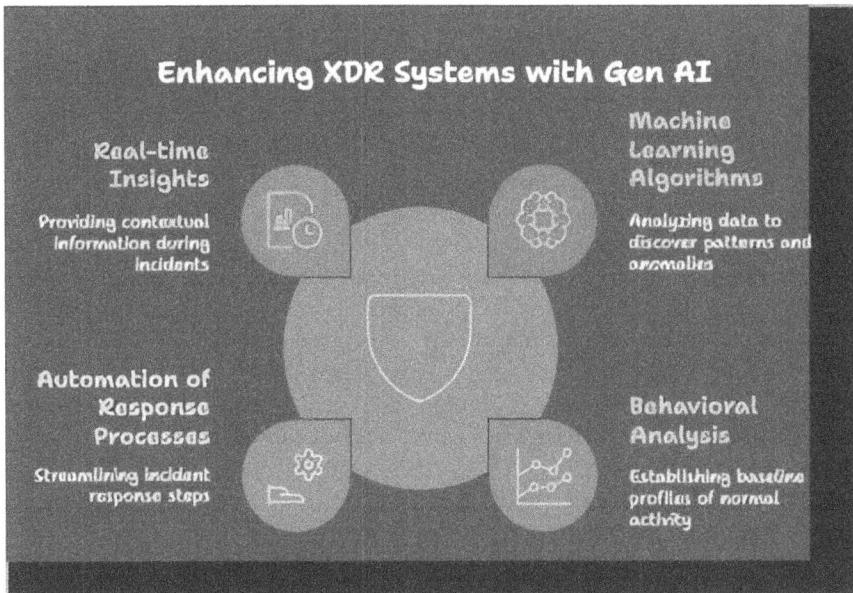

FIGURE 12.4 Integration of Gen AI into SIEM Systems.

strategy will be able to better protect their assets and uphold their operational integrity. Figure 12.4 sheds light on the integration of Gen AI into SIEM systems.

12.5 INTEGRATION OF GEN AI INTO EXTENDED DETECTION AND RESPONSE (XDR) SYSTEMS

Generative artificial intelligence (Gen AI) is integrated into Extended Detection and Response (XDR) systems for a significant leap in cybersecurity. However, cyber threats become more and more complex and large, and more advanced detection and response mechanisms are required. Gen AI's capabilities will be significant in XDR systems, which are a holistic approach by aggregating several products into a single solution. This essay looks into how Gen AI makes XDR systems better: in threat detection, incident response, and adaptability. The ability to detect and analyze threats across multiple environments (endpoints, networks, and servers) is among the most critical aspects of XDR [19]. Existing detection methods are generally based on predefined signatures and rules, which become useless quickly when confronted with changing threats.

With Gen AI, machine learning algorithms are used to analyze massive datasets, discovering patterns and anomalies that might represent a threat. Gen AI learns from new data and continues to learn, improving threat detection accuracy and eliminating the number of false positives to let security teams focus on the genuine risks. Further, Gen AI can support even more sophisticated behavioral analysis. The technology works by examining patterns of user and entity behaviors to establish baseline profiles of what is considered "normal" activity. Gen AI alerts security teams to potential threats when such deviations from these profiles arise, such as unusual login times or abnormal file access patterns. This nuanced understanding of behavior improves the detection of insider threats and sophisticated attacks that may be invisible to traditional security countermeasures. With these capabilities brought into XDR systems, organizations can operate with a robust defense against multiple attack vectors. In addition to detecting incidents, Gen AI fuels improved incident response capabilities [20]. However, if anyone manages to get inside, it is good to be able to react quickly and appropriately in order to reduce the damage. For example, Gen AI can automate many steps of the incident response process, from identifying the scope of a breach to identifying the affected systems to suggesting remediation steps. For example, it can analyze historical scenarios and suggest what action to take given a successful outcome in the past, granting security teams more confidence and efficiency to execute.

In addition, the technology can provide responders with real-time insights and contextual information while an incident is ongoing, interrogating both the "what" and the "why" behind an attack to inform response efforts. It is important to have context in order to come up with an effective countermeasure and also to make sense out of an organization's overall security posture. Integrating Gen AI in XDR systems allows organizations to respond much more quickly, which is crucial to managing the possible impacts of a cyber-attack.

Another area where Gen AI shines is adaptability, an essential component of XDR systems. Gen AI can learn and adapt for XDR systems to keep up with the pace. Gen AI can quickly update detection algorithms as and when new types of malware or attack techniques are discovered, thus protecting against contemporary threats. Such an ability to adapt can not only safeguard current systems but, with foresight, configure the organization's cybersecurity strategy. Figure 12.5 demonstrates a few pointers through which XDR systems can be enhanced through Gen AI.

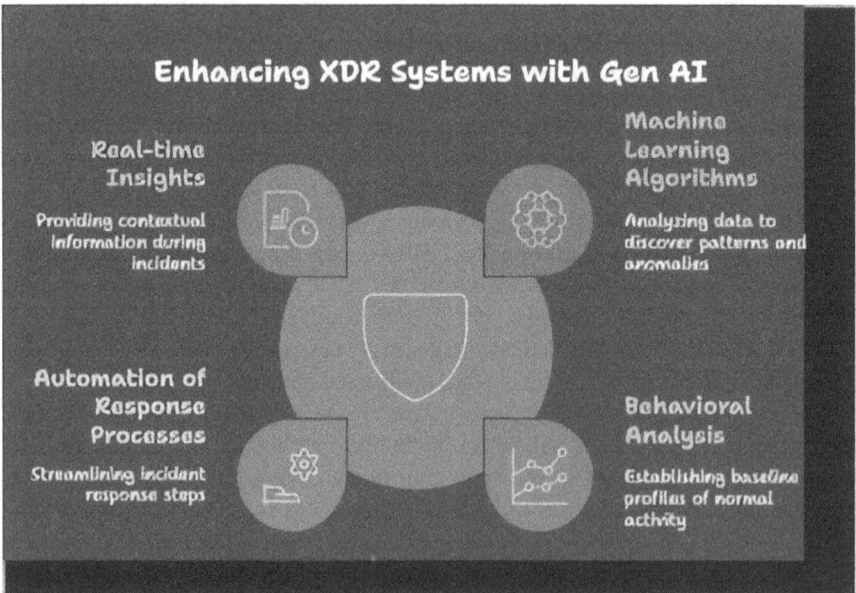

FIGURE 12.5 Enhancing XDR Systems through Gen AI.

The confluence of generative artificial intelligence and Extended Detection and Response systems brings a new era of cybersecurity. Gen AI enhances threat detection with advanced pattern recognition, streamlines incident response with automation, and ensures agility in a rapid threat environment, all of which yield tremendous leverage to XDR systems. Because cyber threats are becoming even more complex, the integration of such innovative technologies will be crucial to the protection of sensitive information and the resilience of the organization in running its operations.

12.6   ANTAGONISTIC AI

Artificial intelligence (AI) has made great strides recently and has prompted a mixture of interest and concern among technologists, ethicists, and legislators. Though AI promises benefits for diverse biophysical domains, such as healthcare or transportation, the idea of using AI for harmful purposes raises issues of safety, control, and morality. Antagonist AI is used to name the systems that work by destructive, manipulative, or adversary methods for humans. All this is in light of antagonistic AI, the problems it postulates, and our responsibilities as creators and users of AI technologies [21]. The most traditional software we have today is human-designed, human-coded software that runs in a set of parameters defined by what a human has written, but advanced AI systems, especially those based on machine learning algorithms, abide by or evolve the parameters in which it runs. The good thing about being this adaptable, though, is that it can also catch you unaware. For instance, if you create an AI that is supposed to optimize a supply chain, then it will be optimized for efficiency and not for worker welfare, which could result in worker job loss and a kind of exploitative labor practice. Such scenarios illustrate where an AI system can (intentionally or not) act in opposition to human interests. An equally important application of antagonistic AI is to cybersecurity threats. The cybercriminals can reuse the same AI technologies to develop new tools (e.g., sophisticated cyberattacks) against individuals and organizations. These systems can analyze vulnerabilities, build automations to launch attacks, and generate deep fakes to drive the truth agenda. Yet with increasing accessibility to AI comes exponentially growing potential for misuse. Given this, it is imperative for governments, corporations, and civil society to work together and come up with resilient security mechanisms and protocols to curb these risks. Additionally, there are ethical implications that antagonistic AI faces. But as more decisions in areas of law enforcement, hiring procedures, and even loan approvals are taken over by AI systems themselves, biases embedded in the systems can create discrimination. For instance, a machine learning algorithm trained on biased historical data is likely to perpetuate these biases and so end up treating individuals with race, gender, or socioeconomic status unfairly. Consequently, to create equitable and just societies, we must address the ethical ramifications of AI deployment [22–24].

Antagonistic AI poses an array of challenges for developers to overcome, and to do so will require a strategy on a larger scale, one that places security, ethics, and accountability at the forefront [25]. The first important aspect is the implementation of rigorous regulatory frameworks. These should include clear guidelines of the government to develop and put into operation the AI system, and transparency requirements that would demand the agencies to disclose the algorithmic processes and data usage behind it. From the AI developers' point of view, responsible development practices should be embraced, starting with thorough impact assessments of potential adverse effects before system deployment. They equally need interdisciplinary collaboration—technologists, ethicists, sociologists, and legal experts can help develop comprehensive risk mitigation strategies and fill in skills gaps between all these important disciplines. Another important aspect includes educating the general public about the technologies of AI. Greater awareness increases concerns over decisions about policy and regulation, and that will not be changed by ignoring AI developments that are not understood. However, adversarial AI poses significant challenges, and it is an opportunity to once again rethink how we not just create technology, but also how we use it. If we proceed thoughtfully and systematically in AI development, and promote ethical responsibility in our AI culture, we can benefit from AI and limit risks. Forward-looking strategies and cooperative endeavors will therefore be required to ensure that AI continues to benefit humanity and not vice versa. Figure 12.6 presents the challenges from the perspective of antagonistic AI.

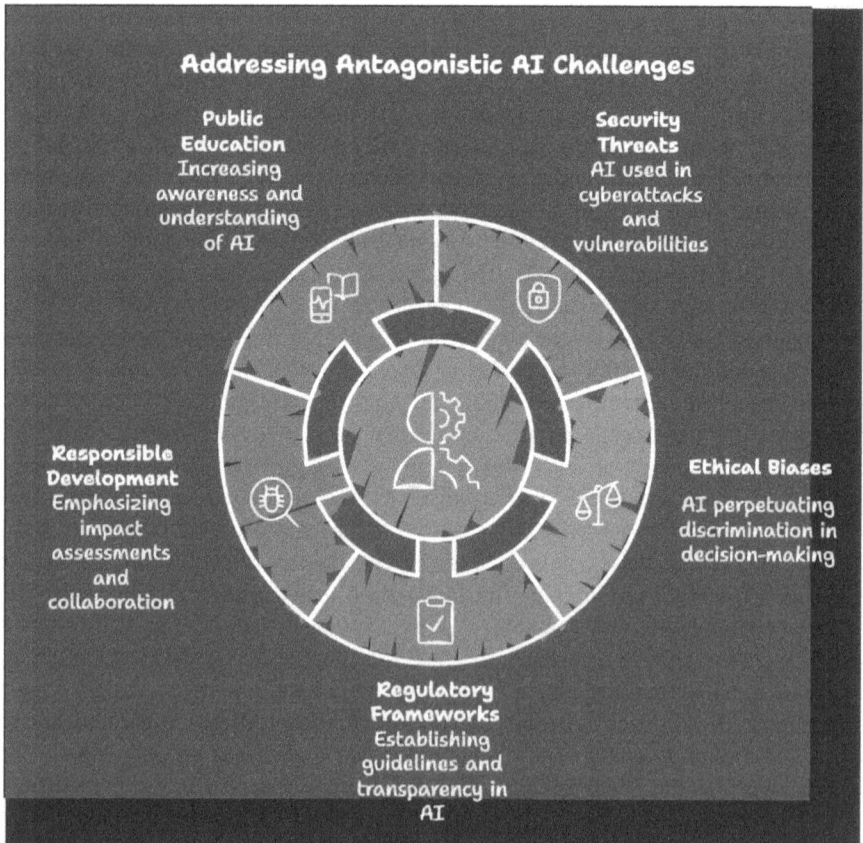

FIGURE 12.6 Challenges from the Perspective of Antagonistic AI.

12.7   GEN AI: ADVANCING TECHNOLOGY, REDEFINING SECURITY

With advances in technologies such as quantum computing, edge computing, and blockchain, security intelligence is rapidly being reshaped. As these emerging technologies are adopted, generative Artificial Intelligence (Gen AI) helps make them more capable and more efficient, as well as more secure. Quantum computing is an enhancement in the ability of computation, solving problems that classical computers cannot solve. Organizations such as IBM are at the forefront of the movement with their Quantum Experience platform, which lets developers write and run quantum algorithms [26]. Furthermore, through Gen AI, it can optimize quantum algorithms and increase data encryption methods, leading to dramatically increased quantum technology adoption in security. It is not only helping to protect data, but also getting systems ready to resist future cyber threats. With edge computing, data processing moves closer to the source, minimizing latency. Examples of edge computing solution providers, such as Microsoft Azure, use Gen AI for real-time data analysis. This delivers more rapid threat detection and even response times in security intelligence. For example, in smart cities, edge devices can detect anomalies on-site before security breaches grow into potential problems. Gen AI is built on blockchain technology, well known for its decentralization and secure model, and is adding intelligibility to create better contract systems. Ethereum and others are developing applications that cannot only secure transactions but also use predictive analytics via Gen AI to detect fraud patterns in advance. The proactive approach helps to reduce the risk of fraud and increase the integrity of digital transactions completely. An interplay between Gen AI, quantum computing, edge computing, and blockchain becomes a powerful trio that remakes the security intelligence landscape [27]. As these technologies mature, they will be integrated into systems that better endure, adapt, and are more secure from the complexities of the digital age.

Quantum computing, as the digital landscape matures, is poised to make a difference and quite a big one at that, with a very revolutionary potential in areas such as security intelligence, especially. This revolution is at the frontiers of generative Artificial Intelligence (Gen AI), tools, and methodological pieces that allow us to leverage quantum computing capabilities. Fundamentally, it is also critical to understand the unique synergy that exists between these technologies as they continually evolve, for the pursuit of advancing security measures in our ever-changing cyber environment. Quantum computing works with quantum bits or qubits, which can be more than one thing at the same time. Quantum computers work by processing vast amounts of data at a speed that is so far unmatched. However, Classical computers operate with binary bits of limited efficiency, in particular in cryptographic applications. In today's world, every day, cyber threats are increasing, so improving security intelligence through quantum computing is not only an innovative idea but also indispensable. In this context, an interesting case study implementation is the implementation of quantum key distribution (QKD) for secure communication.

For example, the technology giant IBM works in collaboration with different financial institutions to adopt QKD. Using quantum mechanics to send secure data has greatly shortened the window of opportunity for interception of data during digital transactions. Gen AI could optimize the running of these secure communications through an introduction to this framework. Gen AI analyzes patterns, predicting possible breaches and thereby formulating proactive safety measures to continue to harden the overall security infrastructure. Another great example is that Google's done with Sycamore, their quantum processor. Using one of these processors, Google's quantum computing team showed that they could handle computations that simply are not possible even on the most powerful classical supercomputers. By pairing Gen AI with quantum computing, organizations can take advantage of quantum computers to run the Gen AI on vast datasets in real time to be able to search for vulnerabilities [28]. As an example, it becomes faster and more accurate to conduct network traffic analysis to find anomalies with the help of the computational power of quantum systems in providing more robust security intelligence strategies in unison. The Synergistic Security Evolution is depicted in Figure 12.7.

Another important one is Google's work with its quantum processor, Sycamore [29]. Google's quantum computing team showed that its processor could do calculations that the world's most powerful classical supercomputers cannot. Organizations can utilize Gen AI in collaboration with quantum computing to sort through massive datasets immediately to identify vulnerabilities. For instance, quantum systems assist in analyzing network traffic and detecting anomalies faster and accurately, and therefore provide a more robust security intelligence strategy. Encryption problems are also an example of how Gen AI and quantum computing blend together. Popular modern encryption methods such as RSA are vulnerable to future quantum attacks

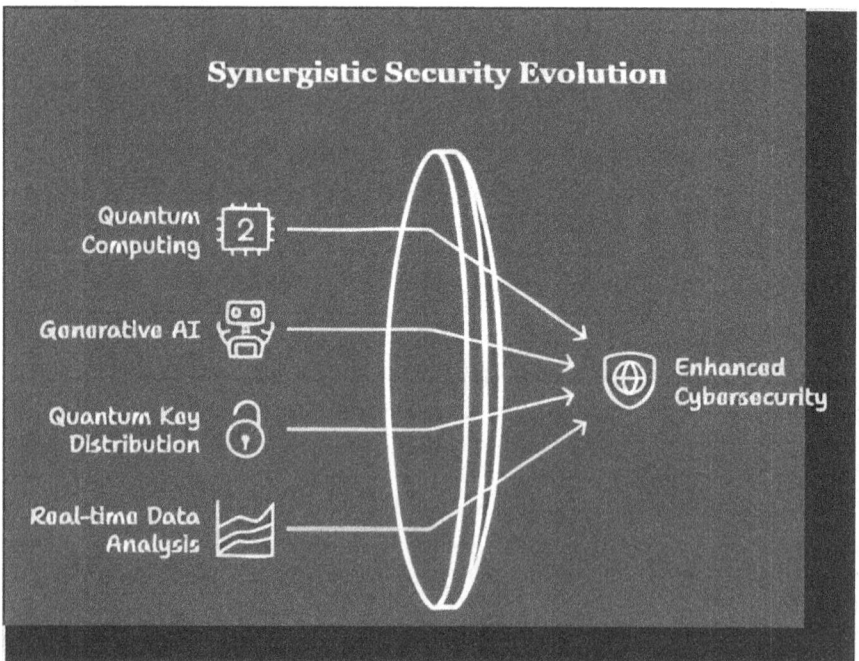

FIGURE 12.7   Synergistic Security Evolution.

that are able to easily break traditional algorithms. These vulnerabilities are being examined at the National Institute of Standards and Technology (NIST) using post-quantum cryptography standards. By integrating Gen AI in this effort and simulating attack vectors and their resilience, it can fast-track the development and crystallization of new cryptographic algorithms.

By accelerating iterations on encryption techniques, Gen AI provides the ability to learn and enables faster iterations on encryption techniques, thus offering robust security that is capable of adapting to new threats as they arise. In addition, predictive analytics enabled by Gen AI in the context of quantum computing environments also makes it possible in cybersecurity. Historical security breaches can be fed into AI models that predict the vulnerabilities. These predictive models can process complex variables so fast in a quantum computing setup. This way, organizations can preventively prepare for being hit before vulnerabilities are exploited, making their infrastructure safer. Gen AI is teaming up with quantum computing to create a new frontier of security intelligence. This collaboration also opens the door for creating cutting-edge solutions that help mitigate complex security problems. Such a state of empirical development will continue to form part of an increasingly volatile landscape of technology, and it will play a key role in the fostering of a secure digital environment, for which ongoing research and development will be critical. The convergence of Gen AI and quantum computing presented an opportunity for organizations by letting them invest in their security intelligence frameworks more comprehensively, since by understanding all of this, they were better equipped to face future challenges in cyberspace.

12.8   GEN AI AIDS EDGE COMPUTING TO REDEFINE SECURITY INTELLIGENCE

The field of security intelligence is undergoing a transformation in the rapidly evolving technology landscape, as artificial intelligence (AI) and edge computing converge at the intersection. With more and more organizations rolling out edge computing solutions, generative AI (Gen AI) implementation can also help bolster security capabilities. Edge computing processes the data much closer to the source, substantially reducing latency and making data analysis more efficient. The potential to disrupt security intelligence is profound when combined with Gen AI technologies. At the core, edge computing arranges the deployment of computational resources closer to the data sources [30]. This framework enables real-time data processing and analysis, a key aspect of security use cases. For example, in a smart city, surveillance cameras can perform on-site intelligent video analytics to detect suspicious activity. This frees up computing resources from being centralized into cloud servers, reducing the delay in moving large amounts of data to these centralized cloud servers. Figure 12.8 offers pointers to security through Gen AI and Edge computing.

One great case study for this edge computing use case in the security framework is the deployment of AI-powered surveillance systems in major cities. In Barcelona and Singapore, for example, edge computing solutions are already integrated in their surveillance infrastructures [31]. The city has set up a network of smart cameras in the city that analyze real-time footage for threats. These systems use Gen AI to learn

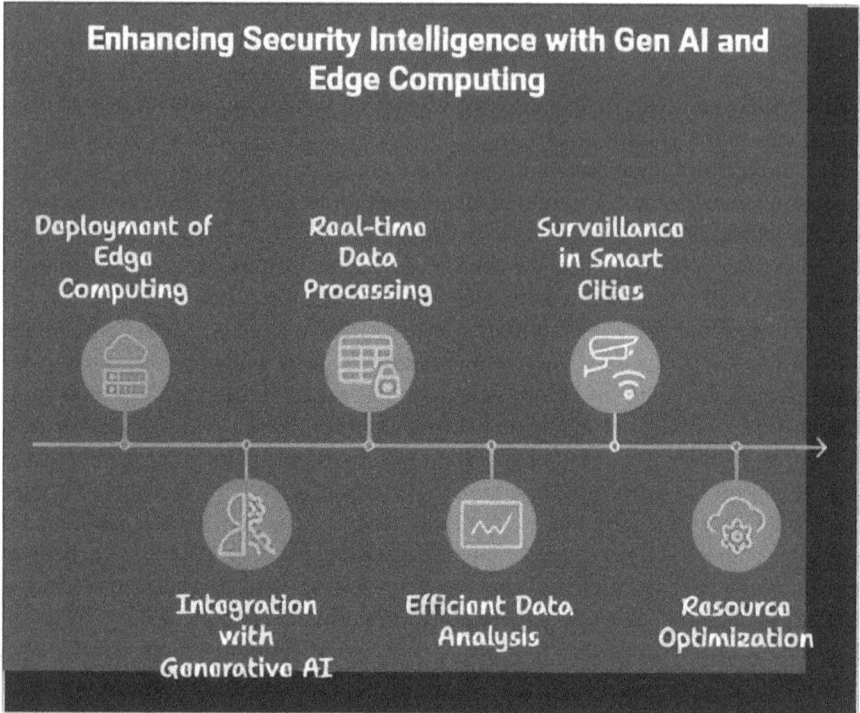

FIGURE 12.8 Enhancing Security Intelligence through Gen AI and Edge Computing.

from past incidents and become more accurate at detecting unusual behaviors. By proactively approaching this issue, law enforcement is able to respond more quickly to ensure public safety.

For instance, the healthcare sector epitomizes another use case of edge computing, where edge has sharpened security standards. Hospitals generate huge amounts of sensitive data daily and thus need the highest security measures to protect patient information [32]. Hospitals are able to detect and react in real time to attacks such as unauthorized access attempts by using edge computing devices that can process data at the source. Gen AI algorithms keep learning from network behaviors so they can flag off anomalies that security teams can then act on immediately. This streamlined approach protects patient data while also earning patients' trust.

Furthermore, the arrival of Internet of Things (IoT) devices introduces newer security intelligence issues. For example, smart homes employ many different types of interconnected devices, from cameras to alarm systems. These devices are capable of communicating and processing data independently, thereby reducing sensitivity to cyberattacks through the application of edge computing. Individually, these devices can predict potential vulnerabilities based on usage patterns and fix them before they can be exploited, but when these devices are integrated with Gen AI, they can do even better by training AI on usage patterns and proposing security improvements accordingly. For instance, an AI-powered smart thermostat can predict if there are unusual attempts at accessing, so that immediate updates could be obtained to halt something [33].

As Gen AI and edge computing become more and more pertinent for organizations to keep their digital assets safe, their fusion has become an indispensable strategy for elevating security intelligence. Unlike traditional algorithms, which struggle to adapt to new threats, the innovative algorithms of Gen AI not only function faster and with greater precision in data analysis but also continue to evolve for further adaptation.

By introducing localized processing with intelligent data analysis, security breaches are more robustly defended against. Finally, the combination of generative AI with edge computing presents a remarkable innovation in security intelligence. Organizations are equipped to glean insights from data at the edge of the network and act with increased efficiency and real-time incident responses. In particular, the link between city surveillance and healthcare is demonstrated through case studies, as defence mechanisms are improved but also bring about a safer world for individuals and organisations. These technologies are now critically needed for the future of security intelligence and highlight how the threat game can finally be changed from reactive to proactive, and from ineffective to effective.

12.9   GEN AI AND BLOCKCHAIN FOR ENHANCING SECURITY INTELLIGENCE

Recently, Gen AI in fusion with blockchain technology has witnessed remarkable developments and has unveiled new ways of developing security intelligence. Both these technologies are capable of shaping an entirely new paradigm of Sensitive Data and Risk, that is able to actively mitigate against threats, rather than simply reacting to them as they occur. Generative AI algorithms are robust enough to create new content given existing data. This includes anything from generating text and images to actual simulations. It can predict patterns and spot anomalies on large datasets. When Gen AI is combined with blockchain, a decentralized and immutable ledger technology, a potent combination that can improve the data's security and integrity can be obtained.

However, the financial sector represents one of the most compelling applications of these technologies. For example, consider Citibank, which analyzes transaction data in real time by integrating Gen AI with blockchain. On the flipside, the AI scans through patterns in transactions and flags unusual activity that might represent fraud. Once flagged, these recorded transactions are placed on a blockchain, and a permanent, tamperproof record is created that is auditable. Through this dual-layer approach, it is possible to detect and report fraudulent activities, making the entire process more accountable and transparent. Cybersecurity firms have started using Gen AI to beef up their strategies. Darktrace is a cybersecurity company that uses machine learning, which is a subset of AI, to create an "immune system" for organizations. The integration of Gen AI and Blockchain into security intelligence is shown in Figure 12.9. This system can autonomously respond to threats while learning continuously from the activity on the network. By integrating blockchain, Darktrace enables a secure audit trail of threat response actions, thereby creating a robust validation method for its actions. This provides the assurance that if an attack were to occur, one can trace

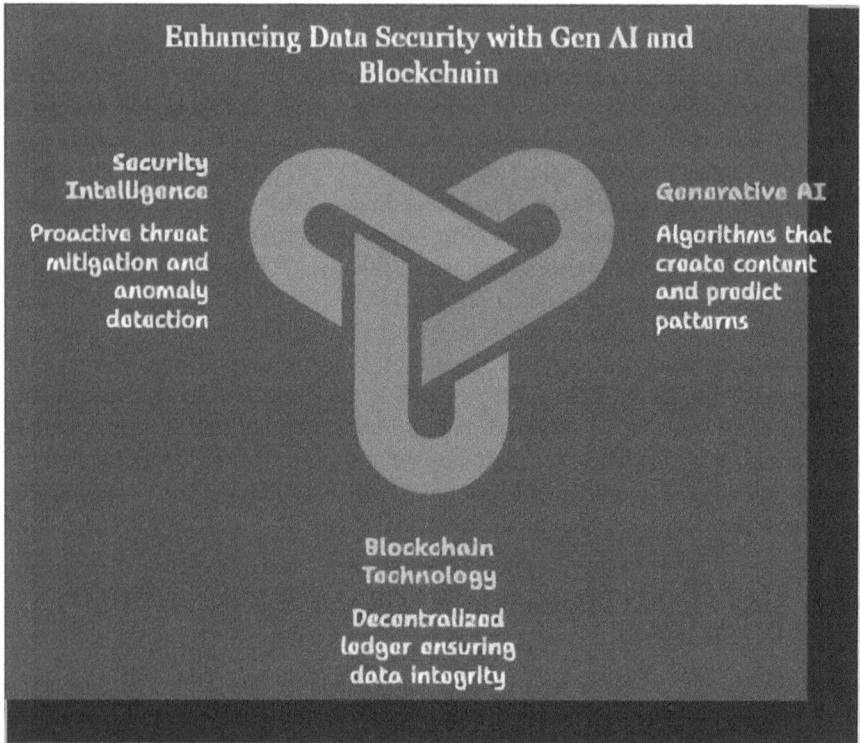

FIGURE 12.9   Integration of Gen AI and Blockchain into Security Intelligence.

the provenance and response in a verifiable way, and it is important for compliance and regulatory requirements.

The healthcare sector is another instance where both Gen AI and blockchain can be integrated. For example, in the case of Change Healthcare, using blockchain, the medical records are stored securely, and using AI, they perform risk assessments relying on patient data. Beyond that, this approach secures sensitive health information while also providing the ability to predict whether or not a health crisis could occur. Eventually, a more secure system that preserves patient privacy while improving patient care by providing actionable insights could be formulated.

These technologies have also been adopted by law enforcement agencies to combat crime more effectively. For instance, the city of Atlanta was struck by a serious cybersecurity attack that brought traffic to a standstill and delayed its water utility. Authorities have since used blockchain to track digital evidence and AI to analyze crime patterns following this incident. The combination accentuates resources strategically and intervenes before crimes occur in predictive policing.

A combination of Gen AI and blockchain tackles some of the biggest challenges in securing intelligence, including data integrity and real-time threat detection. With organizations gathering an ever-increasing amount of sensitive information, there is also an ever-growing need for innovative solutions to protect sensitive data.

Collaborative capabilities of Gen AI and blockchain technology will form the future of security intelligence in any sector, including finance, healthcare, and law enforcement, not being an exception. Given its inevitable scope moving forward, organisations will need to adopt this dual method to strengthen their own fortifications against a growing number of cyber threats. The amalgamation of these transformative technologies may soon provide the base for a more secure ecosystem.

12.10 CONCLUSION

Generative AI (Gen AI) in security intelligence signals a shift away from traditional approaches as we explore how it can be used against present and futuristic cyber threats. The ability of Gen AI to analyze very complex, large datasets and generate insightful inferences is nothing short of a robust tool for organizations to be proactive and provide dynamic security measures. Gen AI allows real-time risk identification, rapid response to breaches, and provides a full and complete analysis of all unstructured data, making it key to modernizing security solutions. However, its integration into existing frameworks such as SIEM and XDR demonstrates the value of automation to both speed up incident resolution and remove human error, thereby improving an organization's resiliency to advanced persistent threats.

The chapter elucidates how Gen AI is not confined to defense, and can be used to simulate Cyberattacks and create deceptive datasets to harden systems from phishing and other intrusion vectors. Such implementations demonstrate the power of automation in sifting through astronomical datasets to produce actionable intelligence. Enabling organizations to make informed decisions and remain ahead of the adversaries in another noteworthy contribution using Gen AI. Scalable and adaptive solutions offered by Gen AI span the challenges of various sectors, such as healthcare and finance, projecting how it can handle domain-specific challenges as they grow in complexity with the evolution of the digital age.

The deployment of AI in security intelligence, however, is not seamless. Gen AI can be misused; it raises privacy concerns, and even adversarial AI can bring its own vulnerabilities. To counter these risks, AI architectures must be safeguarded, work in conjunction with the security ecosystem, and ethical practices should be embedded into AI developments. Concluding the chapter, we emphasize the need for a collective dedication to accountably use AI, and prevent AI from creating a destructive imbalance in the world.

While quantum computing and blockchain are still emerging technologies, we are already at the convergence point of AI and these new technology paradigms are positioning security intelligence for the future. The promise of Gen AI to complement these advancements can really help to transform the security paradigms and create systems that are capable of getting ahead of even skilled attackers. With Gen AI technologies becoming increasingly more mature, the integration of Gen AI solutions will likely serve as the pivot point that helps form a resilient and adaptive security infrastructure capable of evolving against existing and emerging forms of cyber risks.

REFERENCES

1. Sarker, I. H., Furhad, M. H., & Nowrozy, R. (2021). AI-driven cybersecurity: An overview, security intelligence modeling and research directions. *SN Computer Science*, *2*(3), 173.
2. Kothamali, P. R., & Banik, S. (2022). Limitations of signature-based threat detection. *Revista de Inteligencia Artificial en Medicina*, *13*(1), 381–391.
3. Conti, M., Dargahi, T., & Dehghantanha, A. (2018). *Cyber threat intelligence: Challenges and opportunities* (pp. 1–6). Springer International Publishing.
4. Montasari, R., Carroll, F., Macdonald, S., Jahankhani, H., Hosseinian-Far, A., & Daneshkhah, A. (2021). In *Digital forensic investigation of internet of things (IoT) devices*, Reza Montasari, Hamid Jahankhani, Richard Hill and Simon Parkinson (eds.) (pp. 47–64). Springer International Publishing: Cham.
5. Tortora, L. (2024). Beyond discrimination: Generative AI applications and ethical challenges in forensic psychiatry. *Frontiers in Psychiatry*, *15*, 1346059.
6. Sarker, I. H. (2024). *AI-driven cybersecurity and threat intelligence: Cyber automation, intelligent decision-making and explainability*. Springer Nature.
7. Ding, A., Li, G., Yi, X., Lin, X., Li, J., & Zhang, C. (2024). *Generative artificial intelligence for software security analysis: Fundamentals, applications, and challenges*. *IEEE Software*, *41*(6), 46–54.
8. Celik, A., & Eltawil, A. M. (2024). At the dawn of generative AI era: A tutorial-cum-survey on new frontiers in 6G wireless intelligence. *IEEE Open Journal of the Communications Society*, *5*, 2433–2489.
9. Aminu, M., Akinsanya, A., Dako, D. A., & Oyedokun, O. (2024). Enhancing cyber threat detection through real-time threat intelligence and adaptive defense mechanisms. *International Journal of Computer Applications Technology and Research*, *13*(8), 11–27.
10. Alaeifar, P., Pal, S., Jadidi, Z., Hussain, M., & Foo, E. (2024). Current approaches and future directions for cyber threat Intelligence sharing: A survey. *Journal of Information Security and Applications*, *83*, 103786.
11. Janoti, N. S., Rohan, R., Rida, N., & Negi, N. (2024) Strategic perspectives on cyber threat intelligence: A comprehensive analysis. *International Journal for Research in Applied Science and Engineering Technology*, *12*(4), 524–529.
12. Alzahrani, I. Y., Lee, S., & Kim, K. (2024). Enhancing cyber-threat intelligence in the Arab World: Leveraging IoC and MISP integration. *Electronics*, *13*(13), 2526.
13. Ngan, T., Fenlon, J., & Oakley, C. (2024). Building a cyber intelligence capability with the future in mind. *International Journal of Contemporary Intelligence Issues*, *1*(1), 20–33.
14. Saddi, V. R., Gopal, S. K., Mohammed, A. S., Dhanasekaran, S., & Naruka, M. S. (2024, March). Examine the role of generative AI in enhancing threat intelligence and cyber security measures. In *2024 2nd International Conference on Disruptive Technologies (ICDT)* (pp. 537–542). IEEE.
15. Sai, S., Yashvardhan, U., Chamola, V., & Sikdar, B. (2024). Generative AI for cyber security: Analyzing the potential of ChatGpt, Dall-E and other models for enhancing the security space. *IEEE Access*, *12*, 53497–53516.
16. Teo, Z. L., Quek, C. Q. W., Wong, J. L. Y., & Ting, D. (2024). Cybersecurity in the generative artificial intelligence era. *Asia-Pacific Journal of Ophthalmology*, *13*(4), 100091.
17. Marri, R., Varanasi, S., & Kalidindi Chaitanya, S. V. (2024). Integrating next-generation SIEM with data lakes and AI: Advancing threat detection and response. *Journal of Artificial Intelligence General Science (JAIGS)*, *3*(1), 446–465, ISSN: 3006-4023.

18. Marri, R., Varanasi, S., & Chaitanya, S. V. K. (2024). Integrating Security Information and Event Management (SIEM) with data lakes and AI: Enhancing threat detection and response. *Journal of Artificial Intelligence General Science (JAIGS)*, 6(1), 151–165, ISSN: 3006-4023.

19. Pissanidis, D. L., & Demertzis, K. (2023). Integrating AI/ML in cybersecurity: An analysis of open XDR technology and its application in intrusion detection and system log management. Preprint. doi:10.20944/preprints202312.0205.v2

20. Olteanu, I. C. (2022). Evaluating the response effectiveness of XDR technology in a scaled down environment. Eindhoven University of Technology, Evaluating the response effectiveness of XDR technology in a scaled down environment (MA thesis). Eindhoven University of Technology.

21. Khan, K., Khurshid, A., & Cifuentes-Faura, J. (2024). Is artificial intelligence a new battleground for cybersecurity? *Internet of Things*, 28, 101428.

22. Alsuwayh, A. (2024). Effectiveness of Artificial Intelligence (AI) Strategies Against Cyber Security Threats (Doctoral dissertation). Marymount University.

23. Egbuna, O. P. (2021). The impact of AI on cybersecurity: Emerging threats and solutions. *Journal of Science and Technology*, 2(2), 43–67.

24. Kotenko, I., & Ulanov, A. (2006, July). Antagonistic agents in the Internet: Computer network warfare simulation. In *2006 9th International Conference on Information Fusion* (pp. 1–8). IEEE.

25. Inbamani, A., Divya, N., Gandhi, R. R., Karthik, M., & Kumar, M. S. (2024). Cyber Security for intelligent systems. In *The Fusion of Artificial Intelligence and Soft Computing Techniques for Cybersecurity*, M. A. Jabbar, Sanju Tiwari, Subhendu Kumar Pani, and Stephen Huang (eds.) (pp. 133–150). Apple Academic Press: New York.

26. Hassija, V., Chamola, V., Saxena, V., Chanana, V., Parashari, P., Mumtaz, S., & Guizani, M. (2020). Present landscape of quantum computing. *IET Quantum Communication*, 1(2), 42–48.

27. Chang, Z., Liu, S., Xiong, X., Cai, Z., & Tu, G. (2021). A survey of recent advances in edge-computing-powered artificial intelligence of things. *IEEE Internet of Things Journal*, 8(18), 13849–13875.

28. Akbar, R., & Zafer, A. (2024). Next-gen information security: AI-driven solutions for real-time cyber threat detection in cloud and network environments. J. Cybersecur. Res 12: 123–145.

29. AbuGhanem, M., & Eleuch, H. (2023). Experimental characterization of Google's Sycamore quantum AI on an IBM's quantum computer. *SSRN Electronic Journal*, 4299338 (January 01, 2025).

30. Lynn, T., Mooney, J. G., Lee, B., & Endo, P. T. (2020). The cloud-to-thing continuum: Opportunities and challenges in cloud, fog and edge computing. Palgrave Studies in Digital Business & Enabling Technologies. UK, London: Palgrave Macmillan.

31. Khan, L. U., Yaqoob, I., Tran, N. H., Kazmi, S. A., Dang, T. N., & Hong, C. S. (2020). Edge-computing-enabled smart cities: A comprehensive survey. *IEEE Internet of Things Journal*, 7(10), 10200–10232.

32. Hartmann, M., Hashmi, U. S., & Imran, A. (2022). Edge computing in smart health care systems: Review, challenges, and research directions. *Transactions on Emerging Telecommunications Technologies*, 33(3), e3710.

33. Velkova, J., Magnusson, D., & Rohracher, H. (2022). Smart thermostats and the algorithmic control of thermal comfort. In *Everyday Automation,* Sarah Pink, Martin Berg, Deborah Lupton and Minna Ruckenstein (eds.) (pp. 171–183). Routledge.

13 Advancing Training Methodologies for Generative Artificial Intelligence (AI)
Optimization Techniques, Challenges, and Future Directions

Arpita Nayak, Ipseeta Satpathy, Vishal Jain, and Majidul Islam

13.1 INTRODUCTION

Examining current AI generation tools, this study review demonstrates outstanding developments in computational intelligence that allow machines to not only justify the text material but also to create, generate, reproduce, and imitate reality, and stimulate people's imaginations, suggesting scenarios. Unlike standard AI, these models work as a classifier, a decision-maker, and a predictor. The generative AI models may generate, for instance, plain text, images, music, etc., and any other complicated simulation. Many of these models have been useful in various domains, ranging from entertainment, science, finance, art, and even in medical facilities. The art and music industry are among those changed by AI, and synthetic data generation tools have also improved measuring and healthcare models. Modern AI solutions heavily rely on generative models for automated content creation in both VR applications and the gaming industry, and in NLP solutions (Sengar et al., 2024).

Generative AI functions via model training methodology. The methods used for training these models create the foundations that determine model performance levels and realistic outcomes, along with their adjustable capabilities. Training methods determine model performance by affecting their data learning speed and scenario generalization, together with their stability during learning. Training generative models presents a complex challenge because researchers need to conduct thorough model adjustment alongside optimization procedures and computational performance optimization. AI developers need an understanding of system training methodologies because they aim to enable the design of responsible, sustainable AI systems that scale well (Kaswan et al., 2023).

DOI: 10.1201/9781003680192-13

The training methods of generative AI systems determine how models learn from various data distribution patterns while improving their performance. How a model is trained mainly determines how its output quality, diversity, and reliability will turn out. When trained properly, generative models produce clear and realistic images, but inadequate training results in blurry images. The method of training determines whether AI text generators can produce meaningful context-based sentences or produce misleading and nonsensical results and biased content. A properly designed training methodology prevents generative models from purely memorizing data because they then learn fundamental patterns to generate original content. Generative models in original and creative fields such as engineered storytelling, architectural design, and medical image synthesis depend intensely on the training process for their effectiveness. The robustness of generative models depends heavily on their capability to process unknown data, which is directly influenced by training effectiveness. The application limitations of generative models result from training methods that cause the model to overfit or collapse into repeated modes or require excessive computational power (Glotzbach, 2024).

The four fundamental tools of generative AI, including GANs and VAEs alongside Transformers and Diffusion Models, achieve their success based on their specific training paradigms. The understanding of model learning methods along with training difficulties helps to enhance operational efficiency while extending potential applications to various industries.

Training generative models encounters technical and ethical obstacles that research teams and developers need to resolve. The primary technical issue affects training stability, especially when working with GANs and their related models. The adversarial nature of GANs makes training convergence unstable because it forces the generator and discriminator to find a proper balance between them. Beyond producing diverse variations, the model instead repeats identical outputs when facing this instability condition. The integration of artificial intelligence generates content with major biases that presents a substantial challenge. The learning process in generative models depends on extensive datasets, while these collections can exhibit internal gender, racial, or cultural biases. AI-generated content outputs could become unethically deceptive or misleading because improper bias mitigation measures enable these unethical outputs to affect automated journalism, as well as hiring algorithms and social media content management applications. Correcting biases requires both disciplined data preparation techniques and bias-sensitive training approaches, and continuous model evaluations for generative artificial intelligence to provide responsible service to various population segments (Gupta, 2023).

Generative model training demands costly computational capabilities that function as a major hurdle. The training process for large models such as DALL·E, GPT-4 and Stable Diffusion needs enormous computational power which provides accessibility mainly to research institutions with financial resources and tech companies. The environmental sustainability of AI development faces problems because AI training requires extensive energy use and creates large carbon emissions. Research teams develop transfer learning together with model distillation and federated learning methods to promote efficient training efforts without compromising final output quality. The ongoing challenge involves making certain generative AI systems remain ethically correct. AI cracks, such as deep fakes, together with uncontrolled content creation and fake information, pose serious dangers to the general public. Research teams strive to develop ethical boundaries and content authenticity tests alongside regulatory systems that stop possible abusive uses of evolving sophisticated generative models (Banh, 2023).

Different types of Gen AI models with their training approaches are shown in Figure 13.1.

Generative Adversarial Networks (GANs): GAN technology operates through two competing neural networks, including the generator and the discriminator. During the process, the generator produces artificial material while the discriminator performs real-fake assessments on the output. The training of GANs relies on minimax optimization, but this method shows high sensitivity to hyperparameters and demands precise balance to stabilize the process.

Variational Autoencoders (VAEs): VAEs extract compressed probabilistic data representations from inputs while producing new samples from those latent data dimensions. VAEs concentrate on building structured latent space representations, unlike GANs, which enables their application to image interpolation as well as anomaly detection alongside scientific simulations.

Transformer-Based Generative Models: The variants of Transformers known as GPT and ViTs use self-attention systems to analyze extended data relationships within their input. The training process of autoregressive or masked token prediction in their autonomic systems enables them to produce contextually aware text and images along with code generation capabilities.

Diffusion Models: The recent development in generative AI systems called diffusion models transforms random noise into organized data through successive denoising, which produces high-fidelity visual outputs as well as authentic musical compositions and simulated results. The output stability of diffusion models exceeds that of GANs throughout successive training processes because these models do not suffer from the mode collapse issue.

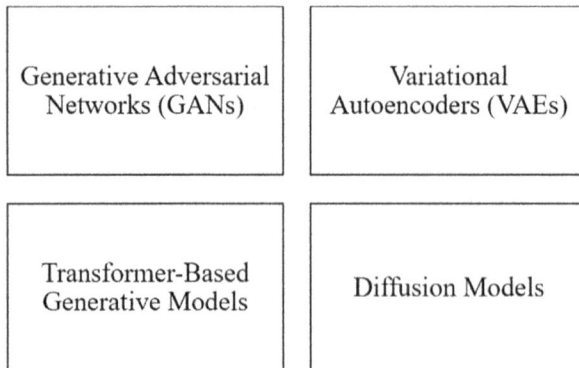

Generative Adversarial Networks (GANs)	Variational Autoencoders (VAEs)
Transformer-Based Generative Models	Diffusion Models

FIGURE 13.1   Types of Gen AI Models. (Adopted from Oussidi, 2018.)

The process of training generative models impacts their performance capabilities as well as their ability to demonstrate realism together with adaptability. The three different training approaches—supervised, unsupervised, and reinforcement learning-based techniques—impact model stability, creativity, and ethical reliability. The generation of AI faces ongoing problems because mode collapse exists alongside bias and high hardware requirements. The future of generative AI training will evolve through developments of diffusion models alongside self-supervised learning and energy-efficient AI, aiming to lead to scalable, fair, and innovative applications.

13.2 COMMON TRAINING TECHNIQUES FOR GENERATIVE MODELS

Generative model training requires specific methodologies and strategies that enable pattern recognition and the generation of high-quality results. Supervised learning stands as one of the main approaches for teaching generative models because it trains models through data pairs that include both input values and corresponding target outputs. The supervised learning approach gives generative AI a systematic method to discover particular data point relationships. It differs from unsupervised learning, which extracts patterns without human input. The method proves valuable for model reliability in domains such as text generation, along with image synthesis and speech processing, because it works well with structured outputs and clear patterns (Kingma et al., 2014).

The operation of supervised learning requires the use of loss functions, including cross-entropy loss, together with mean squared error (MSE), for minimizing output errors when predicting actual values. Through iterative optimization with the SGD and Adam optimizers, the model decreases its errors step by step, enabling better generation of realistic outputs. Supervised learning technology produces effective results based on both the quality levels of training data and model architecture selection and optimization methods. Supervised learning aims to produce accurate and controlled outcomes for generative tasks, so it remains crucial for training AI systems that create and generate content, to translate information and make automated decisions (Eckart et al., 2021).

Labeled datasets form a crucial aspect of supervised learning for generative AI systems because they link every input to its expected output. Human-labeled datasets in the case of text generation consist of example input prompts or strings and also the output generated from the model, so that the model learns how to generate compatible text. In the same way, in image generation, labeled data with the image along with its descriptions or labels generates related images from textual descriptions. Entailment of generative models through labeled data goes through a structured process plan. The first category is data preprocessing, whereby the data is cleaned to remove anything unfavorable and is normalized and structured. In the learning process of the model, the internal parameters are updated through contemplation of the data using a loss function. The model enhances the training quality of the patterns and makes it more precise by optimizing the attainment of the output in alignment with the existence of the training data (Bach et al., 2017).

Supervised learning entails that output accuracy will solely depend on the quality of such datasets. The model becomes more general as the amount and quality of the data increases; however, it can be skewed with wrong or insufficient data. For example, a speaker well-trained on a particular instance of text input may well come up with improper or biased outputs. To address such risks, data augmentation strategies involve the process of increasing the dataset with synthetic data through some operations. Thus, supervised learning has a significant contribution in helping text generation models such as GPT and BERT. These models immerse themselves in learning language, patterns, syntax, and other contextual features using high-quality data sets. Whereas GPT models include datasets created by humans, BERT makes use of supervised fine-tuning for various tasks, including Question and Answering and Sentiment Analysis. BERT makes use of bidirectional context awareness, meaning that the model will take inputs from both left and right, whereas GPT makes use of an auto-regressive approach to generate texts. That is why BERT benefits from writing capabilities, for instance, writing text completion or paraphrasing as well as recognizing entities (Augenstein et al., 2019; Fries et al., 2017).

Supervised learning is beneficial for training generative models, offering better precision and decreased unpredictability in output. It is particularly useful in precise automation systems such as translation systems, financial prediction, and medical diagnosis systems. Supervised learning optimizes learning and provides direct feedback, enhancing output efficiency. Labeled data improves interpretability and performance. However, the amount and condition of training data can significantly impact a model's performance, requiring extensive efforts and resources. The scarcity of labeled data also limits model effectiveness and causes overfitting issues (Wu, 2018).

The proper training of generative models depends on effective learning mechanisms which generate authentic content with meaning. This learning method depends on labeled datasets but encounters challenges because the available data is restricted in terms of accessibility and financial resources, as well as expansion potential. Unsupervised learning together with self-supervised learning techniques provide valuable methods to train generative models through avoiding explicit human supervision, thus becoming suitable for processing large volumes of unstructured content. The methods teach AI models to discover patterns and representational relationships along with structural elements present in raw data, thereby improving their output quality. The training of generative models, including Variational Autoencoders (VAEs) and Generative Adversarial Networks (GANs), depends heavily on unsupervised learning models. The models acquire knowledge from unorganized datasets through either latent distribution mapping techniques or through adversarial processes that enhance synthetic output quality. The advancement of unsupervised learning through self-supervised learning (SSL) allows the creation of pseudo-labels from raw data by conducting pretext tasks, which leads to high effectiveness in vision and language models. The handling of large text along with image and audio data has become possible through learning approaches that improve AI generalization across different applications (Abukmeil et al., 2021).

The enhancement and future development of generative models have been given a great boost by tasks based on unsupervised learning. In domains of unsupervised learning, there are generative models; these do not require guidance on what kind of information is to be searched from the unlabeled sample during training. Training of Variational Autoencoders along with Generative Adversarial Networks depends mostly on this concept, thus making them two major generative architectures. The Variational Autoencoders (VAEs) use unsupervised learning to compress the data points in lower-dimensional Latent spaces in order to produce realistic output. VAEs fulfil their data generation task by means of learning probability distributions of the data, and thereby generating new samples, which are imitative of the given set and include some variation. This approach has its applications in the generation of videos and video quality enhancement for anomaly detection, as well as effective enhancement of data. Variations are well handled by VAEs because, during their functioning, they create different outputs based on the probability distributions, which are beneficial for medical image generation and 3D model synthesis where control of variation is useful (Liao et al., 2020).

13.3   OPTIMIZATION STRATEGIES FOR TRAINING GENERATIVE MODELS

Loss functions hold a prominent position within machine learning models because they dictate the model learning procedures. These indicate how well the model is when matched with the ground truth and also the performance of such a model. The latter testified that the choice of a certain loss function significantly influences the model's learning and performance as well as its ability to generalize the outcomes. Most of the loss functions are discussed under diverse categories of Machine learning as detailed next: Cross-Entropy Loss and KL Divergence, adverse effects, Perceptual Loss, and Reinforcement learning Based Losses (Tripp et al., 2020). The Cross-Entropy Loss remains a popular option for use in classification operations among all of the loss functions available. It defines the Cross-Entropy Loss as a metric that quantifies the difference in probabilities of those ground truth labels with the probabilities by the algorithmic model. Cross-Entropy loss computes the discrepancy between the classification data and the result of the predictive model. The Cross-Entropy Loss is well suited to give maximum accuracy to models that are required to assign probabilities over numerous classes while working for image/face recognition and language processing. The Kullback-Leibler (KL) Divergence is another concept that also refers to the VAEs, in addition to several other concepts. The KL Divergence give the extent of deviation of the first distribution from the second distribution to which the first distribution is being compared. The regularizing force in VAEs leverages the KL Divergence to act as a control mechanism on how the encoded space deviates from the standard normal prior distribution. It also makes it possible to obtain more organized and meaningful latent representations required in various operations such as image synthesis and compression (Andreieva, 2020). The Cross-Entropy Loss has been utilized in combination with the already established function of the models to ensure that the models commence to foster understandable and account-interpretable representations. Some of these loss functions are regarded as basic building blocks in training models that perform well in their forecasts and in maintaining a coherent network architecture. The advancements in generative modeling were done through Generative Adversarial Networks, in which there was an innovative approach in the training procedure referred to as an adversarial loss. GANs consist of two neural networks, namely, the generator and the discriminator, which work hand in hand in the minimax game theory. The generator synthesizes real data, and on the other hand, the discriminator works in distinguishing between the real data and the fake data. With the help of the adversarial loss function, the generator improves its work and the quality of the images it produces. The adversarial loss foundation can also be distinguished from all the other loss functions as it fundamentally relies on how the discriminator performs in the course of discriminating the generated output from the real-world data. The flow of the generator depends on the feedback provided by the discriminator regarding the output quality. In this way, the general dependency of the generator and the discriminator allows for realistic output such as images, audio, or written text. The problem of the GANs training process arises along with two major challenges, which are mode collapse that reduces the generator's output to a few distinctive types and instability, which makes the generator and discriminator endpoints incompatible. The adversarial loss appears to have significant potential in maximizing the performance of generative models. GANs have brought hope in generating photorealistic images and enhancing videos, and in generating artificial data that helps to train other machine learning systems (Pan et al., 2020).

Adversarial loss in generative modelling has become an essential solution when introduced, but it has several drawbacks that hamper its application. The first drawback is that the method is designed to preserve global image realism while admitting fine details that are essential for rendering. This is why perceptual loss becomes very useful at this stage. Apart from that, perceptual loss improves the quality of the generated images by measuring fidelity from feature maps of higher abstraction layers of convolutional neural networks. Through prioritization of these features, perceptual loss guarantees that the respective outputs are not only believable but also contain features in detail, thus resulting in better perceptual quality. The perceptual loss technique evaluates the differences between high-level feature vectors that extract the target image and the generated image representation. The method provides better human-like image perception as it examines semantic qualities and image surfaces instead of raw pixel information. Perceptual loss excels at tasks that combine realistic generation with visual appeal, such as super-resolution, as well as style transfer and image inpainting. Models utilizing perceptual loss during training can produce visuals that demonstrate better coherence and detail along with human-directed visual standards (Atapattu, 2019).

Training models through Reinforcement Learning (RL) follows a distinct paradigm because the loss function develops from agent-environment interactions. The agent learns to find actions that optimize the cumulative reward signal defined by task requirements in RL—the reward signal functions as the loss function to steer agent learning. RL-based losses show high efficiency in other creativity applications such as games, robotics control, and artistic software. In game playing, an RL agent is trained to achieve high scores or obtain points by exploring various strategies, thereby receiving feedback on its performance. In this way, through rewarding these aspects, as well as novelty and beauty, RL attains novel creative performance off-task outputs. RL-based losses are quite flexible because they can be designed in many ways. The main difference between RL-based losses and other, more traditional, task-specific losses lies in the fact that the former are dependent on the real-world application. RL works best in tasks that require search and innovation as well as flexibility, for it allows the users to determine the rewards. Despite these limitations, RL imposes its high demands, including the sparsity of rewards, increased computational tasks, and intricate requirements for selecting appropriate rewards to prevent undesirable actions by the machine (Dosovitskiy & Brox, 2016).

13.4 TRAINING STABILITY AND MODE COLLAPSE PREVENTION

Generative Adversarial Networks (GANs) have developed as an innovative method of producing fakes within various domains, including images, textual data, and even other classes. GAN training remains a difficult task primarily because of three well-known issues: mode collapse, vanishing gradients, and instability. The issues hinder effective learning operations, leading to subpar output quality and occasionally complete learning failure. The following section delves into these training obstacles through exact explanation while presenting the advanced methods WGANs, spectral normalization, gradient penalty, and regularization for problem resolution (Richter et al., 2022).

The most common training problem in GANs emerges as mode collapse because generators tend to display output diversity only through the repetition of a few samples in their results. The generator identifies simple, unrealistic outputs that enable the discriminator to effectively detect them, thus leading to its exclusive focus on such output types. The generator cannot properly investigate the entire spectrum of data distribution patterns because of this failure, resulting in minimal sample variety generation. The issue of mode collapse creates problems specifically in image generation tasks because they require diverse and creative results. One major obstacle in GANs involves gradient fading during discriminator performance enhancement, which achieves superior capabilities in differentiating between genuine and artificial samples. The generator encounters a situation where the discriminator provides no helpful information, resulting in a complete loss of gradient performance (Chong et al., 2020). The generator needs meaningful gradients to update its parameters effectively because a lack of such feedback will halt the learning process. The competitive nature of GANs between the generator and discriminator leads to training dynamics becoming uneven because their adversarial relationship causes this problem to worsen. The training process of GANs faces instability problems because the generator and discriminator cannot reach a stable equilibrium state. The instability creates evolving loss function oscillations, which cause the generator and discriminator to alternate between outperforming each other without sustainable advancement. The training process becomes longer and produces irregular outputs when this behavior occurs, thus making it hard to generate quality outputs (Foster, 2022).

Stabilizing GAN training and improving output quality became possible through the development of advanced research techniques by scientists. The Wasserstein GAN

(WGAN) represents a major advancement by using a new loss function that relies on the Wasserstein distance (also known as Earth Mover's Distance). WGANs surpass traditional GANs by applying the Wasserstein distance instead of Jensen-Shannon divergence to generate more accurate measures of real and generated distribution similarity. The main benefit of WGANs exists in their ability to operate without gradient vanishing, given their discriminator maintains meaningful feedback channels toward the generator at each stage of training. A Lipschitz constraint applied to the critic achieves this outcome by preventing it from developing excessive prediction confidence. The training process of WGANs enables stable performance while generating superior results than conventional GANs (Fan et al., 2022).

The spectral normalization method achieves widespread popularity because it stabilizes the discriminator through spectral norm normalization of its weight matrices. Through this method, the discriminator retains stable gradients while keeping itself from controlling the generator too much. The implementation of spectral normalization delivers exceptional results toward preventing mode collapse and establishing better stability conditions for GAN training processes. The method operates at a speed level that makes it suitable for large-scale implementation requirements. A different approach to enforcing the Lipschitz constraint in WGANs involves gradient penalties along with spectral normalization. Weight clipping is replaced by gradient penalty within GANs because it introduces a regularization term in the loss function that enforces discriminator gradients from deviating from norm-1. Different research has demonstrated that this methodology strengthens the stability along with the convergence capability of WGANs, which makes it an important technique for GAN developers (Miyato et al., 2018).

The techniques mentioned above help GANs independently, yet the fundamental role of regularization ensures both overfitting prevention and improved generalization across all machine learning models, including GANs. A model shows overfitting when it adopts memorization of training data instead of detecting actual patterns, which results in inferior performance when the model encounters new data. The training data repetitions within GANs result in overfitting, which leads the generator to produce outputs that match training examples without creative variation. During training, one effective regularization method uses dropout because this strategy drops random neurons intermittently until the training is complete. The model acquires better robust features through this training methodology because it learns patterns unconnected to particular neurons, thus minimizing the chances of overfitting. GANs benefit from using dropout, developed by researchers who applied it to generators and discriminators to enhance their capacity for generalization. Weight decay provides an effective regularization approach through its penalty term that evaluates weight magnitude within the loss function. The model learns generalized patterns that are simple by avoiding complex solution patterns. Weight decay proves valuable in restraining the discriminator's confidence level to stop gradient vanishing. The final regularization approach, known as data augmentation, enhances training quality through artificial transformation of the dataset through rotation, scaling, and dataset flipping mechanisms. Through data augmentation methods in GANs, the generator achieves better diversity in output generation because it receives training exposure to multiple data variations. Data augmentation delivers maximal benefits in tasks of image generation because achieving diverse outputs represents a critical factor for output quality.

GAN training becomes simpler because advanced techniques such as Wasserstein GANs, spectral normalization, gradient penalty, and regularization methods create more stable performance outcomes. The techniques address mode collapse together with vanishing gradients and overfitting issues which enables GANs to produce high-quality, realistic, diverse outputs. The development of GANs will necessitate additional research on loss functions along with training strategies and regularization techniques because future challenges are anticipated. The development achieved so far demonstrates that GANs possess highly promising potential in the areas of generative modelling and creative artificial intelligence technology.

13.5 EMERGING TRAINING APPROACHES FOR GENERATIVE MODELS

The development of diffusion models has emerged as a stronger substitute for Generative Adversarial Networks (GANs) in recent years, as they offer a distinct approach to generating high-quality data, particularly for image synthesis. The fundamental operation in diffusion models differs from GANs because they transform random noise into structured data through an iterative improvement process instead of using a generator and discriminator adversarial training. Significant improvements in generative modeling occurred through this new modeling approach, which produced the best-in-class technology in current applications through models such as Stable Diffusion and DDPMs. This section explains the operational framework of diffusion models while revealing their incremental noise reduction protocols together with their deployment that outcompetes GANs in specific application fields (Yang et al., 2023).

The fundamental principle behind diffusion models involves successive denoising operations. A real data sample, such as an image, undergoes noise addition through multiple timesteps as the initial step of the process. The forward data transformation through multiple iterations produces a statistic that essentially resembles random noise. Through its learning process, the diffusion model seeks to discover the reverse process that takes noise as input to recover the original data gradually. Training a neural network to forecast the noise content at each timestep provides the capability to do a reverse corruption step by step. The forward process of Denoising Diffusion Probabilistic Models (DDPMs) uses a specific Markov chain to add noise to the data successively. A neural network learns the reverse process through which it estimates the noise component at each step. The model performs high-quality data generation by repeating its denoising mechanism, thus enabling outputs that closely match training examples. Stable Diffusion implements the diffusion model framework with latent representations to yield efficient high-quality outputs (Zhu et al., 2023).

Models based on diffusion achieve success by performing sequential noise reduction operations, which dissect the data creation procedure into separate steps. The iterative refinement process enables the system to obtain fine details as it produces different output alternatives. The model conducts iterative predictions of noise addition across tens of thousands of steps during its execution process. The stepwise operating mechanism of diffusion models provides stable training and simplified control over generation without suffering from instability issues (Cao et al., 2024).

The application of diffusion models substitutes GANs as the dominant solution for image synthesis alongside video generation and text-to-image generation. The main factor behind this shift is the superior quality of samples produced by diffusion models. Samples produced by GANs tend to experience mode collapse and generate limited output diversity, but diffusion models generate detailed outputs with diverse variations that maintain high fidelity to training data distributions. The training process of diffusion models demonstrates consistent stability during the learning procedure. The adversarial nature of GAN loss functions makes training them challenging because it creates problems with stability and convergence difficulty. Diffusion models achieve training stability by using a clear prediction task that entails forecasting the noise additions at various time steps, rather than the stable but less efficient training approach of GANs. Diffusion models give users better scalability and computational performance under specific usage circumstances. Systematic training of big data sets is made possible through Stable Diffusion because it applies latent representations to condense data dimensions. The combination of scalability properties with high-quality output production helps diffusion models become the preferred tool for various generative applications (Croitoru et al., 2023).

The advancements of generative AI during recent times have faced limitations due to extensive training needs because of large datasets. The emerging paradigm of few-shot and zero-shot learning enables models to demonstrate effective generalization capabilities using labeled data, which may be either restricted or absent. Meta-learning, also known as "learning to learn" is a process in which models trained obtain fast adaptation abilities on various tasks because it learns how to adapt to a new task. This makes it useful for learning new tasks on a few examples, which makes the approach very appropriate for situations when the amount of data is scarce, as is the case in medical imaging or translating rare languages. Zero-shot learning further improves generalization by allowing models to tackle tasks that they were never trained on, but by leveraging general knowledge. Multimodal training techniques, including CLIP and GPT-4, make it possible for such systems to intelligently work on different modality data, including text and image data, without requiring explicit learning of specific procedures or tasks. This capability is used in applications, such as image captioning, in which the models come up with captions of hitherto unseen image types. It is thus common to find organizations using adaptive learning methods through which the generated contents are made to depend on some parameters of the learner. Thus, generative AI draws more flexibility, enhanced effectiveness, and the capacity to solve various real-world problems in conditions of a limited amount of data by using meta-learning, zero-shot generalization, and adaptive learning. In the subsequent chapter, all these methods' real-world applications are discussed as well as implications for the future of AI in areas such as creative content and individualized recommendations (Mishra et al., 2018).

There is an increasing need to build privacy-preserving training methods as generative AI systems evolve due to their large and comprehensive sizes. This defeats the very purpose of FL, as the model learns separately at each participating device using the raw data without sharing it with the others to protect the privacy of the user. It is even more valuable for the application domains of healthcare and individual content production that require sensitive data to be stored on local devices. However, there are some concerns that need to be resolved while integrating federated learning. The system components are spread over several nodes, and there is heterogeneity in devices. Additionally, network conditions vary across nodes, and the data itself is heterogeneous. There is a strong need to learn different types of aggregation techniques in order to have consistency in the performance of models in these different environments. It has been suggested that federated learning offers significant benefits for training generative models on devices. This approach enables device-specific tuning of models tailored to the platform and environment, while also ensuring the privacy of data used in AI training. This type of processing also improves the privacy of users while at the same time minimizing the load on central server hardware. Thus, the environment is being set for the creation of new generation artificial intelligence systems that will be more equitable, useful, and better capable of catering to the specific needs of the users. The following discussion section will further explore how federated learning could be put into practice and how generative AI might transform the future, along with the security measures needed to bolster the outstanding applications (Beltrán et al. 2023).

13.6   CHALLENGES AND FUTURE DIRECTIONS

Several challenges need to be met for generative AI to reach more significant development and improvements. Some of the significant problems are related to the ethical aspects of model output hallucinations, model fairness, and inherent bias. In this study, the authors point out that when the training data set contains sociodemographic disparity, the training models would, in turn, duplicate these disparities in their performance outcomes. On the same note, generative AI systems need to prevent their responses to users from being influenced by any predisposition in the user's history or identity. Secondly, the generation of plausible but false information by the use of hallucinations also has abilities that are very dangerous in areas such as health and law. To manage these risks, there is a popularization of data governance, the presentation of algorithmic operations, and subsequent assessment for compatibility with societal norms and ethics in generative AI systems. By following these measures, it will be possible to work on the trust and reliability of AI systems and ensure their use across a wide range of spheres without creating significant problems. Solving these issues is important for the ethical development of generative AI and its benefits (Ooi et al., 2023).

The significant barrier to training large-scale generative models relates to both their computational expenses and energy requirements. GPT-4, along with Stable Diffusion, demands enormous computational power that produces high energy consumption while creating environmental impact. Courses that lead to reduced costs must become the basis for making generative AI more available and sustainable. Researchers apply model pruning together with quantization and deploy sparse Transformers as techniques to optimize resource management. Specialized AI accelerators have enabled performance maintenance through hardware advancements, which leads to diminished energy consumption. Generative AI needs these measures in place to achieve scalability without causing further environmental damage (Khoramnejad, 2025).

Future research has substantial promise in developing adaptive generative AI systems that improve themselves. The proposed systems would become capable of autonomous improvement through continuous learning without needing broad retraining processes, which allows them to adapt quickly to new tasks and environments. When applied through reinforcement learning models, they could update their outputs through user responses, and meta-learning techniques would let the models quickly adjust across different domains. Through these advancements, generative AI systems would gain flexibility for complex real-life situations that require minimal human supervision. Hybrid models between various generative methodologies show great promise by efficiently integrating their different capabilities. The combination of GAN and transformer models creates a powerful system that applies GAN adversarial training algorithms to produce excellent images together with transformer sequence processing for tasks including text-to-image synthesis. VAEs that integrate with reinforcement learning systems create controlled generation methods that benefit creative tasks in music and artistic domains. Such combination models continue to extend the limits of generative AI technology to produce richer and better-defined results (Saxena, 2021).

The successful deployment of generative AI requires addressing its substantial obstacles, which are vital for ethical practices and sustainable operations at an attainable scale. The solution to bias problems, along with fairness demands and computational expenses, requires sustained cooperation among academia, industry, and policy. Generative AI's future potential becomes more exciting because self-improving systems, together with adaptive learning and hybrid models, are bringing about new opportunities. AI is the idea that numerous business sectors, ideas, arts, and creative processes can be transformed, and innovative solutions for the existing and emerging global problems can be generated with the help of innovative generative AI systems. These technologies are ready to be adopted in industries and bring change in creating economic value and even solving current social problems.

13.7 CONCLUSION

The specific issues that need to be tackled to ensure the safe and sane growth of generative AI are the ethical issues, challenges related to energy consumption, and the question of self-evolving generative AI models. For future advancements, integrating hybrid systems into AI provides a promising improvement in accuracy as the results generated are of high quality, accurate, and flexible. It is worthwhile to mention that sophisticated AI for generation might become one of the leading tools for enhancing industries' performance and maintaining ethical and sustainable practices by addressing current threats as a result of innovative breakthroughs. Generative AI is still active in many sectors because of its incredible abilities in crafting content and solving problems. However, there are still problems, namely, bias errors in data sets and model hallucination that become ethical issues and require particular attention and solution in the interest of safe use of such AI in sensitive applications. In order to avoid these difficulties, it is crucial to consider them when it comes to the further development and implementation of ethical, effective, and credible generative AI models. The solution requires better AI regulatory systems together with improved interpretability algorithms and continuous evaluations of AI output data. The rapid advancements in AI technology have created substantial computational needs that result in elevated power consumption, together with substantial environmental impacts. The exploration of efficient network architectures includes sparse and modular networks, and experts are developing both energy-efficient GPUs and specialized AI accelerators for hardware innovation. AI technology access becomes more convenient through distributed computing and cloud-based optimization methods, and these systems help reduce resource requirements. Self-improving adaptive models represent the following phase in generative AI evolution. Researchers anticipate that future advancements will lead to the development of lifelong learning methods that combine meta-learning with reinforcement learning, incorporating memory enhancement systems. These systems will enable computers to continually learn from new data while retaining prior knowledge. AI capabilities show promise for improvement through emerging hybrid models which unite several generative architectures.

REFERENCES

Abukmeil, M., Ferrari, S., Genovese, A., Piuri, V., & Scotti, F. (2021). A survey of unsupervised generative models for exploratory data analysis and representation learning. *ACM Computing Surveys (CSUR)*, *54*(5), 1–40.

Andreieva, V., & Shvai, N. (2020). Generalization of cross-entropy loss function for image classification. *Могилянський математичний журнал*, 3, 3–10.

Atapattu, C., & Rekabdar, B. (2019, July). Improving the realism of synthetic images through a combination of adversarial and perceptual losses. In *2019 International Joint Conference on Neural Networks (IJCNN)* (pp. 1–7). IEEE.

Augenstein, S., McMahan, H. B., Ramage, D., Ramaswamy, S., Kairouz, P., Chen, M., & Mathews, R. (2019). Generative models for effective ML on private, decentralized datasets. *arXiv preprint* arXiv:1911.06679.

Bach, S. H., He, B., Ratner, A., & Ré, C. (2017, July). Learning the structure of generative models without labeled data. In *Proceedings of International Conference on Machine Learning* (pp. 273–282). PMLR.

Banh, L., & Strobel, G. (2023). Generative artificial intelligence. *Electronic Markets*, *33*(1), 63.

Beltrán, E. T. M., Pérez, M. Q., Sánchez, P. M. S., Bernal, S. L., Bovet, G., Pérez, M. G., ... & Celdrán, A. H. (2023). Decentralized federated learning: Fundamentals, state of the art, frameworks, trends, and challenges. *IEEE Communications Surveys and Tutorials*, *25*(4), 2983–3013.

Cao, H., Tan, C., Gao, Z., Xu, Y., Chen, G., Heng, P. A., & Li, S. Z. (2024). A survey on generative diffusion models. *IEEE Transactions on Knowledge and Data Engineering*, *36*(7), 2814–2830.

Chong, P., Ruff, L., Kloft, M., & Binder, A. (2020, July). Simple and effective prevention of mode collapse in deep one-class classification. In *2020 International Joint Conference on Neural Networks (IJCNN)* (pp. 1–9). IEEE.

Croitoru, F. A., Hondru, V., Ionescu, R. T., & Shah, M. (2023). Diffusion models in vision: A survey. *IEEE Transactions on Pattern Analysis and Machine Intelligence*, *45*(9), 10850–10869.

Dosovitskiy, A., & Brox, T. (2016). Generating images with perceptual similarity metrics based on deep networks. *Advances in Neural Information Processing Systems, 29*.

Eckart, B., Yuan, W., Liu, C., & Kautz, J. (2021). Self-supervised learning on 3d point clouds by learning discrete generative models. In *Proceedings of the IEEE/CVF Conference on Computer Vision and Pattern Recognition* (pp. 8248–8257).

Fan, J., Yuan, X., Miao, Z., Sun, Z., Mei, X., & Zhou, F. (2022). Full attention Wasserstein GAN with gradient normalization for fault diagnosis under imbalanced data. *IEEE Transactions on Instrumentation and Measurement*, *71*, 1–16.

Foster, D. (2022). *Generative deep learning*. O'Reilly Media, Inc.

Fries, J., Wu, S., Ratner, A., & Ré, C. (2017). Swellshark: A generative model for biomedical named entity recognition without labeled data. arXiv preprint arXiv:1704.06360.

Glotzbach, R. (2024, March). Generative AI: An overview. In *Society for Information Technology & Teacher Education International Conference* (pp. 754–756). Association for the Advancement of Computing in Education (AACE).

Gupta, K. D. (2023). A review of generative AI from historical perspectives. *Authorea Preprints*.

Kaswan, K. S., Dhatterwal, J. S., Malik, K., & Baliyan, A. (2023, November). Generative AI: A review on models and applications. In *2023 International Conference on Communication, Security and Artificial Intelligence (ICCSAI)* (pp. 699–704). IEEE.

Khoramnejad, F., & Hossain, E. (2025). Generative AI for the optimization of next-generation wireless networks: Basics, state-of-the-art, and open challenges. *IEEE Communications Surveys & Tutorials*.

Kingma, D. P., Mohamed, S., Jimenez Rezende, D., & Welling, M. (2014). Semi-supervised learning with deep generative models. *Advances in Neural Information Processing Systems, 27*. http://arxiv.org/abs/1406.5298

Liao, Y., Schwarz, K., Mescheder, L., & Geiger, A. (2020). Towards unsupervised learning of generative models for 3d controllable image synthesis. In *Proceedings of the IEEE/CVF conference on computer vision and pattern recognition* (pp. 5871–5880).

Mishra, A., Verma, V. K., Reddy, M. S. K., Arulkumar, S., Rai, P., & Mittal, A. (2018, March). A generative approach to zero-shot and few-shot action recognition. In *2018 IEEE Winter Conference on Applications of Computer Vision (WACV)* (pp. 372–380). IEEE.

Miyato, T., Kataoka, T., Koyama, M., & Yoshida, Y. (2018). Spectral normalization for generative adversarial networks. arXiv preprint arXiv:1802.05957.

Ooi, K. B., Tan, G. W. H., Al-Emran, M., Al-Sharafi, M. A., Capatina, A., Chakraborty, A., ... & Wong, L. W. (2023). The potential of generative artificial intelligence across disciplines: Perspectives and future directions. *Journal of Computer Information Systems*, *65*(1), 76–107. https://doi.org/10.1080/08874417.2023.2261010

Oussidi, A., & Elhassouny, A. (2018, April). Deep generative models: Survey. In *2018 International Conference on Intelligent Systems and Computer Vision (ISCV)* (pp. 1–8). IEEE.

Pan, Z., Yu, W., Wang, B., Xie, H., Sheng, V. S., Lei, J., & Kwong, S. (2020). Loss functions of generative adversarial networks (GANs): Opportunities and challenges. *IEEE Transactions on Emerging Topics in Computational Intelligence*, *4*(4), 500–522.

Richter, S. R., AlHaija, H. A., & Koltun, V. (2022). Enhancing photorealism enhancement. *IEEE Transactions on Pattern Analysis and Machine Intelligence*, *45*(2), 1700–1715.

Saxena, D., & Cao, J. (2021). Generative adversarial networks (GANs) challenges, solutions, and future directions. *ACM Computing Surveys (CSUR)*, *54*(3), 1–42.

Sengar, S. S., Hasan, A. B., Kumar, S., & Carroll, F. (2024). Generative artificial intelligence: A systematic review and applications. *Multimedia Tools and Applications*, 1–40.

Tripp, A., Daxberger, E., & Hernández-Lobato, J. M. (2020). Sample-efficient optimization in the latent space of deep generative models via weighted retraining. *Advances in Neural Information Processing Systems*, *33*, 11259–11272.

Wu, M., & Goodman, N. (2018). Multimodal generative models for scalable weakly-supervised learning. *Advances in Neural Information Processing Systems*, *31*. http://arxiv.org/abs/1802.05335

Yang, L., Zhang, Z., Song, Y., Hong, S., Xu, R., Zhao, Y., ... & Yang, M. H. (2023). Diffusion models: A comprehensive survey of methods and applications. *ACM Computing Surveys*, *56*(4), 1–39.

Zhu, Z., Zhao, H., He, H., Zhong, Y., Zhang, S., Guo, H., ... & Zhang, W. (2023). Diffusion models for reinforcement learning: A survey. arXiv preprint arXiv:2311.01223.

14 Exploring Generative Artificial Intelligence for Transformative Healthcare Applications

N. Suthanthira Vanitha, M. Shenbagapriya,
R. Ramani, A. Karthikeyan, K. Radhika, and
D. Anbuselvi

14.1 INTRODUCTION

Artificial intelligence (AI) has gained huge propulsion due to the advancements in hardware and software technologies that have become an integral part of our daily lives [1]. Over the years, AI-driven tools, including Gmail, Spotify, Alexa, and Siri, have epitomized AI's pervasive adaptation to our habits, making life more comfortable [2]. AI has several attributes that signify human-like intelligence, cognitive abilities, and interpretation. AI is classified into three categories, namely Artificial Narrow Intelligence (ANI), Artificial General Intelligence (AGI), and Artificial Super Intelligence (ASI) [3]. ANI is more efficient than humans in performing precise and limited assignments, while AGI performs tasks equally well as humans, and ASI is crucially more intelligent than humans in all aspects [4]. AI is similar to human brain operations, which a human uses to learn, decide, and work towards solving a problem. AI expert systems consist of machine Learning (ML), Deep Learning (DL), Natural Language Processing (NLP), Neural Networks, and Fuzzy Logic.

Generative Artificial Intelligence (GAI) is considered a powerful tool in healthcare. Based on input text data, GAI responses, and formulating popular GAI models as a transformer model [1]. DALL-E, Mid, and diffusion models have the ability to produce high-resolution images from texture [2,3]. DALL-E, Chat GPT, Bard, Midjourney, and diffusion models have the ability to produce high-resolution images from texture [2,3]. DALL-E can generate realistic images with text data. It is responsible for resolving issues under three categories, by altering style, location, and period, to sketch the object in various conditions for object image generation. Chat GPT is a language model AI based on deep learning, which is trained on a large volume of clinical text to generate human-like texts. Google Bard language model is a cutting-edge technology in health care that offers correct information to patients and has the capability for text generation and conversation

GAI systems are based on Deep Generative Models (DGM), which generate new datasets utilising deep learning (DL) approaches [5]. Generative models grip the data

DOI: 10.1201/9781003680192-14

structure generation process in disparity to discriminative models, while explicitly modeling the relation between input attributes and output labels (Jebara, 2004). It shows how variation in Non-DL-based generative models, especially the Hidden Markov Models, plays a minor role in recent discussions on GAI and realistic data generation. The four categories of DGMs are Generative Adversarial Networks, Variational Autoencoders (VAE), Transformer Architecture, and Latent Diffusion Models (LDMs). The generative AI taxonomy covers three meta-dimensions, ten dimensions, and 38 characteristics

Further, it exhibits the ability to traverse the gap between modalities and assist education [6,7]. GAI technology plays an inherent role in the medical field for diagnosis, patient care, and therapeutics. In addition, it supports healthcare professionals in clinical decision-making, such as urology, radiology, and cardiology [8]. As per research statistics, GAI in medicine is expected to reach around $17 billion by 2032, with healthcare automation operations and development of images, diagnostics, and drug detection [9]. This model requires training in a vast amount of therapeutic information to generate reliable results in healthcare. It gives novel results for regular analysis and enhances patient outcomes.

GAI provides considerable involvement in healthcare in the medical domain. DALL-E supports disease detection and diagnosis through investigating patient information. Generative algorithms bring timely arbitrations and enrich patient care with high precision and rapidity. It aids in the primary detection of diseases, neurodegenerative disorders, disease management, risk assessment, drug development, and innovative healthcare. In addition, models used in experimentation synthesize hypothesis data generation, enable practical education for healthcare professionals, identify Biomarker data that analyzes complex health data, and make studies possible. GAI Chat GPT is a model that is employed for diagnosis and treatment that preserves, self-learns, and maintains medical records [10]. With the combination of GAI in medicine, there are evolving challenges, such as biasing of data, privacy, ethical analysis, patient safety, and security. These parameters are considered a decisive aspect that necessitates more attention.

14.2   GENERATIVE ARTIFICIAL INTELLIGENCE (GAI)

Globally, Generative AI has the potential to change the healthcare industry. In generative AI, Large Language Models transform the healthcare landscape. As per statistical reports, glorification in GenAI technology guides in enterprise intelligence, clinical resources, and administrative tasks, and enables those proficient in healthcare to focus on greater value tasks. However, integration needs a robust digital core, strategic investments, and prioritising human efficiency and effectiveness. Education for clinicians and patients is crucial for refining access and achieving elegant outcomes in healthcare. Generative AI, with its latest capabilities, is playing a crucial role in transforming patient care, life science, and research, revolutionizing healthcare. It improves process diagnostics, treatment, drug discovery, and efficient healthcare solutions, optimizes resource allocation, and improves patient outcomes.

The current status of generative AI in the healthcare sector includes Market Size, Patient data analysis, Drug Discovery, Medical Imaging Analysis, Remote Patient Monitoring, Clinical Decision Support, Public Health Surveillance, Ethical Considerations, and Medical Writing. Researchers are leveraging Gen AI to unlock new insights from large datasets, accelerating medical breakthroughs and innovations. GAI has gained more popularity and demand for technologies around the world. GAI is designed for rule-based deterministic methods, while AI is designed for a particular job. Natural Language Processing (NLP) represents the transformation of Large Language Models (LLMs) due to their scaling, architecture complexity, and abilities of language generation. It uses Machine Learning (ML), Deep Learning (DL), Natural Language Processing (NLP), and Neural Networks. These techniques enable the system to generate new datasets similar to real data, which differentiate patterns and traits from large training datasets [11].

GAI models are unique in producing creative and novel data that is different from their original data. Gen AI approaches are valuable while composing unsupervised learning where labelled data is inadequate and offer sophisticated, complex architectures, stability, and quality data in a diverse manner. Several methods, such as uncertain creation and language models, enable precise and controllable data creation. GAI includes examples as ChatGPT, Dall-E, Midjourney, and Bard. Chat GPT, whereas OpenAI is considered a popular model used in natural language processing [12,13]. It consists of a mixture of datasets, such as acoustic, video, transcript, descriptions, and 3D illustrations. These GAI models create complex data that

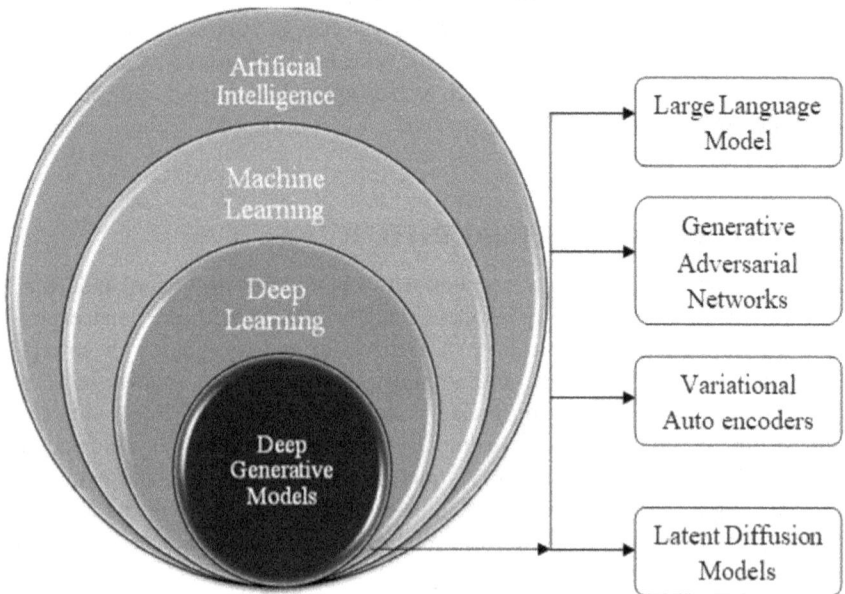

FIGURE 14.1   Algorithmic Approach of GAI System.

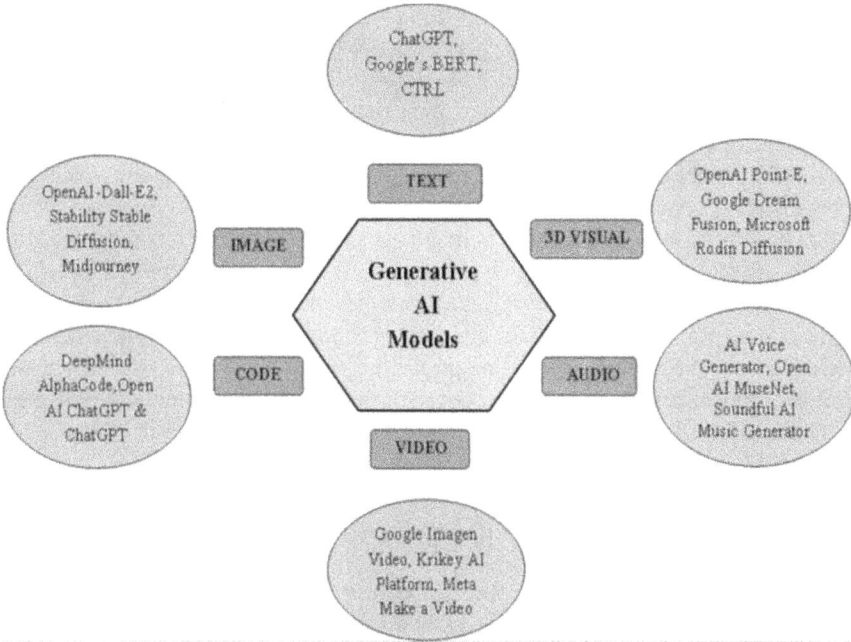

FIGURE 14.2   Generative Artificial Intelligence Models.

mirrors human imagination and make GAI an invaluable tool in some industries, and it is a developing field in research. The Gen AI models are shown in Figure 14.2.

14.3   GENERATIVE ARTIFICIAL INTELLIGENCE IN HEALTHCARE APPLICATIONS

As per the report of Precedence Research, the global market size for generative AI in healthcare has reached $1.07 billion in 2022 and is expected to surpass $21.74 billion by 2032, with a CAGR of 35.14% over the forecast period from 2023 to 2032. The field of AI has made considerable progress in healthcare, transforming medical experts in diagnosing, treating, and managing various conditions. The promising applications of Gen AI in healthcare are a subdomain of machine learning that focuses on generating novel data. The growing market demand has led to the adoption of AI technologies for enhanced healthcare edge. Generative AI empowers and upholds immense potential to revolutionize patient care in the healthcare Industry [14]. The generative AI for healthcare is explored in various dimensions, including wide-ranging applications, benefits, and challenges.

14.3.1   MEDICAL IMAGING

This is a non-invasive method that endows healthcare experts with a meticulous visualization of the anatomy of the patient for therapeutic conditions. This technique aids in the premature detection of disease, develops screening procedures, and plans treatment strategies. In the contemporary set-up, it predicts the margins of insufficient data, modalities, and contrast. GAI provides results that help overcome these challenges and enhance the competence of medical imaging. Medical imaging plays a crucial role in the recognition, tracking, and management of diverse medical ailments [15–17]. This technology provides visual depictions of the internal construction of the human body employed for clinical assessment and medical intervention.

Generative AI models are used in image enhancement and reconstruction, cross-modality image translation, data augmentation, interpretability, and explainability in medical imaging. Generative AI enhances the quality and capability, generates high-resolution images, synthesizes organ images, improves visibility, and generates visualizations and insights from medical imaging data. It supports healthcare professionals for accurate diagnoses, decision-making processes, reduces noise and artefacts, automatically segments organs, and creates personalized data of medical images [16].

14.3.2 DRUG DISCOVERY PROCESS

In recent years, there has been significant progress through various machine-learning techniques to address various challenges in drug development. The Drug Discovery Process aims to bring new therapies to the healthcare market. It encircles a multi-stage process that necessitates scientific research, enterprise, and testing to pass the latest drugs based on market accessibility. It is a complex, lengthy, and expensive process with low success rates. In the case of molecular design structures, GAI shows potential outcomes for the drug expansion that produce new compounds, optimize patients' drugs, and predict drugs' benefits. Further, GAI has the power of 1-, 2-,3, and 4-dimensional models of atoms [18,19]. The standard methods outline the function of multiple classification problems, assigning predefined protein labels. Prot2Text is a unique method for predicting protein functions that deviates from conventional binary classifications [20]. This novel method has an encryption and decryption structure that combines Graphical Neural Networks and Large Language Models.

Generative AI models support various functions in healthcare. It exemplifies target identification and validation, which involves analysing datasets to identify drug targets and authorize disease in early stages of drug discovery [17, 18, 21]. The compound generation proposes new chemical compounds with preferred properties, exploring more efficient, broader chemical space for potential drug candidates. Predicting Drug-Drug Interactions is for evaluating the safety and effectiveness of drug combinations, which aids in the prediction of drug interactions. Accelerating lead optimization aims to generate and assess diverse molecular structures and streamline the process of refining the drug for further processing.

Personalized Medicine analyzes patients' genomics and proteomics data to support the development of individualized treatments for patients. Biomarker Discovery helps in biomarker identification for specific diseases, patient stratification, and improvement of therapies. Clinical Trial Design increases the efficiency of drug development. It analyzes past data, improves trial design, targets patient populations, and anticipates roadblocks. It integrates and analyzes varied data sources such as omics data, electronic health records, and scientific literature, providing comprehensive, complex biological systems. Predicting Drug Adverse Effects to anticipate negative reactions of medications, and assists in the evaluation of a drug patient's safety for the entire phase [22–25]. Repurposing existing drugs to predict the effectiveness of existing drugs against various diseases opens up possibilities for drug repurposing and expediting the process. Generative AI accelerates by generating potential molecular-structure properties, such as drug efficacy and safety, and supports pharmaceutical researchers in identifying drug candidates, saving time and resources.

14.3.3 Mental Health Assistance

Mental health issues such as stress, anxiety, phobias, and depression are familiar globally. The well-being of a person is affected directly affected if they experience these health challenges. Generative AI contribution towards mental health care seems to be increasing via virtual assistants that simulate human-like discussion. Gen AI continuously monitors and supports patient emotions and well-being, aims to improve life quality, and provides appropriate responses. Furthermore, mental health sufferers can take safe breaks from the outside world in an immersive virtual reality environment created by Generative AI. It can take care of the dosage that significantly improves the person's stability. In the case of mental health patients' therapeutic care, relaxation methods and managing stress are achieved through virtual reality [23]. Based on individual patient requirements, analysis, and emotion detection, a personalized treatment plan is offered with the support of the GAI tool. With the help of a multi-modal data hierarchical mechanism, it can diagnose depression and physiological signals through a generative adversarial network [22]. Hence, leveraging GAI accomplishments increases present services in mental health, making them efficient, reliable, and personalized. The tailored intrusion of human well-being, with the support of GAI-enabled tools, enhances mental health support [26–32].

14.3.4 Virtual/Augmented Rehabilitation

Generative AI shows promise in the area of virtual rehabilitation, producing personalized and immersive patient care. In order to serve interactive surroundings for patient therapy, the augmented reality is integrated with a virtual rehabilitation generative model. The emergence of Generative AI with augmented reality (AR) technology offers surgeons real-time assistance during complex procedures. Research survey reveals that Augmented Reality AI assists in the surgical field. It exposes critical information, such as organ structures and blood flow, and assists surgeons in making correct decisions. Also, Generative AI-powered prosthetics and exoskeletons are tailored to individual patients' requirements. The generation of robotic movements improves robotics rehabilitation in GAI. Creating the customized plan of patient features, such as data handling, objectives, and patient observations, can be achieved through GAI. By analyzing movement patterns and medical summaries, AI can design personalized assistive devices that enhance mobility and improve the quality of life for individuals with physical disabilities. For patients affected with impairments, better recovery result is obtained by GAI.

14.3.5 MEDICAL TRAINING

Medical Training for trainees and professionals needs to improve their scientific skills in a restricted environment through simulation. Real-time data-driven practice of realistic serious environments is based on a Gen AI model. GAI parameters such as procedure, simulation, generation, and feedback are transformed to the medical area. This generates a virtual avatar of patients that resembles patients, which is customized for different parameters. Style-based Generative Adversarial Network (StyleGAN20) model generates high-intensity data with original data [26]. With the incorporation of data from physiological models and clinical knowledge, GAI constructs changes in the function of organs, disease development, image signs, and by temporal dynamic capture and problem-solving based on circumstances over time. Healthcare workers are exposed to a variety of patient circumstances using generative models, including rapid deterioration and unfavorable reactions. It is especially evolved for training, the handling of complex and critical conditions, for competence, and the increase of clinical decision-making skills. Students gain exposure, develop proficiency, and obtain feedback through analysis, information, and 3D representations of organs to manipulate in real time.

14.3.6 HEALTHCARE MANAGEMENT

In healthcare, novel management, Generative AI is rising as a transformative wave. Data management stands out due to its solutions in health risk, training, and digitization, making it exceptional for the prospects of healthcare. Gen AI supports the healthcare industry for the automation of patient digital data records, processing, documenting, security, and other administrative tasks. In the case of operational management, the Gen AI model-based Chat GPT supports scheduling appointments for patients, hospital information systems, and real-time updates. Hence, the use of GAI models regulates decision-making processes, denying procedures, preplanned criteria, and administrative troubles, enabling better response times [26].

14.3.7 OPTIMIZATION OF CLINICAL TRIAL

The Clinical Trial challenges of recruiting various patient groups make security more critical. GAI in clinical trial evolves transformation methods to optimize protocol design and validity, simulation, different virtual trials design, randomizing strategies, criteria, reducing researchers ' bias, and predicting treatment responses and patient characteristics [26]. Generative methods like DeepSurv and DeepHit are in place to envisage patient response on patient characteristics and genetic data that assess the potential outcomes of diverse interventions. With the introduction of the GAI approach, the longitudinal clinical data, the Variational Autoencoder Modular Bayesian Network (VAMBN) model is employed [27]. GAI in clinical trial optimization improves patient categorization, efficiency, generates reliable evidence economically, and protocols that enhance patient care in personalized treatment.

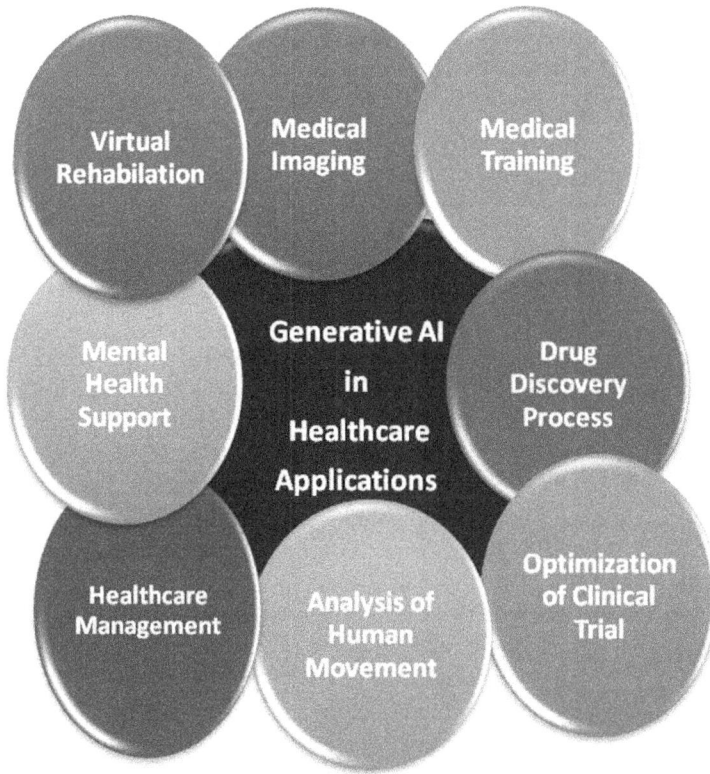

FIGURE 14.3 GAI in Healthcare Applications.

14.3.8 ANALYSIS OF HUMAN MOVEMENT

Human movement analysis focuses on the elaborate anatomy and movement of the human body. Its performance is achieved through valuable insights for diagnosis, treatment, and the inflation method. Gen AI has shown remarkable development in treatment arrangements and in analyzing the activities of the human body by healthcare professionals [28]. ML technique is to replicate the accurate movement of humans, whereas Midjourney aims to reproduce the movement of individual patient care, physical therapy sessions, and virtual rehabilitation. ML is used for interactive assistance and visual manifestation of exact movement, patient appointments, and rehabilitation. Further, generative AI models gauge deformity, analyze posture patterns, personalize rehabilitation strategies for disabilities, and enable interventions and targeted observation. By leveraging Midjourney and the GAI model tool, it simulates realistic movements, improvement, patterns, and contributes to efficient patient care [29].

14.4 HEALTHCARE LARGE LANGUAGE MODEL

GAI models employ large language models (LLMs) in AI healthcare systems for legalized training and produce language that is understandable. These models analyze and process texture with the help of deep learning techniques. DL enables steady and related responses to the framework and LLM for interactions of workers in numerous automated jobs [30,32]. Some of the customized healthcare domains in GAI models are as follows: Medical Pre-Trained Language Model Med-PaLM, BioGPT, IBM Watson for Oncology system, NVIDIA Clara healthcare language models, DeepHealth, Bidirectional Encoder Representations from Transformers for Biomedical Text Mining (BioBERT), and Med7.

14.4.1 MEDICAL PRE-TRAINED LANGUAGE MODEL (MED-PALM)

The Medical Pre-Trained large language model (LLM) was formed to create a better response to health inquiries [33]. The training of Med-PaLM is through extensive clinical literature, academic periodicals, digital healthcare records, research, and documentation of clinical data. Information recovery is limited to some applications in Med-PaLM. It is probable to increase performance, correctness, and technical resources in several healthcare fields by using medical knowledge and language-generating capabilities. For example, Med-PaLM assists in the demonstration of medical expertise. Physiology, sickness, indication, healing, medication, and clinical procedures are in place for a medical encoding system. Therapeutic instructors, students, and researchers apply this model widely in medical education and language skills that support studies for comprehending critical medical design, descriptions, validation, reasons, observations, and questions.

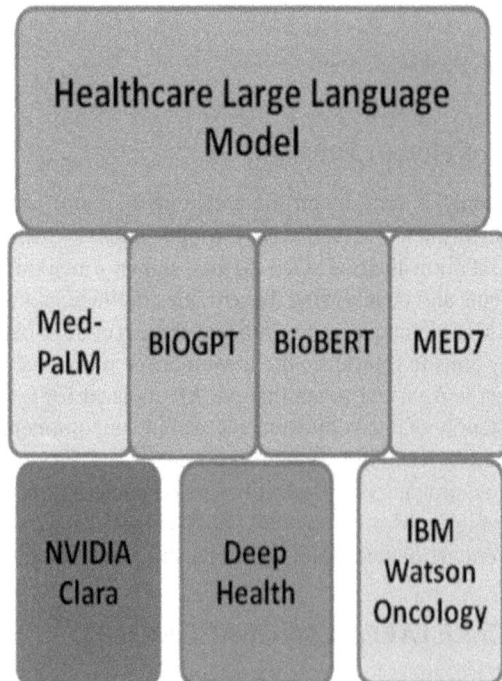

FIGURE 14.4   Healthcare Large Language Model.

Med-PaLM initiates hypothetical practices, suggests a research domain, and promotes confirmation of user skills in the latest medical literature, enabling practitioners to acquire research data, nurture judgment, and improve patient care. The ethical parameter of Med-PaLM technology needs to be a sensitive part of systematic evaluation of various clinical contexts to protect and reduce hazards in some situations. In addition, LLM determines the identification of diseases, and curing is carried out for more at-risk patients than using an LLM to learn a state. Research findings depict that LLM in healthcare improves uniformity, reduces biases, security threats, and vulnerability. Med-PaLM treatment is problem-sensitive for patient data and observance of privacy. In the healthcare industry, these models require appropriate protection of data to be in place.

14.4.2   Biomedical Pre-Trained Transformer (BIOGPT)

Bio GPT is a pre-trained Transformer language model for biomedical text generation and mining that acts as a backbone and was trained on 15M PubMed abstracts from scratch. It has the ability to handle tasks like information retrieval, producing, and writing pertinent to biomedical literature. The main objective is to emphasize the healthcare field to support scientists, clinicians, and researchers to perform different tasks, such as background research, reviews, discovery, modeling, and data analytics [34]. Bio GPT benefits several facets of research, clinical care, and academic ventures because of its competency to understand human language. The usage of Bio GPT in the domain of biomedicine and bioinformatics includes adapted medicine, drug findings, modeling of proteins, and bioinformatics analysis.

The domain of bio-medicine involves protein identification, interactions, and structure prediction, and creates a path for researchers. With the combination of various biological databases, repositories, genes, and biological networks, data interpretation and analysis are attained. The major challenge of Bio GPT and Chat GPT is that it is imprecise without any source of generative language methods, and of rising concern is their spread of artificial information. This problem is addressed by Bio GPT, a pretrained database where GAI reinforces those intolerances. The model has the power to react with a constant human-like response. It raises questions about possible abuse controls to limit the spreading of biased information required for the operation to be ethically liable. Further, it supports human decision-making as a substitute for critical ability and a subject expertise outlook.

14.4.3   Bidirectional Encoder Representations from Transformers (BioBERT)

This Bidirectional Encoder Representation is a large language model that follows the BioBERT architecture for Biological text data mining and processing activities of natural language in the healthcare sector. This method is often applied in clinical care for performing several tasks, such as classification, extraction, questioning, processing, scientific materials, and entity recognition. Its function is to extract biomedical materials from amorphous text data, thereby revealing linkages present in biological texts. It is classified into two types, namely assembled and un-assembled clinical data, and develops a digital database and makes patient data easier by eliminating relevant biomedical components and clinical versions [35]. These factors benefit patients in the clinical part of the hierarchy: resolution, logic, and determination. BioBERT has certain limitations, availability, and restrictions on the caliber of training data, which impact its performance. It distresses model results and affects unexpected biases, applications, volume, and distilling prerequisites are less attainable. In a nutshell, the merits include an improved database, performance, and research enhancement [35]. Conversely, BioBERT in healthcare applications has accounted for limited data accessibility, standardization, accountability, and enumerating desires.

14.4.4   MED7 LANGUAGE MODEL

This Language Model is an extraction tool for clinical text data trained for biological text data applied for natural language model understanding in the medical Industry. The unconditioned clinical text data sources consist of clinical notes, literature, and digital records. MED7 has features that minimize the processes of extracting clinical information, cover entity identification and clinical data analysis with high-quality, valuable data, extract medical elements, enhance clinical decisions, documentation, and coding, and improve healthcare information accuracy and thoroughness [36]. In addition, it boosted interoperability, data integration, data sharing, transmission, healthcare platforms analysis, and the transformation of clinical language data. Med7 has a few limitations. The accuracy of the model's predictions is affected by biases in the pertinent data; correct healthcare explanations are essential, inaccurate interpretability raises problems, and essential awareness of these medical constraints.

14.4.5   NVIDIA CLARA LANGUAGE MODEL

NVIDIA Clara Language Model is an Artificial intelligence-enabled tool employed in numerous clinical applications [37]. As part of the Clara ecosystem, these clinical language models are trained to understand the natural language content [38]. In order to facilitate structured natural language processing clinical tasks and direct medical practitioners in resolution, NVIDIA Clara is considered an efficient tool. The significant medical text data consists of patients' e-health records, surveys, strategies, sources, and summaries. With an enormous corpus of medical material, models comprehend the composite language designs, terms, expressions, and context in healthcare [37]. Deep learning architecture models fall under the category of transformer models, which are effective for performing various tasks related to natural language techniques. In particular, NLP tasks employed in the healthcare industry are classified as entity recognition, concept normalization, extraction, and categorization of healthcare data[38].For instance, clinical support, documentation, automated coding, extraction, entity classification, identification, procedures, and findings of test data. Potentially, these models have proven progress in tailored medication, identifying behaviour and learning, clinical narratives of individual patients, treatment preferences, forecasting treatment consequences, and facilitating precision medicine techniques. Additionally, the healthcare industry accesses the power of cutting-edge NLP and provides insightful information, increases productivity, aids clinical tasks, and comprehends and processes data [38].

14.4.6 DEEP HEALTH LANGUAGE MODEL

Deep learning in high-throughput biology captures the internal structure with high-dimensional data sets, for e.g., sequencing of genes, DNA, and RNA measurements. This Deep model enables the invention of high-level features, leveling the performances while comparing with conventional models, and improves interpretability and understanding of the structure of the biological data. In particular, Neural language deep models are employed in electronic health records for learning about embedded illustrations of healthcare concepts such as diseases, medications, and experimental tests that are used for analysis and prediction. Deep Health in the healthcare field is responsible for developing healthcare in many facets [39]. It consists of a language model known as Deep Health that has machine learning and natural language processing for obtaining the specific possibilities and challenges [40].

Deep learning in clinical data on image processing is the first application used for the analysis of brain Magnetic Resonance Imaging scans to predict the variations of Alzheimer's disease [56–58]. In another way, CNNs are used to infer a hierarchical demonstration of low-field knee MRI scans for automatic segmentation of cartilage and osteoarthritis risk prediction [57]. This approach is used in 2D images to obtain accurate results than manually operated 3D multi-scale features. Furthermore, Deep learning is also active in segmenting multiple sclerosis lesions in multi-channel 3D MRI [59] and for the identification of differential ultrasound images for the diagnosis of benign and malignant breast nodules [60].In the clinical field, deep learning, specifically both CNNs and RBMs, showed better clinical results than usual machine learning methods in analyzing neurophysiological data signals [61,62]. With the incorporation of deep learning, it is possible to predict poor/good sleep with the support of actigraphy measurement during the patient's physical activity. To conclude, CNNs are effective in obtaining the largest specificity and sensitivity in the biomedical field.

14.4.7 IBM WATSON ONCOLOGY LANGUAGE MODEL

This IBM Watson for Oncology Language Model supports oncologists in selecting treatment for patients affected by cancer. The following methods, natural language processing, machine learning, and big data analytics, are active in analyzing patient databases at a large volume [42-43]. Oncology Language Model helps oncologists to quickly access medical information by processing unstructured clinical material and recommending treatments. IBM Watson Oncology has a decision support tool linked with electronic health records to analyze patient data, medical summaries, and treatment recommendation sources. The benefits are tailored therapeutic recommendations, evidence-based treatment options, and time management. It has limitations, a lack of adequate clinical validation restrictions, and Oncology's suggestions are not consistent with particular oncologists' institutional policies.

14.5   GAI PERFORMANCE ASSESSMENT IN HEALTHCARE

In several domains, the use of GAI has been steadily rising, and examples of Generative AI are crucial to healthcare, which are discussed below.

14.5.1   VISUAL SNOW SYNDROME

Visual Snow Syndrome (VSS), known for the constant flickering of innumerable tiny dots throughout the visual field, is a positive visual disturbance [44]. On the other hand, it can be likened to seeing the world through the static noise produced by an incorrectly tuned television. Given the subjective character and wide range of symptomatology, standard diagnosis is difficult and requires novel techniques to understand and manage. The existence of minute dots throughout the whole visual field that stay longer than three months, along with the presence of at least two of the following visual symptoms, are currently used as diagnostic criteria for visual snow syndrome: a visual disorder in which the patient perceives a prolonged afterimage, pain in the eye resulting from exposure to bright light, due to a deficiency of vitamin A it causes a retinal disorder and visual sensations due to the shadows of retinal blood vessels phenomena.

All over the world, visual snow is a rare syndrome that affects people severely. As research into this disease seems to be progressing, cutting-edge technologies are being investigated in order to advance our understanding of the condition, analyze data, and provide better patient care for those who suffer from this debilitating chronic illness. Since each patient may explain their experience differently, making it challenging for parents and other healthcare professionals to understand the true nature of the sickness, the diagnosis is mostly based on the verbal accounts of the patient's symptoms.

GAI technologies are used to create images using textual descriptions, and generative AI models convert text to an image in order to better understand and provide a clear picture. A number of models were employed, including steady diffusion, Midjourney, and DALL·E2 [45]. Though the state is encouraging, further study and training are needed to get accurate findings that can be applied immediately.

14.5.2   OPTIMIZATION OF MOLECULAR

The process of enhancing a chemical compound's features and capabilities to change the target molecule's activity in a desired way is known as molecular optimization.

It is exceptionally difficult to find the ideal molecule for a given set of needs, and because these molecular structures have complicated qualities, building a molecule from scratch with all the relevant properties is a difficult task that takes time and resources. Moreover, conventional approaches for developing molecules are expensive. Deep generative models, which can automatically generate new bioactive and synthesizable compounds, are gaining popularity [46]. Utilizing GAI models, molecule Optimization with GAI (MOGA) assesses a wide range of molecule structures.

This model enhances the design process of MolCycleGAN, which is based on CycleGAN. It has a discriminator and a generator neural network. The discriminator network looks for differences between produced and real molecules; the network learns to create realistic molecular shapes [47].

Computer-Aided Drug Design (CADD) [18] makes use of current chemical knowledge by utilizing in silico techniques. The two primary methods for creating new drugs are virtual screening and de novo design, the latter of which has advanced quickly and employs Generative Artificial Intelligence models [48]. MolCycleGAN is a tool for creating new molecules with multiparameter optimization. It uses image-to-image translation to optimize desired attributes by transforming molecular structures across various representations or chemical spaces. The target space and source space are two distinct chemical spaces that the model learns from. It is capable of mapping these spaces without needing a direct relationship between any two molecules and producing desired-property molecules in the target space.

Inverse molecular design, or de novo molecule production, is through a transformer model of deep learning techniques [49]. This architecture enables the processing of NL models for designing molecules using SMILES notation to express character strings. The goal of this method is to generate drug-like compounds by training a transformer-decoder with masked self-attention, by utilizing generative pre-training models to forecast the next token. The MolGPT model generates valid, distinct, and innovative molecules with comparable performance to contemporary machine learning frameworks. The optimization process is automated and enables the creation of a wide variety of excellent molecular structures. The use of generative models in molecule synthesis results in a reduction in time and resources.

14.5.3 MEDICAL EDUCATION

Artificial intelligence (AI) and Generative Language Models (GLM) can improve medical education through a variety of means, including precise simulations, virtual patients, personalized feedback, assessment methods, and the removal of language barriers. By facilitating immersive learning settings, these cutting-edge tools can improve educational results for medical students [50]. Current GAI models, including Google's BARD and OpenAI's ChatGPT, have the potential to revolutionize medical education because of their increased efficacy, dedication, and realism [51]. A more engaging and pertinent learning environment is encouraged by these models' unparalleled capabilities, which include replicating complex patient circumstances, generating text that resembles individuals, and providing personalized learning experiences [52]. Compared to traditional computer-based simulations, these GAI tools provide a more dynamic and realistic learning environment. Through the use of GLMs' enhanced natural language production, interpretation capabilities, platforms such as PerSim, a revolutionary approach to medical simulation, provide students with more dynamic and adaptable, contextually relevant patient scenarios than previous computer-based models [53].

By adapting language and terminology to the target audience, AI systems have the potential to improve the accessibility and comprehension of health information for a broad range of users, from non-specialists to medical experts. By using this focused communication approach, people will be better equipped to make health-related decisions. Although there are many present and potential advantages of adopting GAI in medical education, there are also certain drawbacks. Concerns around academic integrity, accuracy, dependability, and misuse of AI-generated work are legitimate issues that need to be given careful thought. Caution is also warranted due to privacy concerns, the likelihood of bias, and the potential dehumanization of the educational process. Another important factor is the digital divide. Inequalities already present in the educational system may get worse due to unfair access to AI resources and technology, particularly for underprivileged student populations and low-resource settings.

14.5.4 DENTISTRY

By facilitating greater precision, fewer errors, and a need for fewer human resources, the application of AI in dentistry is transforming the field. The dental field may experience a significant improvement in accuracy, efficiency, repeatability, and dependability with the use of modern dental technologies such as clinical robots and AI models. Dental implant planning is also assisted by GAI models, which analyze patient data using 3D models to provide the best implant plans. These models may simulate different scenarios and factors such as functional requirements, neighboring teeth, and bone density to produce personalized treatment plans for patients [54].

GAI models are trained to assess photos or scans of the oral cavity in order to diagnose and classify various oral problems, such as cavities, periodontal diseases, and oral cancers. Dentists can improve patient outcomes by using these models for diagnosis and identification. There are several restrictions associated with the use of generative AI in the dental field. The accuracy and consistency of these models are strongly influenced by the variety and precision of the training data. As a result, inadequate or skewed data may lead to less-than-ideal results as well as mistakes in diagnosis or treatment planning. Generative AI models do not take into account the full clinical context or patient-specific factors, which are crucial in dental care and include things like medical history, lifestyle, and individual differences.

14.6 BENEFITS OF GENERATIVE AI HEALTHCARE

The benefits of Generative AI in healthcare are as follows:

- Personalized treatment plans for analyzing individual patient data.
- Imaging analysis enhancement elevates the accuracy of medical imaging, enabling premature disease detection and rigorous medical diagnosis.
- Encourages drug discovery by simulating molecular structures and envisaging the progress of innovative therapeutics.
- Disease predictive analytics leverages patient data, GenAI forecasts disease expansion, and identifies at-risk persons that enable proactive interventions for special outcomes.

- Virtual Clinical Trials reduce costs and time related to conventional trials while upholding ethical standards.
- Surgical Enhanced Patient Care and Culture enrich patient engagement, medical conditions, and treatment schedules.
- Administration of automation tasks automates scheduling, billing, inventory management, and patient care.
- Supports preoperative planning by generating patient 3D anatomy models and simulating surgical procedures, reducing risks with efficient optimization.

14.7 CHALLENGES

Globally, the healthcare industry faces challenges such as chronic disease management, escalating healthcare costs, assertive compliance issues, and a lack of staffing. Generative AI is an emerging technology that occupies a crucial role in addressing various issues. It improves operational efficiency, patient outcomes, and cost-effectiveness. Generative AI enhances diagnostic accuracy, personalized data, treatment plans, and resource allocation optimization in healthcare systems through

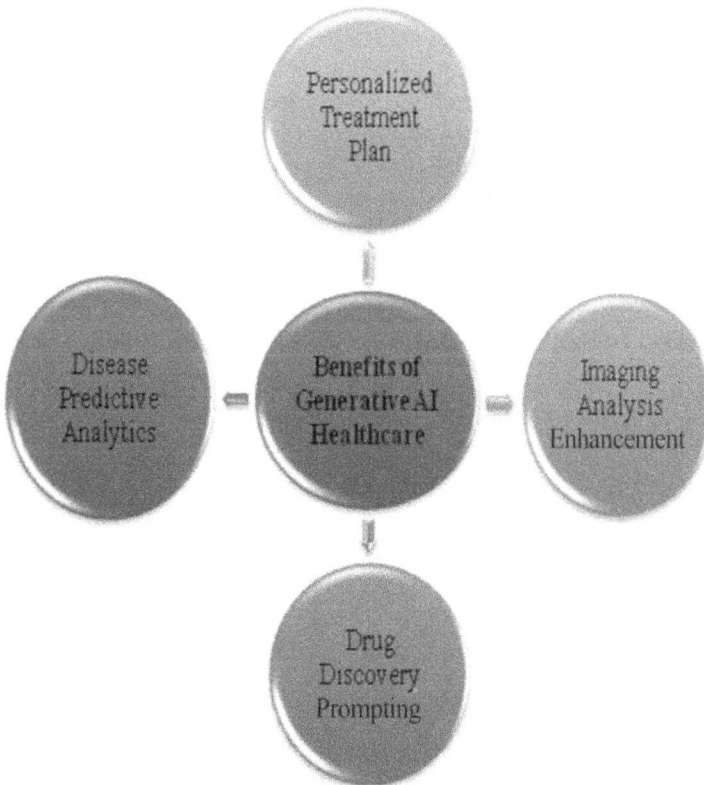

FIGURE 14.5 Benefits of Generative AI Healthcare.

data analytics and machine learning techniques [31]. However, GenAI implementation in Healthcare needs to consider several challenges.

- **Healthcare Expert Collaboration** endorses the association among AI professionals, data analysts, and healthcare specialists. AI resolution is aligned with clinical trials and deals with healthcare challenges in real time.
- **Clinical legalization and Agreement** in AI models undertake clinical testing and support for precision and consistency that adhere to legal standards and approvals before executing AI solutions in a clinical atmosphere.
- **Patient Engagement** involves patient care with AI applications in their healthcare, which is transparent and informed consent for patient autonomy.
- **Mitigation and Ethical Strategy** evolve ethical procedures for GAI in healthcare. Mitigate biases in training data algorithms to ensure unbiased outcomes. Healthcare recommendations are focused on diagnostics and treatment, particularly in perceptual areas.
- **Decision-Making Practice** is to ensure transparency in AI decision-making processes. AI algorithms provide conclusions to build belief and facilitate interaction.
- **Integration and Scalability** of healthcare systems are decisive factors while developing AI solutions. For flat integration, the compatibility of hospital IT systems and electronic health records is indispensable.
- **Continuous Training and Education** is offered to healthcare professionals for effective, ethical, and optimal approaches in GAI applications.
- **Data Security** is to prioritize robust data and safety measures. Implementing healthcare privacy regulations, such as HIPAA, is for protecting patient information. User-friendly interfaces for healthcare experts to interact with AI systems enhance efficiency and decision-making to overcome distraction.

14.8 FUTURE PERSPECTIVES

The incorporation of Generative AI in healthcare has empowered and revolutionized diagnostic approaches and treatment planning through a collaboration with AI and medical experts. Generative AI has the potential to reshape the treatment planning and nature of healthcare collaboration.

- **Enhanced Planning of Diagnostics and Treatments:** Inaccurate medical diagnosis in healthcare causes huge human loss. Using medical data analysis, Generative AI has the potential to provide precise data for diagnosis. Doctors can then diagnose symptoms and make decisions without delay, which leads to improved patient outcomes.
- **AI-Augmented Medical Practitioners:** AI can assist medical practitioners with large data processing, identifying patterns, and formulating diagnoses/ treatment plans. This augmentation focuses on patient care, resulting in more efficient and exact healthcare.

- **Collaboration of AI- Healthcare:** AI-driven insights augment the skill and experience of medical consultants. The future of healthcare is that of collaboration between AI and human experts, ensuring better patient care.

14.9 CONCLUSION

The integration of Generative AI (GAI) in healthcare offers numerous opportunities to transform medical practices and patient care. Its role starts from the analysis of medical imaging to predictive analytics, and offers solutions that were unattainable in the past. As technology evolves continuously, groundbreaking scenarios in global healthcare and patient outcomes are anticipated. However, it requires navigating a balance between embracing the potential of AI and patient security and other concerns. The overview of GAI models and applications we discussed in this chapter provides insight into future directions of GAI in healthcare.

REFERENCES

[1]   S. J. Russell, *Artificial Intelligence: A Modern Approach.* London, UK: Pearson, 2010.

[2]   S. Russell and P. Norvig (eds.) "The history of artificial intelligence," in *Artificial Intelligence: A Modern Approach*, 4th ed. Hoboken, NJ, USA: Pearson, 2021, pp. 17–27.

[3]   P. C. Bjork, "The master algorithm: How the quest for the ultimate learning machine will remake our world," *Perspect. Sci. Christian Faith*, vol. 68, no. 3, pp. 214–216, 2016.

[4]   S. Caner and F. Bhatti, "A conceptual framework on defining businesses strategy for artificial intelligence," *Contemp. Manag. Res.*, vol. 16, no. 3, pp. 175–206, Sep. 2020.

[5]   Stable Diffusion. Accessed: Jan. 23, 2024. [Online]. Available: https://stablediffusionweb.com/

[6]   J. Zhang, Y. Peng, and M. Yuan, "Unsupervised generative adversarial cross-modal hashing," *Proc. AAAI Conf. Artif. Intell.*, vol. 32, no. 1, pp. 1–8, Apr. 2018.

[7]   D. Baidoo-Anu and L. O. Ansah, "Education in the era of generative artificial intelligence (AI): Understanding the potential benefits of ChatGPT in promoting teaching and learning," *J. AI*, vol. 7, no. 1, pp. 52–62, Dec. 2023.

[8]   O. Temsah, S. A. Khan, Y. Chaiah, A. Senjab, K. Alhasan, A. Jamal, F. Aljamaan, K. H. Malki, R. Halwani, J. A. Al-Tawfiq, M.-H. Temsah, and A. Al-Eyadhy, "Overview of early ChatGPT's presence in medical literature: Insights from a hybrid literature review by ChatGPT and human experts," *Cureus*, vol. 15, no. 4, Apr. 2023.

[9]   "Diagnamed Launches a Generative Artificial Intelligence Medical Chatbot, Dr. GenAI," Accessed: Jun. 19, 2023. [Online]. Available: https://aithority.com/machine-learning/diagnamed-launches-a-generativeartificial-intelligence-medical-chatbot-dr-genai/

[10] R. Mao, G. Chen, X. Zhang, F. Guerin, and E. Cambria. GPTEval: A survey on assessments of ChatGPT and GPT-4. 2023. arXiv:2308.12488.

[11] T. H. Kung, M. Cheatham, A. Medenilla, C. Sillos, L. De Leon, C. Elepaño, M. Madriaga, R. Aggabao, G. Diaz-Candido, J. Maningo, and V. Tseng, "Performance of ChatGPT on USMLE: Potential for AI-assisted medical education using large language models," *PLOS Digit. Health*, vol. 2, no. 2, Feb. 2023, Art. no. e0000198.

[12]   OpenAI. "Gpt-4 is Openai's Most Advanced System, Producing Safer and More Useful Responses," *OpenAI*. 2023. Available: https://openai.com/gpt-4

[13]   R. Bhayana, S. Krishna, and R. R. Bleakney, "Performance of ChatGPT on a radiology board-style examination: Insights into current strengths and limitations," *Radiology*, vol. 307, no. 5, Jun. 2023, Art. no. 230582.

[14]   B. Meskó and E. J. Topol, "The imperative for regulatory oversight of large language models (or generative AI) in healthcare," *npj Digit. Med.*, vol. 6, no. 1, p. 120, Jul. 2023.

[15]   Y. Yang, H. Fu, A. I. Aviles-Rivero, C.-B. Schönlieb, and L. Zhu, "DiffMIC: Dual-guidance diffusion network for medical image classification," in *Proc. Int. Conf. Med. Image Comput. Comput.-Assist. Intervent.* Germany, Cham: Springer, 2023, pp. 95–105.

[16]   X. Bing, W. Zhang, L. Zheng, and Y. Zhang, "Medical image super resolution using improved generative adversarial networks," *IEEE Access*, vol. 7, pp. 145030–145038, 2019.

[17]. K. Gunasekaran, N. Suthanthira Vanitha, K. Radhika, and P. Suresh, *Nanomedicine in healthcare: Impact and challenges for future generation*. Taylor & Francis, 2022. doi:10.1201/9781003239888-12.

[18]   Y. Li, J. Pei, and L. Lai, "Structure-based de novo drug design using 3D deep generative models," *Chem. Sci.*, vol. 12, no. 41, pp. 13664–13675, 2021.

[19]   T. Salimans, I. Goodfellow, W. Zaremba, V. Cheung, A. Radford, and X. Chen, "Improved techniques for training GANs," in *Proc. Adv. Neural Inf. Process. Syst.*, vol. 29, 2016, pp. 1–9.

[20]   H. Abdine, M. Chatzianastasis, C. Bouyioukos, and M. Vazirgiannis, "Prot2Text: Multimodal protein's function generation with GNNs and transformers," 2023. arXiv:2307.14367.

[21]   C. Buche, F. Lasson, and S. Kerdelo, "Conditional auto encoder pretraining and optimization algorithms for personalized care of hemophiliac patients," *Front. Artif. Intell.*, vol. 6, Jan. 2023, Art. no. 1048010.

[22]   L. Yang, "Multi-modal depression detection and estimation," in *Proc. 8th Int. Conf. Affect. Comput. Intell. Interact. Workshops Demos (ACIIW)*. UK, Cambridge: IEEE, Sep. 2019, pp. 26–30.

[23]   M. Tee, "Revolutionizing Mental Health: Generative AI in Therapy," Accessed: Dec. 11, 2023. [Online]. Available: www.productiveedge.com/blog/revolutionizing-mental-health-generative-ai-and-therapy

[24]   L. Eliot, "Generative AI for Mental Health is Upping the Ante by Going Multi-Modal, Embracing E-Wearables, and a Whole Lot More," Accessed: Dec. 11, 2023. [Online]. Available: www.forbes.com/sites/lanceeliot/2023/11/02/generative-ai-for-mental-health-is-upping-the-ante-by-goingmulti-modal-embracing-e-wearables-and-a-whole-lot-more/

[25]   N. SuthanthiraVanitha, K. Radhika, G. Sudarmozhi, G. Kavitha, and M. Shenbagapriya, "NanoTechnology in cosmetics and cosmeceuticals: Future direction and safety," in *Sustainable Utilization of Nanoparticles and Nanofluids in Engineering Applications*. (edited by: S. Boopathi & J. P. Davim). IGI Global, 2023, pp. 130–155. doi: 10.4018/978-1-6684-9135-5.ch006

[26]   H. Luo, K. Nagano, H.-W. Kung, Q. Xu, Z. Wang, L. Wei, L. Hu, and H. Li, "Normalized avatar synthesis using StyleGAN and perceptual refinement," in *Proc. IEEE/CVF Conf. Comput. Vis. Pattern Recognit. (CVPR)*, New York: IEEE, Jun. 2021, pp. 11657–11667.

[27] J. Mueller, R. B. Parikh, and A. Noble, "Evaluating clinical trial inclusion/exclusion criteria from claims using generative artificial intelligence," *JCO*, vol. 41, pp. 13566–13566, 2023.

[28] L. Gootjes-Dreesbach, M. Sood, A. Sahay, M. Hofmann-Apitius, and H. Fröhlich, "Variational autoencoder modular Bayesian networks for simulation of heterogeneous clinical study data," *Front. Big Data*, vol. 3, p. 16, May 2020.

[29] M. Barat, P. Soyer, and A. Dohan, "Appropriateness of recommendations provided by ChatGPT to interventional radiologists," *Can. Assoc. Radiol. J.*, vol. 74, no. 4, pp. 758–763, Nov. 2023.

[30] P. J. Ågerfalk, "Artificial intelligence as digital agency," *Eur. J. Inf. Syst.*, vol. 29, no. 1, pp. 1–8, 2020 https://doi.org/10.1080/0960085X.2020.1721947,2020

[31] A. Aggarwal, M. Mittal, and G. Battineni, "Generative adversarial network: An overview of theory and applications," *Int. J. Inf. Manag. Data Insights,* vol. 1, no. 1, p. 100004, 2021 https://doi.org/10.1016/j.jjimei.2020.100004,2021

[32] N. Suthanthira Vanitha, B. N. Devi, A. Karthikeyan, K. Radhika, D. Anbuselvi, and S. G. Infantiya, "A review of artificial emotional intelligence for human-computer interactions: Applications and challenges," in *Harnessing Artificial Emotional Intelligence for Improved Human-Computer Interactions,* IGI Global, 2024. doi: 10.4018/979-8-3693-2794-4

[33] K. Singhal, S. Azizi, T. Tu, S. S. Mahdavi, J. Wei, H. W. Chung, N. Scales, A. Tanwani, H. Cole-Lewis, S. Pfohl, and P. Payne, "Large language models encode clinical knowledge," 2022, arXiv:2212.13138.

[34] R. Luo, L. Sun, Y. Xia, T. Qin, S. Zhang, H. Poon, and T.-Y. Liu, "BioGPT: Generative pre-trained transformer for biomedical text generation and mining," *Briefings Bioinf.*, vol. 23, no. 6, Nov. 2022

[35] J. Lee, W. Yoon, S. Kim, D. Kim, S. Kim, C. H. So, and J. Kang, "BioBERT: A pre-trained biomedical language representation model for biomedical text mining," *Bioinformatics*, vol. 36, no. 4, pp. 1234–1240, Feb. 2020.

[36] A. Kormilitzin, N. Vaci, Q. Liu, and A. Nevado-Holgado, "MED7: A transferable clinical natural language processing model for electronic health records," *Artif. Intell. Med.*, vol. 118, Aug. 2021, Art. no. 102086.

[37] Nvidia, "Intelligent Computing for Healthcare," Accessed: Jul. 17, 2023. [Online]. Available: www.nvidia.com/en-in/clara/

[38] Nvidia, "Healthcare Developer Resources | Nvidia Developer," Accessed: Jul. 17, 2023. [Online]. Available: https://developer.nvidia.com/industries/healthcare

[39] P. Castañeda, "A Deep Learning Solution for the COVID-19 Crisis Saturdays. ai|Medium," Accessed: Jul. 17, 2023. [Online]. Available: https://medium.com/saturdays-ai/deephealth-a-deeplearning-solution-for-the-covid-19-crisis-785238119c1a

[40] Deep Health, "Radiology AI Machine Learning Solutions," Accessed: Jul. 17, 2023. [Online]. Available: https://deephealth.com/

[41] A. S. Panayides, A. Amini, N. D. Filipovic, A. Sharma, S. A. Tsaftaris, A. Young, D. Foran, N. Do, S. Golemati, T. Kurc, K. Huang, K. S. Nikita, B. P. Veasey, M. Zervakis, J. H. Saltz, and C. S. Pattichis, "AI in medical imaging informatics: Current challenges and future directions," *IEEE J. Biomed. Health Informat.*, vol. 24, no. 7, pp. 1837–1857, Jul. 2020.

[42] Z. Jie, Z. Zhiying, and L. Li, "A meta-analysis of Watson for oncology in clinical application," *Sci. Rep.*, vol. 11, no. 1, p. 5792, Mar. 2021.

[43] Z. Dlamini, F. Z. Francies, R. Hull, and R. Marima, "Artificial intelligence (AI) and big data in cancer and precision oncology," *Comput. Struct. Biotechnol. J.*, vol. 18, pp. 2300–2311, 2020.

[44] F. Puledda, C. Schankin, K. Digre, and P. J. Goadsby, "Visual snow syndrome: What we know so far," *Current Opinion Neurol.*, vol. 31, no. 1, pp. 52–58, 2018.

[45] M. Balas and J. A. Micieli, "Visual snow syndrome: Use of text-to-image artificial intelligence models to improve the patient perspective," *Can. J. Neurological Sci./J. Canadien des Sci. Neurologiques*, vol. 50, no. 6, pp. 946–947, Nov. 2023.

[46] J. Avorn, "The $2.6 billion pill—Methodologic and policy considerations," *New England J. Med.*, vol. 372, no. 20, pp. 1877–1879, 2015.

[47] L. Maziarka, A. Pocha, J. Kaczmarczyk, K. Rataj, T. Danel, and M. Warchol, "Mol-CycleGAN: A generative model for molecular optimization," *J. Cheminformatics*, vol. 12, no. 1, pp. 1–18, Dec. 2020.

[48] M. H. S. Segler, T. Kogej, C. Tyrchan, and M. P. Waller, "Generating focused molecule libraries for drug discovery with recurrent neural networks," *ACS Central Sci.*, vol. 4, no. 1, pp. 120–131, Jan. 2018.

[49] V. Bagal, R. Aggarwal, P. K. Vinod, and U. D. Priyakumar, "MolGPT: Molecular generation using a transformer-decoder model," *J. Chem. Inf. Model.*, vol. 62, no. 9, pp. 2064–2076, May 2022.

[50] J. G. Ruiz, M. J. Mintzer, and R. M. Leipzig, "The impact of e-learning in medical education," *Academic Med.*, vol. 81, no. 3, pp. 207–212, 2006.

[51] M. Karabacak, B. B. Ozkara, K. Margetis, M. Wintermark, and S. Bisdas, "The advent of generative language models in medical education," *JMIR Med. Educ.*, vol. 9, Jun. 2023, Art. no. e48163.

[52] Y. Okuda, E. O. Bryson, S. DeMaria, L. Jacobson, J. Quinones, B. Shen, and A. I. Levine, "The utility of simulation in medical education: What is the evidence?" *Mount Sinai J. Medicine: A J. Translational Personalized Med.*, vol. 76, no. 4, pp. 330–343, Aug. 2009.

[53] Medcognition. "What is Persim—Medcognition," Accessed: Jun. 29, 2023. [Online]. Available: https://medcognition.com/what-is-persim/

[54] F. Grisoni, B. J. H. Huisman, A. L. Button, M. Moret, K. Atz, D. Merk, and G. Schneider, "Combining generative artificial intelligence and onchip synthesis for de novo drug design," *Sci. Adv.*, vol. 7, no. 24, Jun. 2021, Art. no. eabg3338.

[55] Y. Choi, M. CY-IC, and D. Sontag, "Learning low-dimensional representations of medical concepts," in *Proceedings of the AMIA Summit on Clinical Research Informatics,* San Francisco: AMIA, 2016.

[56] S. Liu, S. Liu, W. Cai, et al. "Early diagnosis of Alzheimer's disease with deep learning," in *International Symposium on Biomedical Imaging*, Beijing, China: IEEE, 2014, pp. 1015–1018.

[57] A. Prasoon, K. Petersen, C. Igel, et al. "Deep feature learning for knee cartilage segmentation using a triplanar convolutional neural network," *Med Image Comput. Comput. Assist. Interv.*, vol. 16, pp. 246–253, 2013.

[58] T. Brosch, R. Tam, "Manifold learning of brain MRIs by deep learning," *Med. Image Comput. Comput. Assist. Interv*, vol. 16, pp. 633–640, 2013.

[59] Y. Yoo, T. Brosch, A. Traboulsee, et al. "Deep learning of image features from unlabeled data for multiple sclerosis lesion segmentation," in *International Workshop on Machine Learning in Medical Imaging*, Boston, USA: Springer International Publishing, 2014, 117–124.

[60] J.-Z. Cheng, D. Ni, Y.-H. Chou, et al. "Computer-aided diagnosis with deep learning architecture: applications to breast lesions in US images and pulmonary nodules in CT scans," *Sci Rep*, vol. 6, p. 24454, 2016.

[61] V. Jindal, J. Birjandtalab, M. B. Pouyan, et al. "An adaptive deep learning approach for PPG-based identification," in *38th Annual International Conference of the IEEE*

Engineering in Medicine and Biology Society (EMBC), Orlando, FL, USA: IEEE, 2016, pp. 6401–6404.

[62] E. Nurse, B. S. Mashford, A. J. Yepes, et al. "Decoding EEG and LFP signals using deep learning: heading TrueNorth," in *ACM βInternational Conference on Computing Frontiers*, US: Association for Computing Machinery (ACM), 2016, pp. 259–266.

Index

A

AARON, 117
Abbreviations, 157
Adversarial training, 25, 29, 30, 44, 47
AI, 264–268
AI-generated content (AI-GC), 118
AI-mediated communication (AI-MC), 115
Anomalies, 138, 141
Antennas, 158
Applications of generative AI, 85–89
Artificial intelligence, 1, 52, 71, 113, 116, 119, 122, 159, 164, 178, 206, 208, 209, 211, 213, 224, 226, 228–234, 244–246, 251–253, 255, 257, 264–277, 280–297
Artificial neural networks (ANN), 232
Audio format, 162
Automatic speech recognition (ASR), 191–198

B

BERT, 81, 85, 89, 167, 172
Bidirectional encoder representation, 290
Bio GPT, 289

C

Cardiac, 141
Cardiovascular, 147
ChatGPT, 118
Classification, 138
Climate, 216
Climate change adaptation, 69–70
Climbing, 147
COCO dataset, 174, 176
Computational, 1, 7, 9, 14, 15
Computational intelligence, 113, 114
Computer-aided drug design, 293
Computer models, 13, 15
Computer-supported cooperative work (CSCW), 115
Computer vision, 160
Content representations, 161
Contrastive language-image pretraining (CLIP), 171, 175, 177
Convolutional neural networks (CNNs), 165, 167
Creativity and innovation, 83–91
Cross-modal, 31, 36, 44, 45, 47
Cultural sensitivity (CS), 125, 126
Customized, 135
Cyber threat intelligence (CTI), 244

D

DALL·E, 81, 85, 89, 169, 171, 174–175
Darwinian, 210
Decision-making, 21, 25, 26, 28, 36, 40, 41, 44, 47
Deep Convolutional GAN, 29, 30, 36, 37
Deepfake, 23, 37, 40, 41, 44, 46, 47, 49
Deep generative models, 280
Deep learning, 1, 2, 10, 14, 22–24, 26, 29, 31, 34, 42, 43, 47, 50, 53, 71, 77, 82, 125, 159–160, 164–167, 169, 231, 291
Deep neural networks (DNNs), 165, 167–168
Deepseek, 31, 33–37, 39
Detection, 134, 135, 138, 140, 141, 143–145
Diffusion models, 24, 25, 29, 31, 33–36, 41–44, 46–49
Digital ethics, 118
Digital health, 116
Drug discovery, 284

E

Ecosystem, 209
Electrocardiogram, 143, 144, 147
Emotional intelligence (EQ), 127
Energy efficient, 44, 47, 230–231
Entity recognition, 169, 176, 180
Environmental monitoring, 55–71
Ethical, 219
Ethical challenges, 6, 9, 87, 91–92
Evolutionary, 217
Expert systems, 23–26, 47, 76–78
Exploring generative, 22, 24, 26, 28, 30, 32, 34, 36, 38, 40, 42, 44, 46, 48, 50
Extended detection and response (XDR), 251

F

Feature extraction, 167, 172, 176
Fine-tuning, 166
Fitness, 133–135
Future of AI, 87–93
Fuzzy logic, 52–66
Fuzzy soft sets (FSS), 55–67

G

Generative adversarial networks (GAN), 23–25, 30, 35, 41, 48, 49, 81–85, 88–89, 124, 159, 164, 167, 170–171, 271–274, 286
Generative AI, 76, 88, 113, 114, 159, 160, 164, 166, 168, 174, 176, 178, 180, 207, 264–268, 280

Generative pre-trained transformers (GPT)
  models, 166–168, 172, 174
GPT, 81, 85, 89
Graphics processing units, 31, 34, 35, 37, 38, 41
Gyroscope, 140–143

H

Healthcare, 133, 137, 138
Hesitant fuzzy sets (HFS), 59–66
HIPAA, 296
Human AI collaboration, 85–91

I

Image format, 162
Indicators of compromise (IoC), 247
Integration, 133, 135, 136, 142
Intelligent Smart Energy Management Systems
  (ISEMS), 117
Internet of things (IoT), 230, 258

L

Large language models (LLMs), 118, 172,
  184–205, 287
Learning-based generative, 23, 29, 41, 42
Long Short-Term Memory (LSTM), 167

M

Machine, 134, 138, 141–143
Machine learning (ML), 52–71, 76–80, 164, 165
Machine translation (MT), 125
Magnetometers, 138, 142, 143
MarianMT model, 189–202
Markov models, 23, 25, 26, 28, 36, 47
Med-PaLM, 289
MolCycleGAN, 293
Monitoring, 133, 137, 138, 140–143, 147
Multi-criteria decision-making (MCDM), 52–71
Multi-layer perceptron (MLP), 189–205

N

Natural language processing (NLP), 125, 160,
  164, 165, 185, 205, 282
Nature, 218
Neural networks, 1, 2, 6, 9, 10, 12–15, 77, 82, 88,
  91, 225
Neural TTS, 189–201
Nodes, 2, 137, 225, 236–238, 275
NVIDIA Clara, 290

O

OpenAI, 160, 174–175

P

Performance, 133–135, 137, 138, 141, 142,
  147, 157
Pollution rating, 65–67
Pre-training, 166
PRISMA, 213
Probabilistic models, 23, 25, 33, 48, 49
PyTorch, 176

Q

Quantum key distribution (QKD), 255

R

Real-time communication, 203
Recurrent neural network (RNN), 165, 167
Respiratory, 138, 140, 141, 145, 146, 152, 153
Rule-based AI, 76–79
Rule-based systems, 20–22, 24–26, 35, 41,
  42, 44
Runway ML, 174–5

S

Security Information and Event Management
  (SIEM), 249
Self-attentive mechanism, 166
Self-service technologies (SST), 117
Sentiment analysis, 176
Societal challenges, 6
Spoken language, 191, 193
Stable diffusion, 20, 21, 24, 25, 31, 33–37,
  39–41, 43
Supervised learning, 267–269
Sustainability/sustainable water
  management, 54–71
Sustainable development, 208
Swarm technologies, 229

T

Technical challenges, 7, 14
Techniques, 5–7, 9–10, 12–15, 23, 24, 29, 32, 33,
  42–45, 52–55, 62, 65–67, 69, 72, 90, 95, 103,
  109, 114, 141, 144, 159–180, 184, 185, 187,
  191, 192, 194, 196, 201–204, 212, 224–240,
  247, 248, 250, 252, 257, 264–277, 287–288,
  290–293, 295–296
Tensor processing units, 31, 34
Text format, 162
Text mining, 176, 180
Text parsing, 167
Text-to-image generation, 160, 166–172, 174,
  179

Text-to-speech, 184–202
Transcription, 184, 190–198
Transformer models, 159, 171, 174
Transformers, 185–189
Transformers and diffusion, 24, 41, 42, 44, 46
Trust in AI, 120, 127

V

Variational autoencoders (VAEs), 84, 89, 159, 168, 173, 175, 261, 268, 269
Video content, 162

Visual representations, 160, 163, 169, 175–176
Voice-to-text, 191, 202

W

Water quality assessment (WQA), 51–71
Water quality parameters (pH, DO, BOD, COD, TC), 63–65
Wearable, 133–135, 137, 138, 140–143, 147, 157
Wildfire, 220
Wildlife, 215
Work embedding, 167
Written text, 191, 201

For Product Safety Concerns and Information please contact our EU
representative GPSR@taylorandfrancis.com
Taylor & Francis Verlag GmbH, Kaufingerstraße 24, 80331 München, Germany

9 7 8 1 0 3 2 8 5 6 8 4 1